Reflections from the Dog House

by

Kay Kenfield

and

E. Lewis Phillips, Ed D

The *Publishing* *Group*
@ Parson Porch

Parson's Porch Books

Reflections from the Dog House

ISBN: Softcover 978-1-936912-90-2

To order additional copies of this book, contact:

Parson's Porch Books
1-423-475-7308
www.parsonsporch.com

Parson's Porch Books is an imprint of Parson's Porch & Company (PP&C) in Cleveland, Tennessee. PP&C is an innovative non-profit organization which raises money by publishing books of noted authors, representing all genres. All donations from contributors and profits from publishing are shared with the poor

Table of Contents

Foreword

THE SUBTITLE OF THIS BOOK OUGHT TO BE 'THE LEGACY OF BUP and Thane' because, quite simply, if it hadn't been for those two German Shepherd dogs, this book would never, could never, have been written. First, because Bup pulled my adoptive mother out of deep, cold, fast moving irrigation water in the canal when she was three, thus saving her from drowning, and second because Thane, at the age of seven months, fought a house-breaker down a flight of stairs and drove him away one bitter January day when I was living far out and away from town, all alone on a large cattle ranch with no other help within call. Without that big pup, I seriously doubt I would have survived that attack intact, if I had survived it at all. In the first case, I would have been adopted by someone else and might never have grown up with German Shepherd dogs, and in the second case I probably wouldn't have survived at all.

Both Bup and Thane were both heavily endowed with the quality which we today call, quite erroneously, actually, 'genetic obedience'. (It isn't obedience. It's something a whole lot more.) We might as well call it Magic. It is the fairy tale, fantasy aspect of the breed which has enchanted people and drawn them to the German Shepherd dog for over a century in the hope that THEIR dog would have it. Breed pundits of today declare the quality a real fairy tale, a quality all but extinct in the dogs. Maybe it is.

My family was lucky; we had Bup, who came to us in 1918 and who saved both my mother's and grandmother's lives. Then there was Brutus, who virtually invented Search and Rescue in the mountains I grew up in, Katy, who pulled her own kids and all their friends out of a burning barn, my first Shepherd of my own, Thane, who saved my life probably more than once, and his daughter Abby, who went to the hospital (literally) and got the EMTs for my mother when she collapsed, Abby's sister Claire, who, when stolen, made an incredible journey of her own, escaping from her dognappers and making

5

it home despite being bitten by a rattlesnake on the way, down through Mac and Tyr (Mr. Perfect) to Ross, who opened jars of mayonnaise and peanut butter and even my medication for me so I couldn't eat and take my pills when I wrecked my shoulder and had to spend eight weeks with my left arm tied down.

Down through the years the dogs have found lost hikers, fisherman and children, worked stock, become guide dogs for the blind, aide dogs for both brace/balance and wheelchair work, therapy dogs, and, of course, search and rescue. Tyr's brother even became a cop. The genetic component of the magic running through all of these dogs is undeniable—all of them except Bup descended from Brutus, and Thane from Katy as well. 'Obedience'? I don't see how you can call it that. Obedient to what? My mother was barely three when Bup pulled her out of that canal. I was sick as a—well, you know, when Thane met the man who'd just kicked in my front door over the threshold and fought him down the stairs—all the way down, back to ground level again. My mother was unconscious when Abby made the decision to pull the leash out of her hand and go to the emergency room of the hospital to roust out help for her. What 'obedience' was involved when, after watching me wrestle unsuccessfully with the peanut butter jar, and finally give up on it—Ross took the jar off my work space, carried all two pounds of it over to his dog bed and grappled the lid off before, triumphantly, bringing me the now accessible peanut butter to present to me? (With the paper seal still intact!)

On the other hand, what else can we call it? If you figure it out, let me know.

This book grew out of conversations I've had over the years with people on and off dog forums—Lewie, Debbieg, Fred D, Ruby Tuesday, Cliff, Vandal Anne, Carmen of Carm's Pack and others. They've all had input into it, Lewie and Debbie with all their help with the research, Cliff in so many ways, often supplying me with words for what I had only been able to 'feel' before, Fred, with his fulsome encouragement and Ruby with the depth and breadth of the discussions she and Lewie and Debbie so often led me into and Vandal Anne and Carmen with their so helpful validations of things I knew but couldn't quite put my finger on. Without them, this book would never have been written. It needed both, humans and dogs, to make it happen.

Kay Kenfield. February 2014

REFLECTIONS FROM THE DOG HOUSE HAS been in the works for over 100 years. The German shepherd dog sprang on to the scene in the late 1890s and early 1900s when a retired German Army Calvery General made the development of national dog breed his mission. This book traces the development, and what many have lamented to be, the decline of this noble breed we call the German shepherd. The book is divided into six parts containing seventeen (17) chapters.

Part 1 – The Dog - talks in general terms about how dogs came into our lives. As you will read, this section of the book deals with evolution of how a dog fits into our world and how the dog chose humans to form a bond. The section talks a little about the first dogs, what happens when dogs begin to specialize in their evolution and how dogs became a symbol of social class.

Next, the reader encounters what to think about when a decision is made to aquire a dog. Chapter 2 gives the reader an overview as to what to consider when bringing a puppy into their homes as a member of the family. Chapter 3 points out many of the innate characteristics that home owners encounter with puppies.

Part 2 of the book introduces the reader to the German shepherd dog in terms of genetic obedience and the original working tasks the breed was built around. Included in this section are illustrations of the German shepherd being utilized in scent work, Search and Rescue (SAR), herding, and service dogs. The part covering service work includes the origins of the German shepherd in service work and the type of assistance a well trained German shepherd can provide. Last in this section is how to choose a German shepherd pup for service work and what happened to the German shepherd to cause it to fall out of favor in the service industry.

Part 3 looks at The German Shepherd Standard and focuses on the elements of temperament including character and drives. The concept of Functional Conformation is addressed in Chapter 7 and includes the topics Spring of Ribs and Coat Colors. This section is finished out in Chapter 8 with a look at The Actual Standard versus the Consensus standard.

Part 4 addresses the health of German shepherds. In this section genetic diversity is discussed and its role in the current state of the breed. Included are thoughts on line-breeding and how genetic diversity has been lost over the past 100 plus years. Chapter 10 illustrates how genetic conditions are transmitted and gives a list of common genetic condictions effecting the German shepherd. A closer look at Hip dysplasia and cancer finish out this section.

Part 5 is an outline of the German shepherd timeline. Chapter 11 details the origins of the German shepherd dog including the Swabian, Saxony and Burnswick herding dogs, the Northern breed, and the Thuringian "Yard" dogs. Characteristics of each of the 4 originating breeds are given in detail in Chapter 11. Chapter 12 identifies some of the originating dogs that were used to build the foundation of the breed. Chapter 13 looks at the 1930s and the influence Hitler and the Nazis had on the function of the German shepherd. Included in this chapter are names that most people who study this breed will recognize; Utz v Haus Schutting, Nestor v Wiegerfelsen, and Cherusker v Burg Fasanental. Chapter 14 looks at the 1940s post war years and focuses on Lex v Preussenblut and Maja v Osnabrucker Land. Chapter 15 covers what many believe to be the Golden age of German shepherds, especially in the United States, the 1950s and 1960s. Bernd and Bodo Lierburg, Axel v d Deninghauser Heide, Claudis v Hain, and Ingo v Piastendamm are spotlighted. Chapter 17 looks at the modern age of the breed and includes recognizable names in the working lines and show world.

Part 6 closes out this book with some final thoughts about where the breed started and where it is today. The path has been anything but smooth and the result of the rocky road has torn apart the noble breed known as the German shepherd. In this last part, we look at some of the factors that have contributed to the precieved demise of the breed.

The purpose of this book is two fold. One is to record a reflective history of a dog breed that remains one of the most popular in the world today. By understanding history, we can avoid making the mistakes of the past. The question proposed in this book is: Is it too late to return the German shepherd back into the dog it was created to be? The second purposeof this book is to address the current day issues surrounding this breed and suggest steps that should be taken to insure that there will be German shepherds – the versitile working, family companion that was created over 100 years ago – around for many more generations to enjoy.

E. Lewis Phillips Ed D February 2014

We would like to acknowledge the following for permission to use the many photographics included in this book:

East Coast Black Magic German Shepherds (www.east-coast-gsd.com); German Shepherd Dog- The Pedigree Database (www.pedigreedatabase.com); Yvonne Hecht – WinSIS – X Pedigree Program (www.winsis-x-usa.com); Shane A Johnson MD – Cover photograph of Black Magic's Shiloh; Stacy Ransome – Photograph of Black Magic's Beryl's Bladen; Bob Strauss – Prehistoric Dogs. Prehistoric-Dogs-The-Story-Of-Dog-Evolution.htm; Barbara Whitcome – Photographics of Abby, Snotahay Sierra Raine Sensenstein, Snotahay Sierra Ransome Sensenstein, and Snotahay Sierra Ross Sensenstein.

Part I
The Dog Prehistoric Dog

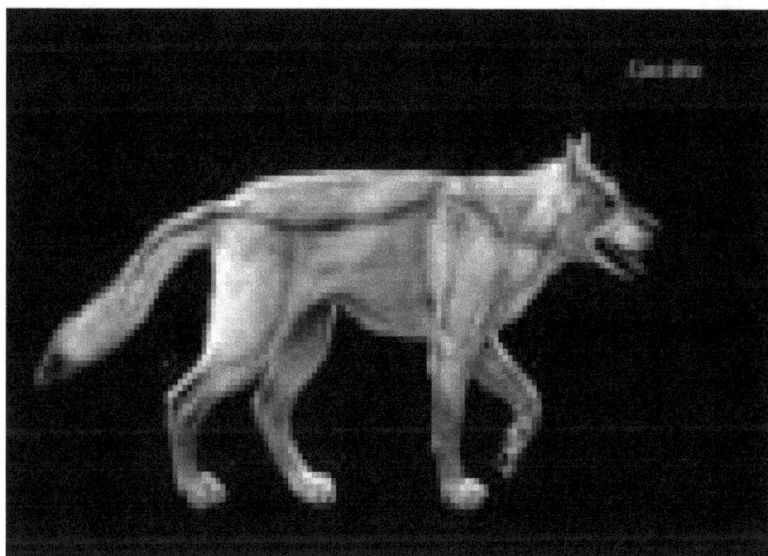

Chapter 1
In the Begining There was the Dog

Black Magic's Sweet Sugar Bear of Rose Hall CGC

THE BIBLE TELLS US THAT IN THE BEGINNING GOD created the heavens and the earth, and then the plants and animals, and after all that, came Mankind. The fossil record agrees. Apparently, the first recognizably dog-like animal is something called cynodesmus,from which wolves, jackals and coyotes all descended, and, in time,canus familiarus, the dog. Archeology tells us that the dog was the first animal to live with mankind in a cooperative manner, and recent discoveries would seem to indicate that dogs chose humans, rather than the other way around.

By the time pictographs and hieroglyphs appeared, dogs had already lived with humans for several thousand years and may very well have been the mechanism by which the other, herd animals were domesticated. Shepherd dogs, war dogs, and hunting 'hound' dogs had already been bred into recognizable types by the time people started keeping track of what they were doing, along with what we now call 'toy' dogs. Some of the first laws we have on record include penalties for injuring or killing someone's dog. Many villages and towns claimed fame for the type of dog they bred and the sale of dogs was an early and important source of revenue in a day when dogs were traded for corn, wheat, goats, and even cattle.

Bone records in archaeological digs around the world, and new DNA records indicate that people and dogs joined destinies wherever people started to live in villages and towns, to hunt in groups, raise crops or herd animals. Dogs have been found buried with humans in Scandinavia, China, the Near East (Tigris-Euphrates river valleys), Africa and even Australia as early as twelve thousand years before Christ. Whenever and wherever people migrated they took dogs along with them, much as they carried food and water. Dogs and people evolved together, survived together, domesticated other animals, together, in a social system of mutual benefit.

Today, dogs help their people to live longer, healthier lives. Contact with dogs can lower blood pressure, relieve stress, motivate us to exercise, and even to help us to stay in social contact with other human beings. But, just as when people started to live in towns, rather than to travel about from cave to cave and water hole to water hole, life has grown ever more complex, and as those first laws would indicate, people who have dogs and the people who live with them need to practice mutual respect and care.

The dog-human connection is literally hard-wired into us. Our ancestors made the best of it in order to survive, so let us do the same to enhance and enrich our lives together so that all of us may live long and prosper once again.

Dogs Chose Us

We all know the story of the kid who comes home from school with a dog and says to his mother, 'He followed me home. Can we keep him?' Something like that happened for the first humans, when dogs followed people who were hunting, driving birds into nets and larger animals into primitive but effective traps. And just as Mom feels, at best, ambivalent about this stray dog, early peoples probably weren't all that happy about their new partners. They probably considered that the dogs were interfering, at first, and then, that they were competing for the scarce game.

But then somebody figured out that the dogs were better at finding the birds and the rabbits they were trying to net, or the wild pigs and sheep they were looking for to drive into their traps. And sombody else realized that when dogs helped to drive the game into the nets or traps, that they were able to net more birds, or trap more animals. Of course, from the dogs' point of view people had skills they could use, since it was people who built the traps and wove the nets. Then, too, people had knives and spears, weapons which complemented dogs' teeth when it came time to kill the game, and this made killing game a less chancy business for the dogs. Today, we'd call it a win-win situation.

The dogs brought their keen sense of smell and fine hearing to the mix, and together, people and dogs were able to find and kill more game than either dogs or people could by themselves. After the game was killed, dogs and people together were better able to drive off the other scavengers, birds and beasts both, who would try to steal the meat and hides so hardly come by. Too, once people started to keep grain and dried meat and berries in baskets so it could be stored for the future, men started trying to steal it. Dogs barked to give warning and even protected the stores of food that made the difference between life and death for people and so the partnership between people and dogs was established.

Of course, in the beginning, the dogs weren't dogs at all, they were wolves, and sometimes jackals, and occasionally even coyotes. We know now, that wolves, coyotes, jackals and dogs can all inter-breed and produce viable young which can, in their turn, inter-breed with any individual of the four groups. It may very well be that early breeders used these four groups to shape the first breeds of dogs. Today we have coy-dogs and wolf-dogs, and the Pharoh hound, which written records from Egypt clearly state was developed from crossing jackals with existing hound-type dogs. It is one of the oldest pure breeds of dog known.

We don't know just when wolves started to include people in the social events called hunts, we just know that they did and that humans prospered because of it. We don't know why they followed us home, or just when, but they did, and because they did, the species called human beings (homo sapiens) survived and prospered when all their competitors (like Neanderthals) fell by the wayside. In turn, humans have created well over 400 breeds of dogs world wide, for all kinds of purposes, as well as no purpose at all beyond pleasing people.

14

First Dogs

The first dogs we have written and pictorial records of are hounds, proto-type Greyhounds, Afgans, the Pharoh Hounds, Salukis, and Borzois, all of them developed in desert climates to hunt hares, antelope, gazelle, deer and any other swift running game by sight. These hounds use their noses to breathe, not to scent, and they can run nearly forty miles an hour. Their coat varies depending on the proximity to the equator with which they originated.

Greyhounds and Pharoh hounds have a very sleek, short coat, while Salukis and Borzois have longer, whispy coats to withstand high desert nights. The Afgan, from the high desert mountains of Afganistan, where temperatures can be bitter, have long, thick coats and are probably closer to their ancestors in temperament than the other sight hounds, who have known more modification by contact with the modern world.

Bloodhounds are the oldest pure type of scent hounds we have records for, but certainly scent hounds would have been used by the earliest hunters to drive small game into nets and to locate larger game. No doubt early scent hounds came in all sizes and shapes much as they do now. They certainly figured in the survival of Stone Age humans.

Bone records found in Scandinavia point to Shepherd dogs being another of the 'first' dogs. Clearly of wolf extraction, many of the breeds still resemble wolves in many ways. One has only to think of German Shepherds, Norweigian elkhounds, Keeshounds, Belgian Sheepdogs, Icelandic dogs, and Dutch Shepherds. The collie breeds, which came to specialize in sheep, lost much of that appearance, but the breeds who kept their early versatility, as hunting dogs, sled dogs, guard dogs, stock dogs, and cart dogs have largely kept their visual kinship with their ancestors. Virtually every country has some kind of national shepherd dog, even today, from the Scots collie of Lassie fame whom everyone knows to the Kuvasz, the Komondor or the Tatra.

These are the dogs of the earliest human migrations, the dogs which, in all likelihood, made those migrations possible. They pulled stores of food on sleds and travois, just as Peary and Amundson used them to explore the North and South Poles and packed hides on their backs to be used to build shelters. They helped find game so everyone could eat, and guarded the baskets of food from thieves of all varieties.

These behaviors, hunting, herding, and guarding, are all hard-wired, so to speak, into our dogs today through fourteen thousand years of natural and human selection. Our ancestors used these traits to help them to survive and even to flourish. Our challenge is to continue to find ways to make these traits work for us, rather than against us, so that we, too, can flourish in partnership with our dogs.

When Dogs Specialize

Sometime around four to five thousand years ago, people started to figure out that they could take the existing dogs they had, scent and sight hounds, and their versatile shepherd dogs, and select for traits they liked better than others. If they bred their smaller dogs to smaller dogs, after several generations, they could pretty much depend upon getting small dogs. And they could do the same thing to get larger dogs. Working traits, like a particularly good nose for birds, or being particularly good with sheep were harder to perpetuate and optimize, but, through observation and trial and error, they managed it.

Soon they had small companion dogs, some of which were particularly good mousers and ratters, the precursors to the dogs we call terriers and those we call toys. The Romans had dogs very similar to our Jack Russells and our bull terriers (sometimes called pit bulls today) to rid their homes, and particularly their store-houses, of rats and mice. Small hunting dogs good for finding birds and driving them into nets, the precursors to our spaniels, were developed. And then there were the war dogs.

Did you know that, as early as four thousand years ago, the dog was the precursor to our modern tanks, and the Great Danes, St Bernards, Newfoundlands, and all of the Mastiffs, as well as a host of lesser known breeds, was recorded by the Greeks and Egyptians? It was called the Mollossus, weighed well over a hundred pounds, and was used as a weapon of war. Great lances were strapped to its back and long spikes were attached to its collar. It was sent in among the men fighting to rip and tear and knock them off their feet where, once downed, they could be quickly and easily killed.

Effective against cavalry and chariots both, the dogs were used by the Greeks and Romans, the Gauls and even to fight lions and tigers to protect livestock and people, and regrettably, in contests for sport. With the development of the Mollossus came the fear of dogs. They had always been the bane of thieves, but the Molossus ushered in the great dogs of superstition and death. The huge mastiffs were expensive to raise, fierce and not always reliable, more guard than companion, and little use for hunting or herding. With the fall of the Roman Empire they became too expensive for most people to keep merely in case of war, and were gradually remanded to the estates of the very wealthy, were they were used to guard gold and game and the bodies of men whose use of their gold and their power had furnished them with too many enemies for men alone to prevail against.

Still, it was perhaps the Mollossus to whom the early Romans referred when they created mosaics that contained the words 'cave canem', with which to decorate their doorsteps. It seems, as long as there have been people who mean other people harm, the first question they ask themselves is, 'how do we get rid of the dog?' Whether it be the great Mollossus, or the lowly rat terrier, dogs have guarded their people throughout almost fifteen thousand years of human existence. Perhaps it is time that we returned the favor, and dedicated ourselves to guarding the dog.

Dogs as Symbols of Social Class

By the middle ages, the kind of dog you had told everyone who you were and what strata of society you belonged to. Toy dogs were the province of wealthy women with nothing better to do than to pet and pamper them. Such women were often little more than prisoners in their husbands' homes. Their children were taken away from them at early ages to be 'fostered', the educational system of the time for the sons of the wealthy, their daughters sent away into early marriages, never to be seen again.

'Stewards' managed their households for them, and they were not allowed in their own kitchens. Their ladies in waiting did most of the sewing for them, with the exception of decorative needlework of one kind or another. Such ladies were commonly tale-bearers as well as jealous and uncongenial. The little companion dogs that warmed their feet were often the only real companions such women had. Who knows how many women owed what little sanity they were able to keep to their small and only friends?

For middle class women, with too much to do and too little time to do it, small dogs in the household meant the energetic little ratter who befriended her sons and kept the stables, or even the pantry, free of vermin. Her husband, depending upon his location and his temperament, might have a fashionable coaching dog to run beside his curricle, or, if he was more of a country gentleman, a spaniel to hunt birds. If he was gentry, he'd have hounds, perhaps the bloodhound we know today, and his wife might have a small spaniel in the house for company.

The aristocracy would have large greyhounds, the great deer-hounds or wolfhounds, to signify their status, and their games- keepers might have some form of the newer, smaller Mollossus, one of the several mastiff breeds developed for taking poachers, or a some- what smaller 'yard' dog, dark and fierce. Much of the prejudice against large dogs today comes from this historical divide, which reaches all the way back to the Romans, when large dogs belonged to the wealthy, who used them to keep the poor disenfranchised and fearful.

The poachers themselves would have small, dark spaniels for taking birds, and small dark hounds for the hunting of fox, badger, otter, and rabbits, precursors to the Cockers, Brittany and Springer spaniels of today, as well as the Dachshunds, a wide variety of small terriers. The lower middle class and the very poor were mostly confined to what we now call terriers, a good many dogs which we would now classify as 'pit bulls'. And yes, they did fight them, just as a distinct sub-class of humans do today.

These little dogs were companions, guards, ratters and fighters. They were pitted against bulls, bears, other dogs, and even men. They sneaked about large estates in the dark to help their masters take the wild game that kept their families from starving. They protected what little food there was from rats and mice, and were the first line of defense against disease, intruders, thieves and fire, with their early alerts and their loud barking.

The dogs of the poor were brash, noisy, ready to bite at the drop of a hat, quarrelsome and utterly loyal to people who would make us cringe today. They ate little, and only what people found too stale, too spoiled, and too foul to eat themselves, yet without them, a great many more people would have died young of disease and fire than did. They were the unsung heroes to which many of us owe our ancestors and even our very being and we can see their descendants any time we visit a shelter for homeless dogs. They are every man's dog, and any man's, as American as apple pie, as British as John Bull, and as stout as any Scot. They are our dogs.

Chapter 2
So Now You Want a Dog

Black Magic's Piper

WHY DO YOU WANT A DOG? What do you want him for? Do you have a yard? Do you work full time (or more)? Where's the dog going to live? Can you afford to feed him? Can you afford his medical care? (Don't worry, dogs aren't as expensive as kids. Quite.) Do you plan to spend time with him? Are you willing to socialize him, play with him, train him? Are you temperamentally capable of fairness and consistency? Do you just want company?

Somebody once said that if a dog was a man's best friend, then that dog had a problem. Don't be some dog's problem. Answer the questions above, then ask some more, and then answer them too. Think about what kind of person you are and what kind of home you live in.

Do you have lots of friends and are you physically active? Or are you basically sedentary? Do you live alone? or with others? Do you have kids, or grandkids? How much will they have to do with the dog? Don't expect a young child, regardless of what they promise, to be able to take care of a dog without lots of help and encouragement from adults.

Dogs have so much to give us, it is imperative that we reciprocate by taking care of them at the very least adequately. Puppies need lots and lots of socialization, particularly between eight and sixteen weeks. During that time, no matter what else you have to do, you must make the time to take them out at least every other day to meet people and other animals and to go places and see things. This is imperative for the proper development of their brains. If you don't do it, you can never get that opportunity back again, and your once delightful puppy may turn into a fearful, shy, unhappy, resentful, even hostile adult dog.

If you don't want to make the commitment to properly socialize a puppy, consider an older dog who somebody else put the time and effort into. Many shelters can introduce you to just such dogs, who have lost their people to illness or even death through no fault of their own who could make you a wonderful pet.

If you do not have a job for a dog, if you are not going to compete in dog shows, or obedience, or Schutzhund or personal protection, if you're not going to do scent work or search and rescue, and you don't need a hunting dog, consider whether you really need a purebred dog. And if you decide you really want one, consider getting one from one of the breed rescues whose people will go the extra mile (literally!) to make sure you get a good fit.

If you decide that you are ready to commit to a dog of many parts, but you aren't entirely certain about picking the best dog for you, try contacting your local dog club to see if they can recommend someone who knows about dogs who could go with you to help you choose. And if you don't think you need help choosing your shelter dog, contact your local dog club anyway to ask when and where puppy socialization classes are held and where you can find good obedience class instruction. They can give you information about the kinds of trainers available for you and what their specialties are.

Some things to keep in mind--dogs with long, fluffy, thick coats require more brushing and washing than dogs with slick, short, tight coats. This is not all bad, if you're willing to do it. The constant grooming the long coat requires can lead to a deep and lasting bond between dog and person. Also, hounds and hound type dogs need room to run, and, perhaps surprisingly, so do the little terrier type dogs. In fact, they may need more exercise than many larger dogs.

Whatever you do, before you actually get a dog or a puppy, do your homework. Talk to people, and read, read, read. The Monks of New Skete have written a great book called 'How to be your Dog's Best Friend' and at the other end of the spectrum, the Purina Dog Chow people have put together some very informative and helpful booklets. People have been writing books about how to live with dogs for close to a hundred years. Colonel S. P. Meek wrote some great books in the 1930s and there are wonderful Barbara Wodehouse books from the 1960s and '70s, and today's books by Patricia McConnell, to offer a mere few of what is available. Enjoy!

First, Consider Yourself

The place to start in choosing your puppy is with yourself. Some people know exactly what they want in a pup because they know what they want to do with that pup. They know because they've done it before and more than once. They know what to look for to get what they want. For someone with less experience the first order of business is to level with themselves, about themselves, to be honest with themselves.

How much time do you really have to spend with your puppy? What kind of commitment do you have to training? To going to classes, joining a club, attending regular activities? Are you really going to do Schutzhund, Personal Protection, KNPV, Mondio, French Ring, PSA, etc.? Really? Is it just a dream? Or are you already attending meetings, becoming a regular, taking your turn at being a helper? If you are, then the leaders of the group will guide you to the dogs they think best for you and it is best that you go along with them, at least for your first dog. (And you'll find, if you are serious about dog sports, that dogs are like potato chips—you have to have more than one!)

Same thing for Search and Rescue. If you're really interested, if you're not just wishfully thinking, join a group, go out regularly, take part in the exercises. Just as Schutzhund people are always in need of good helpers, SAR groups are always in need of tracklayers and people to play lost. Once you become a regular, the people you work with on your SAR team will help you to find the right pup for you.

But what about showing? Well, if you want a show dog, join a dog fanciers' group for the breed of your choice, identify the people in the group who have consistent winners and several champions that they have bred, and allow them to mentor you. Be a regular in your group, go to shows, learn what it takes to make it in the show game (money). Your mentors will get you started with the pup of your dreams. You're going to take up Obedience? Rally-O? Same thing. See above.

As far as lists of what kinds of breeders to look for or what to expect of a breeder, most of those lists are-- Well, I won't quote Cliff. Let's just call them unhelpful. A backyard breeder is just a hobbyist breeder who doesn't breed the kind of dog the person using that phrase likes. Just stay away from pet shops and places you find on the Internet where they have a long list of breeds of dogs available, including a lot of mixed breeds, and they always have a litter on the ground, no waiting necessary. They may be a puppy mill and it would be better not to support one of them.

Pet shop puppies often come from puppy mills as well. They are sold to wholesalers who in turn sell them to retailers—pet shops. These puppies have usually been taken away from their mothers too young, and often their immune systems haven't yet developed enough to protect them from disease. Then they are transported great distances without vaccinations to give them any immunities to the diseases to which they are exposed. (Vaccinations cost money.) As a result they are often sick when you buy them or become sick shortly after you get them home. Because they were taken away from their mother and their sisters and brothers too soon, they have missed valuable socialization that puppies get from those relationships. Because they have been forced to foul the cages in which they are kept, they are often difficult to housebreak.

When you buy a pet shop puppy, you support the system and the people who are willing to commit these abuses for money. If everyone would boycott pet stores who carry puppies, sooner or later they would stop providing them (and breaking the hearts of all those people who bought sick puppies). Don't get your heart broken. Get your puppy from someone who keeps their puppies until they are eight or even ten weeks old, someone who de-worms their puppies and who starts their vaccinations so that they have some immunity built up before they go home with you.

If you are honest with yourself and you find, upon consideration, that you just want a pet, go to someone who has placed a lot of pets successfully in pet homes and always, ALWAYS consider rescues. There are many wonderful dogs out there needing a home and many are excellent pets, or even working dogs. The first heart attack alert dog was a rescue and many seizure alert dogs have come from rescues. The San Francisco ASPCA for years pulled dogs from the shelter to train for hearing ear dogs for the deaf and many of them achieved public access status.

Many dogs wind up in shelters through no fault of their own. I could tell you stories . . . . But whatever you do before selecting a pup—THINK FIRST! Many dogs live 13, 14, or even 15 years and you will be signing on for every day of those years. A buddy who can share your enthusiasms is always better than one who cannot. A few moments of careful thought now can make all the difference in the world in the partnership ahead of you.

Calling Prince Charming

So now you have your perfect puppy. You chose a female because all the dog books assured you that she would be easier to house break, and lo, they were right. They told you that she would be affectionate, and lo, she is. They told you she would be easier to train than a male, and while you don't know about that, she was certainly the smartest puppy in her class. She comes when called and sits and downs and she can catch a ball like Willie Mays. BUT all of a sudden, she's started disappearing.

You blink your eyes and she's gone. She goes over the yard fence, or under it. You can't keep up with her. She's gone for an hour, and then two, while you search the entire neighborhood and call and call and call. Then she turns up, after a couple of hours, and you think it won't happen again, but it does. You didn't put that dog run up next to the back porch, well within your yard fence boundaries, because it was too expensive, too much trouble, and you didn't need it anyway, and now you wonder if it's too late.

It might be. It might not. But even if it's not, your time is running out. Either get that six foot chain link run in, complete with a top, dog house and underpinnings, or take her to the vet and get her spayed. Either way, it will cost just about the same amount. Your girl is simply doing what biology (the part hard-wired into her from her wolf ancestry) demands that she do. As long as she still has her primary source of sex hormones, she's going to do what those hormones tell her to do--put those glass slippers out there for her Prince Charming to use so he can follow her home.

In the wolf pack, when a female reached sexual maturity, if she wanted to mate, she had to found a pack of her own. To do that, she had to put her scent out over a territory which might include several miles, for her Prince Charming to find. She had to get it out there, as close to every day that she could, to optimize her chances of finding a satisfactory mate. That's what your girl is doing.

If you don't want to open your front door one day to find her Prince Charming there to greet you, you have to prevent her from doing that. Some of the earliest dog laws enacted by people have to do with penalties for those people who allowed their female dogs to roam. Females in search of their Prince Charming result in guard dogs who don't guard, herding dogs failing to herd, and hunting dogs who start hunting her instead of game and people get upset about that. And that's not even talking about the cars, people, other dogs, diseases, private property, poisons, (insecticides, motor oils, anti-freeze and toxic foods) to which your dog and theirs may be exposed because of her peregrinations.

23

No matter how wonderful your girl is, the odds that she will reproduce, with any certainty, her good traits, when bred to her idea of Prince Charming are just about nil. (Think of that skinhead your daughter brought home. You know, the one with all the piercings and tatoos!) And remember, too, that puppies come five and ten at a time. Who will want them? Puppies that wind up at the pound are heartbreaking, an expensive burden on taxpayers we shouldn't have to bear, and a reproach to us all.

If you can't make absolutely certain that she is never out of her safety pen, except when she is in the house, then do her, and all of us a favor. Take her to your vet and get her spayed.

To Spay or Not to Spay, that is the Question

Now, you have your girl dog, and she is safe in her pen at the back of your house, and well inside your yard. She is a little yappier than you'd like, (there are bark collars for that) but she has her toys and her chews and bones and she is reasonably content. She stays in the house with you at night, plays and trains with you(it's all part of the same game) in the evenings after work, and has a moment with you in the mornings before you leave, and on weekends she has all kinds of fun with you. She's perfectly lovely, but you know you don't ever want to go to the effort and the expense of raising puppies.

It's more work than you want to do and you realize that there's no real place in the world for more part this-and-part-that puppies. Anybody who wants a lovely pet can go down to the shelter and pick and choose among hundreds in all ages, sizes, colors and hair styles. So what's the best thing to do?

Well, the old timers used to say that you waited until your girl had a litter of puppies and then spayed her, but that's just what you DON'T want to do. The spay 'em while they're still babies group would have you do it at four months, or younger, but this leads to all kinds of health problems they don't want to tell you about--or will outright lie about--like cancer, incontinence, hip dysplasia and even skin problems.

Incontinence is a nuisance, but in most cases giving your girl estrogen pills for the rest of her life will take care of it, if you want to go to all that trouble and expense. Hip dysplasia is more serious. It happens because the sex hormones are responsible for slowing down and finally stopping the growth process and you've cut them off.

When a dog is spayed, (or neutered, for a male) the primary source of sex hormones is removed. This means that it takes the secondary sources of sex hormones longer to produce enough of the hormones necessary to stop the growth process. (Which is why dogs spayed or neutered before one year of age, particularly in the larger breeds of dog tend to be taller than their unspayed and entire sisters and brothers.) The dog's long bones, including the thigh bone, take longer to stop growing and often that little extra bit of growth prevents the thigh bone from fitting snugly into the hip socket, creating a condition referred to as hip dysplasia.

Since we have begun spaying and neutering more and more dogs, younger and younger, we have begun to see a virtual epidemic of hip dysplasia among our larger breeds of dog. Because there is more than one cause of hip dysplasia, and because so many unwanted puppies are born to grow into unwanted dogs, we are reluctant to face the fact that early spaying and neutering causes hip dysplasia. Many people feel it is more important to prevent the birth of unwanted puppies than to prevent hip dysplasia and in many cases they are right.

The female dog who is roaming because she has gotten loose (again) is a far greater danger to herself and to other dogs than hip dysplasia is to her. Disease, the chances that she will be hit by a car (or cause someone else's dog to be hit) are all of more import than the likelihood that early spaying will cause hip dysplasia. Many pet dogs lead full and active lives with hip dysplasia, and there are lots of products on the market which can help the dog with mild hip dysplasia to live a comfortable life.

Hip dysplasia is more serious in working dogs, but that just means that you keep the dog up in her safe secure pen all the time that she is off leash or out of the house until she has stopped growing naturally, then spay her. It is certainly worth the eight to ten good years of work the dog can then offer to go to the trouble of keeping her up safely for that period of time. It doesn't mean that you can't train her or take her out or enjoy her, except during the two to three 'heat' cycles she has before her natural growth cycle is completed. You can, as long as she stays home when she is 'in heat', and you keep her on leash the rest of the time she is out. Virtually all the problems encountered with early spaying can be prevented by doing this.

Remember, spayed females don't have to be lazy, they don't have to be fat, and they don't have to have health problems. Spayed females are quieter, more content, stay home better, and are far steadier to work than unspayed females, and you don't have to worry about those 'accidental' puppies. Unless your girl happens to be one out of a thousand purebred working dogs who should be bred, and you are willing to go to all the trouble and expense of protecting her and getting her health tested, please do spay her responsibly, and don't add to our population of unwanted dogs.

Neutering Male Dogs

Neutering male dogs and spaying female dogs tends to be lumped all together into one single discussion. The subject is even sometimes expressed in the new, compound word sputer. It simply isn't the same. Just to begin, male dogs simply don't get pregnant. They don't die of complications due to whelping, they don't suffer from eclampsia or pyrometra, they don't wind up with perianal fistulas or other life-changing-much-for-the-worse or threatening conditions related to having puppies far too young, and they don't suffer as badly from sexually transmitted diseases as female dogs do. They also mature, in most cases, at a much slower rate than females, both mentally and physically. Their growth plates close much more slowly. About the only things male dogs and female dogs have in common when intact and allowed to escape their yards is that they can both be hit by cars or contract parvovirus or bordetella or any one of another half dozen diseases.

Far from avoiding problems with aggression or reactivity, early neutering actually can cause them, because male puppies need testosterone in order to grow properly, not just physically, but mentally as well. The same is true of health concerns. Early neutering causes far more health problems than it avoids. Studies tell us that the testicular cancer some vets who care more about sticking their hands in your pockets than they do about your pup's health tout as a 'risk' to intact male dogs is a negligible health risk easily detected and easily 'cured' by surgery when caught early. In contrast, the cancers which occur 4 to 6 times more often when puppies are neutered early, thus short circuiting the puppies' natural hormone development, hermangiosarcoma, lymphosarcoma, osteosarcoma, and mast cell tumors, as well as, surprise! prostate cancer, tend to be far more difficult and expensive to treat and far more apt to end in death.

And in an irony founded in Bobbie Burns' idea that the best laid plans 'gang aft agley' those folks who spend all that time and money to find dogs who won't get hip dysplasia because they've been so carefully bred, then turn right around and give the pup hip dysplasia, messing up his natural growth cycle by doing the 'right' thing and neutering the poor pup by 6 months of age. Rescue folks, who in their sincere and wholly understandable desire to stem the tide of unwanted pets filling our shelters and taxing the resources of rescues and shelters all over the country may believe they are doing the right thing for dogs by insisting on early spaying and neutering, but in so doing they are sentencing individual dogs to early and agonizing deaths by cancer as well as to lives plagued by joint infirmaties, allergies and immune deficiencies.

People who don't care about their dog's health and well-being, who just want to be politically correct, will continue to neuter their male dogs at 6 months of age and even younger, and the dogs will continue to die young of a laundry list of cancers and infirmities and suffer with allergies and the like during their lives. People who want their dogs neutered, but who don't want their dogs to suffer, can still neuter, but should wait at least one year for small to middle sized dogs' growth plates to be closed by their natural growth cycle. People who have larger dogs, among them many of the bigger boned, larger German Shepherd dogs, should be waiting until their dogs are 2 years of age, at least, before neutering.

Neutering does not take the place of training. It is not all right to allow your neutered male to run the neighborhood freely just because he's

26

neutered and can't sire any pups. He can still get hit by a car and he can still be a nuisance to your neighbors. Neutered males, in fact, are often aggressive towards intact males and have been known to attack them when allowed the opportunity.

Neutering is not the only cause of the new laundry list of cancers. People demanding that cancer be 'bred out' of their dogs are working the wrong end of the problem. The pesticides and herbicides with which we fill our world are all known carcinogens. If you insist on pouring pesticides on your dog every month to prevent flea and tick infestations and into your dog every month to avoid heart-worm problems you may be creating health problems in your dogs far worse than those a few fleas or a tick or two may bring. Pesticides should be used with care and discretion on an as needed basis, not in a constant attack on the dog's immune system. There are numerous products available to protect your dog against insect infestations which can be used to buttress a sparing use of pesticide treatments, garlic and diatomaceous earth, essential oils, apple cider vinegar washes, and so on. Moderation may be the best program to follow to insure your dogs long- term health, with careful, discriminating use of pesticides in conjunction with more holistic methods of flea, tick and heartworm prevention.

If you wait to neuter your dog until after he's finished growing, and avoid the over-use of pesticides there is no reason he can't live a normal life time in good health and be an active, happy member of your family.

Puppy Mills

We all know that puppy mills are bad, right? But who knows what they are? I can hear you all shout back, Breeders! Well, you're half right. Puppy Mills are places that breed puppies for sale, usually, but not always, in large numbers, without regard to health issues, breed standards, or proper socialization for the puppy. They are only interested in the bottom line.

Some puppy mills turn out at least marginally purebred dogs, while others don't even try, churning out puppies of many parts or breeding one purebred dog to any other dog they have for which they can produce papers, regardless of whether the papers were issued to that dog originally. They have many dogs, often of more than one breed on the premises, and they may boast that puppies are always available. If you are dealing with a reputable breeder, it is likely that you will have to wait for a puppy until a specific, planned breeding, and you may even have to wait in line to get one.

Money is always the issue in puppy mill operations. Now, a reputable breeder may ask you to pay a reasonable amount for a purebred puppy. Health testing is expensive and may run as high as a thousand dollars a dog just for x-rays, blood tests, dna, OFA, and other exams. Then there's the cost of feeding the dog, health care, perhaps purchasing the dog in the beginning, and you can see that it would be easy to have five thousand dollars into a Mom and Dad dog before we even start talking about puppies. The difference is that you will get more than just a puppy for your money from a reputable breeder.

Things start with either UKC or AKC papers certifying that the dog has been registered as a purebred of that particular breed. It doesn't mean a whole lot, since as we've seen, a puppy mill person can say so-and-so dog is the sire of a litter, but who's to know but the puppy mill if he's telling the truth or not? At least it's a place to start. Next we add the certification from either Penn hips or OFA as to the condition of Mom's and Dad's hips and elbows. Again, we have to take the breeder's word that the papers really belong to that dog, but again, it's better than nothing.

Reputable breeders don't have scrawney, starvling Moms nor do they keep them in cages. Their dogs are vaccinated, so the puppies get some immunity from Mom and the puppies don't leave Mom even so much as one day before they're seven weeks old (with the possible exception of some of the terrier breeds, since these puppies sometimes severely injure each other fighting) and many stay with Mom until eight, nine, or even ten weeks of age. Reputable breeders thus socialize their puppies to adult dogs, their litter mates, and people before they leave home and often have them temperament tested.

They also start vaccinations before the puppies leave to give them some immunity against Parvo and distemper when they go to their new home, and they de-worm the puppies. (It will probably need to be done again.) Puppy mills do not do any of these things.

In order to avoid having to feed and vaccinate or de-worm their puppies (which costs money) they often separate puppies from their Moms as early as five weeks of age, denying them socialization both with Mom and their litter mates, as well as people and send them off to shippers and wholesalers before they're fully weaned. This saves the puppy mill a lot of money, but it means that the puppies are at risk of distemper and Parvo and may develop agression problems as adults both with other dogs and people. Puppies may grow up fearful and shy, have difficulty learning and most will have trouble with housebreaking, because from their earliest experience, they were forced to foul their cages.

You never see the home puppy mill puppies come from and if you could find out where they came from you would not be welcome to visit. You would not be allowed to look at your puppy's Mom and Dad. Whereas, if you make arrangements with a reputable breeder beforehand, you will be welcome in their home. They will be proud to show you their dogs--in fact, you may have trouble getting away! Reputable breeders seek to educate you as to nutrition, they are happy to answer your questions about training, equipment, blood-lines, just try to shut 'em up.

Reputable breeders will tell you that if you ever have to let your puppy go, they want first crack at him. They will not allow their puppies to wind up at shelters if they have anything to say about it. Many of them are active in rescue. They fund research into the treatment and eradication of disease, and are constantly seeking to improve the quality of life for dogs and people everywhere. At the end of the day, reputable breeders count the converts they have made to responsible dog ownership. Puppy mills just count the cash.

Back-yard Breeders

If you have heard the term 'Puppy mills', you may also have heard the term 'back-yard breeder'. This is a derogatory term invented so that special interest groups, particularly the bite sport crowd and the show dog fanciers, can use it as a marketing strategy to paint the puppies of all other groups as less desirable than their pups. In German Shepherds the 'working/bite-line' group despise all dogs that don't conform to their particular aberrant version of the breed standard and show-line fanciers live in fear that the huge 'pet' dog market might discover that there are people out there breeding dogs better designed to meet the needs of people who need a dog for work or play than their dog show rejects.

Sport and show dog people make their money selling pups to what they contemptuously call the 'pet' market. With the average litter of puppies numbering from 6 to 10, there simply aren't enough sport or dog show homes for all the pups they produce for sale. (Dog sport and dog shows are an expensive hobby!)

Every breeder out there who is producing nice, stable, solid nerved, high threshold, moderate prey drive, balanced dogs is a threat to their income. If they are to be able to continue to produce their extreme, often mentally and/or physically unsound dogs geared for their particular hobby and get you, the puppy buying public to pay for it, they have to convince you that their puppies are the 'best'. And that those nice, healthy, balanced, sound, moderate dogs the other folks are breeding, because they don't have to conform to the extremes of competition are sub-standard in some way.

This is particularly important to them, because, in order to pay for their hobby, their bite sports or dog shows, they have to charge you a lot more for those pups than the back-yard breeders who just have to worry about good health and mental and physical soundness do. The sport/show breeders have to pay those big stud fees or puppy prices in order to breed to all those popular sires who have won all those championships in the show ring, or scored big on the bite sport trial field. The health tests they tout cost money too. Not that they pay any real attention to them.

Those puppies those sport/show breeders are turning out have to be bred to those 'popular' sires in order to give them a leg up in the competition stakes. When their new young contestant takes to the show ring or the trial field, the judges know who sired that youngster and who the youngster's dam was. If the sire is one of the 'right' names, if the dam is another of the 'right' names, then, in the subjective world of competition, that youngster will have an advantage over contestants whose pedigree the judges don't know, or who the judges do know but consider to have had an 'undistinguished career'. The sons and daughters of champions have a big advantage. So if the person breeding these pups wants to have the name/reputation of turning out 'champion' dogs, they will breed to these 'right' sires and dams. Inevitably, that means the pups will become in-bred.

These days, certain show lines come attached to certain genetic disorders. Some show-line dogs mean that the pups come with EPI, and often vWildebrands as well, while others come attached to SIBO or IBD, while yet others mean Cardiomyeopathy, Seizures, or Juvenile Renal Dysplasia. There are show dogs lines that produce fearful temperaments a rather large percent of the time, and some that are noted for hip dysplasia—for the initiated, secrets that 'pet' people are rigorously sheltered from. 'Working/bite-line' dogs come with their own list of genetic disorders distilled from the pool of 'popular sire' in-breeding, not only vWildebrands, but Degenerative Myeopathy, Pannus, and Juvenile Renal Dysplasia. In addition, they're the progenitors of much of the 'reactivity' being produced today, since they are quite deliberately bred to have high aggression, low thresholds, particularly low bite thresholds, and extremely high prey drive, because those qualities allow the dogs to do well in competition on the bite-sport field (Schutzhund, Mondio, French Ring, Personal Protection, KNPV, PSA and SDA). When people tout their 'titled' dogs, it is usually these sports they have in mind.

I know of one line of 4 generations of National and International 'Working/bite-line' dogs every one of which ended their life suffering from DM and Pannus. Did the breeders care that their dogs carried DM and Pannus? Not at all. Their dogs did well in competition, and that was all that mattered to them. One show-line kennel with a laundry list of 'best in show' and champion dogs turns out a couple of IBD dogs for every champion. But these are 'reputable' breeders in the dog world because their dogs have 'titles'. Many breeders of the German 'High-line' show dogs crank out dogs with EPI, one after the other, with a shrug and the words, 'Oh, you just feed them enzymes and they're fine'.

So what does 'back-yard breeder' really mean? Someone putting any 2 dogs they happen to come across together in the back yard and then selling the pups to make a little extra money now and again without any regard for the temperament, structure or health of the parents? Yes, occasionally. More often the parents are good, healthy dogs sound in mind and body who have proved themselves excellent pets. And sometimes the cross between those two parents is serendipitious in that the pups are all nice, solid, sound and healthy dogs. Sometimes the cross doesn't work out so well, but in both these cases, the dogs are just as likely to be healthy and mentally and physically sound as the competition dogs bred for extremes.

Sometimes 'back-yard breeder' just means someone who breeds dogs for a purpose the bite-sport folks and the show folks don't happen to approve of. This often includes the traditional uses of whatever breed is in question, such as German Shepherds who do herding, search and rescue, and assistance/guide work. Bite-sport folk call search and rescue dogs who save lives 'watered down' and inveigh against breeding them, while they regard all assistance dogs with disgust and consider real herding dogs irrelevant— regardless of the fact that German Shepherd dogs are SUPPOSED to be herding dogs. A little critical thinking is in order, something both the show folks and the bite-sport folks depend upon the folks they want to convince to buy their dogs for their inflated prices being too lazy to do.

Think about it. WHY do they inveigh against the breeding of dogs for the 'pet market' when the 'pet market' consists of 98% of the puppy market? Don't breed dogs appropriate for pets? When that's exactly what 98% of them will be? There's a certain illogic there, and more, some real insanity. The show folks and the bite-sport folks would tell you because 'pet' dogs aren't as good as theirs. But does history and tradition, at least in German Shepherd dogs, support that attitude?

Well, no, it doesn't, actually. In World War I, the German's herding and pet dogs served with such distinction as couriers and sentries and 'ambulance' dogs that both British and American soldiers and ambulance personnel were only too eager to appropriate them for themselves, both during and after the war. After World War I, the German's herding dogs pioneered the use of dogs to guide the blind all around the world, and in World War II, America's and Britain's 'pet' dogs again served with distinction. And, in fact, some of those pet dogs who made it home from the war turned around and helped to re-vitalize the guide dog schools. Others invented the use of dogs for search and rescue, while still others served in our police departments. It was only in Germany and the Communist countries that extreme dogs came into use in Border Patrol where their extreme prey drive and low bite thresholds paired with high aggression served totalitarian goals by terrorizing people in an effort to keep them from defecting.

Pet dogs and 'useful' dogs share many of the same characteristics. Moderate, limited prey drive coupled with high bite thresholds in particular along with high thresholds in general, and sharply disciplined aggression serves good stock handling for the dogs still working sheep and cattle and with horses on the job, just as it serves good family dogs, allowing them to be 'safe' with children as they are 'safe' with livestock. Dogs that care about working in partnership with humans, that dedicate themselves to human tasks and goals not only make good search and rescue dogs, they make good family dogs. The qualities that make a dog a good neighbor are much the same as the qualities that allow a dog to be a good assistance/guide dog. And anyone who wants or needs a dog to work at one of these traditional tasks needs a healthy dog and wants a dog to remain healthy throughout a good, long life. No one wants to lose their partner prematurely, any more than anyone wants to lose their beloved pet prematurely. To breed a dog for qualities which make a good pet is to breed a dog with qualities which will make it a good dog for practical use.

But what about the qualities that serve sport goals? Well, sport goals usually feature a dog with high adrenaline production, a very high, even extreme prey drive, lots and lots of aggression very close to the surface, and a very low bite threshold along with low thresholds in general (so that the dog can access all that adrenaline quickly and easily). If one wants to 'title' a dog in one of the bite sports, this is how the dog has to be bred to succeed. And if one wants a dog to compete in the sport arena, one has to breed to even greater extremes of these qualities. Long term health and long life are not of very great importance to the competitor.

Do some of these dogs make good pets? Well, I suppose that depends on how you define 'good'. Very extreme prey drive means that the dog endowed with it is not going to be easily convinced to live in a household without killing its small prey animal members, like cats or rabbits or hamsters and gerbils. In many cases, it also means that the dog with extreme prey drive is not going to be particularly safe around small children. Add low thresholds, so that the dog becomes easily excited, along with high aggression, and you have the recipe for what is called 'reactivity'. Add low bite thresholds, which make it so easy to train the dog to bite people without any provocation necessary, and you have a dog that in 'real life' out in someone's neighborhood, can be a real liability.

But, if a person is single, or half of a childless couple, with plenty of discretionary income to spend on exorbitant training fees and lots of time to spend training and exercising the dog, that sport bred dog from 'titled' parents may work out very well. For people with little purpose in life, such a dog can give them a focal point to structure their life around. The thing is, if they don't, the dog is not likely to be very successful. And, after all, by the time such folk are ready to have children and form a family in which such a dog may not fit very well, the sport dog is likely not to still be around. Sport dog life expectancy tends not to linger much beyond 10 years and sport dogs tend to become old by 8 or 9. By that time they may be able to co-exist with young children, as long as the children are kept well away from them on most occasions and supervised heavily on those occasions when dog and young children occupy the same space. Judicious use of a crate and outdoor kennel can keep infants safe until the old dog sluffs off his mortal coil due to bloat or one of the cancers heavy pesticide useage and early neutering make so common today.

A pet's family may grieve the passing of their beloved family member, but the sport folks and show ring aficionados are not apt to be so deeply afflicted.

A sport dog has only a very short competitive life to look forward to, and then an equally short breeding life. By the time the dog reaches the age of 8 or 10, the sport competitor is ready to dispense with the older dog so that another up and coming competition dog can take his place. Long life and the kind of sturdy good health that supports long life is not of very great importance to sport people. Older dogs are no longer bringing in the kudos that burnish their reputations and bolster their pride, and they are no longer capable of producing the puppies whose sale lines their owners' pocketbooks. So if DM mandates that they be put down, or Pannus means it's time to say goodbye, or bloat carries them off, or vWildebrands means that one day the sport competitor finds them lying dead in a pool of their own blood in the kennel, well, now there's an open kennel for a dog that can bring in money or prizes.

Show people aren't really much different. Once a dog is too old to show and too old to breed, they really don't have much use for the dog any longer. A long lived dog isn't a positive thing for them. That dog is taking up kennel space they need for their new champion. So if EPI, or SIBO or IBD carries off the dog before they reach their 11th birthday, well, that's not a negative for them. Or Cardiomeyopathy or bloat or whatever. They don't like it if the dog doesn't live long enough to make money for them, but true long life and robust good health are not the show folks' friend. If a female dog doesn't die quickly enough after having 4 or 5 litters of pups for them, they'll 're-home' her. Sometimes that means they dump her in a shelter.

Sometimes it means they dump her on their breed rescue. And sometimes they just put her to sleep. There isn't a lot of room in either the show or the sport world for sentimentality.

So next time you hear someone maligning 'back-yard' breeders, and blaming them for producing less than perfect dogs, or insisting that 'pet' dogs shouldn't be bred, try a little critical thinking about what they're saying (and implying). If you get right down to it, sport dogs are really no more than pet dogs that run down a big field and bite the first person they see as hard as they can for fun and profit. And while it takes a very great deal of very skilled training to get those dogs to do their bite routines just right, none of that training, nor the characteristics that allow them to be trained to do it, are particularly useful. By the same token, what are show dogs but pets who are taught to prance around a ring in a beauty pageant for someone to judge using artificial standards of beauty which again, are of little to no use to anyone? When you get right down to it, the only real thing the so-called 'back-yard' breeders are doing wrong, is costing the sport breeders and the show breeders money.

So Who is a 'Good' Breeder?

A good breeder answers your e-mails when you have questions about their puppy AFTER you've paid your money and taken your puppy home. They lend you an ear when you have concerns, and they can help you to find a good vet, a good diet, a good trainer, good books to read on the subject of dogs, and they do the best they can to answer your questions. They want to teach you as much as you will let them. And most of all, good breeders are THERE.

Good breeders DON'T 'guarantee' puppies. Puppies are not interchangeable parts, like those in your car, they are not washing machines or refrigerators, or any other appliance upon which you get a warranty, they are living beings and MOST of what goes wrong with them after you take them home happens because of things that you did (or didn't do).

Good breeders take their puppy back when you can no longer keep him even long after he is no longer a puppy. They re-train puppies and find them new homes when possible and they bite the bullet and put the puppy to sleep when you have spoiled, poorly fed, failed to exercise, abused and/or otherwise so compromised the pup's mental or physical health that forcing the pup to live a miserable, painful, debilitating life is inhumane.

If you 'broke' one pup, a good breeder does NOT provide you another to destroy.

Good breeders help with rescue in one way or another, by taking in the occasional rescue, by helping people to re-train their rescues, by helping to publicize rescue, by refusing to give/sell puppies to people who they think might wind up dumping their puppy into rescue (or a shelter) and even by occasionally sending people to a rescue who have come to them for puppies because they think that person would benefit by getting an older puppy or an adult dog with some training already.

Good breeders have goals for their pups. That may be simply that the pup achieve the status of beloved family member. It may be assistance work of some kind, or search and rescue or herding or a general purpose ranch or farm dog. Or it may be some form of competition. But they are breeding their pups with a purpose in mind, and they have tailored their breeding in order to suit those purposes. If your purposes don't mesh with theirs, don't get one of their pups!

Good breeders don't try to sell you a 'family' pet if they're breeding for sport purposes, nor do they tell you that any puppy is good for anything. Good breeders know that some of their pups are better for some purposes than others. That puppy of bite-sport 'titled' parentage crammed with extreme prey drive is an appalling choice for a family with young children. A puppy who might be very good at public access assistance work is a rotten choice for bite work, and a puppy who would be good for guide work, brace/balance work or wheelchair aide work would NOT do for the beauty pageant of the dog show world, at least in German Shepherds. The hind leg structure necessary for the work, particularly in wheelchair work and brace/balance work would not be welcomed in the show ring. A puppy bred for bite sports would be a very poor choice for assistance work and is rarely appropriate for search and rescue and no GOOD sport breeder would try to foist one of their pups on you for public access assistance work. The rickety pup wobbling around on his loose hocks and stifle joints might be just the thing for the show ring, but would rarely be successful in the bite sports. (He'd be more apt to fall on his face than to be able to bite the sleeve.) And if possible, he'd be an even worse disaster attempting to turn a ewe or head a cow. Never mind face up to a ram.

No good breeder wants their puppy put in a position in which they can do little else but fail. Breeders who just want your money don't care. They'll tell you anything. And breeders who don't understand the qualities necessary for success in the 'usual' or traditional range of purposes for their breed of dog are not really knowledgeable enough to be considered good.

Good breeders are going to ask you all kinds of questions before you get one of their pups and they may even make you jump through a few hoops. They may make you wait on a list, or they may not, but good breeders don't have puppies available year around.

Good breeders don't mass produce dogs and they don't give you a puppy no questions asked. They may/will want money for their pup but then again, raising pups is an expensive business, if it's done properly. If you want a puppy whose parents have each had a thousand dollars or more of health testing done on them, then you will have to reconcile yourself to paying a healthy price for that pup.

Good breeders spend time with their pups. They imprint their puppies to people and socialize them to different foods, different sounds, different smells and different surfaces and different dogs as well as other animals. (Like cats.) Puppies may not come 'house-broken' (too young) but they will come with the rudiments of an answer to a call, and many will walk on a leash a little bit. Most will be acclimated to a collar.

Good breeders don't let their puppies go to their new homes before they are 8 weeks old, and some of them won't even let their puppies go until 10 weeks. (Puppies receive Mom to pup and pup to pup socialization by staying with Mom and their brothers and sisters that makes a difference in what kind of dog they become. Puppy mill puppies who don't usually get this socialization often have aggression problems because of it.) Also, older puppies have an easier time learning to sleep through the night and to maintain control of their bladder because their little systems are more mature.

Good breeders de-worm their puppies and start their vaccination protocols. (This costs money! And this is part of what you pay for when you buy a puppy.)

And last, but far from least, good breeders will talk your ear off about their dogs and their breed any chance they get. If they don't/won't, then they're probably more into the money than they are the dogs. If you like their dogs anyway—shrug--go for it. High end competition people know what pup they want and why and the only voice they want to hear is their own (in most cases) so they just hand over the money and grab their new competition pup and all is good. Such people have their own opinions about who is a good breeder and why and those reasons might be a little different from those John Q Public cares about. High end police and military are in pretty much the same boat. For most folks, those boats are far out to sea and barely visible so there's no point in discussing them.

Good breeders can be eccentric and they're not always the easiest of folks to get along with. Some of them smoke. Some of them drink. Some of them are computer savvy, some of them couldn't build a decent website to save their souls. Some very bad breeders have very good people skills. Some very good breeders have very bad people skills. Many good breeders are not at all politically correct. None of that has anything to do with what makes them a good breeder, though. If you think it does, maybe you need to re-evaluate. If you don't think you need to re-evaluate, Good Luck!

Chapter 3
Behavior

Black Magic's Beryl's Bladen

When Girl Dogs Fight

Most German Shepherd people will tell you that it is more difficult to keep two female GSDs together than a female and male, or even two males. They're right. It is also pretty well agreed that it is much more difficult to keep two females from fighting, once hostilities have broken out, than it is to deal with a pair of males who fight. I believe this is generally true, and for more than one reason.

Girls are much more subtle in their body language than males, making it a great deal more difficult for their owner/handlers to realize which one is the REAL instigator of the problem. Without the accurate identification of the dog truly instigating the problem, all the owner/handler can do is intensify the problem. (And usually does.)

If that isn't bad enough, the person trying to deal with this is also up against a very essential pack reality. In many packs, only big Momma gets to mate and have puppies. If a junior female wants to mate, she has to either leave the pack, or depose Mama and Dad. If there is a wide range in age--say, if she's coming two and they are say, eight or nine, that may happen naturally, in a gradual, painless fashion. If their ages are close, most females would probably opt to go find their own mate and set up their own pack somewhere else.

The problem is, when we keep two females together in our homes, they can't do that. Sometimes things get so bitter we do it for them, but unfortunately for whichever one of them we choose to re- home, it doesn't often work out for them very well. It isn't always that easy to find a new home for a female known to be a fighter. She's a lot more apt to find herself at the pound, being euthanized. Sometimes that seems to be the only way to go.

Females can get so bitter that they fight to the death, and fights between dogs of sixty pounds and up are dangerous, not just for the dogs, but for any human unfortunate enough to be in the area as well. Any attempt to break up such a fight is virtually taking your own life in your hands, and to do so effectively requires two adults at the least and the ability to lock the dogs out of sight and sound of each other once they have been separated. Never mind the inevitable vet bills.

When male dogs fight, very often it is with a great deal of sound and fury, but very little real, serious injury. When females fight, it is apt to be a bloodbath, with some very serious injuries. Why?

It all stems from the lack of understanding of the dogs' body language, and the person's complete misunderstanding of which dog is really the instigator. Here's a football analogy which may help to illuminate the situation.

In football, offensive and defensive linemen fight over a mythical area of the field called the 'line of scrimmage'. Offensive linemen try to push defensive linemen back from this area and keep them from touching, encroaching on their quarterback. Some offensive linemen accept the rules of the game by which they are supposed to do this. Some don't. (Sort of like the rules of your household.)

The offensive linemen who don't accept the rules try to cheat by kicking, biting, 'rabbit' punching, often at the throat, gouging, especially at eyes, and tripping defensive linemen when-ever they think that the referees can't see them. They know if they can do this and not get called for their infractions of the rules, that they can so frustrate and infuriate the defensive linemen that eventually they can get the defensive player to retaliate. When he does, inevitably, the ref throws a flag on him and hits his team with a 15 yard penalty.

This is a huge advantage for the offensive player's team and can often mean the difference between scoring a touchdown or field goal and not making the first down and therefore having to give up the ball. Most defensive linemen know this and try to control themselves, but as a game wears on, particularly if the score is close, they start to lose patience. Some time in the end of the third quarter, or the beginning of the fourth, they begin to be less tolerant of the ref's incompetence (if it isn't something worse) and they start to retaliate in order to defend themselves.

Bad refs throw the flag then, on the defensive player. This has a tendency to inflame the entire defense, and things can go very bad very quickly. Sometimes you will then see the offensive lineman carried off the field. It isn't always the right one. If they can't get to the offensive player causing the problem, they may take down any offensive lineman they can get to, or even a back or a receiver to 'send a message'. When these things start to happen, it is said that the referees have 'lost control of the game'.

(When things have gotten so bad that the girl in your home being bullied and taunted and harassed can no longer trust you to 'take control of the game' and throw the flag on the right dog, that's when she retaliates, and the fights start.)

Good referees listen to the things players say about one another, and they watch a lot of 'film'. The better the ref, the more 'film' they watch. They learn all the little tell-tale signs of body movements so they can learn when offensive linemen are at their kicking, gouging, punching, biting, tripping activities, and during the game, the first time they detect the least little indication that the known 'cheap-shot artist' is at it again, they throw the flag and call holding.

Now, every sophisticated football fan knows that the way line play is done today, any ref who wants to call a game tight can probably find holding on any play, if he really wants to. So, though our 'artist' may glare at the ref when his number is called, he goes back to work with minimal grumbling. But as soon as things get tight again (and they will get tight, that's the nature of life, and of football) he goes back to rabbit punching throats and biting and everything else.

The good ref throws the flag again. Calls the 'artist's' number again. Now steam starts to rise from the top of the guy's helmet. He stares at the ref. The ref stares back. He's saying that he's going to throw the flag again, unless the 'artist' starts playing by the rules again. The 'artist' gets the message and plays for most of the rest of the game with very few 'cheap-shots'. The defense, confident in the skill and fairness of the ref, slogs it out, doing the best they can. Injuries, if they occur, are accidental. The ref 'has control of the game'.

Oft-times, in the fourth quarter, if the game is close, the ref will have to assert himself again, at least once, to 'keep [the offensive lineman] honest' by throwing another flag on him, which the good ref will not hesitate to do. In such 'clean' games, tempers tend not to flare and injuries are kept to a minimum.

Any person living in a household in which two female dogs are fighting needs to become a 'good ref', and learn to recognize what is really going on. Their home is the 'line of scrimmage'. In it, the dogs are 'scrimmaging' over the resources of the household, most particularly the time and attention of the people in it.

When two females have started fighting, it is because the person in charge of the household is missing the subtle body language of the bully/instigator in the household and is penalizing the dog who is merely defending herself. By the time fights start, a clear pattern (to the dogs' perception) has been established by which the person (ref) has been clearly favoring the instigator/ bully dog for some time and penalizing the victim dog. This results in the victim dog--I'll call her Daisy--losing confidence in their person. She no longer trusts them to take care of her. She's given up on them and now is trying to take care of herself.

At the same time, the bully/instigator dog--I'll call her Diabla--is emboldened to be ever more provocative and threatening to Daisy. She's gotten away with murder and she intends to keep on until she manages to get rid of Daisy--one way or another--permanently. She's lost all respect for the person who is supposed to be in charge, and no longer has any trust or confidence in them because after all, in her view, they're so stupid as to allow her to bully and taunt and threaten Daisy at will without doing a single thing to protect or defend her. Diabla has a whole bag of tricks up her sleeve.

Example: Say person is sitting on the couch, and Daisy is sitting beside her person blissfully, being petted. Diabla joins the duo, sits down in front of the person, edging Daisy ever so subtly out and begins posturing for attention. Tipping her head, flirting, wiggling, she soon has person ignoring Daisy altogether, petting and praising and playing with Diabla, displacing Daisy.

What can person do to defuse this deadly insult/offensive behavior of Diabla's (in Daisy's view). Not much. Any attention given to Diabla what-so-ever, even negative attention (ever heard of negative reinforcement?) is a win for Diabla and a defeat for Daisy. This--if it happens--is a successful challenge to Daisy's position in the household and a serious threat to her status. Diabla may repeat this behavior a thousand times before Daisy finally breaks, but do not be fooled. This is serious stuff and by the time Daisy breaks, it will be a 'the last straw breaks the camel's back' situation and she will be furious.

Prevention is the only successful strategy a person can use to keep Daisy from becoming seriously frustrated and Diabla from 'winning'. Now, if that prevention means that Daisy gets less attention, it won't help matters. If anything, the person needs to increase the number and length of times they sit with Daisy and reassure her that her position in the household is secure. (This only works if person has identified the RIGHT Daisy!)

Example: Daisy is moving from one area of the room to another, moving towards her person. Diabla moves in on her and, without actually blocking Daisy from reaching her destination, turns her shoulder towards Daisy, twists her head, and, on the side away from person, lifts her lip a little and issues a soundless, vibration snarl.

It all happens in an instant. All the person sees is Daisy's reaction, which the person interprets as Daisy being hostile. Diabla is now all innocence, and fakes immediate submissive posture 'Mama, she's being mean to me!' Mama falls for it. Daisy steams. She's been taunted, threatened, and is now being bullied by person at Diabla's instigation. Diabla has triumphed once again.

This scenario can be repeated with a hundred variations: Diabla can use this technique to interfere when Daisy is called and tries to come, when the person is playing with Daisy, when Daisy is attempting to get from one room to the other (usually from the room the person has just exited in order to follow) even whenever Daisy merely tries to change position. When the person erroneously corrects Daisy, for her reaction, it is very strong reinforcement for Diabla, as she is effectively inducing the person to do her bullying for her.

All this stuff is subtle. Diabla has a whole bevy of threats and taunts at her beck and call through which to bully Daisy. Stiff, alert ears can signal harassment towards the other dog. Stiff, braced forelegs, or even more overtly, all four legs stiff and braced, can convey threat. A fixed stare directed towards the other dog conveys a direct threat, and can be re-focused to avoid a person's detection in a fraction of a second.

Diabla can taunt her rival with a laughing eye when she has triumphed, yet again (very similar to those end-zone dances players do when they score a touchdown). A shoulder thrown out in her rival's direction can be a bullying threat or merely harassment meant to make Daisy change directions or to challenge her or just merely to remind her that Diabla can strike at her again at any time.

Identifying which dog is Diabla and which dog is Daisy is crucial. Identify the wrong dog as Diabla, and you are almost certainly condemning the real Daisy to either a miserable life or outright death. Diabla is likely to be the person's favorite—and she knows it! Her person perceives her to be more endearing, more appealing, prettier, possibly even more obedient (she's probably not, she's just flashier about it). She's probably flirtatious. She may be a more subtle dog than Daisy.

Sometimes when Daisy is mis-identified and she ends up in another household, (in the rare instance when re-homing is actually successful) and they later get, or already have, another dog, (who doesn't happen to be a Diabla) then Daisy's first person gets told 'I don't know why you said Daisy doesn't get along with other dogs. She does just fine with Lettuce.' At the same time, if person number one gets another dog, sooner or later, they'll be wondering why their new dog just 'doesn't get along with other dogs!'

Many times a situation that has been simmering under the radar breaks out when one of the girls goes out to the vet to be spayed and comes back in some pain and bereft of her main source of estrogen (also a big source of patience and equanimity). The girl coming back doesn't feel so hot, and when Diabla begins her by now habitual subtle bullying, Daisy retaliates--and immediately gets flagged, merely for defending herself. This is really serious, because the person allowed Daisy to be bullied, taunted, harassed, threatened, just when they should have been protecting her the most and may destroy Daisy's confidence in her person at a time when she truly needs it.

No real improvement in the relationship between the dogs can be achieved until Daisy and Diabla are correctly identified and Diabla starts a strict regimen of correction. However, that does not mean that the situation can be allowed to continue with the girls fighting. It is simply TOO DANGEROUS! If person can't manage to correctly identify Daisy and Diabla, so they can re-train the dogs, they can certainly manage the situation. They'll have to use management to defuse the situation before they can start re-training, anyway.

So, here are some management techniques.

Diabla and Daisy are never to be allowed in the same room—or yard--together again. Diabla by this time is doubtless expert at threatening and taunting with no more than a look--therefore, they may not look at each other any longer, which means they must not be put into a position where they can look at each other. It should go without saying, but I'll say it anyway--these dogs must NEVER meet again at a door or gate or in competition over a person's attention. (throwing a ball, etc)

If person does not have crates, they must get them and use them. Crates should be placed, each one in a different room and the dogs should only occupy those rooms. Dogs should go in and out of the house at different times and by different doors. One dog uses the back door, the other the front. They must never be in the yard together--on leash or off! And in order for this to work, everyone in the household has to get on board with it. Person's house must become a de-militarized zone, complete with a no-fly order.

Feed each dog in her crate with the door closed and the other dog in the other room. Try to make sure each dog gets one on one time with their person, and try to see that the amount of time is as equal as possible. Fairness is a biggee in the dog world. Like young kids watching everything to make sure they get as much as everyone else--'Her piece is bigger'n mine!' they are always on the lookout for what they perceive to be injustice.

Nobody says it will be fun. It'll be inconvenient and time-consuming and irritating. But it will keep the dogs alive and the rest of the household safe.

As to whether the person will ever be able to repair the situation? Unknown. The Diablas of the world lose all respect for their person when they get away with this behavior. Sometimes that doesn't matter much. Sometimes it matters a lot. Some Diablas, once they have successfully routed their Daisy go on to their people and wind up biting them, sometimes quite severely, when the people, still not understanding the dog's body language, do something to 'cross' the dog--to the dog's way of thinking. And since Diabla has proved she is the boss, her perception is that her people should knuckle down and obey her. Her people, having NO clue that this is going on in the dog's mind, almost inevitably do 'cross' her, and whoops! we have dog biting person.

Some Diablas are quite content with routing Daisy and rest on their laurels. They don't respect or trust their people, but it doesn't matter much; they at least like them and they don't have any urge to take charge of them to issue orders which people don't understand.

Perhaps surprisingly, the Daisys of the dog world, even when their people have failed them so egregiously, by bringing Diabla into the household and then refusing to believe she is Diabla, when they get over the worst of their resentment and frustration, are often far more respectful and forgiving of their people than the people perhaps deserve. They can, however, when mis-identified as the instigator, grow sullen, distrustful, resentful and even, finally, disobedient. Why shouldn't they? After all, they're the victim.

So, there you have it, the alternatives for dealing with female on female rivalries.

Re-home

Manage

Manage to defuse the situation and, when tempers have cooled a bit,

Re-train, by correcting the INSTIGATOR when, and only when, correct identification of the instigator is made. Again, I warn-- identify the wrong dog as the instigator, and any attempt at re-training can very easily wind up in disaster. Good Luck!

Reactivity

Reactivity is the modern euphemism for generalized hostility. When I was a kid, reactive dogs were labeled with names like mean, vicious, junkyard dog, and the like. Owning a 'reactive' dog was considered somehow shameful, a proof that you had not brought your dog up properly. It wasn't even considered a real training issue, it had more to do with the kind of basic behavior accepted from the dog in your home to begin with and even more with what kind of behavior you would accept from the dog when you took him into the public eye. Dogs who carried their 'reactivity' too far got pts and nobody indulged in much angst over them.

Today, 'reactive' dogs lucky enough to find themselves with bite sport owners find themselves standing on podiums and becoming popular sires. Is it any wonder that 'reactivity' is on the rise? Today's bite sport dogs are bred to be highly aggressive, with extremes of prey drive and low thresholds, particularly bite thresholds, making them inherently unbalanced and unstable. This is being done quite deliberately, and one could state with some justification that it is done with malice aforethought because for the bite sport people, it creates a dog that scores big points.

Bite sport dogs have to do complex obedience routines in their trials, but those routines do not include having to behave with good manners when another dog is present. The dogs do have to tolerate a judge, but judges certainly do not make any attempt to lay hands on the dogs, and bite sport people see no point in having a dog anyone else can touch, whether or not they, as the handler, sanction it. Bite sport people have little use for the actual, written breed standard of the German Shepherd dog, and they do not breed dogs to conform to the real standard, particularly the portions of the breed standard which regard temperament.

Bite sport people scoff at the AKC's canine good citizen test, disdaining it as simple and basic, and so it is, but there is more than one IPO/Sch 3 dog running around that can't pass it. I've personally met several.

Reactive dogs can't pass the canine good citizen test, but as one second generation Schutzhund exhibitor explains, reactivity doesn't matter in Schutzhund or other bite sports because it doesn't prohibit the dog from getting his title or from advancing through the levels. This does not give the bite sport folks any incentive to eliminate reactivity from their breeding, and when you add that the breeders who have created the plague of reactivity with the very breeding strategies that give them their 'podium' dogs can blithely blame the 'reactive' dogs they created on the so-called 'back-yard' breeders (anyone not a member of their in-crowd) you can see that they can have their cake and eat it too.

Strong handlers don't have much problem with 'reactivity' anyway and most bite sport folks, at least the experienced ones, are strong handlers. When their pups first attempt to experiment with the behavior, the strong handler disagrees with the behavior firmly, re-directs the pup firmly, and then praises the pup fulsomely. The strong handler does this instantaneously, firmly and confidently, without having to stop and think about it, never allowing the pup to get his adrenaline reward for the behavior and the pup soon forgets all about it. The strong handler notes the situation the pup used to trigger his adrenaline production, and the next time such a situation presents itself, the strong handler engages the pup before the situation can develop, keeping the pup too active and intent on what the handler and pup are doing together to repeat the behavior and before very long, the pup has forgotten all about that particular form of misbehavior. He 'out-grows' it.

It is the inexperienced handler trying to fit the square 'working-line' pup into the round pet or family dog hole who has problems with it. Instead of disagreeing with the behavior when the pup first begins to experiment with it, and moving through firm correction to re-direction and praise, the inexperienced handler allows the pup to work through his experimentation and get his reward while they stand by, horrified. Instead of dealing with the pup's misbehavior effectively, the inexperienced handler stops to wonder what's going on, reacts, if they react at all, too late and too weakly, allowing the pup to understand their lack of confidence and confusion.

In the vacuum the handler leaves with his failure in leadership, the pup says to himself, 'boy, this really feels good!' and while the inexperienced handler is busy making all kinds of excuses for the pup 'oh, he just wants to play', or, 'he's not really aggressive, he's just excited' and the like the pup starts looking for the next opportunity to experiment with the behavior again. Actually, while the pup is still in the experimental stage, the handler is somewhat right. The pup is just excited—now. But reactivity is a progressive drug for the pup wired for high adrenaline production, much like any of the drugs people indulge in. Soon enough, the pup becomes habituated to the excited level of adrenaline, and, in the 'working-line' dog bred for the high aggression bite sports require, will soon graduate to hostility. At this point the pup is now mainlining his drug of choice and he is not going to willingly forego his highs any more than the human druggie down the block is going to forego his.

The inexperienced handlers, meanwhile, tell themselves that it was just an aberration, it won't happen again, and decide to ignore what they have no idea how to deal with. Each time the pup exhibits the behavior the inexperienced handler makes excuses for it, blames the behavior on the situation, on other dogs, other handlers, anything but on themselves and their own pup, and denies it is a problem, their pup 'is always perfect, except when—
'

This handler allows the behavior to spiral out of control until it becomes unbearable to them. Unfortunately, by then the dog is hooked, just like any other junkie, and now dealing with the behavior will be a long and difficult process with a prognosis that is far from positive.

My grandmother used to say an ounce of prevention is worth a pound of cure. When it comes to reactive dogs, boy, was she right!

The key to dealing with this behavior (beyond not saddling yourself with a bite sport dog bred from 'titled' parents in the first place) is in that ounce of prevention. Every moment that the pup is out, work at keeping the pup engaged with you, the handler. And, while remaining relaxed and active, you, the handler, must see everything before your pup does and hear everything before he pays any attention to it—and then you prevent him from getting his stimulus. Basically, you, the handler, are preventing him from 'buying' his drug of choice and from 'using' it.

In the beginning this is going to be very hard work. The adrenaline coursing through his system feels better to him and is a more complete experience than the juiciest steak could ever be. No treat will ever compare to that 'hit' of his favorite drug. The fact that his own brain manufactures that drug for him means that it is his brain you have to control.

One of the reasons that electronic collars work—when they do work—is that the brain (yours, your pup's) works on electricity. Thought, impulse, and action are all carried through the brain's synapses and neurons to trigger both voluntary and involuntary nerve and muscle systems via electricity. For many dogs it takes very little electricity to disrupt the spark as it travels along the synaptic pathways of the brain, and that disruption is what prevents the completion of the reactivity circuit. For the mature dog with a confirmed habit of adrenaline loading, electronic collars may not be just the most effective way to interrupt this behavior, it may be the only way. For pups, whose brains are still developing, it should be a last resort. Vigilance, engagement, re-direction and praise should be effective for all but the most addicted pup—if done correctly.

In re-training the reactive pup's brain, (the best time, before the pup becomes a dog and the task becomes a hundred times more difficult) the handler has to act quickly and be vigilant but relaxed. If you're manufacturing adrenaline in your own system all that will do is to trigger the pup to start up his own adrenaline production. It's a mirroring mechanism that has evolved between dogs and people over millennia. Holding that leash tightly, like grim death, is counter-productive. Engage the pup. Get his attention and hold it while keeping him active. Don't ask him to sit still and look at you, ask him to run with you, to walk a zig-zag with you, to concentrate on doing something. Ask him to hold a ball in his mouth while trotting along beside you—in another direction from a situation he has used in the past to get his adrenaline going.

Never let the pup get beyond the focus stage in adrenaline loading. Better yet, never let the pup get focused. At the first suggestion that the pup is starting to focus in on something or someone he might find stimulating, re-direct. Don't wait for him to get to the staring stage, never mind the braced, stiff-legged point. And the very instant the pup re-directs, praise. A lot. Treats are good, praise is better. Use 'em both. Praise builds confidence in the pup and the more confident the pup becomes, the less he needs the 'feel-good' adrenaline his system produces or the aggression he uses to get the adrenaline going.

Dealing with a reactive pup is never easy. Many 'working-line' pups are pre-disposed to high adrenaline production genetically but environment counts for something too, even if the 'everything is genetic' folks would like you to believe otherwise. No 'titled' dog would ever get a title in any bite sport merely because the dog was bred for it. That dog has to be trained to perform, and training is environment. High prey drive, high adrenaline production, lots of aggression and low bite thresholds are bred into bite sport dogs for the simple reason that it is always easier to train in harmony with the dog's genetic heritage than it is to train against it, but training against heredity can be done. Whether the results will justify the effort, only each individual owner/handler can decide for themselves.

If you decide to do it, start early, be consistent, and don't wait to react, be proactive in your approach. Stay out in front of your pup's behavior. Don't try to over-think the why of the behavior. Don't get caught reacting to it— each time your pup manages to get to his barking, snarling, lunging behavior, he's gotten his adrenaline reward. You still have to disagree and re-direct and praise when the pup does re-direct, but you're back to square one. Your pup has had a relapse because you were too late and dropped the ball. Like a druggie who has fallen off the wagon, he now needs to dry out and start all over again.

Dogs use adrenaline to make themselves feel good. They can use it as a coping mechanism to respond to many situations. The bored dog can decide a little adrenaline might liven things up (it will). The dog who is confused or anxious or just doesn't know what to do may decide that adrenaline will 'fix' it. From the dog's point of view, it will. If the dog is already annoyed with another dog's behavior, or finding his handler's behavior irritating, or just incomprehensible, well, adrenaline will at least change the situation and the dog probably figures, with some justification, that it will change it for the better. Once the dog starts mainlining adrenaline, from the dog's point of view, he's now in charge of the situation. Enough adrenaline makes the dog feel like he is king of the world, or at least, his little corner of it.

For those who urge spaying and neutering to get rid of reactivity, good luck. Spaying gets rid of estrogen, which tends to have a calming effect, and neutering gets rid of testosterone, which doesn't. The reasons for spaying a female, keeping her home, preserving her health, so she doesn't get sexually transmitted diseases or distemper or Parvo or the rest, so she doesn't get run over on the road, and so her owner doesn't have to put up with male dogs showing up in his yard and pestering everybody in the neighborhood, and so she doesn't get pregnant, have nothing to do with reactivity.

Neutering may help a male dog because in some cases testosterone may support aggression. Just as often, neutering may increase reactivity

47

because without testosterone, some dogs are less confident, increasing their 'need' for adrenaline loading to replace the confidence they have lost. Some studies suggest that neutering male dogs very young may actually increase the incidence of reactivity, so if you are going to neuter in the hope of diminishing reactive behavior it may be helpful to wait to do it until the dog is at least beyond a year of age.

Remember, anger pushes out fear. Once the dog learns to channel his native aggression to power his adrenaline production, he has his own meth lab situated between his ears, right there to pour his drug of choice into his system anytime he decides he wants it. Any situation which may tend to make him anxious, fearful or uncertain of what is expected of him may trigger his desire to adrenaline load. Any time you can diminish your dog's anxiety, his fear and his uncertainty, you make it less likely that he will attempt to dose himself with his drug of choice.

Dogs can learn reactivity from older dogs in the family. If you have a much beloved older dog and you bring in a puppy to live in your home with that doted on reactive older dog, do not be surprised if your pup learns to be reactive from the senior dog. After all, your new pup will see your older dog getting lots and lots of attention from you for his reactive behavior, and it isn't for nothing that the old adage 'monkey see, monkey do' is a cliché. Pups have been learning how to behave from older, mentor dogs for millennia. Pups learn how to work with sheep by being taken out with an older, experienced dog. In lieu of working sheep, your pup can learn reactivity from your older dog just as easily and negative reinforcement is STILL reinforcement. Or to put it another way, any attention from you may be better, in your dog's opinion, than no attention.

For some reason, the type of dog that is prone to reactivity is very attractive to certain people. Those people will dote upon the reactive dog, spend thousands of dollars on them to 'fix' them and even more hours providing the dogs with lavish attention. Their relationship is sometimes even reminiscent of the alcoholic and his enabler. It doesn't really have 'room' for a pup, and the pup will seldom profit from the experience. So if you have a reactive dog you are devoted to, wait until he is gone before you bring in that new pup—and when you do get your new pup, get a good start with him so that he won't be reactive. Don't let him establish patterns of behavior that supply him with adrenaline.

Most of all, if you've allowed reactivity to develop, for whatever reason, denial, excuses, affection, laziness, ineptitude, whatever, but now it has increased to the point where you can't stand it any longer, don't pass that liability on to some poor unsuspecting innocent. When your dog goes into his act with some unsuspecting body who has no idea what to do with him and somebody's dog gets chewed up, or worse yet, somebody who was just in the wrong place at the wrong time gets bitten, your dog may very well wind up alone and afraid among strangers in a shelter somewhere facing the needle. If you can't tolerate the monster you've created, bite the bullet and put your poor pet to sleep humanely and DON'T get another 'working-line' Shepherd again. Before you get ANY other dog again, LEARN how to live with, socialize and train a dog properly.

The bottom line is that reactivity is a genetic PRE-disposition that we don't have to allow to develop. Heredity and environment work together to create the final result and while the occasional rare individual lives out on one extreme end of the spectrum in which environment and heredity interact or the other, most organisms fall somewhere in the middle. (Think Bell Curve.) In the final analysis, your dog will become whatever you make of him.

Thresholds

In training dogs we talk a lot about something we call thresholds. But what does that mean? In dictionary terms, threshold means the door-way to your house or the entrance to a building. In dog terms, it means the point in a dog's behavior when he is compelled to action by his inner impulses. A dog over threshold in 'prey' drive is a dog who is no longer just thinking about chasing that rabbit—he's actually chasing him, and he's probably not listening to you, either.

Dogs with 'low' thresholds are dogs which can get over their thresholds quickly and easily. Dogs with 'low' thresholds tend to have very poor impulse control and are highly distractable. They may go nuts about the ball, the Frisbee, or some other toy, be unable to resist chasing the neighborhood squirrels—or bite whenever they get excited. Consistent training over relatively long periods of time can help to mitigate the effect of low thresholds, but it will have to be an on-going process and it requires great timing and consistency on the handler's part to do effectively.

Dogs with 'low' thresholds tend to be a very poor choice for family dogs, for Search and Rescue, for herding, and for guide and aide work. Many of them are 'reactive' and others are merely very difficult to live with. 'Low' threshold dogs tend to be unreliable for any work which depends on flexibility of mind or toleration of change; 'low' threshold dogs tend not to tolerate strange people, odd behavior, or general annoyances particularly well. 'Low' threshold dogs often find it difficult to 'stay on track' when tracking, as they are very susceptible to distraction. So why in the world would anyone want one?

The answer lies, of course, in competition. 'Low' threshold dogs make good bite sport competitors. The quicker and more easily the dog can be brought to bite, the better. Any hesitation in delivering the bite will be scored against the dog, regardless of the total lack of threat to the handler which exists. It will be regarded as a lack in nerve, which will be sharply penalized, if not a disqualification altogether. A dog whose 'prey drive' is quickly and easily accessed so he can be compelled to hunt down and attack the decoy with speed and dispatch is a dog who will score high points. A dog who can quickly and easily access their 'fight drive' (aggression) is a dog that can score big points. And a dog who bites readily and hard with no provocation whatsoever from the decoy is a dog who will do well in the point tally. And while all these behaviors have to be trained, point by point, with constant and consistent repetition, still, it takes much longer and is a lot more work to train a dog with moderate or high thresholds to attack and bite in the absence of any real threat to his handler than it does to train a 'low' threshold dog to do the same thing.

The bite sport breeder, trainer, handler, competitor would ask why they should be asked to do so much more work in training, when by producing a dog of 'low' thresholds, the training can be made so much quicker and easier. For the bite sport enthusiast, the question is fair. As long as no possibility exists that any pup bred to bite sport standards would be marketed to pet people, people who need aide dogs, or SAR dogs, the bite sport people could put their dogs' thresholds in the basement and it would not be much of a problem.

The problem occurs when bite sport people discover that there are not enough people in their sport in need of their puppies to pay them what they want to get for them. They need that money so they can pay for the expenses they incur in participating in their chosen sport. The internet is full of bite sport people aggressively marketing their pups to pet people to be 'family' dogs, and then when the pups don't work out, they make the people feel guilty for not somehow doing enough with and for the pup to force that square sport peg into the round family hole. The family is supposed to turn themselves inside out and spend thousands of dollars in training fees to learn how to cope with those low thresholds. After all, it's not the pup at fault, it's the people! Because the pup's parents have bite sport titles, so the pup must be good, right?

Sport people guide forum people, many of whom are very ignorant, into parroting their mantra that only a pup of 'titled' parents is any good and to join them in laying guilt trips on families misguided enough to have fallen for the hype. Understanding what 'low' thresholds are and what they do may help the uninitiated to make up their own minds independent of the pressure the bite sport folks and their adherents bring to bear.

Those thresholds which bite sport people find it helpful to get very low and keep very low in their sport pups have to do with 'prey drive' (that inner compulsion to hunt down and attack prey—or in the sport venue, a human) the dog's willingness to bite quickly and easily in the absence of any real threat, and the dog's ability to become aggressive and to sustain that aggression in a fight with a human. Because the dogs have to perform their actions in the complete absence of any real threat against their handler, 'low' thresholds allow the dog to perform the required actions in a very intense

50

manner despite the lack of threat. In today's bite sport competitions it would be very difficult, not to say impossible, for a dog to attain 'good' scores for their performance without those 'low' thresholds.

Sport people deal with the sport dogs' distractibility when over-threshold by constant repetition, forming wide synaptic pathways in their dogs' brains that amount to super-highways for their carefully sequenced actions. In the same way that soldiers are made to take their weapons apart and put them back together until they can do it by feel in the dark in a matter of minutes, or even, so it is said, in their sleep, so sport dogs are drilled in their routines so that once a dog begins their performance sequence, they will carry it out to the end as they were taught despite being 'over-threshold'.

So what does it mean to the family who 'drank the kool-aide', now that they are saddled with a pup who has 'low' thresholds?

Those people who have had one of these pups with a 'low' bite threshold know what it's like. Herr Eiselen once said that for a Thuringian dog to bite something or someone, all that was necessary was for the dog to see something or someone. A frustrated owner of a bite sport pup with a 'low' bite threshold said almost word for word the same thing more than a hundred years later. 'Low' bite thresholds have been a part of the German Shepherd breed since the very beginning. The big difference is that, in the past, before the Nazis, 'low' bite thresholds were generally not preferred, and the breeding of 'low' bite threshold dogs was not encouraged.

'Low' bite threshold pups do not 'mouth' as the pundits on the forums tell you—they bite out-right, and many of them bite quite severely. They break skin, bruise hands and arms and anywhere else they can reach, tear clothing, and even deliver nasty puncture wounds that can be quite serious, and they can and do start biting as early as 12 weeks of age. They can be very difficult to discourage and many an eight or nine month old pup is still biting and biting severely and seriously.

Some never really do stop biting, and of those, some will wind up being put to sleep. Others will remain a heart-breaking liability and a danger to all around them as long as they live. Those lucky enough to spend their lives as 'bite sport' dogs will wind up on podiums being lauded and become 'popular' sires who create lots more low threshold pups to be sold to unsuspecting families when there aren't enough sport homes for all of them.

Anything can trigger a bite from one of these 'low' bite threshold pups. One bite sport dog owner tells of trying to play ball with her dog with her neighbor and having the dog get so excited that he bit both of them. Another owner of a dog from 'titled' parents tells the story of how her dog bit the mother who regularly car-pooled her kids to school one morning—the dog, who knew the woman well, delivered a nasty bite as a greeting. Then there was the woman with the young dog of bite sport parentage (she was very proud of the Schutzhund titles the parents of her dog had!) who was pulled across the street by her dog so that her dog could make an entirely unprovoked attack on a completely innocent man walking down the other side of the street. Yet another dog from bite sport 'titled' parents, this one in Schutzhund training, escaped from his owner's back yard, then proceeded to get out of the front yard as well. He then ran across the street, where he attacked a lady walking by, bit her, pulling her down and breaking her wrist as well. It took two surgeries to put her wrist back together to anything near 'right'.

The last dog wound up being put to sleep—the dog's owner was unpleasantly surprised to discover that his neighbors had been living in fear of his dog for months and that they uniformly loathed the animal. His total inability to understand the monster his dog had become led to his being sued, as well as to the dog's death.

The moral of all these stories is that if you insist on keeping a 'low' bite threshold dog, you must keep that dog confined securely and manage him well so that your dog cannot victimize your friends, neighbors or innocuous strangers minding their own business on a public thoroughfare. Better yet, don't get one in the first place.

'Low' thresholds on a high prey drive dog can be dangerous as well. While most people won't get too bent out of shape by the wild rabbits and squirrels your dog insists on chasing, if he catches and kills your neighbor's beloved pet cat, or the little Yorkie from next door, as one Schutzhund 3 dog of my acquaintance did, your name will be mud in your neighborhood, and you may even find yourself facing the 'dangerous dog' label. Good luck getting home insurance once the insurance companies find out.

But, you say, he only kills small animals. How can that be dangerous? Well, it can be dangerous in many ways. What happens when the small animal is the new puppy your neighbor just got for his young daughter? And when your dog charges it with intent to kill and she picks the screaming pup up to save it and your dog jumps on her, knocks her over and bites her because her arm got in his way when he was attempting to kill her puppy? What if she breaks her ankle when your dog attacks? Hummm?

What happens when he's trying to kill the newsboy's pug, and you jump in and try to prevent him and he bites you and you wind up at the hospital with some nasty puncture wounds that get infected and keep you from working for two weeks?

Then again, the 'prey drive' bred to extremes in bite sport dogs is, after all, aimed at human targets. Chasing down and attacking people is a major part of virtually every bite sport ever invented. Some of the dogs are trained to take only the bite sleeve, but in some sports, the entire person the dog hunts down and attacks is fair game. Who will be 'prey' for your dog when he goes over threshold? One of the neighborhood kids? Or the eight-year-old nephew you're baby-sitting?

52

Having a 'low' threshold on a 'high prey drive' dog means that the dog can be quickly and easily provoked into beginning a sequence of hunting behaviors which while they are usually directed towards other animals, particularly small 'prey' animals, can also be directed towards other dogs, children and even adults. Because the dog's threshold is 'low' and his 'prey drive' high, that dog's 'prey drive' may be triggered into an attack by sights, sounds, movements or scents that would not normally be considered 'prey-like' behavior.

Notice that in this case the reprehensible behavior is created by the combination of 'low' threshold and 'high' 'prey drive'. 'High' prey drive coupled with moderate to 'high' thresholds means that the dog's 'prey drive' will require considerable stimulation before being activated, giving the dog's handler ample time to perceive the problem and correct it, or for the situation to resolve itself before the dog is actually stimulated to the point of acting. Low 'prey drive' coupled with 'low' thresholds wouldn't be a problem either, since the dog has very little 'prey drive' to be activated. It is the combination of 'low' threshold and 'high' 'prey drive' that causes the problem.

'Low' thresholds and aggression work much the same way. With a lot of aggression the dog likes to fight and is willing, even eager, to attack, but if restrained by a 'high' threshold, the dog is unlikely to do so except in the presence of a real and immediate danger to himself or to his handler or extreme provocation. Add a 'low' threshold to 'high' aggression, and you have a truly dangerous dog requiring scrupulous confinement and the most meticulous handling and management. You may also have a dog who scores big on the bite sport field, IF you know how to train him properly.

That 'reactive' dog we were talking about earlier? Well, he's a dog with a good bit of aggression combined with a 'low' threshold. What triggers he responds to in order to want to reach for that aggression so he can get his hit of adrenaline may differ; the results, unless you stay ahead of him, remain pretty much the same.

So, those are the pros and cons of 'low' thresholds. What about the pros and cons of 'high' thresholds?

Really 'high' thresholds across the board means that the dog is not easily provoked into much. This means the dog can maintain a really even keel; he lives in an easy equilibrium, tolerant of change, flexible of mind and able to put up with quite a bit of inconsistency, irritation and annoyance. Dogs with 'high' thresholds are often very reliable on track, difficult to distract, remain clear-headed and able to listen to and follow directions from the person they are partnering with while herding stock or working as an aide or guide dog. They deal well with the public and tend to be very patient with the family children. In many cases they are able to extend that patience to your neighbors' children and extended family as well.

53

The neighbors' cats don't need to be afraid of your dog, and the Cock-a-poo down the street yaps in the 'high' threshold dog's face with impunity. You're probably more annoyed by this than he is.

Does this mean that the 'high' threshold dog doesn't have any aggression? Or 'prey drive'? That he doesn't have any urge to bite? No, not really.

For instance, the 'high' threshold dog might have a very decent amount of aggression—but until that burglar actually lays hands on you, or points a gun at you so that terror/adrenaline is rolling off of you in a river, he's unlikely to have his aggression 'triggered'. At the point it is 'triggered', however, watch out! Your couch potato may turn out to be capable of ripping that burglar apart.

So why wouldn't everyone want a 'high' threshold dog? Well, difficult as it may be for some people to believe, there are people out there who find a 'high' threshold dog boring. These are the same people who think a reliable dog is 'dull'. Different strokes for different folks.

Not all dogs are 'high' threshold across the board. Not all dogs are 'low' threshold across the board. Some dogs are 'high' threshold in one area while they are 'low' threshold in another, and if you want an 'interesting' dog, these dogs with variable thresholds certainly fill the bill. Just discovering where they are 'high' and where they are 'low' can be a real adventure. People tend to call dogs like this 'unbalanced', but then again, this might be just the dog for someone who finds a nice, 'high' threshold, reliable dog boring.

As a marketing ploy, bite sport people tell prospective buyers that all litters of pups have a variety of characteristics between them, that some will be 'high' threshold and some 'low' threshold and some will have more 'prey drive' and some less, some more aggressive and some less, and so on. This is true. Sort of.

The first problem with this generality is the range within which the pups will fall. Statistically, they will occupy some version of the good old bell curve—that is, a few individuals will fall at one extreme, a few at the other extreme, and the majority of individuals will occupy the mid-ranges. Several anomalies present themselves to the keen observer almost at once. Litters of puppies, even rather large litters, provide only a very small sample of individuals and further, the genetic make-up of those puppies has been skewed in one direction or another.

Old-fashioned pups, for instance, will be born to parents who ordinarily are selected for 'high' thresholds, just for one example and for a second, bite sport pups are bred for 'low' thresholds. This has the effect of setting the curve to one side of the full range of characteristics or the other. This means, for practical purposes, that bite sport puppies will fall from extremely 'low' thresholds to almost moderate, which, by comparison with the other puppies in the litter, will seem 'high' to the breeder, while the old-fashioned pups will range from very high to just above moderate in range.

This means that to the old-fashioned breeder, the pup they identify (if they get it right—it's not all that easy prophesying what an eight week old puppy will grow up to be, never mind factoring in environmental influences, which shouldn't be discounted) as 'low' threshold will be far higher than the pup the bite sport breeder identifies as 'high' threshold. In order to understand the information the puppy breeder is trying to convey to you, you first must understand where the breeder is coming from.

The 'lows' the bite sport breeder considers de rigueur would horrify the old-fashioned breeder, while the 'highs' the old-fashioned breeder is so proud of would horrify the bite sport breeder just as much. And there's more than just thresholds to consider.

Take 'prey drive'. It is far, far away from all bad. The person who wants a dog to be able to handle stock knows that without 'prey drive' the dog won't have any interest in the stock, never mind want to move them. And if the threshold is too high, even with enough 'prey drive' to get the dog interested in stock, he won't be inspired to move them. On the other hand, the stock handler wants a 'high' enough threshold to keep the dog from actually wanting to attack the stock, or even from putting his teeth on them except in case of emergency (threat). So the stock handler wants a dog with moderate 'prey drive' and something better than moderate in thresholds—enough to get well into the reliable range-- without getting too high. To the stock handler, this is 'balanced'.

What makes a good stock dog would not fit today's modern bite sport dog competition at all. The dog, if carefully enough trained, over a long enough time period, might be able to qualify in Schutzhund, but just wouldn't be putting up the kind of scores it takes to make it in competition. On the other hand, the 'prey drive' and thresholds that would make a nicely balanced stock dog, would do quite well for both Search and Rescue and guide and aide dogs, which, you would do well to remember, the sport folk loathe.

Take 'prey drive' again. If you don't have at least moderate 'prey drive' the dog won't have enough of the 'hunt drive' which is a major component of 'prey drive' to be willing to track. A dog lacking in the 'hunt drive' part of 'prey drive' just won't be interested in tracking, any more than he would be interested in moving stock. A 'low' threshold, on the other hand which makes for quick activation of this drive certainly will give you quick activation of whatever of the drive the dog has, pull it up to the surface and make it nicely accessible for use. And 'low' thresholds are fine if you can manage to train in the kind of reliable focus you need to keep the dog on track despite distractions (which will always be there, depend on it!) but a nice, moderate threshold will serve better in the long run. Remember, higher thresholds serve concentration, clear-headed thinking and reliability, lower thresholds serve quickness, distraction, reaction and emotion.

So for a reliable SAR dog, the best recipe may be good 'prey drive' of at least stock handling levels and moderate to slightly above moderate thresholds. Humm. That means that you might be able to get a stock dog or a SAR dog from the uppermost ranges of bite sport dogs, where only a very few puppies will occur with those qualities, and from mid to lower ranges of the old-fashioned. Statistically, that puts the chances of getting a useable stock or SAR dog pretty solidly in the old-fashioned court, since you'll be looking a lot closer to the middle of their bell curve, where the majority of their puppies lie.

What about guide and aide dogs? Well, surprisingly, perhaps, some 'prey drive' is even helpful here, since it can be used to help the dog learn tasks, like looking for your keys or even picking them up once they are found. Maybe this dog doesn't need quite as much as the SAR dog or the stock dog, but they still need some, and they need thresholds low enough so that they can access it when needed while still high enough to keep them safe around small 'prey' animals and other dogs. Generally, however, guide and aide dogs need pretty high thresholds on all three-- 'prey', bite and aggression characteristics.

Stock dogs, SAR dogs, and guide and aide dogs all need a good, 'high' bite threshold. Dogs that bite stock, causing serious, expensive and even life-threatening injuries to stock don't live long. Dogs that bite the people they find on a search get washed out of service very quickly (people file lawsuits about things like that). And guide and aide dogs have to deal with John Q Public all the time. They MUST have a VERY 'high' bite threshold.

So, 'prey drive' and thresholds have varying degrees of value as to 'high' and 'low' depending on what the dog is doing and in relation to each other. Bite thresholds work much the same, with perhaps a greater range of value at the 'high' and 'low' ends of the threshold, again depending upon what the dog is expected to do.

What about aggression? That must be all bad, right? Not at all. Without aggression, the bite sport dog simply won't have what it takes to make the attack that is the keynote of the bite sport competition. Without aggression, the stock dog won't be able to stand up to the stock—it takes aggression as well as 'prey drive' to move stock, and to face them down when they don't want to go where the handler wants them to go. Just try to get stock through a gate without aggression. Hah! Can you say major failure? Some aggression is even necessary to support the 'hunt drive' and supply the determination it takes the SAR dog to work through a difficult track, or over, under, around and through obstacles, in spite of heat, cold, rain, wind and all the rest of the challenges a search dog may face. Channeled aggression, capped by a good, 'high' threshold, can even serve a guide or aide dog, giving him the determination needed to see to their people. Getting a wheelchair through a tricky door can present an aide dog a challenge that takes everything the dog can bring to the task. Without that channeled and capped aggression, the dog might not be up to the struggle. Or consider what it takes for a guide dog to lead his person through a crowd of people. Think aggression isn't involved? Sure, it is a strictly capped, narrowly directed aggression, but never-the-less, it is aggression, even though the bite is NOT involved.

These qualities aren't black or white, good or bad by themselves. These are genetic elements of the dog's character which are useful—or not—for the tasks set for the dog by their human, according to the level of thresholds set by the dog's heredity. Whether they are perceived as good or bad depends far more on the dog's placement on the human continuum than it does on the elements of the dog's character or the thresholds that govern them.

Remember too, that genetics do not account for everything. Environment, what the owner/handler does with the dog in the way of socialization and training have a great deal to do with how the characteristics of 'prey drive', bite reflex and aggression express themselves in the dog. While no training can make a 'low' threshold high, or a 'high' threshold low, skillful, determined training and careful socialization can make a 'low' threshold somewhat higher along the continuum. How much higher will depend not only on the dog's genetics, but on the trainers' skills and the amount of time and effort they are willing to put in. And, by the same token, there are techniques which can lower the dog's thresholds by opening neural pathways to access the dog's own adrenaline production. Dogs can, therefore, be 'adjusted' a little, here and there, to make them better for whatever the work is that they will be expected to perform. That 'adjustment' may be limited, but the possibility that it can be done exists if the person doing the training knows how and sticks to it.

I repeat the caveat, however. 'High' threshold dogs can be taught to be SOMEWHAT lower, yes, but you cannot change the dog altogether. He will still remain relatively high in that threshold, while the same goes for the 'low' threshold dog. He can have his threshold raised SOMEWHAT—but he will still be a generally 'low' threshold dog.

Choose the dog with the characteristics and the thresholds which best suit the work you have for the dog, your own situation and your own handling skills. If you need a guide or an aide dog, for instance, you would be well advised NOT to look for that dog among the 'titled' dogs of the bite sport world. By the same token, don't look for a dog to compete in a bite sport anywhere else. Don't drink anybody's kool-aide. Analyze your needs rationally, and spend your puppy buying dollar accordingly. You'll be much more satisfied with the dog you wind up with in the end.

A Rose By any Other Name . . .

Fifty years ago few people, if any, talked about 'alpha' or 'dominate' dogs. They didn't have to. With the training methods they used in those days, dogs didn't get much of an opportunity to give their owners the finger. It was pretty clearly known what position the dog occupied in the scheme of things, however much they might be loved and valued, it was still understood that they were the dog and people were supposed to be the ones calling the shots.

Now, after forty years of bandying these terms about to describe certain dogs who think they ought to be in charge of their people and giving the orders, we're being told by the so-called 'experts' that 'alpha' theories and ideas about 'dominance' are being debunked. It doesn't matter what you do or do not call the dogs, they still exist. We can call them dogs who would be Kings and Social Climbers if that will make the experts happy.

Some dogs just plain don't like to take orders from anybody and they don't care very much what you want. A sub-set of this group don't mind biting you to get their point across and today's ambiguity about what position the dog occupies in world order doesn't help. All positive training methods with treats dropping around the dog like rain don't help matters.

Trainers today use programs like 'mind games' and 'Nothing in Life is Free' to get these dogs' attention and in combination with the use of crates and muzzles, prong collars and electronic collars and head halters of various types, tons of exercise and careful management, people do manage, but dogs who prefer to be in charge of their world are still a whole lot of extra effort to deal with. It is possible to do it, however and some personalities actually find it fun to have a dog that continually challenges their authority. These folks actually find a good dog boring. For other folks, living with one of these dogs means being locked into a decade long nightmare where they are being bitten for no reason they can discern without any warning they can recognize.

Dogs who would be Kings are hardcore. Call them arrogant, call them egoists, 'dominate', 'alpha' or whatever, they look at people and see staff and it doesn't bother them in the least little bit to bite that staff if they think their servants are getting out of line. People who have these dogs and don't know what they've got are the people who take themselves to trainers and forums tearfully wondering why their dogs bite them. They give lists of all the wonderful things they do for their dogs, the premier dog food, the pricey dog beds (which the dog doesn't use because he's always on the people's furniture) the pretty toys, the boutique treats. They talk about how much they 'love' the dog and everything they've done for him; how could he have bitten them?

In these cases, most of the time the dog has been giving signals that he's going to bite one of these days for weeks, maybe even months and sometimes even years, but nobody in the family paid attention or if they did pay attention, the dog's signs might as well have been Urdu for all the understanding their people have of them. People who have these dogs need to go to a sort of boot camp to learn to deal with their canine dictators. People who have little Napoleons can go to trainers like Caesar Milan. People who have full-sized German Shepherd Hitlers may need to be a little more subtle.

That's where 'Mind Games' and the 'Nothing In Life Is Free' program come into play. They're a start. Doing the kind of 2 week shut-down used when bringing a new rescue into the home can also help, and, if the dog has started biting, a muzzle may help as well. The family needs to learn the dog's body language as soon as possible, so they can head off the dog's train of thought before he gets to the stage where he's chastising his subjects or throwing 'off with their heads' tantrums like the Red Queen in Alice in Wonderland.

Some dogs who haven't managed to plop their butts down into the throne where they think it belongs yet spend all their time thinking about how to get there. For them, it's all about climbing the social ladder. They're constantly trying to tell their people when and how to pet them—'not here, there', 'not now, later' and 'don't touch my feet and 'ooo, I don't like my hair ruffled that way, get away from me' and 'no, I'm not getting off the sofa, you can sit on the floor'—that kind of thing. By the time they've gotten their people to take the floor while they lounge on the couch, they'll pretty much figure they've got it made. They've now crowned themselves King (or Queen) of the house and their family has been relegated to the status of staff.

When their family, who have no idea what is going on in their dog's brains, do something the dog thinks is out of line, the dog responds as he would to another dog—he nips them. If nips don't work, he will eventually graduate to a full on bite. This is often the point at which people declare that the dog has 'turned' on them. 'Turning' has nothing to do with it. The dog has been working up to this bite from the moment he or she walked into the house for the first time. Inevitably, there will have been numerous tipping points where the dog could have been stopped in his progress up the ladder, but because his family had no idea what was really going on and thought everything was going well, the dog was able to climb merrily onward and upward.

Rescue dogs of the Social Climbing persuasion can make very good use of the misapprehension that they were 'abused' to get their new family started on the road to serfdom, if their new family will let them. Very often the dog is in a rescue situation because in their old family they worked their way up the social ladder only they perceived to the point where they became convinced that their family was staff. Then when their family, who had no idea the dog was thinking that way, failed to understand the dog's directions and wound up being nipped a time or two, or maybe even suffered a solid bite, they decided that the dog had to go.

Being deposed from his throne would give any dog pause for thought, but once they've settled into their new home and had time to scope out the social dynamics of the household, the Social Climber will be right back to his old tricks again, climbing the new ladder he's discovered. If his new family doesn't give him something else to think about and something else to do, sooner or later he's going to be laying on the couch while they sit on the floor and when they get out of line, to his way of thinking, he's going to bite them and here we go again. And, should the people of the second family find out that the dog bit before, well—It's not the dog's fault. That, certainly, is true. But it IS this dog's nature.

There are a whole lot of 'working-line' dog folks out there in forum-land who will earnestly assure any newbie who will listen (or anybody else) that 'dominant' dogs are best, and 'hard' 'dominant' dogs are best of all. My answer would be the question, for whom? Certainly there are people out there who would be bored out of their gourd by a dog with good genetic obedience who didn't understand what the hey they were doing if they tried to play 'Mind Games' with them. These dogs, already committed to the dog-human connection, don't need things like 'Mind Games' or 'Nothing In Life Is Free'. They already know all that. Bewildered, they'd do their best to enter into the insanity and like as not, in their confusion, get labeled by the crackpots as having 'bad' nerve.

Dogs who would be King obviously aren't dedicated to the dog-human connection. They're more like cats, always wanting to know 'what's in it for me?' If the reward doesn't suit them, they don't care to play—or cooperate. These are the dogs that have to be 'motivated' by toys and tugs and treats. If you asked them to go out into the pasture and bring in the cows to be milked, they'd probably respond by saying, 'only if I can chew on them on the way.' And forget working stock from dawn to dark through a long, hot summer day. Once things got uncomfortable, and it isn't fun any more, the dog who would be King would find something better to do, like lazing in the shade or laying in the creek.

For those who misguidedly call this kind of dog 'loyal' they should be aware of the exercises some police departments do in training their dogs where, when the 'bad guy' bests the police officer, the dog changes sides and gangs up on his erstwhile handler with the 'bad guy'. It's happened in real life more often than people like to think, with these dogs. That's why some police departments train for it.

Dogs who would be King tend to be too 'smart' for their own good. They get the quick satisfaction in the short run while shooting themselves in the foot in the long run. They're the kind of dog people are thinking about when they tell you to 'be careful what you wish for'.

Folks who like this kind of dog who would be King will tell you that they are confident and have good nerve and that's why they are 'good' dogs and 'better' than other dogs of a different nature. Usually they are right that this kind of dog is confident, particularly in their own milieu. Are they right about the nerve? The answer is, well, maybe . . . and sometimes. The thing is, you always have to remember that for these dogs, it's always take care of number 1 first, and number 1 is always the dog.

When Social Climbers and dogs who would be King deal with other dogs, they often try to show the other dogs what a big deal they are. They march up to other dogs, stretched up on their toes as far as they can go, hackling and bristling and even snarling in an attempt to intimidate and overawe the other dogs. They're quick to take offence at imagined slights and a supposed lack of respect on the other dog's part. They like to start fights, particularly with smaller dogs, and to beat up on puppies. They often have the kind of bullying owner who excuses their behavior by saying that their dog is 'teaching the other dog manners'.

Those people who think these are the best dogs should certainly have them. They don't need to be unnecessarily complicating the lives of good dogs. Better they should stick to the kind of dogs they like and the two of them can play their mind games and with their food and toys happily into the horizon. Each to their own.

For the people who are stuck with dogs who would be King when they wanted a dog who would call them 'Boss', well, they have to make up their minds whether they are going to do the work to make that happen or give up and give in and give the dog over to someone else, either to be put to sleep or, if the dog is very lucky, to find the kind of person who enjoys playing mind games and games with toys and tugs and food and paying for every little bit of cooperation they get.

The fact of the matter is that good dogs are dogs who have found the person who can and does make use of that dog's unique strengths and talents to create a satisfying life for both of them, and bad dogs are the dogs who don't have the qualities and character that suits the person they live with. When someone tells you that 'dominate' dogs are the 'best' dogs, that tells you little to nothing about the dogs but a good deal about the person making the statement. Dogs who would be King suit some people very well indeed; they are the exact worst dogs for other people.

All German Shepherd dogs are not 'dominate'. Some of them still have good Genetic Obedience instead. In fact, Genetic obedience was once one of the qualities for which the German Shepherd dog was best known. Today it is rare and getting rarer, and that quality has often been replaced by dogs who think they ought to be King. People's job is to find the dog that suits them and then to tune out the folks who don't like their kind of dog. The big thing is that as long as the dog who would be King isn't biting the kids or other people and their kids, or other people's dogs, the people who have him and love him can either stage a palace revolution or pledge their allegiance to the throne and obey the dog, whichever they please.

For those trying to make up their mind whether to get that 'best' 'dominate' dog who would be King, or not, consider that one of the reasons that bite sport folk like them is that they are usually willing to use their teeth readily and that people who choose to live with such dogs generally have to commit to a program of mental and physical work-outs for at least the majority of the dog's lifetime. The 'Nothing In Life Is Free' program will become a way of life for them for at least a decade and they really will need to learn to read the dog's body language.

For those who would prefer a dog to commit to learning to read their body language, and would rather have a companion than an adversary or a 'challenge', a dog bred for more biddability and calm cooperation might be the better choice. But make no mistake, it is a choice. And the thing about dogs is, you can have one kind of dog for one decade, and choose another type of dog for another decade.

After all, we're not always the same person from decade to decade. What is just the right dog for us at one stage of our lives might be just the wrong choice for us at another stage. Just make the most of whichever choice you make. Our dogs learn from us, but there is no rule that says that we can't learn from our dogs. Dogs who would be King can teach us how to 'read' our dogs' body language better, and how to be more thoughtful and better leaders. That's not a bad thing.

Reinforcement

And while we're on the subject of training . . . let's talk reinforcment. It isn't just a building block of behavior modification, it's the very foundation of training, regardless of whatever it is you are trying to train the dog to do. This is a long word that means an act or a condition, usually but not always performed or provided by the handler, that serves to strengthen whatever behavior the dog has offered. In behavior terms, there is negative and positive reinforcement. For the average handler, positive reinforcement is the main motivator.

From the handler, positive reinforcement usually consists of things like praise, play, with and without toys, scratches and rubs, petting, verbal congratulation and various varieties of yummy treats. The dog also is able to self-reinforce in a number of ways. The cat's litter box contains what most dogs consider the tastiest of treats, thus reinforcing a behavior most of us find repulsive. Barking and digging stimulate brain chemicals which satisfy the bored dog and mitigate his boredom. In these instances, Grandma's ounce of prevention is worth several pounds of cure, but of course, in order to prevent these behaviors (management) you actually have to pay attention to the dog before he does something so annoying you can't ignore him any longer.

Generally speaking, reward whatever behavior the dog offers you that you want him to repeat. You can sometimes help this process along by creating situations in which the dog is guided into offering the desired behavior; this is what we usually call 'training'. Positive reinforcement generally works better than the old 'yank and crank' methods of the past, and can be very successful, particularly when coupled with a system of correction, re-direction and engagement/ praise/goodies. This does not need to be something severe unless you are doing some kind of bite work where either the training protocol or the dog's temperament requires it. For most dogs and pups a mere disagreement with the unwanted behavior is sufficient, if timed properly and paired with a quick movement on to the next step.

Think of the correction as an explanation to the dog, something to help him and reduce his lack of understanding, sort of like a game of hotter/colder. If a person trying to find something in a room is only given the hotter cues, it will take them longer to find something and be much more frustrating for them than if they are also told they are cold, colder, coldest, when they're going the wrong direction. Dogs are not a whole lot different that way; they like to know how to get their pets and praises and yummies as quickly as possible, too. (Generally.)

The method is pretty simple, on the face of it; you simply drop everything and reinforce whatever behavior you want repeated whenever the dog gives it to you. You can't reward a behavior one time, ignore it another, and disagree with it on a third occasion, and then reward it once again (after the dog has just about given up on offering it) and expect to get any consistency of behavior. All you will get is a confused dog—if not an annoyed one, or a frustrated one, or a discouraged one. Emerson may have said that consistency was the hobgoblin of small minds, but who said dogs had large minds? Consistent reinforcement of desired behavior is the silver bullet of dog training.

So what does positive reinforcement consist of? Basically, something your pup just loves. If an ear rub is bliss, include it in his program. Verbal praise should suit your pup. If you're shouting, jumping around, waving your arms and throwing a party, and your pup turns away, embarrassed for you, that's not positive. On the other hand, 'good dog' declared in a bored monotone is hardly positive and your pup is apt to be as bored over it as you sound. Good praise takes some engagement and some enthusiasm, and takes longer than a couple of blinks of your eye. If anybody can miss it, it isn't good enough.

Goodies, when used, should be, well, goodies, something the dog actually likes. There are people who withhold a significant portion of their dog's kibble and then feed it to them bit by bit as a treat when they're training, and it works, of course. There are even dogs who actually require this kind of handling in order to convince them to cooperate, but it always seems a niggling sort of meanness to me to use kibble as a treat. A good many dogs don't care, though; they think the substitution of their kibble for treats just fine. Certainly the use of a high quality kibble as a treat may be healthier than many of the 'treats' on the market, filled with sugar and artificial 'flavorings' and colors, not to mention preservatives and the rest. Then again, for some dogs with allergies, kibble treats may be necessary, assuming the kibble is the kind of food they aren't allergic to.

Some dogs find squeaky toys or balls or tugs intensely rewarding. If your pup is one of those, go ahead and use it. A good session of play can often get your dog in sync with you so that the two of you can actually reinforce each other and if his attitude towards your training sessions isn't all it should be, a rousing game can do a lot to remedy that in a very short time. Play can also release some of that pent up energy your dog may build up from too much time in the house or the crate or the pen or just without you throughout the long day. There's no reason it can't be a weapon in your arsenal of positives to use in your program of reinforcement.

The second key to successful reinforcement is timing. The reward for the desired behavior has to come quickly enough so that the dog can associate the reward with the behavior it is meant to reinforce. That's why clickers were invented—to get people on board with their timing. Something about clickers seems to work on the human brain to get it to understand that the praise/pets/goodies have to be delivered 'on time' so to speak, not after the adds come on the TV and they can be persuaded to get up off the sofa and find the treat bag.

Clickers make a sound called a 'marker'. The 'marker' essentially tells the dog that they have performed whatever has been asked of them correctly and makes a promise that as soon as their uncoordinated human can get their opposable thumbs to work, praise/play/pets/goodies (reinforcement) will be forthcoming. After a while, the sound the clicker makes becomes a reinforcement in and of itself, if the promise of goodies/praise/pets/play to come has been religiously kept.

This is the Pavlovian principle at work—remember the experiment? Pavlov rang a bell and then delivered the dogs their meals. Before long the dogs started to salivate merely at the sound of the bell. The sound of the clicker is merely substituted for the sound of the bell, triggering the brain not just to anticipate the praise/pets/goodies/ play to come, but to actually start the production of the pleasure hormones the praise/pets/goodies/play trigger. Creating this situation is called 'charging' the clicker.

Used expertly, the clicker can build a mind-set in a dog that allows them to throw out behaviors towards their handlers to see what will generate goodies. It is possible to create the same attitude in the dog without a clicker, but the handler usually needs to know what they're about. Some dogs don't need much encouragement to try this sort of behavioral speculation; others don't want anything to do with it.

64

Some people find clickers awkward and intrusive and feel that they get in the way. Others swear by them. Some dogs, not surprisingly, mirror people's attitudes. If a clicker will get you to respond to your dog in a timely manner and deliver praise/play/pets/goodies appropriately, by all means use it. If it's just one more clumsy apparatus to struggle with, you can always give your pup a verbal 'marker'. 'Thank you,' 'yes!' 'Excellent!' or whatever, will all work, if, again, the verbal marker is used consistently and ALWAYS precedes the IMMEDIATE praise/goodies/pets/play.

Now, that said, not all dogs are alike. They are as varied and as individual as people. Some dogs are less biddable than others, some dogs have attitudes, and some dogs have issues and some dogs would be absolutely perfect if they could just get their person lined out a little. Some people need help with their timing, need reminders to get in their praise/pets/goodies/play, and others just need help getting started. That's what trainers are for. Finding trainers is what dog clubs are for.

If you got a dog from a shelter and you just want a family pet, you want someone who can help you to iron out the little wrinkles in as positive a manner as possible so you and your new dog can have a rewarding relationship. If you got a rescue, well, that rescue should have a list of trainers they can give you to help you to do that. If you want to do something more ambitious with your pup, if you have joined your local dog club, somebody in the club ought to be able to guide you in the right direction.

Different types of dog activities have differing protocols that are not best served by the usual basic training for the family dog; tracking dogs need to be in the habit of pulling, bite sport dogs need to jump up on people enthusiastically, show ring dogs aren't supposed to sit, and obedience dogs are supposed to sit automatically. And that's just a taste of the variations out there. It can be difficult for the nicely mannered dog to forget that he's not allowed to jump on people when it comes time for him to jump up and bite somebody in bite training and it can be utterly embarrassing to have your gorgeous show pup sit and offer to shake with the judge when it comes time for the judge to go over him, and that's just the tip of the iceberg of things that can happen. So if at all possible, get your activity and trainer in place before you start deciding what behavior from your puppy you are going to be reinforcing.

Reinforcement isn't the only method we use to train dogs, but, at least for the simple things, it may be one of the easiest. Certainly trying to train a dog (or a person, for that matter) without it, would be like trying to do wash dishes with one hand tied behind your back. After all, a good word and a few skritches in a favorite place are free. Why not help yourself?

Socialization

Socialization is the word we use for the process of brain growth in the dog that begins at birth and continues for the lifetime of a healthy dog.

65

Recent discussion on the forum has posited that a dog of stable, balanced, confident temperament does not need socialization. Nothing could be farther from the truth. Without socialization, that good stable, balanced, confident puppy will never be able to reach the full potential of his genetic endowment.

So what do we mean when we use the word socialization? We mean a systematic process by which the brain is stimulated to grow and develop, particularly in the cognitive areas. Socialization essentially develops the ability of the dog to think by encouraging the growth of neurons and synapses in the brain. Studies have found that the brains of dogs who underwent the process of socialization as pups developed larger brains with larger cognitive areas and higher numbers of neurons and synapses.

In Siberia, a study was done on large numbers of puppies where three groups were selected. The control group was allowed normal mother/litter socialization followed by normal but not particularly rich or varied pet based socialization. In the second group this socialization was enriched by additional experiences and stimulation. The third group of puppies were given broad, rich opportunities to meet new people and other species of animals, go new places and see new things and to interact with them.

Here's where the study got gross, eww, ick. At periodic intervals a random sampling of each group of puppies were killed, dissected, and their brains weighed, measured and examined in cross sections. Correlations were made for weight and size, that is, the brains of small puppies were only compared to those of puppies of equal size and weight, and the same for large puppies and middle sized pups. (I suspect this study could never have taken place anywhere else!)

The results were perhaps logical. As each group of puppies grew up, their brains grew in size and complexity. The second group of puppies, however, developed larger brains overall, with larger cognitive areas in particular, brains that weighed more than those of the first group, and, when examined in cross-section under a microscope, were found to possess greater numbers of neurons and synapses, with the most densely furbished areas to be found in the cognitive regions.

Those results were duplicated when the brains of the third group were dissected and compared to those of the second and the first groups. In some cases, in fact, the brains of the third group were almost double the size and weight of the brains of dogs of comparable size in the first group. Think about that.

Synapses and neurons are the building blocks of thought. You might compare them to tinker toys. You could even, for the purposes of visualization, think of the neurons as the round pieces and the synapses as the connector pieces. The more limited the numbers of pieces you have to build with, the more limited the size and complexity of the structure you can build. If you have enough pieces, you can build really large, complex structures, or in this case, thoughts. Complex structures of thought are what become, when large enough and complex enough, reasoning.

So how do we go about doing that? You do it by introducing scent, sound, sensation, and finally sights to the developing puppy. The younger the puppy the milder and gentler and less frequent (once or twice a day) the stimuli must be. As the puppies' immature brains develop more complex systems, they can accept more complex stimuli. Avoid loud sounds, bright lights, or harsh touch. Building the senses should be done by gradual, gentle increments.

Some breeders use what they call the 'rule of 7'. By the time the puppies are 7 weeks old, they want the pups to have met at least 7 different animals (other than dogs). They should have met 7 different people, have walked on 7 different surfaces often and long enough to have grown accustomed to them, been 7 different places (but probably not out of the car at all of them) and had the opportunity to sample 7 different foods (textures, flavors, types) and 7 distinctly different sounds. Inherent in this concept is the idea that the puppy is to be taught to accept all these stimuli in a calm, matter-of-fact manner through the calm, matter-of-fact way that they are presented to him and the calm, sensible reaction of the human and the other animals around the puppy when they are presented to him.

This is not as easy as it sounds. You have to do a balancing act between the needs of the puppy for outside stimuli, and the fact that before 7 weeks of age the only real immunity against disease the puppy has are those gotten from Mother's milk--which in most cases is winding down between 5 and 7 weeks but has yet to be supplanted by artificial immunity through vaccination. This makes it very tough to present the puppy with all the stimuli you'd like to safely.

By the time the puppy is 16 weeks old, the majority of the pup's brain development is complete, at least in general. Oh, you can make some improvements at later times in the puppies' life, depending on the pup's base character, but by and large, missed opportunities for brain growth in this period are generally not a hundred percent recoverable. For a bite sport dog, a pet dog, a show dog, this is probably not very significant. For these dogs, what their genetics are at base are probably going to be what determines whether the dog succeeds or fails.

But for the SAR dog, the Guide and Helper/Alert dogs, for Herding dogs who will actually spend their lives working stock, socialization from birth to 16 weeks is often crucial. NOT because the genetics of the dogs are insufficient, but because it is imperative that the dog develop to its full genetic potential. Socialization will give the dog the complex brain structures which will allow them to be flexible, to make good decisions when faced with stark necessity, to respond to people, animals and situations individually, to move beyond rote, trained responses to actually being able to figure out creative solutions to problems.

Seizure and heart attack alert dogs have to make a leap of insight from their response training to the actual alert. Without flexibility of mind, that leap of insight can't be made. SAR dogs have to be able to sort through thousands and even millions of complex combinations of scent; the more complex and highly developed that portion of their cognitive brain is, the better they are able to function. Guide dogs must be able to make a reasoned decision to disobey the instructions of their blind person in order to keep them safe.

If you are a breeder, and you want to make the best decisions regarding which dogs to keep for breeding and what matches to make among those dogs kept for breeding, socialization becomes crucial in its illumination of the genetic potential of your breeding stock. By socializing your puppy and dog you can discover at least some of what the genetic limits of your dog's brain are. Your dog may not be able to pass on the skills which you have trained your dog to exhibit, but she can certainly pass on the ability to learn those skills.

At its best, socialization is not merely exposing the puppy to scents, sounds, sights, and sensations, it is teaching the puppy a set of protocols for dealing with the information the pup is exposed to. Those protocols literally teach the pup what to think and how to think, by forming the structure of the brain. When you allow your pup to respond excitedly to stimuli, you are allowing the pup to develop more structures in the emotional areas of his brain, but when you teach your pup to respond calmly to stimuli, you develop structures in the cognitive, thinking, portion of the brain. You, not genetics, can determine, at least to some extent, which areas of your pup's brain develop the most neurons and synapses.

Allow your pup to drench his brain with adrenaline (the fight or flight hormone) and that pup's brain structure will shift to the action/emotion portions of the brain. Respond to stimuli in an emotional manner yourself and that will immediately shift your puppy to his own emotional center. Get mad, and your puppy will immediately start producing adrenaline of his own. Be anxious, or fearful, and your puppy will catch it from you like a cold germ.

Some people refer to this as emotions going down the leash. They do, most certainly, but your puppy doesn't need a leash to act as a vector for your emotions. All they need is their nose. Our emotions are completely tangible to our dogs through scent. Adrenaline, in all it's permutations, is as obvious to your dog as that scorching pot on the stove is to you.

Your pup's strongest sense is that of smell. It is the first sense your pup gets, and it comes with him down the birth canal. It is the last sense your dog will lose in old age. When the hormonal balance in your body changes it gives off a cloud of scent as obvious to your pup as the cloud of acrid smoke over that scorching pan. If you want to effectively socialize your pup and teach him good manners and how to respond to volatile situations with equanimity, you must begin with YOURSELF.

When your pup is born, start cultivating a Zen state. You might try thinking, 'Don't sweat the small stuff.' And, 'it's all small stuff.' This does not mean that you do not protect your puppy when you are socializing your puppy. Of course you do. And you work at preventing your puppy from landing in situations where you would have to protect him, too. In fact you work at protecting your puppy actively, by being alert to bad situations so you can remove your puppy before they develop, not after. But, at the very least, when working with your pup, you should work on yourself to eliminate anger, anxiety and fear from your emotional vocabulary, whatever the situation. Even irritation and agitation are bad news. Get rid of them.

Instead, go for matter-of-fact. 'Yep,' you say to the pup by your manner, 'that's the way the world works. We just keep going, doing our own thing.' or 'Oh, too bad. Well, onward and upward.' Later, if you want to, you can rant on your chosen forum. Your pup will know you're bent out of shape about something, but it won't be connected by then with any particular event, person or animal, and you can get it out of your system.

Socialization, you see, is your friend. It can do more to repair the cracks in your not-completely-perfect puppy's persona (is any puppy completely perfect?) and actually do more for your puppy than training. It is, in fact, the foundation upon which you will build the edifice of your puppy's training. For puppies who will do guide, helper or alert work, it is absolutely crucial, and it can make the different between a good SAR dog and a great one.

Part II:

The German Shepherd Dog

Hector Linksrhein gen. Horand von Grafrath

Chapter 4
Genetic Obedience

Greif von Sparwasser

Herding and Tracking--A Finite World

Our ancestors lived in a finite world of which we, today can hardly conceive. They lived in a world of limits we can hardly even imagine today. Supermarkets did not exist, and even if they had, most people wouldn't have been able to buy anything in them. Fruit and vegetables arrived in season in sharply limited amounts. Our ancestors lived in a complex balance between what they could keep of what they raised, and what they had to sell for the money to buy what they couldn't raise.

Consider chickens, one of the corner-stones of human survival for thousands of years. Chickens supply meat, eggs and more chickens, any or all of which can be sold to garner enough money to purchase other necessities, such as a doctor's services, in time of need. In societies where money is scarce, chickens themselves are a time honored method of payment. One cannot, however, keep an endless supply of chickens--they must be fed, cleaned up after, (even their manure is an essential component for a thriving garden) and guarded from predators. Like everything else, their numbers must be balanced against the time, effort and money it takes to feed, house and keep them safe yet still have enough to serve the family's needs. Maintaining that balance was often nothing less than a matter of survival.

Eggs, for instance, could be sold down at the General Store, traded for the money to buy clothing or flour or sugar or medicine for a sick child. A dog that killed chickens might as well be killing people. Dead chickens meant no eggs, no food for the family, and no money for necessities, such as medicine from the doctor for a sick child. Dogs that killed chickens were, in their turn killed, because their existence was a direct and dangerous threat to the survival of the family.

Dogs had to have enough prey drive to make them good herding animals, enough hunt so that they would track lost livestock and the occasional wandering child, but those drives had to be sharply modified by pack drives and forms of self-discipline, which were genetically selected for. Depending on the subsistence level of the family and their flexibility, a dog that killed a chicken but quickly learned not to might survive to get into the gene pool. A dog which did not quickly learn to leave the chickens alone would find himself very dead, very quickly. He (or she) would NOT get the chance to reproduce.

Early records tell us that by the time humans had developed a written language, they were already selectively breeding dogs. Top herding and tracking dogs were sought after, and people would pay what amounted to huge prices (things like a dozen chickens, a goat in milk, a ewe with lamb, or even, in the case of a very good pup, a bred heifer) to get one when they could buy one. People traveled miles on foot when they had no other means of transportation to take their female dogs to a top herding or tracking male. Why? They made the effort because a good dog could make or break your family's chances for survival for ten years or more. In fact, if he (or she) could

74

found a dynasty of great dogs, your family's survival could be almost guaranteed for generations as well.

Our ancestors didn't do spay/neuter much. Mostly they did pts and that's a kind way to put it. Today when we say we can't afford something, we mean we might feel the pinch somewhere else, and might not be able to have as much of something else we wanted. When our ancestors said they couldn't afford something they meant they simply did NOT HAVE whatever form of exchange was needed.

Genetic Obedience was not a convenience for them. It was a NECESSITY. They had neither the time nor the energy to deal with training a dog to be useful. The dog had to learn on the job. If he was lucky, he'd have an older dog to learn from, maybe Mom, maybe Dad. Dogs who picked fights with other dogs, dogs who wouldn't cooperate with other dogs (and other humans) weren't considered worth feeding. As soon as he could keep up, the pup was following along as chores were being done, chasing chickens and getting spanked--yes, physically chastised--and if he didn't learn from that not to chase chickens, he might very well find himself tossed into the local river with a stone tied around his neck. Harsh? You bet. But there was no place in our ancestors' world for dogs that didn't learn quickly and easily what they could and could not do with impunity.

Our ancestors were NOT behaviorists. They didn't spend what very, very little spare time they had reading dog books about the newest training methods. They trained their dogs the same way Mom and Dad and Grandma and Grandpa had. Dogs got a 'good dog' when they did right, and, if they were lucky, a pat. They got a thrashing when they did wrong. If they did wrong too many times, they got the rock and the river or hung from a tree. (No, it was not pleasant. But bad dogs threatened not only the survival of the family, but of the community. Getting rid of a bad dog and keeping his genes out of the local dogs' gene pool was considered a man's civic duty.)

The quicker a dog could become useful to the family and the community, the quicker he could start 'earning his keep'. Feeding dogs was a hardship that literally took food out of the mouths of the family's children. That dog had better be worth it.

This is where Genetic Obedience came from. It was created from literally thousands of years of selection for useful traits which would pass genetically from dog to dog through the generations and those traits didn't change much. When asked to track, dogs quickly figured out which scent the person wanted them to follow and then they stuck to it until they made their find. Dogs quickly and easily learned skills geared towards gathering and driving animals much larger than they wherever the herder wanted them to go. Dogs stayed with their person during the day, and they stayed home on the front porch at night. The alternative--death--was pretty absolute.

People didn't have fences other than those which would keep their livestock from harm, and those few tended to be small and close to the house. Fences were expensive in terms of time and effort and the money it took to purchase the materials of which they were made. Dog tight fences were far too expensive in terms of time and effort and materials to be built for the mere purpose of keeping a dog home. A dog simply had to stay home. Dogs which wandered the countryside at night were shot on sight, by guns, by bows and arrows, by slingshots. They were considered predators just like any others and they were not tolerated.

Your neighbor kept his in season female up in a stall in the barn at night and if your dog came courting, he'd better be real sneaky if he expected to get in and out alive. Dogs who stayed home and slept on their porch at night (or in the kitchen behind the stove in bad weather) without having to be confined to keep them home were prized, and got to pass on their genes in approved, and safe, fashion.

Puppies who padded along after Mom and headed that nasty, bunch quitting ewe when Mom was on the other side of the flock were marked for extra care and attention. If, at six months, he had how to help in gathering the sheep, how to keep them together once gathered, or how to drive them pretty well down, he'd get bragged on. By the time he was two, he'd most likely have a litter of pups on the way and those pups would be spoken for and whatever the people who wanted and needed them paid for them would be a boon to the family.

If the neighbor came calling to borrow him to look for a ewe who'd slipped off to have her lamb, or that prize bull calf the neighbor was raising to improve his stock, you'd better believe he'd be siring most of the pups in his immediate neighborhood. In a sheep-based economy, a good sheep dog is worth a flock. For our ancestors, that meant a fortune.

So what qualities went into our ancestors' genetically obedient dogs? Well, they had to have a complex balance of self-reliance, good pack drive, strong biddability, commonsense, a strong sense of responsibility, good hunt drives, good focus and concentration, just enough prey drive to be useful, a touch of play for bonding, a tad bit of sociability, just enough to get along in the neighborhood, and a soupcon of aggression and fight so they could face up to an ornery ewe or that pesky ram, and of course, a foundation of good, strong nerve. Extremes of anything weren't very useful and thus treated accordingly. Dogs who didn't measure up, didn't live long, in most cases.

In German Shepherd dogs, genetic obedience and the balance of qualities that created and sustained it came mostly from the Old Breed, a group of dogs made up of the Saxony and Brunswick and Swabian/Wurttemberger dogs, the older genetic foundation of the breed. The life in the Jura Mountains and the Northern Alps was difficult and demanding, and if it was easier in some ways in the lush river valleys it still meant long days working under a hot sun

76

or in harsh winds and bitter cold. For dogs to survive and thrive, they had to be tough and hardy and to serve the survival of the community as a whole, as well as their masters.

The Thuringian dogs came from the wealthy. They did not have the same stresses and constraints applied to their breeding that the Old Breed had. In their world, there was enough excess so that they could be kept, and even bred on, in order to please the whims of the rich man who owned them. They could specialize, they could support extremes in temperament, as long as the wealthy man who owned them was pleased by those extremes. Rich men could choose dogs for their looks; it is important, I think, to realize that the world of dog shows was created as an amusement for the wealthy, and notions of 'correct' conformation and of beauty itself, were whimsical designs spun out of the imaginations and personal preferences of men and women who never did a day's work in their lives.

For people who work dogs, there is no dog as beautiful as a dog both talented and capable of a good day's work. Their notions of 'correct' conformation come out of pure function, a measure as completely objective as any measure can get. These men (and women) bring an analytical mind to the judgment of dogs, and for them, the temperament reigns supreme, with any good dog a good color, a good size, and a good shape.

Master Shepherd Heyne estimated, just before his death in 2009. that modern breeding aims and practices had eliminated all but about 30% of the genetic obedience of the German Shepherd dog. He lived in Germany. I would speculate that here in America, the state of the Genetic Obedience remaining in the breed is even more dire. If breeders do not start putting the value of Genetic Obedience above extremes like those of prey drive or side-gait soon, in a few more generations, real Genetic Obedience as a practical entity in the breed, will cease to exist.

Tracking--Scent/Search and Rescue/Detection

Scent is the word we use to designate the essence of what the dog follows when he is tracking (trailing, air scenting, etc). It is made up of the detritus shed by all living bodies, human and animal, where-ever they go. The detritus consists of molecules of sweat exuded by our glands, bits of tissue shed like a sort of microscopic dandruff from our skin, bits of hair and even blood. Each microscopic bit of us contains our genetic code, no matter how miniscule, the very essence of each one of us in a sort of micro DNA fingerprint, and dogs can smell it, right down to the molecular level.

When we pass through any environment, we shed our tiny bits all about us. Small and lightweight, they float in the air like dust motes, yet even smaller, invisible to the human eye, swirling about on every current, shifted about by every breeze. In light, dry air conditions, they can stay in the air for hours. In moist, wet conditions, they can be washed downwards and land on grass, bushes, trees and flowers or on buildings, streets and sidewalks. A lot of rain washes these bits of us away. If we pass over a moist area and then it dries out, just a bit, it can 'fix' the scent so it can be identified for hours or even days after our passing. If it stays slightly moist, this 'scent' of us can linger on for close to a week, as long as it is not overlaid by the scent of too many other people mixing with it, or ground into a together powder only the dog with the most discriminating of noses can hope to unravel.

Time is the enemy of scent. Not just because of the action of osmosis, the process by which molecules are spread out into the air, ground and water, but also because some one and some things are always passing over it and shedding their own scent on top of it. Scent in the air dissipates, scent on the ground is overlaid, and scent on structures, be they tress, bushes and flowers or curbs, stair-rails and doors, is knocked off, blown off and washed off as well as buried under layers of additional scent. That means that the older the scent, the less likely a successful conclusion to the hunt will be.

The most successful searches happen when the dogs are the first responders, before human volunteers have stomped all over the scent, burying it, scattering it, and obliterating it as a useful tool for search. Think of the scent as a thread, in this case, ground into the dirt here and there, ripped apart and the pieces scattered so that they no longer make any sense to a dog trying to follow and finding himself jumping from bit of thread to bit of thread and all of the bits pointing every which way. (That is why police and search and rescue groups need to work in close cooperation, so that when the cops don't have a dog they can get to the trail of a lost person quickly, they can call in a SAR dog and handler and get them on the track in minutes, instead of hours--before people have tramped all over it and ruined any possibility that a dog can find anything.)

Dogs smell on the molecular level. Amazing, isn't it? They can smell the changes in cancer cells. They can smell the change in the levels of blood sugar in a diabetic's blood three hours before a machine can register it. Bloodhounds have followed a particular car down a major highway after other cars have traveled over its track for hours. I have had German Shepherds run three day old tracks in the rain. But now stop and think about a sense that keen.

People who wear hearing aids complain about the cacophony of noise that comes with the amplification of their hearing aids. They talk about how difficult it is to re-learn how to pick out particular words or sounds from the chaos of sound around them. Differentiating between different voices is even more difficult for them. Everything is amplified.

Consider then the dog, surrounded by this cacophony of smells, assaulted by sounds and colors in scents we shall never hear and never see. Yet somehow your dog negotiates his way through a feast of scent every day he walks out of your house. Is it any wonder he wants to stop here and there to sample some of it? The way you might bend to savor the rich damask fragrance of a rose, or lift your nose to the heady aroma of barbeque? To your dog, the world outside your house is redolent of scents as varied and pungent as barbeque and roses, fish and cat scat, ammonia and pine needles, sulfur and fresh brewed coffee. The scents are as intense to your dog as wide expanses of garish colors and sharp, loud noises would be to you.

The dog's nose is a wonderful thing, with scent receptors in the roof of the mouth and an entire section of the brain dedicated to sorting out those scents and making, well, sense of them. When sampling scent, a dog may open and shut their mouth to condense the scent and press it up into the scent chambers above their tongue. When you ask a dog to use his nose, for the dog, it is as if he has opened up a kaleidoscope of scents, each one with their own individual signature, like colors overlapping and creating more color, shifting into a new and different pattern of varying 'colors' and intensities with every sniff. Your dog has to identify the ribbon of scent you want him to follow, and then trace it, through every shifting, wavering variation of the pattern.

Only your dog can sense the pattern. To you, his person, the pattern of scent is soundless, invisible, and undetectable. Your dog must discipline himself to remain with that single, solitary ribbon of scent threaded through all the others, however fine it draws, however faint it becomes, until he makes his find for you, or you call him off the track. To do that, he takes responsibility for communicating to you what he finds, however you have taught him to do it, and for remaining on that one and only scent to the exclusion of all others. This, is genetic obedience in action.

Human beings are not very good at taking things on faith. When our ancestors followed a dog after their lost ewe or strayed heifer, they had to take it on faith that their dog was actually tracking the stock they'd asked him to track. They had no choice in the matter. Today's handlers seldom work in the real world, where so many things are out of their control. Instead, they set up the tracks, they mark them, and they control the dog as he tracks. It is that lack of faith, that need for control and obedience they can see and understand that has created the type of tracking done by Schutzhund enthusiasts, where the dog is required to follow the exact footsteps of the track layer, even if the scent has been blown somewhere else entirely. The track becomes then not an exercise in tracking at all, but in obedience, and even those Schutzhund fans not entirely lacking in sense or honesty admit that the kind of tracking done in Schutzhund is not much use in the real world.

Search and Rescue enthusiasts who insist upon air scenting regardless of air conditions or terrain or structures like timber and underbrush or even the age of track are not much better. Too much moisture in the air can knock the scent out of it, too much wind can make air scenting useless, and take a search miles in the wrong direction. Some canny dog handlers use canisters of smoke to make the prevailing air currents visible when they are training their dogs, so they will know where the scent is drifting. Scent that started out in the air can wind up on trees, underbrush, grass, and rocks.

The most accurate and useful tracking allows the dog to follow his nose where-ever it takes him and avoids human interference. The human's job in this instance is to eliminate distractions for the dog, make sure other dogs or livestock or humans don't interfere and to supply water whenever necessary. The dog then air scents or ground scents (trailing) as it seems to him best according to the presence of the scent he is following.

This requires faith on the part of the handler and unfortunately does not translate well to testimony in court, when necessary but one has to ask oneself whether it is more important to find a lost child or impaired adult or whether the possibility of winding up in court after the person has been found—or not—dead or alive is more important. To be most effective the person handling the dog has to let go of their need to be in control every moment and let the dog take control of them. It also requires a dog with real genetic obedience. Too many modern dogs would jump from appealing scent to appealing scent, a squirrel here, a rabbit there, a deer somewhere else, because they have little or no sense of responsibility either to the handler or for the task and less discipline.

This is why, today, many times a softer dog is a better choice for SAR work, because the softer dog cares more about pleasing the handler. It is also why new training methods feature 'motivating' the dog with balls and tugs to get them to track and stay on track, using implied and delivered rewards for the dog's efforts in staying on track in an attempt to replace the genetic obedience which has been lost. (Just think--the very phrase, 'staying on track' long ago became a part of our language, meaning sticking to the desired course of action despite obstacles and distractions.)

True air scenting happens when dogs look for dead people, such as drowning victims. As the body decomposes, it releases scent in the form of gasses, which then rise up through the water as bubbles which burst as they reach the surface. The dog then indicates the location where the scent of decomposition breaks the water membrane. The body itself will, in most cases, be found somewhere upstream, depending upon the current in the water flowing over the body. Colder water, of course, retards decomposition and the stronger the current, the farther upstream from the point where the bubbles of decomposition gases break the surface of the water the body will be.

Human remains detection of bodies either on top of the ground or under it is done in much the same way, although here, the 'current' refers to air instead of water. Again, the dog locates the body by the scent of the gasses released into the air by the body parts as they decompose. Any blood or tissue can be detected in this way, and so can bone although it is more problematical, since it releases less scent into the air and it releases it much more slowly than tissue and blood. To find the body, the dog ranges the area to be searched until they detect a current of air carrying the scent of the decomposing body, and once they locate that current of air, they can then, if the terrain allows, simply home in on the source.

Wind, of course, throws everything off, and rain isn't much better. Rain will knock scent to the ground and hold it there, close, and wash it off and away, too, given long enough. A little bit of moisture on the ground helps the scent to stick there, and seems to act, in the beginning, to intensify scent. (As time goes on, of course, it dilutes it.)

Dogs, of course, as anyone knows who has taken their dog to the beach only to have the dog find something dead and roll in it, have a strong affinity for dead things. A good handler makes use of that affinity.

Time honored methods of foiling tracking dogs include walking up or down-stream in creeks, shaking pepper over a trail, or salt. These stratagems will make it difficult or impossible for a dog to follow a track. So can getting into a car. But dogs, once they understand the concepts involved, have even managed to track individual cars after the person being tracked has entered them. The difficulty inherent in this, beyond getting the dog to understand which car you want tracked, is in stopping traffic on an unknown route in advance of the dog so dog and handler don't get run over. There are cases on record of bloodhounds who have followed cars for hours and miles even on highways. The problem here is less in the tracking itself, than in the logistics of making the tracking possible.

People make a huge distinction between SAR and drug/bomb scenting and the tracking of lost/strayed livestock. This is not correct. SAR tracking is a direct offshoot of livestock tracking and it is the generations, even centuries of livestock tracking from which SAR tracking and drug/bomb detection comes. Without the centuries of livestock tracking from which the discipline of remaining on one specific scent originated, it is unlikely that SAR dogs would exist today. Given the sophisticated training methods we have today, hunting dogs can be and are used, but without the livestock trackers who pioneered Search and Rescue it would have taken SAR a lot longer to get going.

Hunting dogs were originally used to track specific prey, in many cases birds only, or, in the case of some terriers, only rats and mice, or weasels, or badgers. With the exception of bloodhounds, few hunting dogs were bred with the flexibility of mind to add humans to their list of prey to be hunted and for a good many humans, that was just as well since most of the hounds (bloodhounds again excepted) have no genetic stop bred in between the chase and the attack. Most hounds were bred to kill--if possible--whatever it is they were bred to hunt. It is no accident that the hunting dogs used mostly in SAR are bird dogs, where the people they hunt for do any killing to be done and the dog does any retrieving.

81

Livestock trackers, on the other hand, were developed with a full stop between the hunt, and the chase, attack, kill genetic sequence, with sharply modified prey drive to allow them to work safely with livestock and cooperatively with humans. Livestock trackers also had some built in flexibility, being asked to track sheep, cattle, horses, pigs, goats, even birds, so that tracking the neighbor's lost kid wasn't much of a stretch for them. For the livestock tracker, the species the scent belongs to doesn't matter--their genetic back-ground means they'll track most anything that sheds scent once they understand that's what is wanted.

This brings up an interesting point in the use of the modern Schutzhund /bite sport dog for Search and Rescue. As the breeding of these dogs intensifies their prey drive to almost feral heights, and the dogs are bred with ever lower bite thresholds, the safety of any human the dogs seek sooner or later will be put at risk by dogs who no longer possess the stop between hunt, and chase, attack. Even as far back as the 1920s, the trainers of Fortunate Fields, a breeding kennel for search dogs, guide dogs for the blind, and police dogs, opted for the separation of search and attack/bite functions with their dogs because when bite trained dogs searched, they so often attacked and bit the people they searched for. This was all right when the people they were sent after were criminals, but when they were lost children and impaired adults the Dogs' inappropriate attacks upon their innocent victims led to the policy of completely divorcing search dogs from bite dogs. Schutzhund folks who are determined to see their bite dogs used in a search function should limit themselves and their dogs to human remains detection. At least there the human searched for is already dead and cannot be injured any further.

The Nazis and Communists whose dogs form the basis of the 'working-line' dogs of today already obliterated the stop between hunt and bite, of course, quite deliberately. Border Patrol dogs, Prison camp dogs, and Concentration Camp dogs were all bred with feral level prey drive and extremely low bite thresholds quite deliberately (just as the old yard dogs from whom they got their genetic foundation were) to attack and injure, even kill, defectors, smugglers, prisoners and any other people out of favor with whatever government was in charge. Too often today, people talk about Border Patrol dogs, or bite sport dogs, without understanding what those terms mean.

Dogs with titled parents 'all the way back' are genetically programmed to bite humans. That is what having titled parents 'all the way back' in a bite sport, means. Too often bite sport and 'working-line' people regard that as a good thing without ever allowing themselves to understand what it means in terms of the genetic inheritance of the dogs. Many of them do not understand because they do not WANT to understand and refuse to face what they have created. If anyone tries to get them to understand the dog they've created they get mad and call those people names and refuse to listen to them and try to silence them so no one will be able to hear them.

When their 'working-line' dogs wash out of SAR for 'reactivity' (dogs that lack the genetic stop that prevents them from attacking other dogs and people) they are quick to point out that it is just that single, particular dog washing out. They refuse to face the reality that it is not just that particular dog at fault but their breeding that created the dog as well. With training methods that emphasize using prey drive to train modern Search and Rescue dogs, the genetic stop between hunt, chase, and attack needs to be defined and emphasized in both breeding and training SAR dogs, with any dog trained to follow through to the bite prohibited from doing any search work other than human remains detection. If it isn't, some day a tragedy will occur that no one wants to see that will bring the entire use of dogs for Search and Rescue into question and may very well wind up disqualifying the German Shepherd from use.

Hunting dogs are already proving effective in drug, bomb and arson detection. Does anybody really care if a Beagle chews up a bag of cocaine? other than the danger to the dog itself? Beagles already do an excellent job. Small (so they can fit into tight places) cute and often people friendly, beagles are only dangerous to foxes and small rodents. They find ready acceptance with the public and their use in customs would seem a great fit, in more ways than one.

As far as training goes, if balls won't do it for them, food usually will, but an off-lead Beagle on a scent is a lost Beagle, except in confined spaces, (like airplanes). Beagles have served well in airplanes in Guam, for example, to prevent small poisonous snakes from stowing away and infesting Hawaii, where they would decimate the local bird populations (as they already have on Guam).

Beagles would find much more work as earthquake dogs if it weren't for their penchant for just disappearing once off lead. Beagles have been bred for centuries to work independently of humans. A Beagle with a rock solid recall, especially when on a scent, is an anomaly. Where-ever dogs have to work off lead yet still in close cooperation with a human, Labs, German Shepherds, Dutch Shepherds, Malinois, Goldens and the occasional Border Collie are still going to be the dogs of choice.

Tracking then, as the dog follows the ribbon of scent through air, around trees and undergrowth, and over terrain, is the essence of genetic obedience, a showcase of the dog's ability and willingness to cooperate with a human and commit to the attainment of a human goal, to the point of even adopting that goal as their own. The discipline, focus, concentration and the assumption of responsibility in communicating where to go in leading the handler is the gift of all those who went before us, selecting and nurturing the dogs through the ages. Now it is our responsibility to select, nurture and preserve such dogs ourselves.

Genetic Obedience: Herding

It has been said that we do not train dogs to herd, that we train dogs to help us to herd. Virtually every country in the old world has some type of herding dog, and many of those dogs are very old breed types. The 'Old Breed' Swabian, Saxony and Brunswick herding dogs used to create the German Shepherd Dog has a written history going back nine hundred years. Oral traditions hold that the 'Old Breed' herding dogs have existed as a breed type for more than a millennium, making them very old, indeed. For human purposes, herding dogs go back to the beginning of time.

The modification of dogs' prey drive to serve herding purposes is the very foundation of the domestication of prey animals by humans. It began when dogs 'herded' those same prey animals into crude traps so that humans could kill them and grew from that to 'holding' the animals so that they could be killed and eaten later, say, in the middle of the winter, when game would otherwise be scarce, thus allowing more people (and more dogs) to survive. Dogs have been used all around the world to herd sheep, goats, cattle, poultry, horses, pigs, and even donkeys and camels.

Herding dogs the world around tend to share certain physical and mental characteristics —a deep, double, weather proof coat and a willingness to work closely with humans may be among the most universal. (The Queensland Blue Heeler is one of the few exceptions to the double coat rule, but it is well to remember that the Queensland is an Australian breed, from an environment where adaptation for heat is all that is necessary. Cold is not usually an issue for them.) A sharply modified prey drive which allows the dog to interact with the prey animal safely even when humans are not present and taking responsibility for getting the job done, however unpleasant or difficult, are others.

Most herding dog breeds are in decline today, as their traditional jobs on farms and ranches are marginalized, but they still exist and they are still working. People just don't talk about them they way that they once did. We hear little about Hungarian Kuvasz or the Greek Tatra, the Pyranees and others of their kind because, while they are still out there working, we don't see them in dog shows often, and it is rare that they appear in our neighborhoods. Some breeds, like the Scots Collie, have deteriorated from valuable working dogs to beauty pageant contestants thanks to more than a hundred years of dog show breeding for 'fancy' dogs, rather than working dogs. Other dog breeds in this group, like the German Shepherd and the Belgian Shepherd, have prospered through their versatility. Their use as police dogs, military and service dogs, sport dogs, and pet dogs, have kept their numbers high and encouraged their spread around the world.

84

Border Collies have thrived as they emigrated to places like Canada and the United States, Australia, and even Africa. They flourish, not because they became less specialized (because they haven't) but because they do one thing as well or better than any other dog—they work sheep. It may not be an exaggeration to say that as long as people keep sheep, there will be Border Collies.

As a herding dog, the German Shepherd draws primarily from two foundations, the Swabian Shepherds from the Northern Alps, the Jura Mountains and the Black Forest (Wurttemberg) and the Brunswick and Saxony dogs from the lowlands and river valleys of the central part of Germany. The Swabian were the larger and the more flexible of the two, with ancient origins and an ancestral ability to handle all kinds of stock and to suit their herding styles to the specific needs of the stock they tended, the situation and the tasks they needed to accomplish. The Brunswick and Saxony dogs herded sheep almost exclusively and usually in large numbers. They drove sheep from point to point and kept them from straying from pre-set boundaries once they reached the grazing areas.

Different types of herding styles have developed through the centuries in answer to the differing situations and, of course, the differing styles of handling livestock developed by humans. Today, these types of herding are generally referred to as DRIVING, MUSTERING (gathering) and TENDING.

Today, dogs working in 'real life' situations would only very rarely find themselves in an artificial 'trial' situation. Trials for sheep dogs are generally set up in one of two ways —to test/showcase either tending or driving. Most dogs who herd livestock today as a real job do some form of each of all three types of herding as they work. The difference is found mostly in what the dogs spend the majority of their time doing. Because most people today spend very little time doing herding as actual work, and instead set up artificial situations for the dogs to 'herd' in, people tend to make hard and fast differentiations between styles of work that on a real job would tend to be a much more fluid and flexible as the dog switches from one technique to another according to the type and number of animals worked and the necessities of the situation with which the dog is presented from moment to moment.

DRIVING

Driving is something almost all herding dogs do at some time or another, whatever stock they work and in whatever situation. Sheep dogs may herd, ie, drive the sheep out to pasture in the morning and drive them back to the fold at night. Usually this would be a smaller flock, but not always. A cattle dog might bring in the cows to be milked—'driving' them into the barn. Or they might 'drive' beeves into a loading chute to be trucked to market.

Driving is usually seen as moving animals together in a cohesive group from point A to point B while moving them over, under, around or through whatever obstacles present themselves on the way. Sheep dog trials often feature a single dog driving a small group (three to five) of sheep through a pre-determined course over a fair distance and then penning them, with the sheepherder's help, at the end of the course.

MUSTERING

This is what it is called when a dog gathers any number of stock when they are scattered over a wide area. The dog brings the stock to the herder to 'hold' and then goes out to gather more until all the animals of that type (or which the dog knows belongs to the group in the case of mixed herds) in the area are collected. The dog then drives the stock to another area, usually, once they are collected.

TENDING

This is usually thought of as the more typically German Shepherd type of herding. In tending, the dog establishes boundaries by creating a moving fence with their own body to keep the sheep in marked areas. When sheep were established upon their pastures, dogs continued to patrol boundary lines sometimes called 'furrows' to keep the sheep away from crops, even in the absence of fences, repelling all attempts by the sheep to trespass beyond the set boundaries. Some dogs were even able to continue to keep the sheep to their proper pasture even when the shepherd was not present.

In some regions and situations the dogs have to combine driving and tending at one and the same time, moving a flock of sheep along a pre-determined course while patrolling the verges of the flock to keep them from trespassing on fields along the route. The larger number of sheep the tending dog is asked to contain, the tougher the dog must be to repel all challenges to his authority.

The German Shepherd style of herding comes from the old Swabian/Wurttemberger and Saxony and Brunswick dogs taking their herds of livestock out to pasture and bringing them home morning and evening, while holding them to the designated portion of the family's ancestral grazing areas during the days. In Swabia (Wurttemberg) the 'flocks' would be made up of large sheep and cattle and goats and even some horses, pigs and geese now and again. The actual number of such a group might be relatively small, with no more than a couple of dozen animals altogether. In Brunswick and Saxony, the herds would be large flocks, and number into the hundreds, but the dog would still be responsible for keeping the sheep within their proper boundaries.

The tending style of herding intensified as Germany became oriented more towards crop production and mechanization and predators became less numerous. Land available for sheep to graze became more limited and more sharply defined. Sheep could no longer be driven to a particular area and just left. The danger that they would get into the fields and damage crops was now too great. Dogs had to change their style from just mustering and driving and a more relaxed watching brief for predators to one more intense. Dogs had to patrol the verges of the flock and keep the sheep together at all times, and to do this dogs had to change their focus from outwards, away form the sheep in protection against predators, to inwards, towards the sheep. Now the dog protected the boundary FROM the sheep, instead of the sheep from outside threats.

Many people who work sheep with German Shepherd dogs today are inclined to emphasize that German Shepherd dogs have a 'different' style of herding than, say, Border Collies or Aussies or Queensland Blues. They often talk about the tending portion of the German Shepherd's stock work as if it is all the German Shepherd does or did do. Nothing could be farther from the truth. Their emphasis may come from the ignorance of their audience of the tending style in which the German Shepherd dog works at times, but in accounts of the daytime activities of at least two of the last remaining Master Shepherds of the breed, both mustering (gathering) and driving the stock remained an integral part of each day's work for the dog.

Dogs and their Master Shepherd began by gathering up the stock from their bed ground and driving them to the grazing areas, in much the same ways that other herding dogs gather and drive stock. Only after arriving at the grazing areas did the dogs take up the quintessential 'tending' work, pacing along shallow ditches cut into the ground called 'furrows' which mark the boundaries of their grazing areas so their bodies became essentially moving fences, as they turn back any livestock attempting to cross the boundary the dog is policing. German Shepherds are not the only dogs who have done this kind of boundary work.

For centuries, in Great Britain, homes with large lawns and garden areas often used sheep to keep the lawns trimmed long before the day of riding lawn mowers. These gardens had shallow ditches cut into the ground to keep the sheep out of the flower beds and kitchen gardens. Rather than being called 'furrows', in Britain these boundaries were called 'hah-hahs' (who knows why) and they were patrolled by collies who served the same function as German Shepherds to keep the sheep out of areas of the garden they didn't belong in. The idea that collies never 'tend' stock and that German Shepherds never 'drive' or 'muster' stock, are simply products of our modern mentality of specialization, not artifacts of historical reality or even present day reality.

Dogs dealing with large individual sheep, or large flocks of sheep used different techniques to control and intimidate them to keep the sheep from defying them and leaving their designated areas. Some sheep were grabbed by the wool at the neck, others the side, while still others were trained to grab the wool at the flank. A dog grabbing the lower leg of the sheep would be severely disciplined or dispensed with altogether—the risk of injury to the sheep was too high. And, as Master Shepherd Heyne reiterated, over and over, the shepherd had to pay the value of any sheep his dog injured or killed back to the owner. (Back to that finite world again!)

So how does a dog control a sheep with thirty or forty pounds on him, or a cow with six or eight hundred? If he's smart he starts with force of personality. An intense, threat-filled stare is the hallmark of the herding dog, sometimes delivered from a crouching stalk, sometimes through a mere passing glance. And it works—IF the dog has backed it up with a stout charge and a willingness to use his teeth, IF the animal has made the fulfillment of his threat necessary. The most effective dogs are those who rarely, if ever, have to use their teeth. The more moral authority the dog can exert, the better for everyone involved.

Mustering, (gathering) is just as useful a maneuver for cattle as it is for sheep. Cattle, at least in much of the western US, are kept on 'ranges' where they are allowed to scatter at will. 'Drift' fences may limit that scatter to specific areas, but those fences may be miles apart (and usually are). They do not keep the animals together. It is common for the cattle to splinter into small groups of half a dozen or even less and settle into certain areas where grass, water and shady places to rest please them. The behavior of sheep in predator free areas is not too much different.

In such a situation, dogs are invaluable. In fact, while many a cattle rancher has replaced their horse with an ATV, the dog is still a vital part of working cattle. On the range, cows hide. I don't know what they're thinking. The old cows know very well that they move down out of the high pasture in the fall and travel down to the lower ranges closer to the ranch, where they can be fed through the winter and watched over, and that they go back up to the high country in the spring. Some (few) of them accept this and show up when they hear the ATVs or horses coming and sort of present themselves to be gathered up. Most of them do not.

They hide. They tuck themselves and their calves into the underbrush and watch you go by and just keep chewing their cud. They slip into gullies and in among the trees usually clustered there, and keep a low profile. Without dogs, you'd never find them all and rooting them out of the brush and up out of the gullies would be a sweaty, dangerous nightmare and take forever. But they can't hide from the dogs.

The dogs use air scenting to detect their presence, track them down and root them out and then drive them up to where you're gathering them together. Then the dogs help to keep them together while you're moving them through the pastures. It is commonplace to work two dogs at a time, one to sift through the underbrush and the gullies and the other to hold the cattle together. Good dogs seldom require much direction during this phase of the work. You take a young dog out with an older dog who knows the routine, and in a few hours you'd think the young dog was an old hand.

Later on, when you're sorting cattle—this old cow belongs to my boss, that one to the neighbors—or separating the old cows from their coming yearling calves, the dogs work off signals, a shout, a waving arm, a gesture. Point to a gate—the dog will head the group of calves he's driving towards the gate. All you have to do is open and close it. Want the neighbor's cow excused from your herd? Point towards her and then follow it with a hand gesture in the direction you want her taken. Dogs with genetic obedience pick the signals up quickly and with little effort, seemingly. (Dogs that don't pick them up quickly don't come back—and are a source of endless joshing.)

A cow dog does NOT grip. The animals a cow dog works do not outweigh him by a few pounds, but by hundreds of pounds. And grip on a cow would have to pierce hide and cause considerable damage, a technique to be used only in an absolute emergency, when lives are on the line. Even then, it is better for the dog to find another, better way to get the job done.

A cow dog slashes across the cow's sensitive nose, and across the cow's heels. They dart in and out—cows kick, as well as butt and they often have horns. Cow dogs have to have plenty of nerve; cows are not small animals, and they are many times larger than the dog. Working cattle is not for the dog faint of heart.

A herding dog, whether they are herding cattle or sheep or goats or whatever, needs to be able to cut quickly, to make abrupt changes in direction in the blink of an eye, have the ability to work all day and the smarts to use only as much effort and energy as needed to get the job done. They need to be able to learn to take a break any moment an opportunity to take a breather presents itself. The physical types of dogs that have this kind of ability would find their closest human equivalent on basketball courts and football fields.

It is no accident of history that so many of both the Northern and Swabian dogs bred for stock work for centuries were big, tall dogs, because they had to be natural athletes and they had to stand up to large animals. If you stop and think about it, a linebacker or defensive back in a football game moves in ways very like to those a working stock dog uses. As the back and the receiver attempt to run their routes, the linebacker and the defensive back try to stop and interfere with their movement and finally direct it by blocking them, pushing them and cutting off their movements. Just the way a dog does when gathering cattle or mustering sheep or holding a flock of sheep or a herd of cattle.

A dog patrolling a 'furrow' is like a basketball player in guard mode, watching, ever watching, for an opponent looking for an opening into which to leap. Well, the patrolling dog watches as he moves in the equivalent of the basketball player's down-court loafing jog, ready, ever ready, to block any dive towards the 'furrow' the sheep might make, ready to dart and dive in front of the sheep the moment the ewe turns away from the flock. The sheep tries a head fake —the dog tenses, and then, the moment she commits herself, spins to counter.

This is no place for the long, stringy muscles of a marathoner, nor for the lean, narrow frame of a GQ model. The dog needs a bone structure that can support the kind of short, powerful musculature which produces the quick, forward thrust needed, the rapid, sharp cuts and pivots so essential for the dog to use in turning to face either sheep or cattle. The dog needs explosive, physical force to back up his mental and moral authority over both cattle and sheep. He needs to be able to move crisply, even sharply, with authority. If he's going to bluff, it needs to be a good one, and convincing, and if he's going to threaten, it better be a threat he can fulfill, if he as to. A wimpy, floppy hocked dog, a loose-legged, creeping, crawling show dog with a misshapen back just isn't going to cut it, for oh, so many reasons, and that is why for stock work, in the real world, the show dog need not apply.

For all their similarities, working cattle as opposed to working sheep has certain fundamental differences. Sheep are smaller, quicker, and a lot flightier. They are far more likely to be preyed upon, even by the dogs charged with protecting them, than cattle. They move away from the dog more quickly, usually, than cattle do, and gather into a tighter knot of animals than cattle do, In most cases a dog uses less threat on sheep than cattle and, in general, works farther off them. Even in sheep there are very large differences between breeds. Working a flock of Barbados would be very different than working a flock of Lincolns; the difference would be a lot more than just size. A dog would have to treat them quite differently.

In general, you wouldn't see that much difference between breeds of cattle unless you were trying to work Long-horns. Long-horned cattle are big time dangerous; that's why hardly anybody raises 'em any more, even though they're superb beef producers, big-framed, very low in cholesterol and virtually impervious to predators.

Cattle are dumb; sheep are dumber.

Cattle dogs seldom have to protect the cattle; though prey animals, cattle are large and to some extent capable of taking care of themselves. Coyotes may take a calf here and there, but it takes a pack of wolves or a bear to take down a cow. Once out on the range, cattle are pretty much on their own.

Sheep have to be watched continuously, with rest for people and dogs coming only at night when the sheep are safely penned up until morning. In both cases the dogs move the stock from one place to the other, but in the case of cattle, dogs often (usually) have to hunt actively for them, in many cases on ranges where cattle are spread out over hundreds and even thousands of acres.

Dogs learn to anticipate the work. They read our body language and get the hang of our routines, and stop needing direction to do what needs to be done when. Each time you're ready for the next step, there's your dog, ready to get started, if he hasn't started already. In the old days, when people didn't have clocks, dogs moved from task to task when they understood it was time for the next task to begin. They often still do, if they have the chance to do work in a routine manner.

How do the dogs know to heel your stirrup? I don't know, but every German Shepherd in my line I've ever worked has picked it up quickly and easily. I don't remember ever making any effort to 'train' the dog to do so. I was always busy working, with, more often than not, a green colt under me needing attention as well as the cows to tend to. I didn't have any left over attention to spend training the dog to stick close. Genetic obedience took care of it for me.

Ever wonder when your older dog pushes your young dog around to make him go where he's supposed to or do what he's supposed to? There's your inheritance from your dog's herding ancestor, right there. This inheritance isn't going to mean much on the modern Schutzhund field. Maybe in the old days it did, but not any more. But for a service dog for the disabled, the tracking and herding behaviors and the complex web of characteristics that produced them have direct and valuable applications. The blend of softness and nerve, the genetic obedience, the self-reliance, the discipline and the ability to take responsibility reliably, are all tailor-made for the service dog.

Only one problem remains—are there enough of the dogs with these qualities left? How do we find dogs to identify? And how do we know when we've found a dog who still has them? What test do we use if we don't have sheep or cattle or goats to try them on? Schutzhund's no good, not as it is done today, with its emphasis on prey drive, low bite thresholds—the bite sports of today are geared towards producing a dog genetically engineered to bite humans quickly and without hesitation regardless of threat levels. A herding dog needs much higher thresholds and much more moderate prey drive than a bite sport dog has—an actual bite has to be his very last resort, for emergency use only when all else fails. His forte is to be found in presenting a solid and believable threat of his own.

Herding itself is a long old haul, literally, as you seek to find a herding group to train with and then drive to get there. Distances are daunting, and the experience, once you find a group and join them, limited to pushing a few animals around a pen.

Better than nothing. Perhaps the test is the thing, to see if the dogs will take responsibility for moving the animals, to see if they will discipline themselves not to chase. Do they get the hang of it quickly, or do they need a long period of direction? How biddable is the dog?

91

Then there are the value judgments. Be honest here. Could you leave that dog with the sheep and come back and find that every sheep was there and not one had been harmed? Or is the prey drive just a little too high for him to be around the sheep on his own recognizance?

How about his clear-headedness? Or does he just get so excited he can't contain himself? Does he adopt a proprietary manner towards the sheep? Does he dislike it when other dogs wade in on them with too much excitement or prey drive? Does he want to get between the sheep and the other dog?

Do the sheep intimidate the dog? Can he stand his ground and learn to intimidate them? Or is he a bully, rough on the sheep, too sharp with them? Or fearful? Unable to stand in and push back? Does he bark like a maniac? The Schutzhund people would call that leaking drive. Too much excitement and fear can be very close and neither works well on stock.

How about cattle? Can he regard them with equanimity? Can he sit quietly while cattle are moving around more or less quietly on the other side of a fence? Can he be around horses without misbehaving? (barking, rushing at them, trying to bite, getting so excited he forgets to mind, that sort of thing?) Do large animals intimidate him? Can he learn, relatively quickly, to move around them quietly and without fuss? Or is he vibrating with drive, hardly able to bear not chasing them?

Stock dogs don't work on a leash. How's your dog's off-leash heeling? Just how hard and fast is his recall? How willing is your dog to work off hand signals? And here's the biggie— does your dog need NLIF to mind you?

People who have sheep can try their puppies on them to see how attractive the sheep are to them. Some people start with puppies and lambs and get them together, young puppy to young lamb and so on. Most people don't have those options. Here are some ideas.

Look for the puppy who minds more often than not even when you don't have a leash on him. Look for the puppy who doesn't need a prong collar to walk quietly on the leash with you, the puppy who can hold it together mentally when things are getting exciting. Look a for a puppy who picks up hands signal quickly and easily and minds them without a lot of work on the handler's part. Try to avoid the brash puppy who blows the handler off, the puppies who rebel when you ask for a sit or down when they don't want to. If your puppy does better on NLIF, he's not a good candidate for stock work. If you have to use a clicker and treats to get his attention or his cooperation, he's probably not a good prospect for stock work.

As in everything else, solid nerve is your friend. Dogs without solid nerve have worked stock before and will again, but those dogs have nerve that only fails in the artificial world of humans. Put 'em on stock and they've got no problems. The best sheep dogs have a strain of softness in 'em. Think Border Collies and Kirschental dogs. All stock dogs are biddable, if they aren't, they aren't useful. You need a puppy who WANTS to come to you when you call him, a puppy who WANTS to work with you.

The fulfillment of the predisposition for cooperation with a human partner in the dog is not something that appears instantly between handler and dog, in most cases; it has to evolve. The bond between the handler and dog becomes like a very successful marriage of give and take. The handler has to learn to trust and respect the dog and to 'lean' upon the dog to get the job done. In some circumstances, such as guide dogs, military and police dogs, and service dogs for the disabled, the handler has to depend upon the dog for their life and future. This creates a higher level of bond than that of sport dog work, as the reliance of the handler on the dog is felt in an emotional realm that supersedes training. When that occurs, the true measure of 'Genetic Obedience' becomes clear.

But here's the bottom line—if you don't or can't understand the work, then you can't judge the dog as to whether or not he's capable of the work, never mind if he may or may not be good for it. It is the total ignorance of the work—be it search and rescue, herding, police or military work, which makes both the show ring and the bite sport world so helpless, hapless and hopeless in judging whether a dog is good for the work or not. The idea that the flying trot, so beloved of the show ring fanciers and created from weak, loose hocks and elongated, weak stifles attached to long, loose thighs somehow translates to a dog who does work requiring sudden stops and starts, quick turns, spins and pivots at the drop of a hat, as well as the ability to take up a threat- filled stalking posture, is downright idiocy. The idea that effective public access dogs, either guide dogs for the blind, wheel-chair aide dogs, or brace/balance dogs can be made from dogs bred with high prey drive and low bite thresholds to bite people quickly and easily in the absence of any real threat to their handler is equally moronic.

People advancing these ideas are merely showcasing their ignorance of what the job the dog needs to do consists. In fact, the celebrated and much desired show championship pretty much guarantees a dog physically incapable of doing a real, day after day, job of herding and quite possibly mentally incapable as well. Just as certainly, the bite sport person is going to be far out and away when touting their bite sport titled dogs for public access work. Can some bite sport dogs make it as police dogs? Yes. Can some do military work? Maybe. Can some even do Search and Rescue work? Occasionally. But history and studies from World War I to 1934 all tell us that the best source of all of these dogs and more is herding.

Tracking down and finding lost stock is an integral part of every herding dog's repertoire, and always has been, making them the obvious choice for SAR work. Whether the dog is tracking down a lost lamb or keeping the stock gathered up or moving along and the handler/herder safe, the person working with the dog has to trust the dog. There is no place here for prong collars or even leashes, no place for dogs that have to be forced to work with their handler by stratagems such as 'nothing in life is free' or clickers and treats.

The work is all about the dog-person bond, the dog's willingness, even eagerness to serve the human and work in cooperation with that human as a partner—not a slave, or a servant, nor even an employee, but as a member of a team striving towards a common goal. That partnership is what makes a dog effective as a law enforcement officer, as a guide dog, as a search dog. And while a police dog may have to be able to bite, and a search dog know when NOT to bite, and a public access dog that no matter how insane John Q Public may be they CANNOT, must NOT bite, the source of all of that 'obedience' is to be found in the dog's dedication to the partnership he has with the human with whom the dog is partnered.

In order for a dog to carry the kind of genetic obedience which is the heritage of herding dog ancestors, they must have solid nerve and a bite threshold that is at least moderate. When breeders erode the bite threshold in order to create dogs which bite people readily in the absence of any threat from them they must first minimize the human-dog connection present in genetic obedience. In today's bite sport dog, herding types of genetic obedience have been minimized or even outright eliminated, in favor of a dog whose levels of prey drive have been elevated to a degree which would make the dog unsafe around stock and lowered bite thresholds to allow the dog to bite readily.

Nor have show dog fanciers done any better. Just as the show dog no longer possesses a physical structure capable of real work, the preferred temperament for which the dog show fancier breeds has little to nothing to do with work and everything to do with competition and exhibition. The dog show person wants a dog which, far from being focused on work, with outward attention split between the stock and the herder, is focused on himself. The dog who exudes charisma, that 'look at me!' attitude, the ham who shows off relentlessly, who plays to every admiring member of the audience, as well as the judge, who never relaxes, who relentlessly preens and poses and prances, is the epitome of the great show ring temperament. Many a dog with such a temperament has won many a show ribbon over a dog of much greater solid worth, dogs of much better working temperament and working structure but when it comes time to get down to real work, to stop prancing and preening and get down and dirty, to hang in when it's hot, and when it isn't fun any more and when no one is clapping and cheering such dogs have failed ever and over since the day that dog shows were invented.

As far back as 1920, studies of the German Shepherd dog have found that the choices made in the show ring damage the working ability of the dogs. Even Stephanitz himself declared that the best dogs for breeding were seldom those who did best in the show ring. Unfortunately, though he may have talked a good line, his choices in the show ring proved, over and over, when the rubber met the road, he failed to put his money, so to speak, where his mouth was. From Horand v Grafath through Roland v Starkenburg to Klodo v Boxberg and on, his show ring choices were damaging to the working ability of the breed. At least he pretended to value working ability in his dogs. Show judges since his death haven't even bothered to do that. They simply mouth platitudes about the flying trot being needed to herd sheep which only proves how little they know about the work, and go on their merry way celebrating their mental and physical cripples with lauds like champion and best in show, with the result that show dogs have become synonymous with genetic disorder, physical disability and mental instability.

While the show community whines about unfairness and points to one dog in a thousand who can spend two minutes in the presence of stock without falling down, the bite sport people pretty much just ignore their dogs' deficiencies. Some of them even brag that their dogs aren't guide dogs, those German Shepherd colored Labs, in their parlance and they simply deny that dogs are ever used on stock these days so why should they be concerned about losing the qualities that make a good stock dog? The entire herding mystique is irrelevant to them. Neither group has any intention of changing anything that they are doing and both breeding pools are becoming ever more constrained as dogs of genetically diverse inheritance become ever more completely excluded.

Master Shepherd Heyne estimated before his death in 2009 that such breeding strategies have produced a modern German Shepherd dog which has lost 70% of what had been the breed's genetic obedience. He may have minimized the problem. Most German Shepherd breeders today do not even know what the phrase 'genetic obedience' means, and the idea that it occupies any position in their breeding strategies, never mind a position of priority, would be a form of insanity—unless you mean dogs breed to bite people indiscriminately and without reserve or hesitation regardless of the lack of threat. The bite sport people have produced plenty of that kind of genetic predisposition, and the presence of the German Shepherd dog on breed ban lists and the difficulty of getting home insurance for homes in which German Shepherd dogs live do not deter them in the slightest from their production of ever more 'reactive' and 'aggressive' dogs bereft of the kinds of checks and balances necessary for the production of stable, useful dogs.

That leaves the prognosis for the future of the German Shepherd dog as one of great 'genetic obedience' a poor one. The 'title' mania, whether from the show ring or the sport field has no room for the consideration of 'genetic obedience' and it does not occupy a position of importance on either the sport breeders' or the show breeders' lists of priorities. In fact, in both cases, it seldom even makes the list of what they breed for. Until it does, until 'genetic obedience' and nerve occupy the top spots on the majority of breeders of German Shepherd dogs' list of priorities, along with genetic diversity, not much good can happen for the breed. In fact, as long as the so-called 'expert' breeders of German Shepherd dogs continue to ignore priorities like genetic obedience and genetic diversity, the much maligned back yard breeders will continue to produce better all-around dogs with a greater possibility for the real improvement of the breed than those show dogs and sport dogs the 'experts' produce. At least the back yard breeders generally choose dogs they like—and mostly they 'like' dogs with a nice stable temperament and good health, with reasonably functional physical structure who are easy to train and live with, which is what genetic obedience produces, as opposed to the sport and show breeders who often deliberately and knowingly breed dogs who are mentally unstable and unsound physically, as well as short lived and unhealthy.

After all, even if John Q Public may not know much, the common man has sense enough to know that dogs staggering around with hind legs doubled up like a kangaroo's, or bent double so that the dog walks on the lower half of his hind legs instead of his feet, a back humped like a camel's or running downhill like a ski slope have something wrong with them, and that ravening maniacs frothing at the mouth and barely restrained by a prong collar also have something wrong with them, no matter what the sport aficionado and the show dog fancier tell them. P. T. Barnum may have said that there's one gullible fool born every moment, a fool who will swallow that garbage and believe that such dogs are good and what a German Shepherd really ought to look and act like, but for every such idiot, there are ten people who know a pile of manure when they see it.

Sensible people are going to continue to buy reasonably priced puppies from people who may not know what the words 'genetic obedience' mean, but who do value dogs easy to house- train, easy to train to behave well around the house and even to do the occasional task who manage to behave personably with friends and family and strangers and even in public without a great deal of angst or hundreds (or thousands) of dollars and hours spent attempting to train them to do so. Because that's what 'genetic obedience' means to the pet person who doesn't have livestock in his back yard, who doesn't desire to spend hundreds of hours training his dog to do 'nose work' or search and rescue, and who doesn't want a dog who is a liability around the house or the neighborhood.

Silly people are going to swallow the BS spouted by the 'title' fanatics and pay inflated prices to support hobby breeders in the sport and the show world. They'll continue to get aggressive, unbalanced, fearful, unstable sport and show world dogs plagued with an alphabet soup of mental ailments such as DA, FA, HA, and 'reactivity' because they have parents who have 'titles'. (Dog Aggressive, Fear Aggressive, Human Aggressive) Their sport puppies will need weeks and months of serious effort to be trained not to bite them (euphemistically called 'mouthing' by the sport crowd who typically aren't honest about the dogs they're producing).

Just as an aside, 'mouthing' is the experimental mild chewing action of a teething puppy which is easy to discourage and is not damaging either to skin or clothing. If a puppy is 'mouthing' the behavior does not outlast the teething phase. If your puppy is biting due to his inborn genetic pre-disposition to bite people, he will not be easily discouraged, and the behavior will persist long past the period of time the puppy is teething, often to his eighth or ninth month and sometimes even to a year of age, when he can deliver a severe bite and his biting behavior can become dangerous.

Sport bred puppies from 'titled' parents bite, they don't mouth. While the behavior usually begins around 12 weeks of age (around the same time 'teething' does) the sport bred puppy does not mess around with any mild 'mouthing'—this puppy is bred to bite humans and that is exactly what he does, shredding clothing, puncturing and slashing skin, drawing blood and creating nice, deep bruises that turn all colors. Nor is the sport puppy easily deterred from this behavior. He bounces quickly back from any attempt at correction to bite again, usually even harder, the very behavior prized on the sport field. It may take months, even years to discourage him from biting, and he may never reliably leave it behind, biting friends and family indiscriminately whenever he gets excited about something.

The sport puppy from 'titled' parents is BRED to BITE PEOPLE!!! He is genetically programmed to do so. That is what a bite sport title means, people!! If your puppy is from generations of Schutzhund titled dogs, then your puppy is from generations of dogs who got their titles for biting people! That is what a Schutzhund title IS, and that is what it MEANS! This doesn't mean not to get a puppy from Schutzhund titled parents, if that is what you want and you know what you're getting into—but it does mean NOT to be foolish and get this kind of dog without understanding just what kind of puppy you're getting and what kind of dog he will grow up to be—a dog who will ALWAYS require careful supervision around people, particularly children and one who will require extensive (and often expensive!) training to keep him from becoming a serious liability for you and a danger to your family, your friends, and your neighbors.

The show world produces its own problems, from show champions and lists of best in show dogs which come attached to SIBO and EPI and IBD to Cardiomyopathy, von Wildebrand's, DM and JRD, that show world 'title' is a virtual guarantee of health problems. Puppies from the show world who are both healthy and not plagued by fear issues are both rare and unusual. A show 'title' means that the parent or parents of your dog won a beauty contest—it doesn't mean that they're intelligent, or healthy, or mentally sound, or that they have any 'genetic obedience' of any kind. It means several somebodies thought they looked pretty—and that is ALL it means beyond the near certainty that the puppy will have come from parents heavily in-bred on a small number of individuals .

If you seriously want a dog with 'genetic obedience' you need to go to someone who breeds their dogs for a real world purpose, NOT 'titles'. Find someone who has dogs who can work stock, dogs who do search and rescue, dogs who can be a wheelchair aide, dogs who do brace/balance or guide dogs for the blind. If you want a police dog or a dog for military work, go to someone who specializes in producing dogs for those purposes. Breeding programs for guide dogs face the dichotomy that the genetic foundation that produces the best temperaments for guide dogs is going to produce the occasional dog too large to fit on public transportation. A reasonable donation to the program may get you one of those oversize dogs—who may turn out to be the best dog you ever had.

You may have to do some looking around for this dog, because the people who breed, raise and train these dogs are not thick on the ground and you won't find them blowing their horns on the forums, in most cases, with the 'title' folks, but they're out there. You'll know their dogs when you see them—those nice, healthy, sound dogs with their straight, level backs and strong hind legs well placed within the plane of their bodies, steady, well-behaved dogs meeting other dogs without difficulties and people without UNfriendliness. And I'll give you a clue—the people will have temperaments much like the dogs, well-mannered, mildly friendly, knowledgeable and steady and the first question they ask you about your dog WON'T be whether your dog can bite!

Genetic Obedience: Service Dogs Origins

People here and there through time have used dogs to help them when they had disabilities. Records going as far back as 2,000 years before Christ show us dogs leading the blind and pulling wheeled carts of primitive design for people no longer able to walk. But, until 1916, in Germany, we have no record of a concerted, organized effort to breed and train dogs to help humans with disabilities.

Sometime around 1914, the Germans perfected a type of biological 'poison' gas commonly called 'mustard' gas. This 'gas' was sprayed over troops and the trenches that protected them, in a fine, mist like spray. On contact, it burned the skin, and if it got into a man's eyes, it blinded him. If it got into his lungs, it did permanent damage there. Men exposed to a full 'dosage' of the gas, died. Gas Masks of the time were only somewhat effective, and many men survived, only to live with disfiguring burns, blindness and lung conditions that eventually killed them. The Germans eventually stopped using it because it was difficult to control—it went wherever the wind blew, killing and blinding as many Germans as Americans and Brits. The result was, however, that by the end of the 'Great War' otherwise known as WWI, tens of thousands of young men around the world were faced with living the rest of their lives in darkness.

Anytime that many men are affected by something, someone usually comes up with an idea to deal with it. My guess is that Stephanitz started it, after all, he was always looking for another job for his dogs, and he had the energy and the money and position to do things that others didn't, but he was no dog trainer. The idea might have stayed in Germany, if it hadn't been for a lady named Dorothy Eustis, who went to Germany and established the first breeding and training guide dog school, Fortunate Fields. She used her own money to do this, and from the beginning until her death in 1946, she promoted the use of Guide dogs worldwide.

In 1927 she wrote an article 'The Seeing Eye' which was read by an American named Morris Frank. He subsequently went to Germany to Fortunate Fields where he trained with a dog Dorothy provided for him, named Buddy, who he brought back to the United States. Morris then established Seeing Eye, Inc, here in the US which settled in New Jersey in 1932.

Morris Frank and Buddy lobbied tirelessly for seeing eye dogs to be granted the kind of public access they enjoyed in Great Britain and Europe without needing legal privilege, and testified before Congress itself in support of such legislation. Thanks to their efforts, and a dramatic demonstration by Buddy, the legislation was passed, and guide dogs gained the right to take their people everywhere a person without a dog might go in public.

Today there are 'seeing eye' dog breeding and training schools all over the United States. Most of them are non-profit, receive their funding from public and private donations and supply dogs to blind people for free, though in many cases the waiting time for a dog is 2 to 3 years. Some schools still prefer to use German Shepherd dogs, although today they are in the minority. Other breeds commonly used for the work are Golden Retrievers and Labrador Retrievers, though people who have had a German Shepherd will often wait a year or two longer to get another Shepherd, if necessary, in order to get one. Statistics on German Shepherds working as guide dogs indicate that no woman working one has ever been successfully mugged or raped, something that cannot be said for either Labs or Goldens.

The San Rafael school for Guide dogs for the blind, here in Northern California was established by a man named Clarence Pfaffenberger using dogs from the Longworth Kennels in New York and dogs from Fortunate Fields to create his breeding program. For decades, the German Shepherd was the only breed used there. After Pfaffenberger's death, the school branched out into other breeds and now they now no longer breed or train German Shepherds.

Guide dogs for the blind are considered the 'gold standard' of assistance dogs today, and it is to the guide dogs that everyone else who uses an assistance dog owes their privileges in being able to have a dog to help them to go about in public.

As Dorothy Eustis is the mother of guide dogs for the blind, a lady by the name of Bonnie Bergin is pretty much the mother of assistance dogs for the disabled. It is she who created Canine Companions for Independence nationally and worked towards the establishment of Assistance Dogs International, as the international umbrella organization to codify what an assistance dog should be and to register organizations who produced assistance dogs. She has worked tirelessly to see that other assistance dogs were able to take advantage of the same public access privileges guide dogs enjoy.

As a young woman posted overseas, Bonnie was struck by the number of people who were able to take advantage of the helpfulness of dogs and the variety of their disabilities. She saw dogs helping people to walk, dogs who dragged small wheeled carts carrying people who did not have wheelchairs, and dogs fetching and carrying for people. She also noted that these dogs were able to do as much as they did for their people because they were able to go just about anywhere in public that people went. She noted that, not only in many third world countries, but in Great Britain and Europe, dogs had a freedom of public access that they did not know here in the States and that if she was going to be able to duplicate the feats dogs performed for their disabled people, they were going to have to have public access of the same type granted to them that guide dogs for the blind had.

Just as guide dogs for the blind were the answer to WWI and an idea whose time had come, dogs for the disabled was another idea whose time had come. People were already individually using dogs here for things like heart attack alert, blood sugar alert, seizure alert, brace-balance work (although we had no name for it) and there were even a few dogs who had proved that they were able to detect cancer and alert on it. No one, however, had any hope of being able to reliably replace that dog when they (inevitably) lost it. Along came Bonne.

She has established the Bonnie Bergin Institute in Santa Rosa, California, with a 2 year program to train the trainers of assistance dogs, as well as the dogs themselves, and gives one of the only Master's Degrees in Assistance dog training and breeding in the world. She has pioneered the imprinting of dogs on certain scents, early task training, codified what needs to be achieved for public access and even champions teaching dogs to read hieroglyphs and simple words to help them develop cognitively and in the hope that someday they will be able to read simple signs for those who are visually impaired and cannot read the signs for themselves.

Today we have dogs helping people with wheelchairs, both manual and electric, seizure and blood sugar and heart attack alert/response dogs, some of whom can even use a specially designed telephone. Brace/balance dogs assist people in walking, we have dogs that 'hear' for us, dogs who can help their Alzheimer's partners stay anchored in reality as well as get them home when they wander, and, of course, guide dogs.

We have the Delta Society which is the umbrella agency for therapy dogs, Assistance Dogs International, which can help you to find an accredited group training assistance dogs in your area, as well as Guide dogs. Tomorrow we may have dogs that read signs for their blind partners, dogs that screen you for cancer, and dogs that tell you when to take your pills. With a little technology, lots of training, and some real imagination, who knows? The day after tomorrow, the sky may be the limit.

Service Dogs: Types of Assistance Dogs

Guide dogs for the blind, also called Seeing Eye dogs, were the first official assistance dog to be bred, raised and trained specifically for the work that they do just as hunting and herding dogs have always been. They are also the first dog to receive legislated privileges for public access. Other dogs have followed in their footsteps through the decades since Guide Dogs first achieved prominence.

Guide dogs are chosen from the larger dog breeds because they need some physical strength and to be structurally sound. Guiding is a physical labor, as the dog pulls firmly on the hand in the act of guiding. Even halts require some physical signal. As a result, guide dogs are usually between 22" and 26" and selected from a physically strong breed, such as German Shepherd dogs, Labrador Retriever or Golden Retriever. Doberman Pinschers have also been used but this breed has been unable to consistently produce the necessary temperament for the job.

The upper levels of size are limited not by the physical demands of their job, but by the fact that most blind people are constrained to use public transportation and the larger dogs (above 26") simply won't fit. Many taller men would prefer a guide dog of greater size to do the actual guiding, but unless they have access to van transportation virtually a hundred percent of the time, the day will come when they have to use public transportation and they will be right back with the same problem everyone else has. If the day ever comes when the transportation problem is solved for the blind, you will see larger, taller guide dogs working because bigger dogs provide a better sense of security to larger people than the smaller dogs do.

Hearing Ear dogs for the deaf were developed starting in the 1980s. They perform 5 basic tasks for the hearing impaired, beginning with the alarm clock to get people up in the morning, the buzzer on the stove to help with cooking, the telephone ringing, a knock on the door or doorbell ringing, and name recognition to alert their person that someone is speaking to them. Hearing ear dogs can be any size and any breed or mixed breed. The tasks are easy to train and come naturally to most dogs. The trick is to find the dogs which can achieve public access standards. For decades, the ASPCA in San Francisco ran a program to train hearing ear dogs where they selected dogs from the shelter population and trained them successfully for the work, but they lost their funding and have now closed their doors. This is unfortunate;

hearing ear work is the venue best suited for the use of shelter dogs for assistance work.

Brace/balance dogs have been around, without a name, for centuries. Their tasks, on the highest level, are closest to those of guide dogs both in complexity and degree of difficulty. Their basic job is to keep people from falling. That may mean bracing them to help them to reach things or getting those things for the people themselves. It often means coping with a cane or a walker and it can mean shifting from a walker to a wheelchair with the attendant change in tasks.

Basically, they get people up in the morning, help them in and out of the bath, help them to get up off of chairs, help with grocery shopping and with household tasks like getting clothes out of the washer and dryer. It may be as simple as sitting up against the person's legs to help them to stand, or they may pull the clothes out of the machines themselves. They can open doors, turn out lights, and have been taught to use the telephone (with a little technological help). To be at their most helpful, brace/balance dogs need to work at the public access level and to do that, they must be virtually bomb proof even more so, if possible, than their guide dog cousins.

This is the place where the big dogs shine. Depending on the size of the person they are assisting and the level of help they need, dogs need to be 24" at least and go up. Even Great Danes are used here, when both temperamentally and structurally sound dogs are available. Dobermans have been used, the big German Shepherds are wonderful, Labs and Goldens, when large enough, and even English Mastiffs have been bred for the job. People who just need a 'little' help can get by with a smaller dog. People who need a lot of help need a big dog. Since most of these people still do most of their own driving and have vans or SUVs, the size of the dogs is not an issue except as they help their person.

Wheelchair aide dogs vary from the smaller dogs who work with electric chairs to the big dogs who muscle around manual chairs. The smaller dogs do stuff, like opening doors, picking up things, and turning lights on and off. The big dogs with the manual chairs do the heavy work. Literally. They pull, push, balance and brace both chairs and people. They get people out of bed and into their chairs, help them to use public rest rooms (or private ones) help them to get in and out of the bath, and often do all or most of the sorts of things the smaller dogs do for the people in the electric chairs.

The smaller dogs can be any breed and for children, collies, border collies and poodles and even smaller dogs have been used. The most common are the big 3 again, Goldens, Labs and German Shepherd Dogss. I prefer my dogs to be within 25" to 27" to fit with the wheel of my chair and big framed and powerful. A shorter, big-framed, powerful dog would probably do the job better than a tall, willowy dog could. People in a higher chair might want a taller dog. Strength and power in the dog, for someone active like me, is a must.

Wheelchair aide dogs come in 2 levels, like many other assistance dogs--the companion level, for use in the home, and public access level. German Shepherd dogs have a history of achieving a higher percentage of dogs attaining public access level than any other breed, with Labs being the second most successful. Someone wishing to home train a service dog, I would advise choosing one or the other of these 2 breeds.

Alert/Response dogs can alert on or respond to seizures, blood sugar highs and lows, and heart attacks. Psychiatric support dogs exist, too, although these dogs have a harder time getting public access rights as the disabilities their people have are less visible to the public. Like the other dogs, all these dogs come in 2 levels--companion level for use in the home and public access level. Unlike the other dogs, size is not really a consideration here. These dogs can be of any breed or even no breed at all, and dogs from shelters can and have done very well here.

Seizure dogs come in 2 flavors, alert dogs, who alert their person when a seizure is eminent, and response dogs who do something after the seizure has occurred, like calling in help. Many of these dogs aretrained to use specially designed telephones which, when activated by the dog, automatically call a list of names until someone answers, at which time a pre-recorded message plays alerting the person on the other end of the line that help is needed. Many of the first alert dogs came from shelters. The trick of alerting on seizures cannot be trained, partly because who would induce a seizure just to train a dog, and partly because not all seizures start the same way.

Response dogs of course can be trained and are. Larger dogs can actually help to prevent injuries by at least partially immobilizing the person during their seizure. They can help to re-orient a person coming out of a seizure and they can retrieve medication for the person. They can help, if the dog is large enough and strong enough, to get the person sitting up again, or even to a chair.

Most dogs start as a seizure response dog and graduate to an alert dog as they learn their own person's particular seizure precursors. Some response dogs never do graduate to alerting. Some of this simply rests on the dog, other factors include the person-dog bond and the general environment in which the dog was raised. Handler sensitive dogs are more likely, of course, to develop the knack of alerting.

Heart attack alert/response dogs are very like seizure alert/response dogs, in that the response can be trained but the alert must come to the dog on its own. Heart attack response dogs are taught to use the telephone to call 911 in case of a heart attack and most have a specific command the person can give to tell them to do so. In fact, there is a news story about a dog who did just exactly that, and who was able to pant and bark and whine with enough urgency to convince the dispatcher to send someone to check it out and thus actually saved his person's life. It happens, it's real.

The first recognized heart attack alert/response dog was a senior shelter dog named Dakota, a predominantly Golden Retriever. After being rescued from a shelter, he responded by alerting on his new person's heart attacks so successfully that he became celebrated for his life-saving talents.

Blood sugar alert dogs, on the other hand, can be taught the job and may even be the wave of the future for diabetics. After using the dogs at a summer camp for adolescent diabetics, one pediatrician working for Kaiser Permanente stated that the dogs were the best new break through in treatment he had seen for this group.

Teenagers who would never pay any attention to a person will pay attention to a nagging dog. In this age group, the dogs can prevent seizures and comas and much of the damage suffered by diabetics with out-of-control blood sugar variations. Dogs can detect blood sugar changes for up to 3 hours before blood sugar meters can. The likelihood is that you will be seeing a lot more of these dogs in future. So far, German Shepherds and Labs are the leading breeds from this work, but truthfully, any conscientious dog with a good nose could do the work at the companion level.

Psychiatric support dogs are a harder sell to the public, but they are no less valuable. Dogs actually have a better record of combating depression than medication does (forget Prozac, get a puppy) and can delay the onset of the last stages of Alzheimer's by keeping people anchored in the here and now. They can also help to keep a person home (from wandering) or if they do wander, they can often get the person home again. Dogs have proven valuable in nursing homes as residents and as incoming therapists for the human residents. Currently, dogs are finding a use as support for people with PTSD and as the need for them rises, you will see more and more of them with war veterans, helping them to reintegrate into a peaceful society.

Legitimate concerns do exist, however as to how well people struggling with psychiatric problems can care for a dog, though it has been proven over and over that caring for a dog can keep the elderly functioning on a higher level than they would otherwise be able to without the dog. Psychiatric support dogs are now being prescribed for people with post-traumatic stress disorder and are again proving to be valuable therapeutic tools. I think we will see more of them in the future being used for anyone needing help either at home or out and about. Perhaps someday arrangements can be made to provide a safety net for in these situations which would allow the dogs to do their jobs and still have some security in their care.

Levels for psychiatric support dogs vary from companion levels to therapy dog levels to public access levels and can be done by any dog with the correct temperament. Successful dogs can come from any breed or from shelters. Mutts may apply and should be welcome. Healthy, structurally sound, long-lived dogs preferred.

As our population grows older, we will need more help for the elderly and the disabled. Like it or not, dogs are able to provide more cost-effective care 24/7 than people are, and with timely and adequate support from humans they can be very effective. We will have to change how we think about dogs and what they can do for us if we are to reap the full benefits of the dog-human bond, but we have set foot on this path already. We have a long way to go, but the journey can be a wonderful odyssey of discovery if only we will open our minds and our hearts and let ourselves explore it fully, without prejudice.

Service Dogs: How to Choose a Pup

In the 'New Knowledge of Dog Behavior' by Clarence Pfaffenberger, he posits a series of tests for Guide Dogs, but that was a long time ago and the only one of the tests that has stood the test of time, so to speak, is that of retrieving. Since so many tasks a dog does these days are based on retrieving behaviors (with modifications) you will want a pup who retrieves. It is quite possible, we now know, to build in a retrieve by starting with a puppy at the imprinting stage. In order to do this, however, you will have to have a relationship with a breeder of dogs suitable for service work. This may be the best way to obtain puppy to train, if that is the route to your service dog you choose to take.

Tests can be problematical. Puppies do not always show to best advantage in tests. They may have just eaten, or just played themselves into readiness for a nap. They may just have awakened from one, and not be quite awake yet. All sorts of things can skew the results of tests. I know several adult dogs who are excellent retrievers with very good retrieving task work who tested out as having no retrieving instinct at all. Puppies, especially GSD puppies, have been known to blow off testers who don't strike them just right, so you will need to visit the puppies early and often in order to make a well-informed decision as to which puppies in the litter will work best for you.

Working with a breeder is the best way to go to choose a puppy for service work, because, like retrieving, some things can be enhanced at the imprinting level that will be helpful. Puppies can be exposed to different surfaces to walk, stand and lay on at a very early age which can help them to develop a good sense of what kind of surface their people will have to take care on later. Breeders can introduce their puppies to a wide variety of food types, raw, dehydrated, kibble, eggs (boiled), milk, cottage cheese, yogurt, and all sorts of treats, thus 'hooking' the pup on the use of 'treats' for later ease of training. Breeders can also get their puppies accustomed to a wide variety of toys, like tugs, balls, etc which later can be used as training tools (tugs can be used to open doors, for instance).

Note, however, that I use the word enhanced. The puppy must have innate, genetically inherited characteristics for obedience and biddability, as well as steady nerve and what is usually referred to as 'handler sensitivity'. Imprinting alone will not produce an appropriate puppy for service work.

In a day when behavioral training is so sophisticated, it is tempting to think that any 'good' puppy can be taught to perform as a service dog. Unfortunately, this leads to what are called 'meltdowns' somewhere along the line when the puppy, now a dog, suffers the canine version of a 'nervous breakdown' when the real world stresses of public access collide with genetic limitations.

Most people who understand public access, will tell you that if you want a dog to succeed in dealing with all that the public can dish out--and they can dish out a lot, from the obnoxious to the bizarre through the unexpected --the dog needs a 'steady' nerve and they are right. However, 'steady' nerve can mean very different things to different people with different purposes in mind. 'Steady' nerve to someone experienced in working with public access dogs will mean something very different from that which is valued by those for whom the sine qua non of the dog world is the sport dog.

'Steady' nerve comes from two places, adrenaline and serotonin. Both hormones mask pain, decrease fear and lend the dog confidence. Some dogs are genetically endowed with adrenal glands which produce the hormone adrenaline in greater amounts than middle range dogs. Other dogs produce more serotonin than mid-range dogs.

Adrenaline is the 'fight or flight' response hormone. Dogs who secrete greater than average amounts of adrenaline or secrete them in response to lower levels of stimulus often seem very bright and quick and are often appealing and endearing. Very little stimulus is required to activate a dump of the hormone into their systems and many grow to crave the feeling of enhanced confidence and well-being the hormone imparts. Such dogs often appear very bold, courageous, impervious to pain, and they are, in the sense that the adrenaline actually does make it more difficult for them to feel pain. Dogs in this state may either over-react to stimulus or under-react to it during training, requiring either very harsh corrections to get their attention, or alternatively, respond quickly to any correction with great negativity. These dogs are often (assuming the other characteristics are in place) VERY good for sport. High adrenaline output very often translates directly into high scores and happy handlers who very soon get a reputation for 'knowing' dogs, being 'outstanding' trainers and the like. IN THEIR SPORT that may all very well be true.

Outside their sport, it can translate into disaster. When people concerned with sport breed dogs, they breed them for the sport they love and are successful in, and that is perfectly acceptable. They breed, if they are wise, successful dogs of the type best suited to their handling methods to successful dogs of the same type, thus producing more adrenaline-based dogs. Some of the puppies they produce will not be as strongly adrenaline-based as they like for their sport and they will sell those puppies to pet homes (where they are often not very successful) and they will try (in the case of the ignorant, chauvinistic or those lacking in integrity) to convince those in search of a service dog that their puppies would be suitable for the task. They seldom are.

DO NOT select one of these pups to be your prospective service dog no matter how attractive they may appear. They are NOT suitable. Your odds of getting a suitable puppy for service work are better at the pound than they are in trying to select a puppy out of a sport-based litter with sport 'titled' parents. Even a pup from a crap for structure 'titled' show litter with their iffy temperaments would have a better chance of successfully making a service dog. Remember--Adrenaline is a Fight or Flight based hormone. It does NOT create appropriate responses for a service dog.

So, the next place to look for steady nerves is with the serotonin-based crowd. You will NOT find any of these dogs with the sport crowd. They don't like them. Serotonin is calming. It creates dogs for whom life's blows are cushioned by generalized good feelings, dogs who look at life through 'rose-colored' glasses, so to speak. Serotonin allows dogs to 'savor' experiences, enhancing learning (so you'd better make certain they have 'good' experiences through which to learn!)

Serotonin dogs tend to be serious, calm, thoughtful, rather than reactive. This could be characterized as the 'think about it' hormone. The cognitive center of Serotonin based dogs' brains tend to be larger than those of the Adrenaline based dogs. They tend to have a 'bite threshold' of higher levels than that found in most dogs. For a service dog, this is very good.

The Serotonin based dog, when told to run around and bite somebody would probably ask, if he had words, 'why?' And he'd probably be sitting down when he asked it. Since the same command given to an Adrenaline based dog would probably result in someone getting bitten, and rather quickly at that, it can be readily seen that the Sport crowd would have no use for a serotonin-based dog. Therefore, it is no use talking to sport people about the selection of service dogs. Only the very few and rarest few at that are even capable of thinking with any kind of accuracy about the qualities a service dog needs to possess because these qualities are so antithetical to the qualities they prize. Service dogs at the public access level have to be able to multi-task. Think about how difficult it is for a human to do, and then realize that we're asking our dogs to quite literally do two or even three things at once.

1) They are responsible for staying in position (whatever that position may be) despite any physical or human obstacles with which they may be confronted. This they must do while watching out for these obstacles, which means they CANNOT walk around curved around their person's leg while staring slavishly up into their person's face.

2) They must try to stay on task--keeping their concentration on what they're doing (different from just maintaining position) such as guiding, actually

bracing or balancing or pulling their person in a wheelchair, despite people getting in their way, greeting them, petting them, asking about them, and generally making a nuisance of themselves.

3) They must hold themselves ready to hear/see/feel any direction/ changing need from their person and be ready and able to make whatever adjustment is called for, perhaps even instantly, despite the cacophony of sights, sounds, scents and movement by which they are being bombarded. Is it any wonder that dogs 'meltdown'?

Serotonin helps a dog to stay calm and to cope. Adrenaline urges the dog to react, to fight, to flee, to charge, to bark, to bite, to DO SOMETHING! If you want to give your puppy the best possible chance to achieve success as a public access level service dog, it is best to choose a pup from NON-titled, serotonin based parents.

But how do you do that? How do you find and choose a serotonin based pup? Well, we already know you are going to begin by eliminating any pup from parents who have sport based titles, especially bite-sport based titles. It will be tough. Not only are the arguments the chauvinistic sport based crowd can muster persuasive (however inaccurate or illogical), their pups, with their appealing looks and happy bouncing brashness with their 'damn the torpedoes, full speed ahead!' attitudes are ever so enticing. Try to remember that such an attitude can result in a nasty fall, or a tipped over chair, not to mention a dog that just finds it impossible to stay on task among all those distractions which are so much more interesting and fun than actually working. Try, also, to remember that such pups usually require the use of prong collars and some physical strength to handle, and that many, many of these pups will require both the prong collar and the strength even after they are 'trained' because they are simply not reliable even to walk on a leash without pulling without a prong collar.

If you need help resisting these delightful charmers, Remember, sport is, at base, a game, and work is, at base, well--WORK. Sport drive is one thing. True work ethic is often something quite different.

Forget the fearful, shy, timid puppy. Look for the steady, thoughtful, look-before-he-leaps pup. The one who stops to find a way around the obstacle instead of throwing himself into it full speed ahead. You want a pup who thinks before he leaps. That's not shyness or fear, it's just good sense. Sense may not make him the most attractive, appealing pup, but it will make him a much safer pup for his person, and this pup will be able to instill a sense of security in a person that the bolder pup won't.

Some Sociability, or Friendliness, is necessary in a good public access dog, since the dog will have to be able to cope with the public and stay even-tempered and ON TASK. Too much sociability interferes with the work, but any hostility or suspicion should be a complete disqualification. A 'neutral' or 'aloof' dog MIGHT be all right, if a marginal choice for the work, but a dog with a basically friendly mind-set is better. They are much less apt to have a 'meltdown' when confronted with public idiocy. (Which is why people use Labs and Goldens. Very few Labs or Goldens are hostile or suspicious/shy and this helps to make up for their shortcomings in other areas of the work rather well.) And sooner or later, John Q Public will behave in an idiotic way. Count on it.

Brace/balance dogs and to a somewhat lesser extent, wheelchair aide dogs need to be almost bomb-proof. Reactive, adrenaline based dogs need not apply. The dog needs to not respond much to sudden noises or movements and they cannot be reactive to other animals, dogs or people or even squirrels or rabbits or objects. Sudden sounds should not produce an adrenaline fueled response, such as fight (aggression) or flight (shyness, fear). High thresholds not found in most sport dogs, should be de rigueur.

There will be times when avoidance or extreme caution is the absolutely correct response, so try to keep that in mind and don't wash reasonably cautious pups out. They may be just what is needed. (Some examples that come to mind--gratings which could trap the wheel of a walker or a chair or a cane and cause a painful jolt or even a fall, mud or water that could prove dangerously slippery, wet grass, ditto, or wet stone or linoleum floors, just to begin.)

You want a dog whose first reaction is to stand and look and then think before he does something about whatever it is. Try not to confuse a handler sensitive dog, who might be very good at the job with the reactive dog, who just likes to be excited about stuff. Again, the kind of dog a sport person would find appealing is probably NOT a good choice. The puppy who loves to run around you in circles, or who just adores leaping after toys is the WRONG choice. The puppy who startles a little at a gunshot or other loud noise and looks around a little to see where it came from is ok. The pup who jumps up and yanks you over to either run away or go see, either way, is out.

Seizure dogs, whether alert or response, need to be able to tolerate a grand mal seizure. A dog has to be able to stay on task even when the person is behaving in ways which to the dog must seem wildly out of the ordinary. The same dog, however, would have to be very observant, the kind who would notice any little variation in behavior or scent or activity level, because they watch their person closely. They need to be very handler sensitive, while being bomb- proof at the same time.

This is something of a paradox and seizure alert dogs always seem like a gift because there is simply no way to train the alert. The dog just has to figure it out for themselves. I would look for a pup with steady nerves and some resilience who likes to sit and watch people. You know, the one who listens and tips his head this way and that while he tries to figure stuff out about people, rather than things as long as he isn't whining while doing it. (Whining is either anxiety, excitability, or dominance. He isn't interested in you, he wants you to do something for him.) Look for the pup that stays with this behavior,

109

who doesn't bail out when he doesn't find the answers right away and go jumping around forgetting all about you.

Blood sugar alert dogs need to combine a nose-oriented world view with high handler sensitivity. These dogs need to sit around and watch, listen and most of all, smell their person. They have to have a great deal of patience and the stick-to-it-tivity to stay on task and find it enthralling enough to remain sensitive, through long hours, to the slightest change in the scent of their person's body. This makes it very important to match the energy level of the person and the pup so that the pup is always either the same or just a little less energetic than their person. They must be able to fix their attention on their person, and not on whatever activity is going on around them. Most service dogs are trained with treats, but these dogs, because they need their noses to stay clear, should only get intermittent treats and not the fragrant kind, so they need to find toys and tugs rewarding as well.

Hearing ear dogs can be somewhat reactive. Your hearing ear puppy should find sound exciting. He's got to do something about it. He wants you to know about it. This can be a little bolder dog, unless the person is older or has other issues beyond just hearing loss. Terriers and French bulldogs have done well at this. Achieving public access with a hearing ear dog means striking a balance between reactivity and calmness. Well, so much of service dog work is about striking a balance between qualities. This is just one more area where you need to find it.

Matching energy levels between people and their dogs is really important. Too many trainers make the mistake of matching their own energy levels and thinking that because the dog is fine for them that he will be fine for the disabled person. WRONG. The other mistake often made, particularly by sport/ so-called 'working-line' dog people, is to equate energy with work ethic. They think that if the dog isn't bouncing around like electrified frog legs that the dog is a couch potato. They CANNOT think in terms of balance; there is no in-between in their thinking between insane energy and the moderate dog they mislabel a couch potato.

The world of the service dog is the world of the MODERATE dog. Too often even the lowest pup in the sport-dog litter is way, WAY too energetic for either the people or the work. The pup only appears to be moderate because the rest of the litter is so extreme. And, too, what seems to the sport person as 'moderate' prey drive is often actually W-A-Y too much for the work or the person. Part of this is the sport person personality. They like WOW! dogs. They think there is something wrong with anyone who doesn't. In some instances, as with the disabled, they are exactly right. The person using the service dog is often doing so because they have something physically wrong with their body.

Sport dog people tend to be athletic, active, and more physically fit than the norm. People with disabilities are at the opposite end of the spectrum.

110

This is often very difficult for the sport dog breeder/trainer to internalize. They want their dog to fit so they try to cram a square peg into a round hole or vice versa. Disabled people and their families wind up getting short changed and thinking the whole thing about service dogs is a bunch of hooey. Especially when the sport person tells them that it's their fault that the dog didn't work out the way it was supposed to. It isn't their fault, it is that they were stuck with the WRONG dog in the first place!

Service dogs for brace/balance and wheelchair work in particular and the alerts as well, need to have work ethic, rather than what the sport person thinks of when they use the word drive. These dogs are the poster children for 'they also serve who only stand and wait'. The brace/balance dog who takes one step, waits a beat, and then another, and then waits another beat, may be working very hard. That pause beat may be the brace as they shore their person up and prepare them to take that next step. It's not a driving kind of action. It takes a lot of patience and care and self-discipline on the dog's part to achieve that perfect willingness to SLOW DOWN.

The alert dog may spend hours every day sitting around and watching intently. If they're lucky, they have an owner who can do a little physical activity and can play with them. Not all people with seizures or diabetes can play actively with their dogs for several hours a day. They still need a service dog and it is perfectly acceptable for them to have one—just as long as they are not saddled with a sport dog who simply will not fit their needs. So when you look for a puppy for someone, you have to think about the person the puppy is for and the tasks they're going to be asked to perform, not what you like yourself.

With a GSD you almost can't get too low an energy level for brace/balance, but you sure can get a dog who has way too low a caring level. The dog that just HAS to chase that squirrel because his prey drive is so intense? His prey drive may be too high, but his caring level is also too low.

Structure, in most of the alert dogs, isn't too crucial. However, in guide dogs, brace/balance dogs, and manual wheelchair aide dogs, it is very important. Strong hind end assemblies are critical. Show dog hind ends simply do NOT belong here. Many a show type dog can work as an alert dog or with an electric wheelchair. But when the dogs start pulling someone, or holding them up, the dog needs strength and stability. To get this, the dog's hind legs MUST fit comfortably within the plane of the dog's body and he MUST walk on his feet, NOT his hind legs. This is a LOT more than simply a dog with OFA good or excellent hips! The entire structure of the dog's hind leg MUST be functionally correct, which lets out all those over-agulated show dogs and all those sickle hocked show dogs, and all those show dogs with hind legs sticking out behind their bodies, all the show dogs who can't stand up, who wobble when they walk, or crouch, or squat.

111

Those elegant, long thighs, long stifles, horizontal 'second' thighs and loose ligaments so beloved by the show world along with the fancy 'side-gait' they produce, are hopeless. Thighs should be moderate to short, rounded with muscle, and UPRIGHT. Hocks should be open and upright, atop vertical metatarsals. Front legs should be straight with forearms which do not turn in or out, not bow-legged, not pigeon-toed. They don't have to be pretty. They DO have to be functional.

Far better to have a lop ear than a long stifle or an over-angulated hock. Even puppies should be straight and tight when they stand and move. NOT wobbly, NOT loose, NOT low in back. I know it's sometimes difficult to see. We've been presented with so much aberrant conformation for so long, we have difficulty recognizing correct hind-quarter assemblies when we see them, but we must educate our eyes and work at seeing correct conformation on the rare occasions when we're presented with it if we are to make successful choices.

To sum it all up, 1) Avoid dogs bred for sport--eliminate all sport 'titles' from your prospective puppy parent list. Try to find dogs bred to produce serotonin rather than adrenaline. 2) Look for a natural retriever. 3) Fit the dog's energy level first and then 4) the tasks (genetic obedience), remembering to factor in structure for the physical stuff. (No show dogs.)

This is done by what? close observation over time, not a one or two time test which may or may not be accurate and working with a breeder who knows what service dogs are, if you are lucky enough to find one. Which leads me to . . . .

Service Dogs: What Happened to German Shepherds?

German Shepherd dogs, as we all know (or ought to know) were the pioneers of service work done by dogs. They were the first police dogs, the first ambulance dogs (in WWI when they located wounded soldiers for ambulance crews), the first war dogs, and the first Guide Dogs for the Blind. They were the first dogs to locate and get help for lost hikers in this country ('a la St Bernard dogs in the Alps), what we now call Search and Rescue dogs. They were certainly among the first Brace/balance dogs and the first wheelchair aide dogs. Until the training of German Shepherd Dogs was discontinued at San Rafael, blind people would wait a year or even two in order to get a German Shepherd instead of a Lab or Golden.

Lame excuses proffered to the public blaming 'health concerns' is exposed as just how lame when statistics regarding washouts for reasons of health in the three main service dog breeds (GSDs, Labs, and Goldens) used for the work are consulted. Labs and Goldens wash out at a much higher rate for hip dysplasia and other genetic health conditions than GSDs do. Additionally, success rates for GSDs at San Rafael under Clarence Pfaffenberger's breeding program varied from year to year from 80% of puppies finishing successfully to 85% working successfully. No other breed has ever even come close. Labs and Goldens at their best have only achieved 65% success rates, and 60% is more common, while many programs using Labs and Goldens can do no better than 35% of dogs completing their program and successfully partnering someone with disabilities at the public access level.

So why are the first and the best dogs bred for service work either being phased out of most programs, or completely ignored as a possibility for the work in the first place?

The short answer is pretty stark in its simplicity. Clarence Pfaffenberger is dead. So are most of the other successful designers of German Shepherd breeding programs for service work. Most of those who are still alive are at least in their sixties. Very, VERY few are still breeding.

Breeders coming up for the most part, have no idea of how to breed a dog for the kind of functional structure and temperament a service dog requires, and neither the show folk nor the sport folk have anything to teach service dog breeders that is of any positive benefit. Therein lies the long answer to the question of why German Shepherds are no longer bred for service work by so many organizations.

The vast majority of dogs today with a title for working sheep are competition dogs who work a limited number of sheep for a very short period of time under artificial conditions. The few people still breeding dogs for working stock in the real world under conditions where the dog actually does a job, rather than gets a title, are rare, and almost completely unknown. Almost without exception, they don't have websites and don't spend time on forums. (They'd probably say they don't have the time to waste on fools.) They don't have a lot of disposable income, and they're just too busy to be bothered.

Search and Rescue has been taken over by the Schutzhund crowd with their craving for 'titles'. It's now dominated by people who choose their dog first for what is called 'ball-drive' and actual considerations of dogs that stick to their track through thick and thin until they actually find somebody have been marginalized, or sometimes disregarded completely. The sport crowd has taken over, and run out any of the real old real-work dogs, which is why so many of these groups no longer get called out on real searches and why 'human remains detection' dogs get most of the work today. But they know it all, and it's their way--and their dog--or the highway.

Sport dogs are now called 'working' dogs--a complete misnomer quite deliberately adopted by their proponents as a marketing tool which has been very effective. Show dogs have been reaping the whirlwind of their short-sighted generations of in-breeding, so that if it's an American champion, odds are it has either SIBO or IBD or Cardio or von Wildebrand's or DM or a selection of the above. If it's a German high-line show dog, it probably has

EPI at the least, and quite possibly vWildebrand's and JRD as well, with a soupcon of DM just to make things interesting.

Both Show and Sport groups are prone to bloat. Both groups will occasionally throw out a pup with hip or elbow dysplasia, always keeping in mind that about 50% of these are environmentally created.

In the era from the 1940s to the 1960s, no real split existed in the breed between working dogs and show dogs and sport dogs didn't exist. Schutzhund was NOT a competition, it was a pass-fail test to which breeding advice was appended. Dogs didn't get scored, nor were they rated on their Schutzhund tests separately from their conformation exam, which, if one looks at the early Siegers critically, was weighted far more heavily towards conformation than to Schutzhund performance. (Just as it is today.) Dogs who actually worked stock were just as prized as dogs who did well at Schutzhund, and dogs who excelled at tracking got FHs and kudos.

Breeders selecting dogs to go into programs for Guide Dogs, or military dogs, or stock dogs, could judge whether they wanted to add dogs to their programs by using the judgments of other dog people as expressed through terms whose meaning was understood by most people using them to mean pretty much the same thing. Misleading terms like 'working-line' for sport dogs hadn't yet been invented. When someone called a dog a 'real working dog' they meant the dog actually worked, and at a real job. Today, a 'real working dog' runs down a football field and bites somebody. Show dogs' structure was still relevant to function, and people still believed that when they line bred for one generation, they were supposed to out-breed the next.

This made picking and choosing among elements of temperament and structure relatively simple in juxtaposition with the quagmire it is today, when you have to figure out who is talking before you can interpret what they're saying. We have the show group, who have their own language and their own concerns and the bite sport group with theirs. Unfortunately the show people are so far out in la-la land with their total disregard for anything having to do with temperament or health in their in-bred cripples that they're simply irrelevant to anyone who seriously intends to attempt to breed German Shepherds for service work.

Unfortunately, the working line crowd, with their penchant for extremes of temperament are in pretty much the same boat, if for different reasons. Extremes of prey drive, low bite thresholds, dogs which require two to three hours of extreme exercise every day, dogs whose adrenaline levels create reactivity reminiscent of an electrified frog's legs, or worse, dogs with severe aggression issues, called 'reactivity' along with dogs which consider any correction they don't like excuse enough to attack their handler are worse than useless for service work.

So what has anyone wishing to start or even to continue a established breeding program of GSDs have to work with? A sport dog reject is still far too extreme in prey drive, adrenaline reactivity, and far too lacking in bite inhibition to be a candidate for any realistic service dog breeding program. And any dog of show breeding is an equally rotten candidate, whether it is a show reject for the 'pet' market or even a more expensive show prospect. The health concerns for genetic conditions due to extreme in-breeding ought to be enough to disqualify the dogs, even if their structure hadn't gone to unreliable extremes.

Well . . . that leaves the smallest group of all, the proponents of the old fashion Germand Shepherd dog, bred to resemble in both physical and mental structure the early dogs of the breed up through the 1950s with an emphasis on selection for the ability to perform the traditional tasks of the breed, such as herding, search work and guide work, with the occasional police dog here and there. The fact that these folks are such a small group is a concern in and of itself from the standpoint of genetic diversity. Can a person find enough unrelated adequately temperamented, basically correct functionally structured dogs in this group to create a successful breeding program? On the up side, this is the group which is statistically the most free of in-breeding and its resultant genetic conditions. So that's a plus. But this is the least sophisticated group of the three, as well as the smallest.

Worst of all, perhaps, is that the bloodlines in this group have been marginalized. No readily available body of knowledge regarding the characteristics of temperament or structure exists. No one can say, 'oh, dog A, this is what he throws in his sons, and this is what he throws in his daughters'. When we look at the old lines, we can say things like, 'oh, line-breeding on Lex/Maja tends to give you sharp pups' or 'Axel tends to throw over-size, particularly on Arras or Onyx grand-daughters' or 'Bernd v Kallengarten throws the occasional incomplete hip socket'.

Working-line people can tell you this stuff. Show people can tell you at least what kind of structure their dogs will produce. If the old-fashioned people have a clue, so far that knowledge doesn't seem to have reached a point where it can be called a common body of information. And without that knowledge, how are service dog breeders supposed to know how to breed to get what they need to do the job?

To this group, all pups are 'good' pups. They're right, of course, but how many of these breeders can recognize elements of temperament when they see them? Or see them to recognize in the first place? (Well, those are questions which could just as validly be asked of the first two groups, but--oh, well, never mind.) And how many of these breeders would recognize correct structure in their pups if they saw it. (Ok, not very many of the so-called 'working-line' group could do this, either, and the show crowd would think all the wrong things were right, so--back to never mind.)

The only answer, of course, is for the prospective breeders to familiarize themselves with what they're breeding. To go and look at the dogs these breeders have. Handle the dogs if they'll allow it (and wash them out if they won't). Make four or five visits to get acquainted with the puppies and talk for several hours on the 'phone (or face to face) with the breeder (e-mails are only for supplement--you will need to 'hear' what the breeder is saying, intonations, inflections, emphasis, all those important nuances that are left out of written communications).

And one breeder isn't enough. Anyone attempting to breed GSDs for service work is going to have to create a network of breeders from whom to get pups through the years. (Yes, years--a breeding program is a matter of decades.) They will need to go back to certain dogs to create the 'nicks' that set in the characteristics they need to turn out successful dogs. (Sort of like the old Axel/Lex-Maja nick of the 1950s, which produced so many great real world working dogs.) And they'll have to be continually on the look-out for quality out-lines to keep their genetic diversity and away from the extremes that seem to be the inevitable result of repeated in-breeding, both in structure and temperament.

Which brings us back to reality again. All service dog breeders have a very tight budget. Private individuals who do it out of something very like true altruism get pretty much nothing out of their dogs. If the pup's recipients can kick in something to help out with expenses, that's about the best they can hope for. First, because this is a very small and specialized 'market' populated by people on very tightly fixed incomes (sometimes SSI, oft-times some form of disability payment, almost always something not really adequate to meet comfortable living standards without a spouse's or parent's supplementation). Secondly, because the number of people who are disabled yet still capable of training their own dogs is so small. And third because few people know what is possible, selling these dogs for any kind of competitive price would be virtually impossible.

Most organizations who breed, train and place dogs, like CCI, Dogs 4 Diabetics and San Rafael Guide Dogs for the Blind, operate on grants from the public sector and private grants and thus provide their dogs for free. Either way, money for the purchase of pups with which to either begin or continue their breeding programs is very scanty. Money to travel around and meet dogs and interact with them is virtually nil. Even the cost of long-distance calls can be a strain.

In the 1950s and '60s show breeders donated pups to various Guide Dogs' breeding programs for the bragging rights of being able to say, "I breed Guide dogs." Effective programs like the one at San Rafael picked and chose the dogs they would take, and put them through the entire two year training program before assessing them for breeding. Top show breeders made every effort to get their top dogs into such breeding programs. Today, no one would use one of their dogs in their program if they could avoid it, given the EPI, IBD, Cardio, vWildebrand's and SIBO they are riddled with, never mind their structural problems.

Today, the 'working-line' breeders arrogantly shrug off the complaints that their dogs are not appropriate for service work with the words-- "Get a Lab, then". In fact, the day when Schutzhund had anything of value to add to the breeding of a versatile, 'useful' dog is long gone.

The result is that it is nearly impossible even for an established breeding program for German Shepherd dogs to find appropriate out-lines by which to carry on their programs in a cost-effective manner. Without adequate sources of genetic diversity, these programs simply cannot continue to turn out dogs of sound character and constitution.

So far, the Lab community and the Golden community can still give service dog breeding programs the support and structure such programs require. Administrators making breeding decisions for their service organizations may not be as successful as Pfaffenberger and his GSDs but at least they don't have to deal with two competing groups telling them out-right lies and a third group with no clue what claims to make, other than the unsophisticated claim that their dogs are 'good', which, however accurate it may be, is unhelpful in making breeding decisions. I don't blame them for giving up on German Shepherds.

Part III:

The German Shepherd and The Breed Standard

Peffer von Bern

Chapter 5
Temperament

Bodo vom Lierberg

The Breed Standard Temperament

The breed standard through the years has NOT waxed eloquent about what it expects in a German Shepherd Dog's temperament. The 1929 standard was NOT hung up on details. It says, "The traits and special characteristics of the Shepherd are watchfulness, loyalty, honesty, and an aristocratic bearing, forming a combination which makes the purebred Shepherd Dog an ideal guard and companion. It is desirable to try to improve his appearance, but nothing must be done which in any way detracts from his usefulness." (I particularly like that last sentence. Too bad it wasn't included in the latest Standard, from 1978.)

1978: "The breed has a distinct personality marked by direct and fearless, but NOT hostile expression, self-confidence, and a certain aloofness that does not lend itself to immediate and indiscriminate friendships. The dog must be approachable, quietly standing its ground and showing confidence and willingness to meet overtures [from strangers] without itself making them. It is poised, but when the occasion demands, eager and alert; both fit and willing to serve in its capacity as companion, watchdog, blind leader, herding dog, or guardian, whichever the circumstances may demand.

"The dog must not be timid, shrinking behind its master or handler, it should not be nervous, looking about or upward with anxious expression or showing nervous reactions, such as tucking of tail, to strange sounds or sights. Lack of confidence under any surroundings is not typical of good character. Any of the above deficiencies in character which indicate shyness must be penalized as very serious faults and any dog exhibiting pronounced indications of these must be excused from the ring.

"It must be possible for the judge to observe the teeth and to determine that both testicles are descended. Any dog that attempts to bite the judge must be disqualified. The ideal dog is a working animal with an incorruptible character combined with a body and gait suitable for the arduous work that constitutes its primary purpose."

So much for the show rings full of spooks and modern Schutzhund's penchant for Civil Aggression and 'good' suspicion. I doubt that the standard really matters any longer, since no one pays any attention to what it actually says. German Shepherd judges dare not put their hands on a dog in the ring, dogs bite judges with impunity and garner awards, and it has surely been at least thirty years since a dog was excused from the show ring for 'shyness', if ever.

Schutzhund folks and the rest of the bite sport people in general think their dogs should not have to allow a strange judge to touch them, never mind check their teeth; many of them do not even require their dogs to allow a vet to examine them. They believe there is no need for any stranger to be putting their hands on their dog, or even to come within six feet of them and they see no value in the type of temperament which would allow it.

Standards as to what is desired in temperament have changed so drastically through the last two or three decades, as well as the meaning of the language used to define the elements of temperament, that attempting to compare modern dogs to the breed standard, even the 1978 standard, amounts to attempting to compare apples and oranges.

Today's Schutzhund sport, with its emphasis on the long bite and point scoring has even less resemblance to the Schutzhund used to 'test' the temperament of dogs in Stephanitz' time than modern baseball, with its 'intimate' parks, 'juiced' balls, and steroid enhanced home run hitters has with the baseball played by the infamous 'Black Socks', or Cy Young, Ty Cobb, and Rogers Hornsby. Just as the old baseball teams played what is now called 'small ball', with the emphasis on bunts, sacrifice, and moving the base-runners over, Stephanitz' Schutzhund focused on obedience, strength and agility and identifying dogs who could stand in against a threat to their handler. The 'courage' test involved standing firm when a gun was fired and stepping up to stand between the handler and a strangely dressed man playing the 'bad guy'. NOT running down a football field or a cow pasture to bite the first person they find!

They had no 'long bite' and Stephanitz and his cronies wouldn't have considered it a positive thing if a dog had offered it to them. The actual bite counted for no more than any other obedience exercise and probably less than some of the obstacles, at least until the Nazis came to power and started fighting with Stephanitz about the type of temperament they wanted on their dogs, as opposed to what he wanted on his.

Some people who have been active in Schutzhund for thirty to forty years, have said that the changes in the rules, the judging and training of the Schutzhund dog have turned what was once all about putting the traits and characteristics of the German Shepherd Dog on display into an exhibition of the skill of the trainers. The score has become more important than the comments, and many judges, according to them, no longer bother with comments at all. These changes in the sport have resulted in substantive changes being made in the dogs which perform in sport.

Temperament is subjective, always has been and always will be. Modern bite sport people want a sharp--the quickness with which a dog will bite when his bite threshold is exceeded--dog with a very low bite threshold (the amount of provocation a dog needs to bite). People who raise, train and use dogs for service to the disabled don't want a dog with any sharpness at all and they want/need a very high bite threshold on their dogs.

Police departments and the military are currently using sharp dogs with a low bite threshold. They seem to be all right for the military personnel, but police departments who are now using Malinois who are typically sharp/low threshold are finding that they can be a liability on the job. The

Malinois customs dog who bit the toddler is just one example of what can happen using this kind of dog around the public.

Pet people tend to be with the service dogs for the disabled crowd, and when they get conned into the sport-type sharp, low bite threshold dog, quite often bad things happen. Dogs drag their handlers across streets to bite innocent pedestrians, attack neighbors, friends and family members and otherwise prove how inappropriate they are for average family life while giving a colossal black eye to the breed as a whole.

People talk about the elements of character in two ways—as a combination of drives, which they may variously label as fight, defense, flight, protection, food, resource, prey/play, retrieving, hunt, and so on, or as a combination of personality traits. High drive to this crowd generally refers to prey/play drive, usually blended with high adrenaline levels which drive the dog to high levels of activity. These 'drives' are routinely confused with work ethic, which is something else entirely and which a good many of the people who describe dogs in terms of drives don't recognize.

Other people qualify temperament in terms of essences of character, hardness, softness, nerve, resilience, biddability, sociability, focus/ concentration, civility, aggression, timidity, suspicion (timidity by another name) work ethic, sharpness, bite threshold, clear head, common-sense, nobility, ability to forgive, patience, equanimity, loyalty, stuff that is quintessentially subjective. People who like to think and talk in terms of drive tend not to be comfortable with the concept of character as an essential element of a dog's temperament. People who tend to think of their dogs in terms of the essence of their character, tend not to care much about the concepts of drives. A few people realize the dog's temperament is made up of a complex web of all of these, all of which are variably inherited genetically and all of which are impacted by environmental conditions.

Tracking and herding are inborn skills created by thousands of years of selective breeding. Some people call this genetic pre-disposition for certain skill-sets 'genetic obedience' though such a label is not entirely accurate. It is, however, a handy way of referring to such talents as herding and tracking and the commitment to working in cooperation with humans which underlie herding and tracking skills. Dogs may have these genetic endowments to a greater or lesser extent, and dogs with extremely strong genetic proclivities for tracking or herding are often visibly affected by this. Dogs with lesser genetic 'programming' are often still affected, if less visibly, by this inheritance.

ALL of these elements influence the temperament of the dog. They combine in an infinite number of ways to make an infinite variety of temperaments. Think in terms of a kaleidoscope. A finite number of elements in different sizes (types) and colors (intensity) shift about into different snowflake patterns with every variation of the combination. No two temperaments are exactly alike any more than any two snowflakes are exactly

124

alike, although some can be remarkably similar and others can be remarkably dissimilar.

Consider the ideal sport dog, which combines sharpness and low bite threshold with high prey drive. Sharpness is the quickness with which a dog reacts to bite. Get over the sharp dog's bite threshold and the dog's head whips around and CHOMP! Bite threshold is the point at which the dog is stimulated to bite. Sharpness itself, if the bite threshold is high, might not be too bad for pet homes. But lower the bite threshold, and the result for a service dog or a pet dog can be disastrous. In a police or working drug or contraband detection dog this can result in inappropriate bites, like the Malinois that bit the toddler. This is a perfect example of a sharp dog with a low bite threshold.

Bite sport dogs are deliberately bred to be sharp and to have a very low bite threshold. These are the land sharks one hears about on the various forums, pups who bite to play, bite often, bite hard, and are extremely difficult to discourage, so that they're still biting and biting hard at eight months, a year, even, sometimes, at eighteen months, breaking the skin and causing bruises and puncture wounds. These are the dogs who run across streets to bite complete strangers who are minding their own business. No fear is attached to the act of biting, nor is any animosity, nor has the person provided any provocation.

These dogs are simply bred to bite. They get excited? They bite. They're playing, having a good time? They bite. They're happy? They bite. In 1896 Herr Eiselen commented that all that was necessary for a Thuringian dog to bite a person was for that dog to see a person. In 2010, a writer said of her 'working-line' dog that all he needed in the way of motivation to bite something or someone was for him to see something or someone. A hundred and fourteen years, and nothing had changed. Both were describing the epitome of a sharp dog with a low bite threshold.

The reason these dogs are bred to bite are myriad. The Nazis bred them that way to intimidate crowds, guard concentration camps, and later, POW camps. The Communists came along and found them good for border patrol. Their purpose was to bite anyone their handler indicated they should bite, or when on patrol, any person they found, regardless of how little threat that person presented to them or their handler. These dogs are ideal for the new Schutzhund where the dog is simply to run full tilt around a football field and bite the heck out of the first person they find.

I would argue that such sharpness and low bite threshold are not good for the breed for many reasons, and I know a lot of people who have worked dogs for decades agree with me, but people breeding for sport are going to keep on doing it as long as sharp dogs with low bite thresholds score big and get them to the podium. Even so, sharpness and low bite threshold dogs are not much of a problem as long as they remain limited to the province of the bite sports.

The problem ensues when the sport people market their dogs to the general public. They do this because litters tend to be large and they do not have sufficient numbers of sport homes to purchase all their puppies. Sport dog people have come up with a number of vary effective marketing strategies to sell their surplus sport dogs to the ever gullible public. ("There's one born every minute!" P. T. Barnum)

From the forums which tout their dogs and put all other dogs down, disseminating an organized program of misinformation regarding the breed standard in favor of their own revised standard, to the mantra that only puppies from 'titled' dogs, mainly Schutzhund titled dogs, are any good, they brainwash people into buying from them. These strategies have been, unfortunately, very effective, driving the breed's bite statistics ever upwards.

Individual people's struggle with inappropriate pets can be heart-rending, but it is when the dogs are marketed to police departments, Search and Rescue and Customs and the like that the you-know-what really starts to hit the fan. Police departments have the resources to protect and defend their dogs that private individuals don't. When those department heads lack the integrity, as they so often do, to root out such dogs from their programs, and the intelligence to learn from the occurrences, the inevitable events like the Customs dog and the toddler, or the dog in Spokane that chewed off a guy's foot, strike at the very heart of agencies' ability to use dogs in public.

Service dogs for the disabled, who have to struggle every day to retain their rights to public access, have to be selected with extreme care to have HIGH bite thresholds and NO sharpness, in order to safeguard those rights. That is why the marketing of their cast-offs to people for service dogs by bite sport people is of such grave concern in the service industry, and one of the many reasons why such dogs are inappropriate for the work.

So what are the elements of temperament dog people talk about and what do they mean by the words they use? Well, here is a discussion of some of the most common terms in use. Note that in some instances, they bear NO relation to the dictionary definitions of the same words.

Elements of Temperament: Character

NERVE

The most important part of the temperament is nerve, and it is the easiest quality to lose and the most difficult to regain because in terms of the dog's temperament, nerve is global. It is the anchor thread that sits at the center of the web of elements that make up temperament, and it influences how each and every one of those elements is expressed in the behavior of the dog. Nerve is more important than hips or structure because a dog with good nerve but moderate hip dysplasia can still be of service. A dog with weak nerves that is OFA excellent cannot be of use because stress will make the dog unreliable.

Nerve allows the dog to handle the stress of being faced with new people, places and things and still function, and it allows the dog to be trained to high levels of usefulness. Without nerve, you have only a shell of a German Shepherd dog without the essence of one.

Nerve is the foundation-stone upon which public access is secured. It is therefore of extreme importance to the service dog, of just about any kind, whether it be police work, military work, or work for the disabled.

But what is nerve? The sport people see nerve as a dog so high on adrenaline that he doesn't even register being hit with a stick. They have no use for 'courage', the quality of performing a purposeful act despite fear; most don't even believe dogs are or could be courageous. They aim for 'fearlessness' itself.

Debates as to the value of this kind of 'fearlessness' between the 'old-timers', who find it less valuable and the new sport people who are all for it don't matter much. Of greater importance is acknowledging the source of this kind of 'nerve'.

Adrenaline is the fight or flight hormone. Blend adrenaline with aggression, and you get fight, blend it with fear, and you get flight. All dogs have adrenal glands and produce adrenaline under the right circumstances. Dogs with high 'drives' are easier to get to producing adrenaline. By combining adrenaline, aggression and prey drive, sport breeders get dogs which, when their adrenaline is up, do not feel pain and therefore do not register fear when they are being hit with the stick and 'fighting' the 'decoy'.

Dogs in an adrenalized state in which aggression is combined with the adrenaline do not react fearfully to much; gunshots, strangers armed with weapons, loud noises, whatever. They are, unfortunately, prone to violence. For the sport people, violence is the whole point, so this is a positive form of nerve for them and it is useful for their purpose, which is to score big points.

On the downside, highly adrenalized dogs may be very excitable, and 'reactivity' is merely the expression of a sport dog who is not trained to channel his adrenaline into sport purposes. Another problem is that many, if not all, dogs who produce large amounts of adrenaline have difficulty remaining what is referred to as 'clear-headed' when they are active. Some of these dogs can be trained into an appearance of 'clear-headedness' by consistent corrections and frequent, regimented training, with lots of repetition of what they are supposed to do, and when. Some of them can't. For sport purposes, this is NOT of any particular importance. The dog merely performs a routine by rote. He doesn't really need a 'clear' head.

For police and the military, it occasionally can be important for the dog to remain clear-headed, when what the military call a SNAFU occurs-- which is where the old-timers start arguing their case.

127

'Nerve' produced by adrenaline is extremely attractive to the sport person. Dogs with this kind of 'nerve' usually appear very confident, even happy-go-lucky, scoring big points for their bright attitude. They actually get 'high' on adrenaline when excited, or anticipating any kind of action. They appear to work with zest, verve, even delight, though they can become serious as well, depending upon the sport discipline within which they were trained.

One caveat applies to adrenaline-based nerve. Adrenaline is the fight or FLIGHT hormone, a coin with two sides. For those dogs who get the fear response to the hormone a life of misery and fear lies ahead of them. Depending on their levels of aggression and the intensity with which they respond to the hormone levels with fear, they can be fear reactive, in which case sharpness and low bite thresholds are commonplace, or just merely fearful. Anyone breeding for high adrenaline production in their dogs WILL produce fearFUL dogs as well as fearLESS dogs.

'Nerve' of this sort is obviously ideal for sport work. It is not so great for the pet dog, and not at all good for the service dog dealing with someone disabled. Fortunately, 'nerve' from the adrenaline source is not the only 'nerve' available. Just as dogs inherit a predisposition to produce an outsize amount of adrenaline, dogs can inherit a predisposition to produce more serotonin than usual.

Serotonin is entirely different from adrenaline. It is a calming hormone, and it, too, produces pleasure and, to some extent, masks pain, though not as completely as adrenaline. (Adrenaline is a survival hormone. Serotonin is more a quality of life hormone.) The pleasure it produces, however, is a source of quiet content rather than leaping delight. Serotonin is subtle in its effects, rather than violent. It influences bonding, and helps to create equanimity, patience, and a forgiving attitude. Serotonin supports a high bite threshold. Dogs whose bodies produce a good, consistent supply of serotonin are characterized as calm, steady, quiet, and sometimes even as gentle or kind.

Dogs whose bodies produce lower than normal levels of serotonin are often irritable, quick to bite, difficult, even morose. Such dogs are often easier to deal with in the morning when their bodies produce something close to a normal amount of serotonin. Unfortunately, their bodies' production of the hormone usually decreases during the day until by evening the dogs are snappish and angry.

Dogs who produce just a little bit more of the hormone than normal tend to be just the opposite; mellow, easy to live with and very easily trained, in a low-key way. Since relatively 'good' serotonin production tends to be linked to the quality called genetic obedience, the dogs often anticipate the household routines so that they seem to train themselves, but they are not usually flashy about it. It is common for such dogs to be serious, rather than happy-go-lucky. They study their lessons and though they are forgiving, it is easier to go wrong with them, more because they 'take things to heart'. Lessons once learned are learned thoroughly and well. Teach them the wrong lesson, and they have it just as firmly as the right one.

Just as adrenaline based dogs are ideal for sport, serotonin based dogs are ideal for service dogs for the disabled. It needs to be understood, however, that these dogs come from two different genetic founts. It would be unlikely for a sport-based breeding to produce serotonin based brains, and just as unlikely for a breeding of dogs high in serotonin production to produce puppies high in adrenaline. Only by crossing the two types do you get the possibility for both and the results in these cases tend to be very uneven.

Serotonin nerve provides cognizance of loud noises but equanimity in the face of them. These dogs will hear gunshots or other loud noises but will react very little to them, perhaps turning towards them, but with little startle. They will flinch when being hit, but depending on the amount of aggression they possess as well as the reason they are fighting, may respond by fighting very seriously and with considerable ferocity. These dogs generally require significant threat in order to attack, but when they do, they are not playing a game.

GENETIC OBEDIENCE

Discipline/Sense of Responsibility/Self-Reliance

The very label for this quality, Genetic Obedience, is a misnomer. Dogs simply are not genetically OBEDIENT. They aren't born knowing how to sit or down and they aren't born knowing what the word come means. The very idea of such a circumstance has been called magical thinking and a fairy tale, and the people making those complaints for the title of Genetic Obedience are absolutely right to call it that. Studies of both human and dog brains show us that certain areas of the brain, such as those areas in which emotions are seated or those which activate when cognitive thinking occurs are pre-disposed, among certain people or dogs, to light up with activity when stimulated. The same studies, however, clearly indicate that it is ENVIRONMENT, ie socialization and training and general all around treatment, which dictate the final development of those areas of the brain.

A dog's brain CAN be genetically pre-disposed to work closely in partnership with a person and to internalize their person's goals as their own as a result of generations of natural and artificial selection for that pre-disposition, but if that dog's brain is not nurtured, socialized, and trained so that the portions of the brain which mandate that kind of behavior are GROWN, it will NOT develop the neurons and synapses to fulfill that potential. In other words, in order for a dog to exhibit what we call Genetic Obedience (for lack of a better label) they must not only be born with the genetic pre-disposition to use certain areas of their brains at a higher level of activity than the norm, but those areas of their brains MUST receive adequate stimulation to develop the structure to support that higher level of activity.

Many dog people today want to believe that all of the dog's temperament is decided by the genetic structure of the brain that they are born with, but today's studies of the brain simply don't support that premise. At the same time, what we're learning about the way brains work clearly presents evidence that not every brain works the same way and that equally clearly shows that pre-dispositions for certain patterns of brain activity run in families. How those patterns display themselves, however, is expressed largely by how the brain is acted upon by environmental factors.

Certainly there are dogs who manage to triumph over lives of apparently unmitigated abuse and somehow manage to remain sociable and even forgiving of the humans who have mistreated them. And just as surely there are dogs who have been well treated all their lives who the genetic breaks of the game have betrayed to fear and misery regardless of how carefully they are nurtured and cared for and trained, but these dogs are at the extreme ends of the spectrum where heredity and environment meet. Even in these dogs good environment provides for better brain structure than they otherwise would have had. Who knows what greatness the first dog might have achieved with a good environment or how truly horrid the life of the second dog might have been without the good environment with which they were gifted?

Dogs, whether 'genetically obedient' or not, are ALWAYS the product of both their genetic heritage and their environment.

Some dog people are very skeptical of the use of the term genetic 'obedience' because the very term tends to make some people think that if the dog is supposed to have 'genetic obedience' it means they don't have to nurture, socialize or train the dog to perform at the levels of behavior they desire. People who expect their dog to somehow train themselves because the dog is 'genetically obedient' are just plain wrong. And people who have to deal with people who don't want to do the work getting a well-behaved and well-trained dog requires can certainly be forgiven for their impatience with the term.

However, for some people, such as those who work stock for a living, or those who work with service dogs for the disabled or SAR dogs often find that cluster of hereditary pre-dispositions called genetic obedience scarcely less crucial than nerve. Others, such as the bite sport people, desire no other genetic pre-disposition than that to bite quickly and easily and hard and you can take everything else and shove it, they'll TRAIN their dogs to do whatever else they want.

For the people to whom genetic obedience is important, it means a dog with a strong hereditary pre-disposition to work cooperatively in partnership with a person in order to achieve a common goal. Genetic obedience is the well from which the dog/person relationship springs. It has been developed through more than fourteen thousand years of dog-person evolution and it was distilled to 20th century levels through the process of the domestication of herd animals.

Genetic obedience—for lack of a better term—genetic pre-disposition for cooperative bonding and partnership with people is the stuff of Lassie and Rin-Tin-Tin and many of our fantasies about our dogs. It produces the dogs who call 911 for their people when they have a heart attack, dogs that get their families out of burning houses and dogs that watch over diabetic children so they can alert on blood sugar spikes and sudden lows. Without at least some genetic obedience there would be no guide dogs for the blind, no wheel-chair aide or brace/balance dogs, no hearing ear or blood sugar alert dogs, no herding dogs, no SAR dogs, and hunting dogs would run off and leave their human companions in the dust instead of waiting for them to make the shot.

Self-discipline, self-reliance and a sense of responsibility in the German Shepherd dog all come from the genetic obedience for herding and tracking, and it is the foundation of biddability, which is merely a lower level of genetic obedience. A dog can exhibit biddability without reaching the level at which a dog is considered to be genetically obedient. A dog can also be 'biddable' without having any proclivity for herding or the kind of focus, determination or hunt drive, however you choose to define it, to stay on a track when the track becomes difficult.

In herding and tracking, dogs have to operate on their own recognizance, in a very real sense, so they must have the self-discipline to do what they have been taught to do, the sense of responsibility to both the shepherd and the livestock to do it, and the self-reliance to be able to decide how to carry it through. It is genetic obedience that activates the other qualities necessary to the work.

In tracking, people have no realistic way to check up on what the dog is actually doing, despite all their attempts to do so. Neither do they have any realistic way to control whether the dog is actually doing what they ask. In the world of scent, the dog is sighted and the human handler might as well be blind--just as a truly blind person must depend upon the dog to lead them, the SAR handler must TRUST the dog to lead them. The dog must trust himself to be able to take the lead and to guide his person and he must make his own decisions about how to do that.

For the tracking dog to become a guide dog for the blind is hardly a stretch. In both cases, the dog is leading the person along a track the person CANNOT see. The dog takes responsibility for remaining on the track the person has asked him to take, ACCORDING TO THEIR TRAINING, whether that track is a scent, or a direction that the person has specified. Dogs who refuse to make the effort to stay on the track their person has asked them to follow, who go off 'crittering' after squirrels or rabbits or whatever, are dogs showing their lack of genetic obedience. While training can to some degree mitigate this inclination on the dog's part, it can seldom eradicate it reliably.

Herding dogs must exhibit self-discipline as well. They are a great deal more than merely dogs with prey drive pointed at sheep (or cattle, etc). They care for, direct, discipline, and protect sheep. Their prey drive, though often intense, is sharply modified by softness, self-discipline, and a sense of responsibility, and they have to be able to rely on their own decisions about what to do in order to manage the task. When a person is training a herding dog, what they are teaching is NOT how to herd sheep, but how to understand their human's communication regarding where the person wants the sheep (or cattle or goats) to go or to stay and how to help their person get or keep the stock where they're supposed to go or stay. Good herding dogs can be left with the sheep (or cattle, or goats, etc) to watch over them and take care of them on their own for hours at a time.

Dogs on small farms have taken responsibility for bringing the dairy cows in to be milked morning and evening for centuries. Herding dogs have baby-sat for children, guarded flocks, searched for lost lambs and fought predators, for as long as there have been shepherd dogs. Lassie may be over-blown and exaggerated, but in a very realistic sense, Lassie has lived among us for as long as we have used dogs to herd our livestock.

According to Master Shepherd Manfred Hayne genetic obedience is one of the two defining characteristics of the German Shepherd Dog. (The other being nerve.) When genetic obedience is lost the dog becomes no longer biddable, his temperament becomes unbalanced and unstable, leading to reactivity and unmodified aggression. The Master Shepherd believed that retaining genetic obedience is more important than hip dysplasia, prey drive, coat, color, or nuances of structure because it is crucial to the dog's ability to be of service to humans in a way that no other characteristic of the dog other than nerve, is. He believed that no more than thirty percent of the breed's original genetic obedience remains, and that the lack of it is due to the ignorance of breeders who do not work their dogs. He feared that if the present trends continue, that only a miracle can save the breed as a true working dog.

CLEAR-HEADEDNESS

Clear-headedness is a characteristic that goes along with nerve provided by serotonin, as the hormone tends to enhance cognitive intelligence. Adrenaline, on the other hand, tends to shut down the cognitive brain in order to enhance the odds of survival by emphasizing physical response. A dog that is clear-headed is one who is able to continue thinking and making reasoned decisions based on their training and genetic inheritance when all hell is breaking loose around them. The clear-headed dog is the one who minds their handler when all the other dogs are running around and barking (or worse). It is part of and belongs with, genetic obedience.

COMMONSENSE

Commonsense is also a part of the serotonin cluster of characteristics. Because serotonin supports reason over reaction, dogs with more serotonin tend to be able to 'think' better, and therefore respond to situations in a more measured manner, as well as to connect cause and effect more successfully. It goes along with genetic obedience.

SOCIABILITY

Sociability is another of the basic elements of temperament. When people talk about having a German Shepherd coated Lab or Golden, it is sociability to which they are referring. Sociability tempered with a touch of aloofness may express itself in great benignity, while socia-bility combined with adrenaline results in the dog that jumps all over everybody demanding attention. Combined with serotonin, it makes the dog feel content, so the dog is also apt to be friendly towards people and other dogs, and more accepting of their foibles.

Sociability to some degree is very valuable for the service dog working with the disabled. In order for the person to be able to go places in public, move along crowded sidewalks calmly and cheerfully, go into stores or restaurants or attend any event where people congregate, they must have a dog comfortable around people. (Which is why so many Labs and Goldens are used. Their high degree of sociability to a large extent prevents the 'meltdowns' which other breeds sometimes suffer from when the public, inevitably, commits some idiocy around the dog or even directly upon the poor dog.)

The confidence, approachability, and willingness to meet the overtures of strangers called for in the breed standard comes from the genetic combination of nerve and sociability. And while too much sociability can interfere with task work, too little can actually result in a faulty character. Better to have to train the dog to temper his sociability and remain on task than to have too little. Training cannot replace what isn't there.

SUSPICION

Many sport dog people prefer what they call 'good suspicion' to sociability. I consider suspicion perilously close to hostility and timidity, both of which the standard clearly and unequivocally enjoins against. This is just one of the many areas where the sport people, while insisting that the 'breed standard' is holy writ have in fact, deviated from it significantly, and hold to that deviation. Some suspicion may be good in military and police dogs, it may even help to get good scores in sport (though I wonder about that) but it does

NOT belong in a service dog for the disabled, or the therapy dog, and it has NO place in the breeding of service dogs for the disabled.

SOFTNESS

This is a quality absolutely necessary for a service dog for the disabled and makes a good herding dog, but which sport dogs, military dogs and police dogs do not value. (Ever notice how soft Border Collies are?)

Softness supports biddability, patience, high bite thresholds, forgiveness and caring. Without some softness, a dog will not be able to work for and with someone with disabilities with forbearance. Softness turns tricks into tasks and supports reliability in doing those tasks. A hard dog does tricks for treats; a soft dog does tasks for love.

Soft dogs anticipate your needs and try to help you do the things you want to do without being asked. Hard dogs make you MAKE them do whatever it is you want them to do, and if you haven't the physical strength or the coordination to do so, well, too bad. A soft dog can be asked to help other people, as well as their own person, and they will comply, often gladly. Soft dogs tolerate handlers unable to do things perfectly. Soft dogs will even LEARN from handlers unable to do things perfectly. Dogs with a touch of softness have been called 'empathic'.

Soft dogs can do SAR quite well but are not usually much use for police or military work, and they usually have high bite thresholds which makes them inappropriate for bite sports. They are often ideal for therapy work and of course they are excellent, as long as they are not too soft, for service work with the handicapped. Dogs with good softness make wonderful companion/pets.

So, why wouldn't everyone want softness with their dogs? Answer: a little softness can go a long ways. Sport people, military and police do NOT want a high bite threshold and soft dogs can be very difficult to get to bite unless they perceive a serious threat. Too much softness can spiral down into a lack of nerve. It can fall into fearfulness. It tends to flatten out resilience and discourage persistence.

Soft dogs NEED strong handler approval in order to be confident in their work. The softer the dog is, the more approval they need and if they are too soft, they can never get enough approval to be confident. A dog needs confidence in order to be able to work adequately, especially in public access situations. It takes confidence for a dog to even attempt to manage a shopping cart and wheelchair or a walker in a grocery store, never mind to do it in a crowded grocery store. And that's just one task. It takes confidence to do them well--heck, it takes confidence in many cases to attempt them at all! Think about it!

HARDNESS

Ok, you ask, why would anyone in their right mind choose a HARD dog? Well, they would do it because hardness supports confidence, nerve, low bite thresholds, sharpness, resilience and persistence and often goes hand in hand with civility, aggression and fight drive. Hard dogs can maintain their sense of purpose under rough handling and in the face of bad weather and obstacles, IF you can instill a sense of purpose in them in the first place. Hardness is valuable to support sport work, attack and bite work for the police and the military and can keep a dog from folding under the pressure of disapproval. Some hardness is necessary for all dogs in order for them to be able to work, but like softness, a little bit of it can go a long ways.

Hard dogs demand strong, skilled, athletic handlers who can and will correct them when necessary. They don't care a whole lot about what their people want, they aren't willing, in many cases, to accommodate them, and they require relatively strong aversive/corrections in order to create caring. The Nothing in Life is Free (NLIF) program, which at base is the no work/no eat training method, was designed just for hard dogs. Hard dogs can be dominant as well, in which case they can be bad news, but they are not necessarily. Hard dogs that are aggressive belong in sport, police and the military and pretty much nowhere else. Hard dogs in general do NOT belong in service to the disabled, and seldom make good companions. Hard dogs can be a nightmare in a family.

Hard dogs have been called German Shepherd colored cats. The typical hard dog's attitude is 'what's in it for me?' They don't care a lot about pleasing their people. Hard dogs don't care a lot about praise, in many instances, give them treats to gain their cooperation—and it may be helpful to keep them a little bit hungry so they'll care about the treats.

Sometimes hard dogs get dumped and live a hard life that teaches them to care a little. Other times the exposure to a little 'real' life ruins them completely and they must be pts. Hard dogs seem to be able to make the transformation to feral more easily than softer dogs, (a soft dog will keep trying to go back to people) and when they do, they can be very, very dangerous. Which brings me to

CIVIL/Civility/Civil Aggression

This is very close to hard. Civil dogs are, according to the descriptions I have read of dogs which were designated as Civil, very sharp, with very low bite thresholds (almost zero) and is usually combined with aggression. Civil apparently means the exact opposite of the dictionary definition, when applied to dogs.

Civil, when applied to German Shepherd dogs, does NOT mean friendly, civilized, amiable, or courteous. Given every description of a 'civil' dog that I've ever read, it means hostile, suspicious, ready to bite at the drop

135

of a hat, and under only the most tenuous control of their handler. One account of a celebrated 'civil' dog explained that he could not be examined by a vet as he would not tolerate it. Other accounts of dogs labeled 'civil' indicate that a trip to the vet is a major ordeal involving muzzles and other extraordinary measures, such as being examined by the vet while in a crate.

Several accounts detail dogs who cannot be approached when they are in their kennels and therefore have to be viewed from afar. Yet another account lauded a 'civil' dog who put not only a helper into the hospital, but his own handler there as well, a dog who could only be taken out of his kennel to be handled wearing a muzzle.

One detailed account of an afternoon spent by a sport enthusiast in the company of a 'civil' dog and his handler included the person's explanation that she had to change clothes so that her outline would be less provocative to the dog. She also had to remove her hat and dark glasses so as not to be bitten. Her movements had to be very slow and deliberate at all times, she could not approach closer than twenty feet to the dog and she had to be very careful of the tones of her voice. At the end of two hours, after she had survived without being bitten, she was very elated that she had behaved with such perfect propriety that she had escaped unscathed.

In every account of a 'civil' dog, although it was not outright said, the limits of the handlers' control over the dog's behavior appeared to be perceived as very minimal, and tenuous at best. Far from being able to prevent the 'civil' dogs from biting, the handlers appeared only able to do so if other people were kept out of reach of the dog. 'Civil' dogs clearly do NOT adhere to the strictures of the breed standard to be approachable, willingly meeting the friendly overtures of strangers and which calls for dogs not to be hostile. Civil dogs appear NOT to be merely aloof, but to actively be unfriendly towards anyone outside of their own personal handler and, possibly, his immediate family. Some accounts of 'civil' dogs indicate that those particular dogs do not even tolerate their handler's family.

For whatever reason, bite sport people tend to be much in awe of and very reverent of dogs described as 'civil' or having 'good civil aggression'. Apparently, it is perceived to be valuable in military and police and sport dogs and there are definite indications that many winning bite sport dogs are perceived to be 'civil.'

Civil aggression, or simple civility, in dog terms, has no place in the makeup of dogs working with the disabled and should not be included in breeding stock where public access is a goal, nor is it appropriate for companion/pet dogs. 'Civil' dogs should be considered a danger to the family and do not belong in the company of children. 'Civil' dogs should be limited to the bite sport people, military and police dog breeding where they may have some viable use and where they will spend their lives in kennels and crates when not actively working or at least confined to the immediate family of their handlers. It should be noted that not all police or military dogs are 'civil'. Many police and military dogs are adequately sociable to be around not only their own immediate families but among friends, neighbors and extended family. Police and military groups often have very different views of the kind of dog with which they wish to work. One group may wish one kind of dog while another group may want an entirely different dog, depending upon the uses to which the dog is to be put and the people with whom the dog is to deal.

AGGRESSION

All that said, dogs must have some aggression. How much they need depends almost entirely on what people are going to ask them to do. Bite sport dogs MUST be aggressive in order to be willing to run down a football field and bite some complete stranger minding his own business merely because someone said to. If the dog has not sufficient aggression in his make-up, he's going to say, in dog language 'You want me to do WHAT?'

Aggression supports sharpness and the willingness to bite. It gives the dog the fuel to fight, defend and protect. Without it dogs would not protect anyone, could not herd stock, nor be any use for the police or the military. Without aggression bite sports could not exist. But aggression is a double-edged sword. In combination with the right elements of character, it's a life-saver. In the wrong combinations it's dangerous, and lethal to the dog.

Police, Border Patrol, the Military, Prison Camps, all need dogs with lots of Aggression in order to exhibit the kinds of offensive action their particular jobs require. Without Aggression dogs simply cannot do these jobs. Even defensive protection requires Aggression. The dog with no Aggression is the dog who will let his person be physically attacked while they are present and they will do nothing about it except perhaps to run around and whimper or bark in distress.

A little aggression goes a long way. Military and police dogs need more. Sport dogs often get more. Herding dogs need enough to face up to the stock, but SAR dogs don't need much, and service dogs for the disabled and therapy dogs don't even need that much.

If aggression is a problem, it is because it is affiliated with low bite threshold and sharpness or hardness without adequate amounts of the elements of nerve and biddability to restrain it. Those dogs, however good they might be for bite sports, don't belong in pet homes or with people needing service dogs for their disabilities. Dogs with high levels of aggression are fine in bite sports, police work and military work. A dog with a medium amount of aggression who also possesses good nerve and biddability, a high bite threshold, NO sharpness and only moderate hardness is not a problem in much of any environment, as long as it is not an abusive one.

Overall, Aggression is a single element which is not good or bad in and of itself. It is what it is combined with in the dog's temperament, and its

137

intensity which makes it good or bad, and even more, where the dog is placed to live his life. A dog of low to moderate aggression in a bite sport household would have a miserable time of it, never quite measuring up to what his person expected, while the same dog, with an appropriately high bite threshold might be able to live a long and happy life as a pet or a service animal for someone with disabilities. By the same token, a dog with high aggression and low bite threshold in a pet household might very well find itself being pts, while if the poor dog could only be swapped out with the low to moderate dog in the sport household, both dogs could live long and happy lives.

BIDDABILITY

This goes along with 'willing to serve' in the breed standard. Being biddable means being obedient, willing to take direction and comes out of genetic obedience, though it doesn't go quite that far. A dog could have some degree of biddability without possessing much real genetic obedience. It is deceptively simple. Hardness obviously mitigates biddability. Biddability is necessary for all real work in which dogs and humans work together. A degree of it is even necessary for sport. If a dog is to work with a person with disabilities, that dog will need a high level of biddability and that level would have to be one which moved into the zone of 'genetic obedience'. The complementary characteristic to biddability is

HANDLER SENSITIVITY

This is a very narrow form of softness in which the dog is very responsive to the handler. A handler sensitive dog does not require strong corrections for much of anything, does not need prong collars or electronic collars in order to care about what the handler wants, nor do they need to live on programs of NLIF. They are quick to respond to their handler's communications and to accommodate them.

Handler Sensitivity seems to exist independently of hardness or other forms of softness. It is biddability exclusive to the relationship between the handler and dog. Handler sensitivity is a requirement for a good service dog for the disabled, but not at all necessary for a bite sport dog or a police or military dog. With the right combination of other characteristics a handler sensitive dog can be a good therapy dog.

FOCUS

Focus is an integral element of the cluster of elements that creates the genetic pre-disposition we call 'genetic obedience'. This is the dog's ability to focus on their handler and concentrate on their signals. Focus is also a strong support for self-discipline in the dog. Focus can provide a nice tight heeling exercise, or give the dog the desire to pay such close attention to their person that they can detect changes in blood sugar or in brain activity. Focus helps a dog in tracking to stay on the desired track. In herding, it keeps the dog's attention on the stock despite distractions.

Good focus supports good obedience, biddability, handler sensitivity, and is an element of each of those qualities. It also supports good tracking and herding and is an element inherent in those skills. Good focus carried into the better realm is the basis of all alert work. Hearing ear dogs focus on sound. Blood sugar dogs focus on scent. Who knows what seizure alert dogs focus on. Electrical energy? Auras? Scent? All three? At any rate, it certainly should be a consideration in breeding for service dogs for the disabled.

RESILIENCE/Persistence

Resilience is crucial to the dog's ability to learn and perform tasks. Resilience gives a dog the 'right stuff' to keep on trying when something is difficult to learn or hard to do. It is one of the foundations of work ethic. It's stick-to-it-tivity, pick-yourself-up, dust-yourself-off and start-right-over-again. Resilience has some elements of hardness but is essentially different from hardness and independent from it in that a resilient dog may care a great deal about what their person wants or needs and that caring may actually be a part of the force motivating them to try-try again.

Resilience by itself is great and you want lots of it. It is when resilience leaks over into persistence (resilience plus hardness) that resilience crosses the line into annoying and unwelcome in most homes. Persistent is the dog that WILL NOT stop barking, pulling, biting, chasing the cat, etc. because they really don't care what you want and they want to do it regardless (whatever you want). Resilience is good and necessary and desirable for just about everything. Persistence may be valued in military and police work and is valued in bite sport work, but may be less valued in service work for the disabled. Resilience/Persistence is absolutely necessary for SAR work and herding. It will keep a dog on track when the track is old, difficult, or weather conditions are uncomfortable and will keep a dog after that old bunch quitting cow no matter how many times she tries to duck out and away with her calf. Which leads us nicely into

WORK ETHIC

This is the willingness of the dog to work when it is not pleasant to do whatever it is he is asked to do. A dog with drive works when it's fun and when it's easy, and when it's a game. He works for rewards like balls and tugs and treats and good stuff like that. He works when it's exciting, and when he's happy. A dog with work ethic will carry on working a difficult track in the rain and wind and even into darkness when there's nothing fun or easy about it. A dog with work ethic will handle a shopping cart and wheelchair through crowded store aisles, will pull a wheelchair up a steep ramp, or jockey it over a difficult door-sill while holding the door open with his shoulder when the work requires pin-point concentration, patience, or even tolerating some pain.

Work ethic is for dogs with real jobs in the real world. SAR dogs, herding dogs, police dogs, military dogs, service dogs for the disabled. Dogs with work ethic are serious. They work when it isn't fun any more, or never was fun in the beginning. Dogs with work ethic aren't playing games. They may not do it with zest, they may not do it prettily, but they do get the job done. (Many occasions call for the dog to work with care and consideration that zest, verve, and that delightful happy-go-lucky attitude simply don't support.) Work ethic comes out of 'genetic obedience'.

ON/OFF Switches

The ON switch is the ability of the dog to go from a state of relaxation to a state of excitement/arousal quickly and easily without needing much in the way of stimuli. The OFF Switch is the ability of the dog to change from a state of excitement/arousal in some variety of drive to a state of relaxation. Dogs with a lot of adrenaline find it difficult to turn Off.

Dogs with a lot of serotonin turn on too subtly for sport people, that is, their level of excitement is not high enough to satisfy the sport person's need for excitement. Sport people call such dogs couch potatoes.

Elements of Temperament: Drives

Sport people use the concept of drives to explain the complex interactions they use to trigger the behaviors they want to exploit. The word drive is used to describe the impulse to action. Drive includes an element of force, i e, the dog is compelled by his essential nature to act in certain genetically set manners developed through thousands of years of artificial and natural selection. The description of the intensity of the drive (extreme, very good, good, moderate, low) also describes the intensity of the inner compulsion forcing the dog to comply.

Some basic drives:
Food
Prey (closely affiliated with food)
Play (closely affiliated with . . .
Retrieving
Pack
Sex/Reproduction
Hunt (supports tracking)
Defense (protection)
Fight (supports defense/protection)
Flight

FOOD drive in its essence is merely the sign of a healthy animal. It is the will to eat and drink and survive. It can be used to harness the will of a hard dog, or to motivate a less biddable animal to work for his handler.

PREY drive is the natural drive to hunt, chase and kill live animals for food. It was necessary for the survival of the species for thousands of years, even long after dogs had affiliated themselves with human-kind. It can be enhanced to extreme levels, as all these drives can be, by selective breeding. It is enhanced to those levels, in fact, by bite sport enthusiasts, in order to use as a training aide by which to achieve such things as the dramatic 'long bite' and to allow the dog to regard humans as 'prey' and to hunt them in the blind search and to carry out an attack on the human when found by the dog.

PLAY drive is another natural drive. Wolves, coyotes and wild dogs all teach their offspring through play. Play also provides social interaction, enhances bonding among members of the pack and helps to set the social order of the pack. Some humans have learned to use play in the same ways. People also have a tendency to be amused and entertained by play so they tend to select for it when breeding. Because of that, many dogs have an increased play drive over their feral cousins.

RETRIEVING drive is a subsidiary to prey which hunters, in particular bird hunters, have selected for artificially for centuries, perhaps even thousands of years, to get their dogs to bring the game they kill back to them. Retrieving drive has been of value to humans for thousands of years. It is directly useful in and of itself, and has application for driving other useful behaviors. It should definitely be included in any breeding program for service dogs for the disabled and it is valuable for SAR work.

PACK drive is a survival mechanism naturally selected for to allow several related or unrelated members of the same species to bond together, thus allowing for enhanced survival of the group as well as for each individual in the group. Strong pack drive keeps some individuals in the group even if by so doing they give up the right to mate and reproduce. By doing so, they strengthen the group and give the group's young a better chance at survival. Pack drive supports the development of self-discipline in the dog.

Individuals in the group whose reproductive drives are more intense than their pack drive leave the pack and go out to find a mate and carve out new territories and reproduce. New packs are necessary to retain genetic diversity in the population as a whole, so both strong pack drive and strong reproductive drives in differing individuals of the same species support both short term survival of the group and individual survival as well as the long term survival of the species.

Humans use pack drive to their advantage when they make their dogs a part of their family packs. Pack drive compels the dog to be biddable, to conform to the pack social order and is what underlies all obedience. Pack drive is what keeps our dogs with us when off leash. Pack drive keeps dogs home, instead of constantly fighting fences. Pack drive underlies herding--the dog is raised to view the sheep as part of his 'pack'. Humans have selected for this, when they have selected for it, pretty much unconsciously. For service work, particularly that with the disabled, it might not be a bad idea to keep pack drive in mind when breeding.

SEX/Reproductive drive is about as basic as it gets. It's survival of the species. If people mess with this too much, we're apt to lose our dogs altogether.

HUNT drive is what happens when the dog gets hungry or goes looking for a mate. The dog then hunts for food/prey/mate, using, in the case of scent trackers, their nose. Hunt drive underlies all tracking work, both scent tracking and sight tracking and supports task work in the service dog for the disabled. People commonly use phrases like, 'Go find' or 'Seek', in putting dogs on a scent or asking them to do tasks like finding their keys.

Once the prey is found through hunt drive, then prey drive takes over with the chase and kill. Prey drive has been modified in some breeds of bird dogs with artificially selected stops: from the hunt, the pointer who freezes when game is found, to the spaniel who chases just to the point where the birds are 'flushed' and rise into flight, to the retriever who goes through the chase all the way to the catch and then stops the prey progression and changes it to the retrieve instead.

In the same way, Bloodhounds and certain tracking lines of the GSD have been artificially selected for strong 'hunt' drives. When activated, the dog latches onto the particular scent the person has indicated to them, and follows it until they are no longer able to discern the scent, or until they find the originator of the scent, or alternatively, are pulled off the scent by their handler. Dogs with strong hunt drives tend not to like being pulled off the scent they are following. In these dogs, quitting before making their 'find' goes against their basic instinct.

DEFENSE drive is pretty simple. It's the drive for self-defense, that is, the basic drive of the individual to survive. It is occasionally also the drive to defend members of the pack, such as the pack youngsters, which is where protection comes from.

FIGHT drive supports the kill in the hunt, chase, kill sequence as well as defense and stock work. While small prey can be overwhelmed easily enough, large prey has to be fought. Sport, military and police use this drive in order to score big points, in the case of sport, or stop the bad guy, for the military and the police. Fight drive supports Defense and allows the dog to stand off stock when they attempt to break away from the herd/flock. Without Fight, Defense is just an empty bluff.

FLIGHT drive is almost too obvious to bother explaining. It arises in the fearful dog who produces the hormone adrenaline in greater than average quantities. In this fearful dog, the fight or flight adrenal response is translated into flight in some or all circumstances in which the dog is physically able to flee whatever is causing him discomfort. When unable to flee their discomfort in real terms, these dogs will attempt to dig themselves out of their confinement, sometimes they will attempt to bury their heads, rather like an ostrich, even going to the extreme of tucking their heads under their bodies. They will hide under beds, behind sofas, under tables, desks and even climb into bath-tubs or cower behind the bath-room commode.

Fearful dogs in physical flight can take their owners on long runs across country, drag them into trees, mud puddles and through rocks. In full flight they seldom watch where they are going and are almost never 'clear-headed', with the result that they run out in front of cars, into the sides of buildings, and they can create havoc and injure anyone unlucky enough to be on the end of their leash quite badly. Add low bite threshold, sharpness, or both, and you have a dangerous dog heading down a straight path to being put to sleep. Most people agree that flight drive is bad, and I don't know of any viable use for it but it is the other side of the adrenaline coin and if you use adrenaline in your breeding, almost inevitably, sooner or later, you will get fearful dogs as well as fearless dogs.

It is important to remember that extreme drives, where one drive over-rides all the rest and over-shadows every other element of the dog's temperament creates an unbalanced dog. Too much drive can over-ride the brain, making it difficult or impossible for the dog to think once his drive is activated.

All of these elements operate together in a complex web of support and complementary qualities, and in some cases opposition. In those cases where elements of the dog's nature oppose each other, the dog can live within an essential tension--or an internal balance. When we say that a dog is well-balanced, we mean that these qualities interact harmoniously to create a dog that we find pleasing and useful, without extremes or great deficits in character or drives, and that the dog lives in equilibrium. (Note: Dogs whose balance is achieved through opposition, and who, therefore, live within that essential tension tend to live shorter lives than those dogs whose balance is achieved harmoniously and to suffer from 'bloat' quite often.)

Now, what we consider balanced differs considerably, depending upon what we consider pleasing and useful. Someone in the police or military might require a dog with more fight drive and more aggression and hardness than say, a SAR handler would want, or could use, never mind someone who uses their dog for therapy or service work for say, brace/ balance. By the same token, the person in the wheelchair considers a dog as having a nice balance when they have plenty of softness and bid-ability matched with good retrieving and, perhaps, some hunt skills. The sport dog is well-balanced to the bite sport enthusiast when the dog has strong prey drive underlying the fight and

143

aggression, but they would have little use for softness, and only limited use for biddability.

Everyone's needs in 'balance' are different. Everyone agrees, at least in principle, that extremes are wrong, but to the bite sport person, the softness and handler sensitivity necessary for therapy and service work for the disabled is an extreme they don't like one little bit. For the therapy and service dog people, the hardness of the bite sport dog and the aggression of the police and military dog are extremes equally reprehensible, beaten out only by the extreme prey drive of the bite sport dog in degree of disfavor. And everyone out at the fringes hates the moderates in the middle while the show crowd ignores matters of temperament altogether or merely mouth platitudes which pay lip service to 'good temperament' without ever really paying any attention to what it is, or is not.

At the least, we need to learn that litters bred for high intensity of drives are not likely to turn out dogs appropriate for work where softness, biddability and handler sensitivity are high priorities. While it is true that litters generally cover a range of these qualities, the range they cover may be entirely unlikely to produce appropriate balances of necessary qualities for an activity at the opposite end of the spectrum. A litter of puppies bred for qualities essential to service dogs for the disabled and therapy dog community is unlikely, even at its highest end, to produce adequate hardness, prey drive and low bite threshold to satisfy even the most uncritical of the sport crowd.

By the same token, the pup in the sport litter who is the lowest in prey drive and hardness, and the highest in bite threshold is unlikely to be low enough in prey drive and hardness or high enough in bite threshold to be able to make it as a service dog for the disabled or for a therapy dog. There may be exceptions to this general rule, but those exceptions will be few.

The attempts by 'working-line' breeders to market their dogs as companion/pets, therapy dogs and even service dogs for the disabled benefits no one but the breeders who collect money for dogs which will never suit their new owners. This practice does the new owners a disservice, it does the individual dogs a disservice, and it does the breed a disservice.

The time-worn practice of show breeders of dumping their cast-offs on the general public without the slightest regard for the dog's suitability for the purpose they will serve for a very nice price is equally reprehensible. It, too, is damaging to the dogs, the new owners, and the breed itself. Only the show breeder pocketing the innocent's cash benefits from this practice.

The best way to create dogs for certain tasks is to analyze the tasks the dog will be asked to perform and the type of handler they will be working with, and then to slant your breeding to the characteristics most useful for those tasks. For instance, any dog to be used in any form of tracking or scent discrimination should have a strong hunt drive as one of it's foundations, along with nerve, focus and biddability/ genetic obedience for tracking. And since

144

SAR dogs have to pass at the very least a variant of the cgc, they need a tad bit of softness as well.

Service dogs for the disabled need to balance on a foundation made up of nerve, biddability/softness and hunt/retrieving and food drives. Genetic obedience for herding and tracking are good places to get these qualities, along with self-discipline and a sense of responsibility.

A police dog, in addition to nerve, hardness and some biddability, would need aggression and fight drive as well as good hunt drive and some prey for detection work. A bite sport dog needs prey up the wazoo, along with hardness, some fight and a soupcon of biddability along with their nerve.

You'll notice that the two threads running through all of these requirements are nerve and biddability/genetic obedience. That's why Cliff is so strongly entrenched in his position on nerve. Everything else is variable. Nerve is NOT. It sustains all the other characteristics of the dog's temperament, supports the drives, reinforces skills and buttresses confidence. Without nerve and genetic obedience a dog cannot achieve a 'balanced' character. For example, Softness balanced by nerve can be superbly functional, and Sociability balanced by nerve can make a dog great.

Nerve is the anchor of the temperament, the center of the web of qualities that make up temperament and genetic obedience is the thread with which it binds them together. As Cliff so aptly reminds us, only by holding to that center can we preserve the functional ability of the German Shepherd temperament. (Thanks to Vandal Anne, Cliff Anderson, and Master Shepherd Manfred Heyne for their contributions on temperament.)

Chapter 6
Functional Conformation

Onyx vom Forellenbach SchH III/FH

Functional Conformation

The original American breed standard for the German Shepherd dog was codified in 1929 and the text of that standard is presented in Fred Lanting's book 'The Total Gherman Shepherd Dog', along with the changes and modifications made in 1943, 1958, 1965 and 1978. The original standard for the breed written by Captain v Stephanitz in 1922 and translated to English and published in America in 1925 appears in Chapter 4 of his work, 'The GermanShsepherd Dog in Word and Picture' with photographs, diagrams and pictures of skeletons to illustrate his points.

Stephanitz stated the the dog should be shown 'standing easily and naturally, never over- stretched nor unnaturally placed in a special position'. (So much for modern show stances, which are both over-stretched and unnatural.) He decrees that the hind legs and feet should fall naturally directly beneath the hindquarters and provide support for the body in a 'free and natural' condition. Denlinger, in 1952, concurs-- 'The dog should be permitted to stand normally during its examinaton. The efforts on the part of some exhibitors to stretch the hindquarters . . . as far back as possible deceives nobody.' [That was then. Now, things are entirely different.] 'Many judges rightly resent this artificial posing of the dog and in the effort to examine the dog in his normal position ask that the handler break the pose by moving the dog a step or two.' [Too bad today's judges don't share this viewpoint!]

As for size, Stephanitz himself chose many large-sized Siegers and Siegerins, beginning with the first Sieger in 1899, Jorg v d Krone. Jorg, who carried heavy infusions of Northern herding blood, stood close to 27 inches as a mature dog. He was followed by Hektor v Schwaben in the next two years and Siegerin Elsa v Schwaben, both of whom were big-framed, broad dogs of, in Elsa's case, close to 26 inches, and in Hektor's, a good 27 inches and at maturity, perhaps a bit more. 1908's Sieger, Luchs v Kalsmunt-Wetzlar, ranged upwards of 28 inches, and was a robust, big-framed dog, as well. Hettel Uckermark and Tell v d Kriminal Polizei, who followed him in 1909 and 1910 respectively, were both big-framed, tall dogs, with Hettel heading upwards from 27 inches and Tell 28. Hettel was noted as a big, stout, strong dog, descriptions of him given by Stephanitz as well as others. Holland's champion of 1913, the Tell son, Jung Tell v d Kriminal Polizei, was described by Stephanitz as 'the ideal German Shepherd dog'. Jung Tell, at maturity, was well over 28 inches tall.

The most popular sire in the early years of the breed, the fount of both great genetic obedience and working ability for stock work, search and rescue and police work, Horst v Boll, was surveyed at well over 28 inches in height before he reached maturity. In 1913 his exquisitely elegant daughter, Frigga v Scharenstetten, was chosen Siegerin by Stephanitz despite being over 27 inches in height. Of course, that same year, Stephanitz chose the Tell son, Arno v d Eichenburg as Sieger over the far more elegant Falko v

147

Scharenstetten, though both dogs were over 28 inches in height and Arno looked as if he carried some Great Dane in his ancestry!

Frigga, in her turn, followed the two Kriminal Polizei girls, Flora and Hella, who were both quite tall girls themselves. And they followed Gretel Uckermark and Hulda Siegestor, Siegerins of 1906 and 1907, both of whom were big-framed, solid girls of upwards of 25 inches in height.

The Sieger of 1919, Dolf v Dusternbrook, looked back on 27 inches from his mature height, and 1921's Harras v d Juch was sired by the 29 inch Nores v d Kriminal Polizei, a very popular sire of his time and son of Horst v Boll, and he, too, was well over 27 inches in height at maturity. The Sieger for 1924, Donor Overholzen, was another dog who could look down on 27 inches from maturity, and he was followed by a Siegerin, Seffe v Blasienberg, who came very close to 27 inches herself. Her brother Sultan, runner-up to Sieger Klodo v Boxberg, in 1925, was over 28 inches at maturity. All of these dogs were chosen to be siegers and siegerins by Stephanitz himself.

The v d Krone, v Schwaben, v Brenztal, v Boll, v d Kriminal Polizei, Secretainerie and Blasienberg dogs were all 'big' dogs by any measure, with most of the females maturing out in the 26 to 27 inch range and most of the males running upwards of 27 inches to 29 inches, and far from being discriminated against, they were some of the most popular dogs of their time and far more popular among stock-dog users than the smaller dogs, particularly Horand v Grafath and Roland v Starkenburg. The most popular lines to Roland among people who worked their dogs went most often through Roland's large, stout, strong, stock-working sons, Guntar and Hettel Uckermark and police trained grandson Tell v d Kriminal Polizei.

In fact, the most popular of the early German Shepherd dogs among stock-working people were big dogs, dogs with breadth as well as height and stout, strong bone structures. Dogs like Schafermadchen were excoriated as too small and fit only to herd geese, among stock-working folk, and Horand and Roland were pretty much roundly despised by all the stock-working folk who knew them. Stephanitz may have personally preferred a smaller dog—well, he preferred the small Thuringians, personally, as well as the dark colors which also came from the Thuringians—but Stephanitz was not a stock-working dog handler, nor a police-dog handler, nor a handler of search and resue dogs, nor a trainer of guide dogs. In fact, Stephanitz did not train any of the dogs he had, nor did he work any of them. When he wanted a good dog, he bought one bred and trained by Herr Eiselen, and then changed the dog's name from v d Krone to v Grafath, which, to give him his due, was common practice then.

In the early 1920s, with dogs like Nores v d Kriminal Polizei (29 inches at maturity) so popular, and so heavily used (180 litters were recorded from Nores alone) Stephanitz deliberately chose a small (24 and 1/2 inch) but very correct Klodo v Boxberg as Sieger in 1925. He knew that people would turn to him and that his use as a stud would inevitably bring the dogs back towards the middle ground in size. Choosing the Klodo son Utz v Haus Schutting as Sieger in 1929 to follow Klodo merely solidified that modification. Stephanitz knew that he could depend upon people breeding heavily to whatever dog he chose as Sieger, and he was right. His choice did serve to keep the size of his dogs from heading towards the stratosphere with sizes over 30 inches.

There is no evidence, however, that Stephanitz, though he declared the height of 25 inches 'ideal' felt in any way constrained to that size. Indeed, going by the proof of his repeated choices of much larger dogs as Siegers, he found dogs of varying sizes, from middling to large, 'breed- worthy' to use a modern phrase, and quite 'ideal', and he used the word 'ideal' to describe big dogs such as Jung Tell v d Kriminal Polizei, Holland's champion in 1913 despite the fact that Jung Tell fell into the 28 to 29 inch range. Given the historical data we have on the early dogs, there is no doubt that those early breeders who actually worked their dogs on either stock, or for search work or police work, even guide work, actually PREFERRED the large dogs for the work they had for them to do. (There were no bite 'sports' then for people to obsess over. Schutzhund was merely a 'test' then, and it had not yet superseded actual work in importance. Dogs who actually worked at one of the above mentioned tasks were considered first rank dogs, while dogs who merely did Schutzhund were considered second rank dogs.)

Early American breeders shared the same preferences. One thing is utterly clear; German Shepherd dogs were never intended to be limited to a narrow range of size. The point should not be the size of the dog as long as the height does not shoot upwards of 29 inches or below 21 inches. The point should be the correctness of the dog's structure and his mental and physical ability to do useful work. (Bite sports, including Schutzhund, are SPORTS, not WORK.)

In looking at a dog, think about fitting the dog within a box, as if you were going to photoshop the picture the dog makes. Place the first corner of the square (ok, it's slightly more of a rectangle, but you get the idea) at the place where the dog's neck fits into their shoulders so that the straight, horizontal line skims over the dog's back. (You're not even going to look at the head! Old-timers used to say that 'Heads don't make no miles' and they were right. Heads distract us and keep us from seeing the things that are really important about the dog's physical structure. Pretty faces are a distraction we need to avoid fixing our attention on.)

Then draw a level, straight, horizontal line towards the base of the dog's tail and then add a vertical line at a ninety degree angle from the base of the dog's tail to the ground. Another straight, level, horizontal line goes back to the front of the dog. Complete the rectangle by adding the fourth, vertical line, and connect it at the top of the box where you started. There. You now have your dog in a box. Well, maybe. And more or less.

This is going to make some things very simple to see. If the line of the back, which is supposed to be straight and level is not, then the dog is NOT correct. If the dog's back rises over the line, the dog has a 'roach' back, and despite show ring considerations, this is NOT correct conformation for work. If the dog's back curves downward, in an upside down half moon, the dog is 'sway' backed. This is NOT correct. (The topline is not as it should be.) If the hind legs are sticking out behind the vertical line, the dog is NOT correct. If the dog's front feet are markedly in front of, or behind the vertical line at the front of the dog, the dog is NOT correct. The dog's feet should fall right where the front vertical line meets the bottom horizontal line, directly underneath the point of shoulder. The hind feet should fall before the vertical line in back, directly under the dog's hips, putting the dog's feet firmly WITHIN the plane of the dog's body.

The angle of the dog's shoulder should describe a diagonal line somewhere around a 45 degree line from the point of shoulder at the dog's chest to the dog's withers. The dog's front feet should point straight forward, not inwards or to the outside (easty-westy).

The dog should not be overlong in the thighs or pasterns, thighs should be upright and rounded at the top, with short, strong stifles (knees) strong, open, upright hocks, neither loose, nor weak, nor over-angulated. You will note, in an over-angulated dog, that the hock joint looks rather like a V laying on it's side and when the dog moves, and even sometimes when the dog merely stands, a portion of the dog's hind leg touches the ground. Dogs with severely faulty hock angulation often stand or move with a large portion of the hind leg between the foot and the hock in contact with the ground.

This is a SEVERE and disqualifying fault for a working dog. As long as such a dog moves through soft dirt or on a manicured lawn, he can do so in relative safety, but should the same dog have to travel in rocky or even merely gravelly terrain, never mind in hills or truly rugged going, the hind leg would be badly abraded or torn or both in no time. Such a dog could not travel any real distance without doing real damage to his hind legs, and his collapsing hocks make it impossible for him to move with any crispness or power. Whether such a dog is called upon to pivot, charge, duck in and out on stock, or to launch himself forward and upwards in an attack on a human or climb over a rubble field in an earthquake search, such weak, faulty hocks are not able to support the dog in such activities for any length of time or with any durability.

Today it is commonplace to see dogs in the show ring who stand and move with their entire lower leg in contact with the ground, from their foot all the way to their hocks, and just as common to see dogs whose thighs are so long and weak and wobbly that they cannot stand without bracing one hind leg against the other. Just as often, when such dogs move, they push off both hind legs at the same time in order to get any forward thrust out of their hind legs — one leg alone is not sufficient in strengh to be able to launch the dog into any truly vigorous motion. These are all SEVERE faults which compromise the dog's ability to do useful work.

Hind legs should not be overlong, so that in order to stand or to walk the dog has to fold its hind leg into an awkward, clumsy doubled over position. The dog's thighs should be upright and rounded at the top, with short, strong stifles (knees) positioned close to the underline of the body

where the dog's rib cage can support the joint and protect it from lateral movement which would tend to stretch and tear the ligaments in the joint. The body of the dog should have good breadth as well as depth, with a good spring of ribs, and a chest which provides plenty of room for the lungs and heart to expand. The front legs should not be close together either at the top where they come out of the chest, or at ground level and the space between them should be pretty much the same top and bottom.

The breed standard calls for a dog to have a back that is both STRAIGHT and LEVEL. It uses those exact words. It also says that the back should dip slightly down from the withers (this is EXACTLY what is called for by the breed standard, it is NOT a sway back). And ideally, the croup--the area that extends from the hips to the base of the tail—should slope gently to the base of the tail. The dog should be slightly longer than he is tall, thus the rectangle instead of a true square, but should not be much longer than slightly off square. Too much length of back leads to weakness and injury. Better, for working ability, to be square rather than too long.

Today, too many people see a good spring of ribs as 'fat'. This is NOT the case at all. A dog's rib cage should be rounded, with the spine comfortably suppported by a musculature and ligaments which create a distinct breadth along the top of the dog's body. This allows space for the dog's internal organs, the heart, lungs, stomach, liver and pancreas, as well as the intestines and etc. Some studies even show that a good spring of ribs in a dog mitigate against bloat as well as provide a dog with endurance. Dogs that are narrow and deep tend to suffer more from bloat than dogs with more breadth to balance their depth of body. Dogs that have breadth across their backs as they should, and as provided for them by a correct spring of ribs, are NOT sway- backed.

Dogs with over-long thighs of the sort so common among German 'high-line' dogs today and becoming more common in American line show dogs were castigated by Stephanitz as 'over- built' and 'weak' and 'faulty'. All his diagrams and photographs and skeletons given as examples of 'correct' conformation show dogs walking on their hind feet and ONLY their hind feet, with the section of the hind leg between the feet and the hock perpendicular to the ground. Over- angulated hocks of the sort so popular in the American show-lines today Stephanitz denigrates, and the well-known dog judge of the 1940s, '50s, and 60s, Milo Denlinger agrees with him. Stephanitz merely says that dogs that are thus made cease to correspond to the racial (breed) type. He says that though they may look fine, they are no longer Shepherd dogs because their suitability for use is absent from the structure of their body.

Denlinger is more specific. He describes the over-angulated hock as resulting in weakness. He describes the correct conformation of the hind leg as the leg dropping 'vertically' from the hock to the foot. According to him, this formation gives the dog the maximum of leverage and propulsive power. He says it is of 'supreme importance'. 'The craze for excessive angulation . . . weakens the hock joint, an added tension upon the muscles.' He adds that 'they are spectacular and may fool the uninitiated, but they exemplify weakness rather than strength.' From the 'Complete German Shepherd' by Milo G Denlinger, c1952.

From the beginnings of the breed in the 1890s through the 1950s, hip dysplasia was no more than a minor problem at most, and dogs routinely worked comfortably despite some degree of dysplasia in their hips. Conditions like pre-rickets, caused by inadequate digestible calcium in dogs' diets, injuries and early work all contributed to the creation of this condition quite as much as the occasional genetic abnormality but dogs still worked, and they worked all day, every day, without particular discomfort. They did such work for more years than most of our dogs live, today. They were able to do this because, unlike today's Shepherds, with their grotesquely long thighs, their fragile, loose, low stifle joints, and weak, over-angulated hocks they had correctly structured hind legs .

A correctly structured hind leg contacts the ground with the foot, and only with the foot, pushing off from the ground with some force. That motion is amplified by the open, upright, hock acting as a powerful spring. The short, strong stifle (knee) joint, situated close to the body at the top of the vertical, short, upright 'second' thigh, translates the motion to the body through the short, angled upper thigh connecting the stifle to the hip. Both the hock and the stifle act as shock absorbers, to some extent, and protect the hip from the impact created by the foot meeting the ground. A slight angulation in the hock gives the hock greater 'spring' and allows the dog to power forward with more propulsion. BUT, angulation of the hock beyond 'slight' weakens the 'spring' effect of the hock and robs it of power. Today's show dogs in the American lines are virtually ALL over-angulated, and not by a small amount, either. Virtually all of them have hocks so weak that the slightest stress or shift of weight towards the dog's hindquarters results in the dog's hind leg hitting the ground.

This is a fault so serious it over-rides all considerations of color or size. It unfits the dog for work, robs the dog of any approximation of endurance, and makes a travesty of the dog's structure. Without a correctly

152

structured hind leg, a dog is incapable of any truly functional forward motion. The weakness of the hocks is a good part of the reason why show dogs cannot do well in bite sports—they simply lack the physical ability to power forward and upward into the sleeve. The show dogs' weak hocks simply won't support the kind of forward thrust necessary to allow the dog to launch an attack onto the sleeve—and without that launch, the dog is incapable of any kind of solid bite.

Dogs which add long, loose thighs and long, low, loose, fragile stifle joints to the problem, as the German High-line do, and as some of the American dogs are beginning to do as well, simply exacerbate the problem. Not only do these dogs lack the ability to push themselves forward with any impulsion, their entire hind leg has been weakened even more by the long, loose thighs and stifle joints. In the show ring, these dogs are typically shown moving as quickly at a trot as their handlers can manage, in order to make the excessive movement of their hind legs less obvious to the observer, but the moment the dogs slow down, or when slow-motion photography is used, the loose ligamentation and the extreme lateral movement of the thighs and stifle joints becomes readily apparent.

Because the over-long thighs do not 'fit' within the plane of the dog's bodies, the dog's legs must make adjustments in their motions in order to move forward. The first adjustment made is that the dog's lower leg, from the foot to the hock joint, comes into contact with the ground, becoming the carrying point for the dog's weight, instead of the dog's foot. (Slow motion photography often show the dogs' feet flopping in the air, as the dog's weight strikes the ground as much as 6 inches behind the dog's foot.)

In order to allow this, the hock must flex so it can come into contact with the ground as well, thus mitigating and sometimes completely negating, its ability to absorb the shock of that impact. The stifle, at the end of a long upper thigh, no longer protected by the underline of the dog's body or the hock joint, now sustains considerable impact which it is not designed to fully disperse. Meant as a secondary shock absorber, rather than a primary one, it is unable to discharge the full extent of the impact imparted to it by the dog's forward motion.

Loose ligamentation is absolutely necessary to allow these adjustments to take place, but this adaptation means that the stifle joint is no longer able to minimize the lateral movements generated by the dog's motion any more than it is able to entirely mitigate the impact of the lower leg coming in contact with the ground. The result is that the hips now are subjected to not only additional impact stress from the lower leg coming into contact with the ground as the dog moves forward, but is also subjected to the lateral wobbles created by the movements of the long, loosely ligamented thighs. Even the most perfectly fitted hip socket must suffer from the distress of this kind of impact joined with the strain of attempting to hold together in the face of such excessive upper thigh movement.

The dog's body is not designed to work that way. Is it any wonder that tendon, ligament and cartilege tears around the stifle joint are now as common as hip dysplasia?

When the dog walks, trots, and runs on his FEET instead of his lower leg, and when his hock joint is strong and upright and open, when his stifle joints are protected from lateral movement by being connected to SHORT thighs so that they fit close to the dog's body, and the dog's legs fit comfortably within the plane of the dog's body, the hock and the stifle joint protect the hips from impact stress and from the strains of excessive lateral movement the way they are supposed to. The result? Hips don't need to be perfect in order to function comfortably for the life of the dog.

It makes no sense to complain about a dog's supposed lack of nerve, or drive, both temperament issues, when a dog simply does not possess the structure to support the actions which supposedly demonstrate that nerve, or drive. When a dog's hind leg is so badly constructed that it sticks out behind his body even when he's standing at rest, there is no possibility that the dog can move forward with any kind of impulsion. It doesn't matter whether the dog is trying to hit a sleeve or face off with a ram, the poor dog is more likely to find himself doing a face plant than succeeding. One of these dogs trying to make a sharp cut is more likely to find himself on an operating table getting a torn ligament repaired than he is to actually manage to turn a ewe.

Ski-slope toplines are created by collapsed hocks and roach backs are created by people whose perverted tastes run to dogs that look like camels instead of dogs. Show people who consider correct structure boring and who prefer bizarre and grotesque angles and lines in their dogs do the breed a major disservice by indulging themselves in such abberationsbut as long as the show world caters to such folks, expecting changes for the better in the dogs' structure would be foolish. These people lost any recognition of correct working structure a long time ago and since they do not work their dogs in any real fashion they are unlikely to learn anything about functional structure in the future.

Given Stephanitz' diagrams and photos and skeletons, he would be appalled by the toplines of today. He considered roach backs seriously faulty (and they've been associated with spinal chord problems) and sloping backs completely improper and unfit for any real work. Stephanitz' over-arching concern was always that the dog be conformed in a manner to fit him for work, firstly as a herding dog and secondly as what he called an 'ambulance' dog (and what we would call, today, a search and rescue dog) and as a guide dog and police dog.

In a world where champions spend their lives in a kennel staring at chain link fence, or at best on the family couch (if they're very, very lucky) and bite sport champions seldom 'work' for more than ten minutes at a time, truly correct conformation may not be very important. But if you insist upon obsessing over hips, it might be instructive for you to understand that your dog's 'hip dysplasia' or at least, his hip discomfort, has more to do with his aberrantly structured hind legs than with the actual fit of his hips, in most cases.

If you want a dog to do actual work in the real world it is perhaps beneficial to go back to the old arbiters of the breed, to Stephanitz and others both before and after him who actually worked their dogs, for ideas as to how you want your dog to look. If, of course, you are only interested in a show animal, then, by all means, choose your dog for his red and black color, roach back, grotesquely elongated thighs, or the Am-line black and gold show dogs with their sloping backs created by their weak, over-angulated hocks. A good working structure in a dog is not going to get a look in the show ring any more than a show ring dog will be effective on the job in the real world (as opposed to the artificial world of 'titles').

The breed standard is not holy writ. It has been written and re-written through the years by influential show breeders who had no regard for temperament or working ability of the dog and according to whatever the fashion in dogs was in force at the time among the rich dilettantes of the dog show world. (And to what advantage to them the revised breed standard could be!) It has been and is open to interpretation by judges and breeders whose only interest is in dog shows and in addition, one must beware of those who use the breed standard, often very inaccurately, as an argument winner. Very often what the breed standard actually says and what a certain group agrees that it says, can be two entirely different things, and that is when they don't ignore it entirely, which, it seems, they very often do.

Functional Conformation: Spring of Rib and Bloat

Yesterday I read a post from a woman on the gsd forum bragging about how flat her dog's rib cage is and how narrow and lean he is. No one told her this wasn't anything to brag about. People seemed, in fact, to agree that this is a good thing, attractive and proper conformation. Nothing could be farther from the truth. This is, in fact, a serious fault.

A month or so back, another poster to that forum wrote that the breed standard called for dogs to be narrow, lean and deep-chested. She was aware that such a structure had been implicated in the frequency of bloat, so she supposed that as long as dogs were bred to the 'breed standard' German Shepherd owners were just going to have to bite the bullet and accept that their dogs were going to die of bloat now and again.

No one disagreed with her. In fact, not only did NO ONE disagree with her, but a number of folks regretfully allowed that she was RIGHT!

This is a perfect example of that sometimes nebulous and sometimes not so nebulous Consensus of what the Breed Standard says which is

ABSOLUTELY INCORRECT. I can't believe I'm defending the Actual Breed Standard yet again, but here goes. This is what the Breed Standard, American, 1943, and echoed word for word in 1978, has to say about the correct structure of the rib cage for German Shepherd Dogs.

"Ribs-- Well sprung and long, neither barrel-shaped nor too flat, and carried down to a sternum which reaches to the elbows. Correct ribbing allows the elbows to move back freely when the dog is at a trot. . . . too flat or short causes pinched elbows. Ribbing is carried well back so that the loin is relatively short."

I will elaborate. (You knew I would.) Each rib connects at the top to the spine, and SHOULD curve outwards in a slightly shallow half circle, so that the top of each rib bone is slightly horizontal at the top and each bone should be spaced slightly apart from each other rib bone so that there is a slight indentation between ribs.

Spring of ribs means just that—the ribs must spring outwards, in order to do their job properly. The slightly horizontal top portion of the rib is shaped in such a way so it can support the muscles, tendons and ligaments that in their turn, support the spinal column. Dogs with 'flat' rib cages cannot support this muscle structure and therefore tend to weakness in the back.

But that is not all these outwardly curved ribs do. That full, gracefully rounding curve creates room for the dog's internal organs, as well as room for bitches to carry their puppies comfortably and safely and the muscle structure to support their pregnancies. It supports the muscle structure needed to sustain the bitch while she's carrying. (Maybe the lack of correct spring of ribs is one of the reasons why so many 'working-line' dog people talk so much about difficult pregnancies and bitches dying during whelping?)

In order to work to their fullest capacity, your dog's heart and lungs need to be able to expand as well as to contract. Flat, straight ribs limit that ability and cramp the internal organs, heart, lungs, stomach and intestines, liver, kidneys, pancreas and all. These organs quite simply need room in order to work properly and when the ribs do not provide that room then the dog's entire system is stressed.

It is the LACK of decent spring of ribs which has people saying that the German Shepherd Dog is no longer a good choice for someone to run with. Yet all those years I did SAR and worked dogs on cattle, we routinely expected our dogs to either lead or follow our horses for twenty and thirty miles a day, often in terrain and often at speed, even in high elevations and over rugged mountain trails. But now, apparently, German Shepherd Dogs are unable to go jogging with their people??? How could this happen?

It happened because people decided that a narrower, leaner dog was prettier, and started breeding to get that narrow, deep, lean, greyhound-y look. To get it, they took the curve out of the ribs. Now, any dog with an even halfway decent spring of ribs, if pictured on the forums, will be castigated as 'fat' and some pundit will opine that the dog has a 'sway' back and call it weak, despite the fact that it is the very opposite of weak because those outwardly curving ribs support the spine. And, as we all know, to be 'fat' in today's culture, is the ultimate sin.

And so our dogs die of a condition completely unknown 40 years ago, when a good spring of ribs was de rigueur on our dogs. Well, that's what happens when rigors of real work are forgotten, or worse yet, treated with the kind of contempt poured over anyone who gives the principles of function developed over centuries of work and observation any kind of priority in today's breeding. Today, people know nothing about the function of dogs engaged in real work and have no intention of learning. For them, the subjective and artificial judgments of sport have taken precedence, and these temporary fads (one fad will always be supplanted, sooner or later, by another) have replaced the function of real work with their artificial and illusory standards.

It doesn't matter if all the studies in the world—and there are already 2 well-respected, large studies of multiple breeds of dogs on the books—show that flat-ribbed dogs are prone to bloat , and that their chances of dying are increased by raising their stress levels by breeding them to be highly adrenalized (extremely driven). As long as people want their narrow, lean, deep dogs with their extremes of drive, the dogs will continue to pay the price of human egoism with their lives.

Functional Conformation: Coat Colors

The first thing most folks say when they talk about getting a German Shepherd puppy is 'I want a---' and the blank is filled in by a color, black and tan, black sable, white or black. Instead of talking about the temperament they want, the use they have for the pup, or the structure they prefer, they talk color. As if the color of the dog has any real significance as to what kind of a dog it will actually be. Actually, the very fact that the first specification they have for their dog is the color it will be says more about them than it does about the dog.

In the beginning, the first German Shepherd dogs came in a rainbow of colors, all of them perfectly acceptable, though the colors herding people preferred in their dogs were predominantly light. Various shepherds and regions had their favorites, of course—the Brunswick and Saxony areas featured 'tiger' dogs in brindle for herding, with lots of a light silver-grey or a light orange-y color interspersed with black and brown stripes over the body and 'leopard' grey and red-spotted dogs we'd probably call merle today. In Brandenburg, the city's most prized 'yard' dogs came in predominantly black with tan legs and white or tan splotches on the chest, sometimes including white toes, splotches and toes that today's purists would scorn.

One of the foundation dogs of the breed, the Northern herding dog, Greif, was white, and he was not merely well-received when he was exhibited with his two white daughers as examples of German herding dogs, but highly touted as an even better dog than the Phylax Society's flagship dog, Phylax. Greif was highly considered, not just because he was a real herding dog but because he was well put together for herding and colored well to endure the long, hot summer days with the flocks. (For those who have swallowed the idiocy regarding white dogs being hard for the herder to distinguish from the sheep to excuse the mindless prejudices spouted against white dogs, bear in mind that the national herding breeds such as the Greek Tatra, the Italian Maremma, the Hungarian Kuvasz, the Pyranees Shepherd dogs, the Great Pyranees, and the Anatolian, the latter two breeds sentinel dogs, all, have the base color of white for their breed, with variations to biscuit and gold and pale grey. Even the Bearded collie and the Old English Sheepdog are grey and white.)

The original generally PREFERRED colors for the actual working German Shepherd herding dogs were grey, sometimes called 'wolf' grey and white. The grey was oft-times a salt and pepper combination or colored hairs, grey overcoat with light undercoat and points (legs) shading from tan to white. Today, this once very much preferred working color called 'grey and tan', the color of Horand v Grafath, Horst v Boll and Klodo v Boxberg, is now considered a 'fault' by people with no idea of what it takes to do a day's work in the sun, particularly where daytime temperatures are high. Outside of being just nuts, to declare a color which was preferred in working herding dogs for centuries a 'fault' betrays serious ignorance in the the ruling body which made such a declaration and an equally serious contempt for the history of the breed as well as for the strictures of real work.

'Dark' dogs, the black dogs, black-sable dogs, and black and tan bi-colors and blanket- backs, were the PERSONAL preference of Stephanitz. It should be remembered that Stephanitz did NO work with his dogs. The dogs he had with the HGH designation identifying the dogs as master herding dogs came to him with that accomplishment already achieved. Dogs of his which achieved other designations did so by being trained and handled by other people. People who worked stock with their dogs through long, hot summer days knew that dark dogs simply could not tolerate long afternoons in the heat and the hard glare of summer sun-light. For them, it wasn't a preference, it was simply a fact of nature.

The advantage of grey dogs with a light undercoat and light points had to do with the conditions in which they worked. Light 'points' (legs and undercarriage and highlights on the cheeks and around the eyes) reflect the sunlight off snow, one of the hardest, most glaring natural lights there is, while the occasional black or grey shafted hair absorbed just enough light to keep the dog warm enough in cold, bright winter days to be able to work. Grey dogs with light undercoats and points are best for climes where the dogs work in snow and ice in the winter and hard sun in the summer, while the light/white dogs do best in areas which stay comparatively warm year around. Far from being 'washed out' or in some way less desirable, as the black/dark dog proponents would aver, these light undercoats are a more desirable adaptation for actual work. People who use terms like 'washed out' for these lighter undercoats are merely expressing their own prejudices and exposing their ignorance of or contempt for true working qualitites as opposed to the qualities preferred for dogs to be used for intimidation.

If you work your herding dog in New Jersey, upstate New York or Ontario, where the sunlight is pale and thin, you can get by with a dark colored dog. If you try the same thing in the Great Plains, never mind the American Southwest, or the sunnier parts of California (as opposed to, say, the Bay Area) trying to work a blanket-back or otherwise dark colored dog through the summer would be to endanger the dog's health. Obviously in these regions, a dark colored dog is NOT an appropriate choice to work stock. In Germany, in the warm river valleys and the high, hard sunlit mountain slopes, light colored dogs were de rigueur.

The reason has to do with how light works. Light, on Earth, is provided by the sun. It reaches the earth after passing through the atmosphere and it expresses itself through a broad spectrum of color some of which we can see when we see a rainbow. Pigment is the element in most organic matter which reflects the colors of the light spectrum back to our eyes. Chlorophyll, for instance, reflects the color green back to us. White is produced by the reflection of a broad spectrum of the colors in light to our eyes. If we see the pale 'gold' of, say, a Golden Retriever, it is because 'gold' is the primary color of the spectrum reflected back to us. Dark colors and solid black are what we see when the pigment absorbs a wide spectrum of the light available. What we would call 'solid' black means that the pigment is collecting ALL the visible range of light.

On a sunny day, the dark portion of a black and tan's coat, usually the back, can become so hot it becomes uncomfortable to touch. Prolonged contact with the black hair of the dog's back can 'burn' your skin under such conditions. Imagine, if you can, what it would be like for the dog to be exposed to that hard, unrelenting light and heat for hours while the dog attempts to work with stock or to follow a track. (A panting dog is not a scenting dog!) Then compare that with the salt and pepper grey dog, the one with the light undercoat, where little light is absorbed by the shaft of the hair and the light undercoat reflects that hard light away from the dog's skin. This is the reason that whenever herding bloodlines are added back to the breed, the so-called 'color paling' effect occurs.

If you're a reasonable person, you can understand the ramifications of how the light spectrum works, and you can understand that a working stock

159

dog, a public access dog that needs to be outdoors year around in sunny climes, and dogs that do search and rescue in warmer regions, should be chosen with regard for those conditions and the lighter, grey sable, white and grey and tan colors favored. Those people who continue to insist that only dark colored dogs need apply for those uses are people so mired in their personal prejudices that they cannot make rational decisions anyway—which leaves rational people to simply ignore them. Continuing to argue with them once the facts of the matter have been explained to them is a waste of time and breath.

A secondary condition exists for public access dogs, one which has everything to do with people's prejudices and nothing to do with actual aptitude for the work, and that is that light-colored dogs find more acceptance from the public than dark-colored or black dogs. This is no more reasonable than the prejudice some German Shpherd people insist upon in favor of the dark -colored dogs, but it is real, none-the-less. (Just let the rescue people show you the statistics for adoption of dark-colored dogs versus light-colored dogs in shelters—as difficult as it is for any dog to get out of one of those places alive, the odds are all with the light-colored dogs!)

If the light-colored dog is the right choice for day work, it stands to reason that the dark-colored dog is the right choice for night work. A light-colored dog is a beacon at night. He's a target for the bad guys, or a sign for the good guys that you are up to no good. Either way, for any kind of police or military work, you want a dark-colored dog. At night, light is not a problem. You don't have to worry about it over-heating your dog and limiting his usefulness or creating a hazard to his health. You do have to worry about the wrong people being able to see him.

For police, dark-colored dogs are simply more intimidating. In the more or less 'recent' past, dark-colored German Shepherds were used for border patrol in the no man's land of the Iron Curtains of the Communist countries, as prison and POW camp guards and as concentration camp guards. Dark-colored dogs were used as agents of terror by the Nazis and by the earlier gamekeepers for Germany's large estates. Used as manhunters at night, they were set on poor men and women gathering wood and roots and herbs to keep warm and to eat, and to search for poachers stealing game from the wealthy, well-fed men for whose tables the birds were intended.

The fear of black/dark dogs goes way back, all the way to pre-historic times, and is virtually atavistic. The light-colored dog of the day is the partner with which shepherds watched their flocks and hunters sought for the birds to bag for the table. Can you imagine the cop with a yellow Lab? Or a Golden Retriever? 'Come out with your hands up or I'll send in the dog!' the cop shouts but when the perp sees the dog, what's he going to think? Oh, I'm so afraid? Or 'Oh, hey, buddy, come say hi?'

People who do military and police work have a very reasonable and useful preference for dark-colored dogs. People who breed dogs for police

160

and the military know that and therefore seek to slant their breeding to produce black and dark-colored dogs. For them, it is no more a prejudice than the shepherds' preference for light-white-grey dogs. It is mere practicality.

The problem is that very few people base their preferences for color on rational grounds, especially when they challenge the preferences of people who use their dogs for practical purposes with their ignorant bigotry. Color preferences today seldom seem to have anything to do with yesterday's useful fact-based partialities. People are excoriated for their preferences for the good old-fashioned working dog colors by other people who have no idea beyond their ignorant prejudices why they're doing it. People who have what was once called 'just enough knowledge to be dangerous' inveigh against the old colors because they're now 'faults' according to an ignorant and short-sighted breed standard.

In 1965 the German Shepherd Dog Club of America voted to make the traditional coat colors grey and tan and red and tan (liver) disqualifying faults for purposes of the judging of dogs at dog shows. The SV had apparently already done so through both grey and tan (referred to these days as 'blue') and liver (red) and tan were traditional colors belonging to the breed from its very incipiency, colors far better for working sheep through long days in the heat than colors featuring a lot of black, especially solid black over the dog's back. Too bad they forgot that a good dog can never be a bad color.

My first take on this was that the decision to disqualify the colors for showing was political, one of the small-minded meannesses with which people who have ascended to positions of power squeeze out their rivals, once those positions are achieved. After all, there were several successful kennels with generations of champions of those colors, and this was one way to squeeze them out and make their entire strains of dog obsolete. I thought also that it was short- sighted and displayed a good deal of ignorance about working dogs and the conditions under which they work, the sort of thing which can be expected of wealthy men who have never spent a day out with the flocks or on the range under a hot sun in their lives. I thought it would have unintended consequences beyond just the bad feeling and the colossal black eye people making such decisions inevitably give themselves in the sight of knowledgeable people who understand the breed and its history.

And, of course, being American, my conclusion was that I would breed grey and tans or red and tans if I wanted to. If I found a dog of great character, good health, and outstanding structure whose characteristics I want to perpetuate in my dogs, I would use them and the GSDCA could take a flying leap. Thank God I'm not German, end of story.

The decision WAS short-sighted, and we are suffering the consequences now.

Too many people think that genetic diversity merely means large numbers. If you have a lot of dogs, they think, they must be genetically diverse.

161

It is possible for a large number of dogs to have genetic diversity, of course, but diversity means differences. Unless those large numbers of dogs are different from each other in some way, they are not genetically diverse. For those differences to be genetic, they must create observable differences. Therefore, the more different coat types, colors and sizes your breed accepts and utilizes in breeding, in simple terms, the greater your breed's genetic diversity.

The idea that a breed of dogs should all look alike is a relatively modern notion beginning in the end of the nineteenth century when the first dog shows began to occur. Prior to that time, dogs were judged by their usefulness to mankind, and by the types of work that they could do and did do. Breed types were classified by labels that reflected the work they did, some of which we still retain, ie, pit bulls and rat terriers and such like. Uniformity, the notion that all dogs who did the same types of work ought to look similar, never mind exactly the same, had not yet dawned on the dog person's consciousness.

Then wealthy people with too much money and too much time on their hands got hold of dogs and started using them as a way to occupy their time, money and minds. They didn't work the dogs. They didn't concern themselves with matters of stock or connect form to function. It was all about looking pretty. Dogs became an adjunct to the male ego in whole new ways.

Men, and to a lesser extent, women, have always taken pride in the work dogs did for them. Wealthy men who hunted for 'sport' and poor poachers who hunted to survive took much the same delight in their respective bird dogs. Men and women with top herding dogs had been holding sheep dog trials for centuries, though many were pretty informal and when cattlemen do a round-up in the spring and fall to move cattle from summer to winter pastures and back again those informal trials may even be accompanied by a few side bets here and there. But the judgments in these cases tended to be relentlessly practical and objective, based on the job the dog did and only the job the dog did. Numbers, like how many birds the dog bagged, or how many sheep the dog penned, how well they handled the cattle, and whether they were able to find all of them, and time—how long it took to do it—provided concrete parameters by which dogs and people were judged.

That all changed with the advent of 'the fancy,' as dog shows were called, and as the world of dog shows is still referred to. People who breed and show and own dog show dogs are called 'fanciers'. Dogs used for show by almost exclusively rich men were called 'fancy' dogs. Some of the earliest breeds to be irrevocably changed by this new phenomenon were the Sots Collie and the Irish Setter. Rare indeed would be the bird hunter you found today still hunting with an Irish Setter and if there is anyone still out there working sheep with a Scots Rough Collie I doubt anyone has ever heard of them. The German Shepherd is now well along that same road, and one of the reasons the dogs have gone so far from their roots has little to do with the lessening of jobs working stock for dogs and everything to do with the decisions made by the ruling bodies of the breed, ruling bodies always made up of the wealthy who do little or no real work with their dogs and who often substitute artificial 'tests' like Schutzhund, which just become another competition, for real work.

In fact, people's preferences in the way of color, at least in German Shepherd dogs, seem to have more to do with their own temperaments than they have to do with real qualities of the dogs'. People like my friend, Debbie, who celebrate their dogs whatever color they happen to be and choose them based on preferences as to health, temperament and structure rather than color, are few. Instead, people's preferences in color seem to be based on their own cast of mind.

The people who want a dog to intimidate and bully people of course want a black/dark colored dog. People who are willing to go to the trouble and effort of training their dogs to bite people are people who over-whelmingly favor dark colored dogs. And people who over- whelmingly favor black-dark dogs also seem to over-whelmingly favor gun ownership and signs for their yards that say things like, 'Forget the dog. Beware of the GUN'.

People drawn to the lighter, less mainstream old herding colors when they choose their dogs tend to be more liberal, more open-minded and information oriented than those who prefer the dark/black dogs. People who strongly prefer the lighter colors of the breed seldom have any interest in training their dogs to bite other people, never mind spend the kind of time, money and effort the dark-colored dog people put into the activity. Is it any wonder that light-colored dogs seldom excel in a sport requiring a minimum of two years of dedicated training?

In other words, the reason you don't see light/white dogs in Schutzhund as a rule, is because the kind of PEOPLE drawn to light/white dogs are NOT often drawn to the bite sports. Dark- colored dogs do well at the sport, particularly dark sable dogs, because the people who spend their time, money and effort on training bite sport dogs almost uniformly prefer black and dark sable dogs and choose them to train in the first place. If you go to a bite sport group with a light colored dog, you are likely to be shunned and your dog excoriated on sight. The likelihood that you will stay and perservere in the training with such uncongenial people is not high. Go to a training meet with a black/dark dog, and you may, at least, be given a chance. Remember, bite sport judging, like all judging, is subjective, a place where people are free to indulge in their prejudices. Black/dark dogs excel at bite sports because of their PEOPLE, not because of their color.

And then there are the folks who wouldn't have any German Shepherd other than a black and tan no matter what and don't think German Shepherd dogs should come in any other colors. They tend to be more conventional than either of the other two groups.

This brings us to the reality of what the breed standard is—a standard that limits the number and type of colors now favored for the breed and which clearly prefers the dark-colored dogs. That standard does NOT support the genetics of true working dogs, it does NOT support genetic diversity, and it does NOT support the physical health of our dogs. It does NOT help the breed to segregate the white dogs into a separate breed—it hurts the breed by denying it the diversity those genes represent. Declaring the old herding colors of liver (red) and tan and grey and tan faults marginalized the old herding genes, eliminating them from the gene pool-- despite the fact that those 'old breed' genes support genetic obedience, good nerve, and healthy bodies for our dogs.

What no one seems to have stopped and considered, is that for the entire history of the breed, whenever the show breeders or the Nazis or the Communists have gotten themselves into trouble with their constant in-breeding to produce the dogs that salved their egos and savaged people, they have had to go back to the well of the old herding dogs in order to reclaim their dogs from genetic adversity and from the decimation of war time and time again. The old Swabian/ Wurttembergers and Brunswick and Saxony dogs repaired their breeding mistakes and they saved the breed from extinction after two world wars. Without them the breed would have languished in genetic disorder and the simple lack of sufficient numbers necessary to survive. Scorning the colors of the herding dogs from which the breed originated is simply not good sense.

Today we have something which is euphemistically called 'the split' but which is a great deal more than that. It is, in fact, the intolerance displayed by the breeders and the aficionados of all the particular varieties of the breed for every other variety, to the major detriment of the breed as a whole.

The German show dogs, called 'high line', are so heavily in-bred on so few individuals that they come in only one color, black and red, and are riddled with genetic disorders. EPI is the norm--'oh, that's nothing,' they say, 'you just add enzymes to their food', vWildebrand's is commonplace, ('you just get the clotting agent') Degenerative Myeopathy occurs more often than anyone wants to admit, Juvenile Renal Dysplasia has everyone burying their heads in the sand and people are just starting to notice anal fistulas. Hind legs are so long and wobbly, with fragile stifle joints so far from the body and therefore so prone to ligament, tendon and cartilage damage that hip dysplasia seems hardly worth noticing. And the obsession with hips doesn't seem to preclude the in-breeding on a number of the 'high-line' show champions for generations despite the fact that those very champions were noted for having bad hips and producing them.

Breeders of the 'high-line' would no more think of adding outside German Shepherds of the 'wrong' color or the 'wrong' type or the 'wrong' lines to improve their breeding stock than they would think of adding Dobermans

164

or Great Danes to the mix. (Not that Dobermans and Great Danes don't have their own problems—they do!) They think all other kinds and colors of German Shepherd are ugly and that their dogs are perfect, anyway, and don't need improving, mentally or physically and they close their eyes to the devolution of their dogs' mental and physical health and pretend it isn't happening. At least that way they can just keep on in- breeding for their champions.

American show-line breeders are no different than the 'high-line' folks when it comes right down to it. For them it's all their in-bred variants of black and tan, with SIBO and IBD running rampant through their vaunted champions and best in show dogs, along with Degenerative Myeopathy and Cardiomyeopathy and even anal fistulas are starting to appear along with more and more dogs prone to epileptic fits. With a back that runs downhill like a ski slope thanks to weak hocks and hind legs that are so structurally unsound that hip dysplasia seems a minor consideration, few people are willing to pay their inflated prices for the ego satisfaction of bragging on the crippled champions from which their pups originate and STILL the show people don't care enough to do anything substantive to stop in-breeding and start improving their dogs.

Though the American show people swear up and down that they really are going to improve their dogs, like the 'high-line' folks, they have no intention of adding any outside blood from which to do it, never mind changing their in-breeding ways. After all, as far as they're concerned, no other dogs are good enough to add to theirs. They fully intend to go right on in- breeding on the same old dogs for ten more generations until the dogs can't stand up, can't breed naturally and drop dead the day after they achieve their championships—as puppies. And when that day comes, as it inevitably will, the show folks will tell you earnestly that German Shepherds are supposed to be that way, that only really GOOD German Shepherd dogs stagger around and collapse like that. They'll tell you it's a real sign of quality when a dog looks like a famine victim because of SIBO or IBD and you'll be advised to get preventative surgery on your new puppy to fix his stifle joints to keep his hind legs from falling apart—but his hips will be perfect!

Don't bother these folks with the truth, you're just 'picking' on them and being 'unfair' and any example you show them must be invalid—you just chose 'a poor example'. It doesn't matter to them how many championships your examples boast, or even how many 'best in shows' they are still 'a poor example' as long as they typify what you are pointing out. They are sure there are plenty of show dogs out there who are just fine, never mind that any example they tout inevitably carries the same problems as the 'poor example' you offered; the only difference between the 'poor example' and their dog is that the dog they think is fine is their own.

West German so-called 'working' (bite)-lines, which are really sport dogs, will soon be as saturated on a different set of bloodlines as the 'high-lines' are on their bloodlines. Already it is difficult to find dogs without certain competition winning stud dogs in their bloodlines, stud dogs already related to each other, in some cases, very closely. And virtually all 'working'-line dogs are back-massed heavily on Lex v Preussenblut and Maja v Osnabrucker Land, mostly through Rolf v OsnabruckerLand, but also through Rosel, Rena, Reina, Roland, Racker and Ina v OsnabruckerLand. Degernative Myeopathy is commonplace in their dogs, though they don't admit it and Juvenile Renal Dysplasia is rearing its unlovely head while they ignore it. Cardiomyeopathy is making an appearance here and there and vWildebrand's is endemic among them while bloat shortens the lives of way too many 'working' (bite)-line dogs, a not so silent killer.

Some of the 'working' (bite)-line folks have tentatively begun to absorb the DDR and Czech lines into their own which would be more helpful if these lines didn't all wind up back at the same place—Lex and Maja—and they weren't so in-bred themselves. The Czech dogs do have the advantage of the outside Northern breed dogs they assimilated after World War II and the West German dogs pulled in some outside 'old breed' Saxony and Brunswick dogs to shore up their gene pool, but the DDR dogs don't even have those advantages.

The white dog people are the poor relations of the breed, perennially being shoved to the side and marginalized. Even though they have some of the most knowledgeable breeders, when it comes to genetic diversity, people open to learning about genetics and dedicated to preventing their gene pool from becoming too constrained by popular sires and the exigencies of their color, they are plagued by schisms in their own ranks which further narrow their already dangerously small gene pool for breeders who adhere too closely to one faction or another.

The last group, the old-fashioned dogs, have so far been able to add judiciously to their lines from DDR dogs, old American and West German show lines, old working lines (where working means real work rather than bite sports) and even some of the white dogs. They'll even accept some of the much-maligned back yard bred dogs to help them to create a diverse and relatively healthy gene pool. This group accepts a wider range of sizes and colors than any of the other varieties of the breed, but if possible, are even more vilified for doing it than the white dog folks. Their dogs tend to be healthy and long-lived, compared to the rest, relatively free of genetic disorders and bloat and many of them make good guide dogs for the blind, while others do well as wheelchair aide dogs, brace/balance dogs, and even occasionally do blood sugar alert work. Many of them work stock and others make good SAR dogs, while the occasional dog even works as a Police Officer for departments where the emphasis is on community policing and extreme dogs are not wanted.

166

If the other lines, the show lines, the 'working' (bite) lines, want to produce a healthier dog, they need to borrow strategies from the 'old-fashioned' group (which is about as likely to happen as an ice cube is likely to survive a stint in hell!). They need to welcome more variety over all, particularly in size and colors, minimize the influence of 'popular' sires successful in competition, and make a strenuous effort to bring in outside lines of unrelated dogs to add to their breeding stock.

Will the breeders of the various lines do this? Outside of the white dog people who routinely bring in outside dogs of color to add to their lines, and the 'old-fashioned' dog people, who work together in breeding circles to keep their lines open and diverse, I don't see it happening. Merely broach the subject to any 'working' (bite)-line dog group and they will go ballistic on you. It's a toss up which groups, the various show-line groups of the working'-line groups are the most elitist and the most snobbish. After all, making good health through genetic diversity a priority does not serve competition aims and good health and long life do not serve competition people, whatever their form of competition, well. In fact, competition folks are set to screw the breed's standards for uniformity down even tighter, further limiting the dogs' sizes and segregating the white dogs even further from the breed by labeling them a different breed altogether. (Can you say idiocy?) According to all of these groups, their own dogs are perfect and everybody else's dogs are garbage, which attitude helps no one, least of all the dogs.

The 1965 decision to disqualify the grey and tans and the red and tans from the show ring had a truly disastrous effect we are just beginning to recognize. (Well, some of us are. Most of us have our heads firmly buried in the sand!) In barring these colors from the show ring, they were also barring the old herding dogs' blood from the breed. And maybe they intended to do exactly that. If they did, they were condemning the breed to genetic disorder and compromising the entire character of the breed.

Then again, they were people whose entire focus is on competition. What did they care about the character of the breed? Or genetic disorders, either, for that matter? As long as the dogs could still stagger around the ring or hit that sleeve for a year or so and get that 'title', and shell out puppies for a couple of years more, did they really care if the dogs died comparatively young or had to be put down when they could no longer produce puppies? Quite possibly, for the sport and show ring folks, that empty kennel is just a place for the new up and coming competitor, more of a blessing than a reminder of a dog who died before his time.

Disqualifying grey and tans (blues) and red and tans, therefore, was not just a self-serving political maneuver by people lacking integrity, it was a move away from the genetic health of the breed, a move away from the practical working ability and character of the breed and a move away from breed's historic roots. It may just have started as a way to cut out competitors, or as a marketing strategy, but making that decision revealed a total lack of understanding of the genetics of the breed and how they worked, as well as either out and out ignorance of the history of the breed, or just an arrogant disrespect for it. (Never mind a total disregard for good, functional, all-weather, heat resistant real world working dogs.)

Short sighted? Certainly. We are paying the price for that decision now, as we face the plague of genetic disorders visited upon us by the dwindling genetic diversity these decisions produce. When the people of the so-called 'working'-line dog forums repeat the party-line mindlessly, as they do, that all breeding dogs have to be exactly the same size and the same colors, black and tan and sable with only the occasional black allowed, they are saying, in their utter ignorance, that they want unhealthy dogs riddled with genetic disorders who die young after living lives made miserable by fear and reactivity and discomfort, plagued by allergies, immune deficiencies, digestive disorders and heart failure. Those dogs may be miserable, sick, fearful and 'reactive', but by golly they'll be the 'right' size—small--and the 'right' color!

Functional Conformation: Size

Way back in the beginning of the breed, the dogs were a wide variety of sizes. The Northern 'wolf' and herding dog types were large boned, big framed and tall, as were the Swabian/ Wurttemberger herding dogs of the Jura Mountains and the Northern Alps. They needed to be in order to withstand the cold of their collective climes—their bigger bodies maintained the body heat necessary to survival in their harsh environments better than smaller bodied dogs could have and the people who owned them tended to be independent families, many of them semi-nomadic for most of the dogs' existance, who could and usually did feed their dogs the same thing everyone else was eating. In the river valleys and on the large estates where dogs were sheltered in stables, smaller dogs could survive just as well, since maintaining body heat was not as difficult and still do the work, particularly when that work was merely alerting on intruders to the stable yard. Additionally, the people who cared for them, the gameskeepers and shepherds, were usually relatively poor, and smaller dogs could be maintained in working condition on both less food and food which was of a lesser quality. (Not that the people, dependent as they were on the largess of the wealthy, were not surviving on food of a 'lesser' quality as well!)

The Northern dog people, and the people of Southern Germany, and even many of the Saxony and Brunswick people, felt that larger dogs were better for work in general. When Schafermadchen and Stoppelhofer were exhibited in 1891 in Frankfurt, critics declared that they were too small and 'fit only to herd geese'. Later many herding folks would level the same criticism at Horand v Grafath (24½ inches tall) and his small size was a common complaint given by herders during his lifetime as one of the several reasons they did not want to breed to him.

The early dogs exhibited, Greif, Phylax and Pollux, as examples of what the new German Shepherd should be, were all large, big-framed dogs, with Greif being white and Phylax and Pollux both what was then called 'wolf-grey'. Although no exact measurement as to their size is given, all three were described as both large and tall, with the additional comment made of Phylax that he was raw-boned and angular. The consensus of the early opinion of what the breed should be, among those who worked their dogs on stock, was that male dogs should be at least 26 inches in height at the withers and bigger was better. This preference may have lingered on because until the mid nineteenth century, herding dogs had to be guardian dogs as well, matching up against wolves and even bear now and again, and it should always be remembered that the 'Old Breed' as the Swabian/Wurttemberger and Saxony and Brunswick dogs were called, had been around for a thousand years before Stephanitz took over the effort to meld these various regional types into a single breed.

At any rate, many of the early dogs of the breed, Max and Jorg v d Krone (Jorg was the first Sieger of the breed in 1899) conformed to the larger size the working people of the time preferred. Hektor v Schwaben (Sieger 1900-01) was no small packet, nor was Elsa v Schwaben (Siegerin 1901). These were big dogs in every way, big-framed dogs, broad of chest and strong, dogs that carried their breadth all the way through, from front to back. So was Audifax v Grafath (v d Krone), who Stephanitz described not only as a 'big' dog, but as a 'mighty' dog as well, with the big head so prized by today's Czech-line folks. 1908, 1909, and 1910 Siegers might be described as the trifecta of big dogs, with Luchs v Kalsmunt-Wetzlar, Hettel Uckermark (that 'big, sturdy, stout fellow') and Tell v d Kriminal Polizei winning the honors, respectively. Hettel, who was a working herding dog, with the HGH, was no one's lightweight, and both Luchs and Tell were measured at more than 28 inches while still less than fully mature.

When it came to the girls, Hella Memmingen might have been in the smaller size ranges, but the girls who followed Hella as Siegerin, Regina v Schaben (1904), Gretel Uckermark (1906 and mother of Hettel), Hulda Siegestor (1907) and the Kriminal Polizei girls, Flora (1910) and Hella (1911-12) were none of them small packets. And one might as well call 1913 the year of the big dog, with Arno v d Eichenburg taking the prize as Sieger at well over 28 inches and looking a bit like a Great Dane, Frigga v Scharenstetten being named Siegerin, at something better than 27 inches and 28 inch plus Jung Tell v d Kriminal Polizei being named the Champion of Holland— and described by Stephanitz as the 'ideal' German Shepherd. Frigga's brother, Falko, as elegant as his sister, and even taller, was one of the runners-up to Arno. 1921's

Sieger, Harras v d Juch, and 1924's Sieger, Donor Overholzen, were both over 27 inches in height before they were fully mature.

One of the most popular sires of the time, Horst v Boll, stood over 28 inches in height and was, as well, both grey and tan and a fount of great working temperament, while his son, Nores v d Kriminal Polizei, was even taller and just as popular, though his temperament was not nearly as good. In fact, the pillars of great working ability in the breed were, almost without exception, the big dogs, Carex and Mores Pleiningen, Hektor v Schwaben, Audifax and Horst and Luchs v Kalsmunt-Wetzlar, and Falko and the rest of the F litter Scharenstetten and Tell and Jung Tell v d Kriminal Polizei. These are the dogs you want to see in your dog's pedigree, if you want your dog to be able to work.

It is actually from many of the smaller dogs, Roland v Starkenburg, Horand v Grafath, Sali v d Krone, Hella Memmingen and Alex v Westfalenheim (though neither Alex nor Roland were all that small) that the fearful, shy, timid dogs come. It may be an irony few of the bite sport people can fully appreciate that the small size they revere is the font of the German Shepherd breed's poor nerve, while it is the big dogs they so love to hate who are the fountainhead of the solid nerve they so loudly espouse.

In the early 1920s, with so much herding blood being added back into the breed to bring it back after the decimation of World War I, the size of the dogs inevitably began to increase. In combination with the heavy use of both Horst v Boll and his son, Nores, the size of the dogs was pushed ever upwards. More and more of the big dogs were produced, to the distinct satisfaction of the stock working contingent. In 1922, more than 30 male and female dogs out of the 239 submitted to be surveyed stood 28 inches or more in height, while another 30 some stood 27 inches in height or more, in all, almost a quarter of the dogs presented, in fact. One can only surmise how many dogs deliberately not presented at that event exceeded those heights.

Today, people on the forums will tell you that the older dogs were smaller. Some of them, like the noted Schafermadchen and her kennel mate Stoppelhofer, were smaller, but the middling sizes have always comprized the larger group, with dogs of 25 and 26 inches and females of 23 and 24 and 25 inches in height. Most notably, the dogs of the Nazis, which drew heavily on the old Thuringian lines, were of the smaller size, but considering their record of attacking and terrorizing women and children that is no recommendation for the smaller dogs of the breed. Horand v Grafath was definitely not large (at 24 1/2 inches) and he was not so nice, either.

The decision to name Klodo v Boxberg Sieger in 1925 was not made on the trial grounds, or in the conformation ring, as most people who know of that change in direction in the breed, think it occurred. Rather, it took place during a long, closed door meeting Stephanitz called his cohorts to before the annual Sieger show. Oh, when the trial came along, Stephanitz made it look good—he worked the top class of dogs for two solid hours in the ring, gaiting all the while, with only ten second breaks for water and changes of handlers, and people bought the charade, though for many people at the time, Stephanitz' decision was inexplicable.

Stephanitz wanted to make a substantive change in the direction the height of the dogs of his breed were going. With the over-use of Nores v d Kriminal Polizei and the use of other dogs of his type who carried large percentages of the 'Old Blood,' the height of a great many dogs in the breed was heading upwards of 30 inches, excluding the smaller dogs from the gene pool, and that needed to be stopped if the breed was to continue to be active and agile and versatile. He felt that the range of the dogs' sizes needed to remain between 21" and 29", and Klodo split the difference nicely. It certainly did not hurt his feelings that the dog best suited to his purpose was heavily in-bred on his beloved Horand.

Did he intend to eliminate diversity of height in dogs of his breed? Not at all. He made his choice in order to RETAIN diversity of size within the breed. People who point to Stephanitz' praise of his Horand as an ideal example of the breed are deliberately forgetting that he also hailed the 28" Jung Tell v d Kriminal Polizei as an ideal specimen of the breed. And perhaps they never knew the list of big Siegers and Siegerins from the first 26 years of the breed, or the names of Audifax, Hettel Uckermark, Arno v d Eichenburg and Luchs v Kalsmunt-Wetzlar, or the rest. And even in 1925 he named Seffe v Blasienberg, a tall bitch, as Sigerin, though she was taller than Klodo, and the even taller Sultan v Blasienberg as first runner-up to Klodo.

They are also completely discounting his approval of the choice of that same Sultan to be a foundation sire at Fortunate Fields, the first breeding facility for guide dogs for the blind.

That Stephanitz' decision that day in 1925 had the unintended consequence of turning the breed away from the working abilities of the 'Old Breed' as the Wurttemberger/Swabian dogs were so often called, and away from the very diversity of size he was attempting to preserve would not, I think, have pleased him. But then, I doubt he foresaw, in 1925, the ascendancy of the Nazis, who would turn to the Thuringian dogs, with their smaller stature, crossed with the Saxony and Brunswick dogs in order to obtain their ferocity and willingness to bite indiscriminately and thus create a problem by re-setting the acceptable range of size to far smaller levels than he could ever have anticipated. It isn't unusual for people to find their attempts to do one thing have a snowball effect that winds up doing something they never dreamed of and wouldn't have wanted to have happen if they had.

Certainly, Stephanitz must have felt deeply about his opposition to the extremes to which the Nazis were taking his dogs. One didn't oppose the Nazis lightly, as he did over the direction they took 'his' breed. They killed men, or arrested them and threw them in concentration camps for a lot less.

Even so, the Captain's daughter believed that his struggles against the direction in which they took his dogs shortened his life and even caused his death. Maybe it did.

Captain Stephanitz chose to spend his life in the struggle to create one single breed out of a wide variety of dogs, some of them already breeds in their own right, as the 'Old Breed' and the Thuringian yard dogs, some of them merely types and old blood lines, like the Northern 'wolf' dogs and herding dogs, and the Brandenburg 'yard' dogs. To do that he had to encourage a certain amount of uniformity in color and size and structure. By the time of his death, he had more than managed to do that. Today, a few of us are beginning to learn that too much uniformity will destroy our breed. We need the genetic diversity of all those original dogs, of the big dogs, the middling dogs, the small dogs, of the old, light, herding colors and the old, dark, man hunting colors. We need their athletic ability, their agility, and their good, stout, durable physical and mental structures.

If people want dogs of stable, balanced temperament, and good character, healthy, strong dogs who live active, vigorous lives, then they MUST go back to the fount of that health. The first steps in doing so will be thumbing their noses at the self-serving edicts of ignorant, arrogant and elitist ruling bodies of the breed. The decisions these men have made to tighten down the range of sizes acceptable in German Shepherd Dogs (again) eliminate traditional 'Old Breed' colors, white, grey and tan and red and tan, and the good, double weather-proof coats of old in favor of a slick, undercoat-less short coats, have caused the problems the breed is now having. If we allow them to continue to mandate the production of cookie cutter dogs created by in-breeding on dogs already compromised by the back-massing caused by two world wars, then we are essentially allowing them to foist unhealthy dogs on us, dogs riddled with EPI, JRD, cardiomyeopathy, IBD, SIBO, DM, von Wildebrand's and allergies, prone to fearfulness and reactivity and all the rest.

If people want to again repair the health of the dogs and bring back their character, they are going to have to ignore the strictures of the egoists with their mean-spirits, who have to announce to the world that anyone who gets a grey and tan (blue) or red and tan (liver) puppy that they must be stupid because they don't know that the colors are supposedly 'bad', declared faulty and disqualified from the show ring and God help you if you breed one of them! Bear in mind, when you see/ hear these self-righteous prigs who just can't resist raining on someone else's parade, that they are merely showing off how shallow their little bit of dangerous knowledge is. That when they're scolding innocent newbies for actually finding these old, traditional colors in their dogs pretty, or enjoying the stout good health and sensible temperament of their big dog, that the know-it-alls are, in fact, merely demonstrating their ignorance of the history of the breed, and their complete lack of understanding of what the words genetic diversity really mean.

Perhaps it will help to remember that it is the short-sighted, snobbish, elitist, market-driven policies of the SV and the GSDCA which have gotten us into the genetic pit we are in now. Only by rejecting their policies and strictures as to the size and the color of our dogs, can we dig ourselves out. All the genetic tests in the world cannot help us if we will not increase the range of sizes we consider breedworthy, and if we will not add back the traditional colors of the breed, white, grey and tan, and red and tan we will never be able to reverse the trend we are in. The brindle and merle colors once so common in the breed are gone. To add them back we would have to go outside the breed, but white, grey and tan and red and tan do still exist inside the breed, although the latter two are becoming ever more rare (despite the downright deceitful statements of the pundits on the forums who swear they are not rare).

The future of the breed is in our hands. We can choose to study the history of the breed, we can learn about the old dogs who brought the breed its health, longevity and versatility in the past and take those lessons to heart. We can then use them in our own breeding to preserve and repair our dogs' health and character, or we can continue to allow elitist ruling groups to tell us what to think and what to do so that we continue to serve their own selfish, short term goals at the expense of our dogs.

I think I know what the regulars on the major forums are going to do, and it isn't anything good. One of these days, when they are picking among the three or four genetic disorders their dogs all suffer from—'oh, EPI? That's normal. You just feed enzymes'. And 'v Wildebrand's? Oh, no problem, you just give the dog clotting agents, and you don't have to worry'. I can see the questions and answers on the forums now. 'Oh, your dog's reactive? Never mind, all German Shepherd Dogs are reactive. It's normal. You can still get a Schutzhund title on him, if you're willing to work hard enough. Just give up any idea of getting a cgc on him.' Come to think of it, I've already read that last one a couple of dozen times.

Maybe they will wake up and realize they need to do something different, then, but I'm not holding my breath. Even if they do, which I doubt they will, by then, there won't be any genetic diversity left for them to fight for good health or decent temperament with. When people talk about the healthy, noble Shepherds of their youth, the people on the forums will say, 'Oh, they weren't really like that. You're just imagining things, because you were young then, and you didn't know any better. And besides, they weren't really purebred German Shepherd Dogs, anyway.'

You know, the way they talk to people who remember the Shepherds of the '50s and '60s now. Sturdy, healthy German Shepherds of good character will be a myth of the past, long gone and far away, their very existence denied so that people can sell their wimpy, wiry, small, nasty- tempered, wobbly, sick dogs to people too gullible and gutless to demand anything more or better.

173

The Actual Standard versus the Consensus Standard

Often, I have noticed that certain statements were made about the breed standard for German Shepherd dogs as articles of faith, that, when the actual breed standard was consulted, turned out not to be true. Sometimes, in fact, it turned out to say something entirely different than whatever it was that people agreed it said. For instance, the coat type agreed upon as 'standard' has been stated, even in a number of supposedly authoritative places, to be short, harsh and tight to the dog's body, with little or no undercoat.

It turns out that this is absolutely and categorically INcorrect. The breed standard actually calls for a 'full double coat' and states that a coat without a 'full' undercoat is faulty.

The issue of straight, level backs, is another instance where people have agreed upon something entirely different from what the actual standard says, with both most show groups and the so-called 'working-line' group agreeing that the standard calls for a sloping back, while other show groups declare a 'roach' back (where the dog is humped up like a camel) is correct. In actuality, it calls for nothing of the kind. The actual breed standard, as regards to the back, (America breed standard, both 1943 through 1978, written by the forebears of the show people who ignore everything it says today) is, 'The withers are higher than and sloping into the LEVEL (my caps) back. The back is STRAIGHT (my caps again, but so much for the people who say they can find neither word in the breed standard) very strongly developed, WITHOUT sag or ROACH, and relatively short.'

Surprise! Pictures on the AKC site support this standard and illustrate it with a drawing of a dog with a stock (fully double) coat and level back. How clear can you get? And yet, visit any dog show, and what do you see? Depending on the type of show, you will have a choice between ski slopes and camels, but one thing you can be sure of—you won't see anything resembling a real German Shepherd dog!

Is it any wonder that on a recent German Shepherd dog forum, the so-called 'working-line' group and the show folks loftily asserted that the breed standard called for a sloping back and that the STRAIGHT and LEVEL back the breed standard calls for was FAULTY! Anyone attending an American show-line dog show would quickly see only too clearly which standard the show ring supports and it wouldn't be the official written one!

This is what I mean by consensus. A specific group has decided what their idea of the breed standard shall be and they will verbalize it or write it as if it is gospel, defend it religiously and even believe the lie—well, some of them don't know any better—and they don't care what the actual standard is. Sometimes that false standard serves them to help them market their dogs more effectively to an ignorant public. Sometimes it serves their ego. Sometimes people accept the consensus because if they do not, they cannot belong to the group.

174

The show consensus was built over a long period of time and is carefully supported by a framework created by the big breeders so that judges would be thoroughly brainwashed by the time they became judges. In order to become an AKC judge, a person must have bred 25 champions in that breed. 25! That's one champion every year for 25 years!

Think about the time and effort and the MONEY that took to achieve! By the time a person has accomplished something like that, they are so invested in that consensus of the standard, both in money and in ego, never mind time, that I doubt it would be possible for them to perceive anything wrong with the results they have created. Their brain has been trained to see only those shapes in conformation as acceptable.

Today the show standards agreed to by the show people are not serving them well. Although German Shepherd numbers are up world wide, the numbers of German Shepherd dogs in the American show ring keep going down. The show ring people have not gotten the message that dog people in general don't like their dogs and I doubt they are going to get it any time soon. Even if they did, I doubt they'd care. They are completely disdainful of anyone not of their particular elite in-crowd and have only contempt for other German Shepherd people (and all the dog pet people—the only use the show people have for pet people is to separate the pet people from their money when they dump their cast-off show dogs onto them!) who do not partake of their own particular consensus. They believe that anyone who prefers a different kind of German Shepherd dog from the one they foist off on us is just a stupid ignoramus who needs to be straightened out and forced to partake of their consensus of what a German Shepherd dog ought to be.

The show crowd is by no means the only group with these attitudes towards their own consensus of what the breed standard is. The 'working' (bite)-line crowd has their own consensus of what the breed standard is for them. In their case, they're not much concerned with physical matters, they have made up their own breed standard as to what German Shepherd dogs' temperaments should be, although they are the group that also came up with the 'standard' coat, no doubt as a result of so much Thuringian (low-country) blood in their dogs. The proponents of the new slick, no undercoat coat calls all dogs with a true stock coat 'fluffy' and quickly (and incorrectly) labels all long stock coat dogs, long coats.

The kind of coat their dog has, must, in their minds, be the right one, The actual written breed standard which labels the kind of coat their dog has, faulty, simply cannot be! After all, they, the 'working' bite-line people breed their dogs to the breed standard—they insist on it! So, therefore, the standard must be re-created in order to support the kind of coat their dog has. Never mind the truth, their dog is the right dog so that's their standard and who cares what the actual standard says, it doesn't matter. Some (few, I think) people do

175

this consciously, as a very effective marketing ploy. Most are just along for the ride, following the leaders.

The matter of height comes, I believe, from the same fountainhead of Thuringian and Saxony and Brunswick blood that permeates the 'working' (bite) lines. Dogs of predominantly Thuringian, Saxony and Brunswick blood tend to be lighter framed and smaller than dogs of the old Swabian blood or of the Northern lines, though the largely Swabian dogs are the ones older people remember from their childhood as the 'great' old dogs of their youth. That's the dog many people want. They don't want today's bite line dogs descended from Hitler's concentration camp weapons that the 'working' line dog folks are pushing at them because these dogs have neither the look nor the temperament of the dogs they remember but they don't want the modern show dog, either. They don't like the way they look they don't like the way they move, and they don't like their temperaments.

In order to force these people to accept dogs they don't really want, the 'working' (bite)-line dog people have to first somehow destroy the memory the people have of the dogs of their youth by convincing them that the dogs either never existed as they remember them ('you were just a kid, the dog just seemed that big') or that they were never pure-bred German Shepherd dogs in the first place. I believe that the working line dog people who are so offensive and so violent and bullying in their attacks against the old-fashioned dogs do so because it is these dogs with whom they must compete to sell their dogs to that most despised and derided market—the pet people.

The actual breed standard for male German Shepherd dogs is 24" to 26" in height and states in so many words that dogs a little over this limit are not to be discriminated against. A 26" dog is not at all 'over-sized', yet 'working'-line people will hotly insist that he is, don't bother them with the facts. Neither is a 24" bitch over-sized, though they will tell you that, too. Bitches can be 22" to 24" in height, that is the actual 1943, 1965 and 1978 standard. (It remains unchanged from 1943 to the present.)

Earlier standards allowed for a one inch variance either way and stated that such dogs should not be discriminated against in judging. Even the 1978 standard pays lip service to this additional height with a statement that taller dogs are often favored in the show ring and does not state that such a practice should be discouraged. Originally, dogs from 21" to 29" were acceptable.

As a marketing ploy to make their smaller dogs more acceptable to the American consumer using a breed standard that is agreed upon by an influential group of breeders (no matter how inaccurate) and then using public forums to publicize it is a stroke of pure genius. How well it works can be seen by the hundreds of sycophants endlessly repeating their catechism so faithfully. They've sold a lot of dogs that way.

The oft-stated article of faith that only 'titled' dogs of the absolutely 'ideal' height, weight, color, etc (according to their own extremely narrow and genetically Undiverse agreed upon breed standard—never mind the real one) is 'breedworthy' is another superb marketing strategy. Get rid of the competition before they are even born! And this one plays right into the PETA and Animal Rights people's agenda so perfectly that they can even get behind it! It's perfect! It's just not the breed standard.

Since the dogs they breed are not appropriate for service and Sar work, they denigrate Sar dogs, calling them 'watered down' and public access level guide, assistance and alert dogs 'German Shepherd colored Labs', ignoring the breed standard that calls for a German Shepherd to be a leader dog for the blind. They sneer at dogs that actually adhere to the breed standard for temperament. People who want a service dog are supposed to take the cast-offs of the 'title' world and make do with them as best they can, however inappropriate they are for the tasks they are needed to do, and however divergent from the actual breed standard they are. They are most particularly NOT supposed to breed a dog according to the actual breed standard suitable for public access work. Nothing will make the 'working'-line dog crowd froth at the mouth faster than the words 'suitable for service work' as applied to a German Shepherd dog.

In fact, the entire 'breed standard' for temperament adhered to by the 'working' (bite)-line people is entirely different from the actual written standard and even in some cases diametrically opposed to it. Where the actual breed standard inveighs against hostility and says that the dog must be approachable and must show willingness to meet [friendly] overtures, the 'working' (bite)-line standard calls for a dog to be edgy, aloof and borderline hostile, ready, willing and able to demonstrate a pronounced 'fight' drive at the drop of a hat and sees no need for the dog to accept friendly overtures from anyone. And where the actual standard sees any sign of hostility as a severe fault, the 'working' (bite)-line standard sees nothing wrong with a little hostility. The 'reactivity' which would be a disqualifying fault in the actual written breed standard, is just fine with the 'working' (bite)-line folks because after all, 'reactive' dogs can get their 'titles' just fine.

In place of the 'quiet confidence' and 'poised, eager and alert' qualities the actual breed standard calls for, the bite folks want a dog that is 'naturally suspicious'. The 'working' (bite)-line folks want a dog with 'over the top', extreme prey drive, low thresholds, with low bite thresholds in particular and extremely high over-all 'drive' and insist that this is the breed standard, when it bears no relation to the actual, written breed standard for temperament which has been in effect in almost unchanged form since 1943.

Then contrast the actual written breed standard which calls for a dog that is 'fit and willing to serve' as either a 'blind leader or herding dog' with the attitude of the 'working' (bite)-line folks when they excoriate guide dogs as

177

'German Shepherd colored Labs' or out and out state 'we don't have any stinkin' guide dogs here!' and it is pretty easy to understand that the 'working' (bite)-line folks don't mean the real, actual written breed standard when they tout their dogs as adhering to the 'breed standard'. Add their attitude towards herding dogs, that who cares if their dogs would rather kill sheep than herd them because herding dogs don't count anyway, and that anybody who is anybody would prefer a dog with extreme prey drive, because they're much easier to train to hunt down and bite people than a dog who is 'fit and willing' to herd stock would be, and their insistence that they're the only people who breed dogs that adhere to the breed standard starts to seem just a little bit 'off'.

And if you don't like the dog you get for tracking, if he won't stay on track, but keeps getting off onto other, more enticing scents than that of the lost person you're trying to find, well, change the goal of the training you do so that the purpose is no longer to track and find someone who is lost, but to train endlessly and play with a ball and get a title. Who cares about lost people (or livestock), you're never going to get a call-out anyway. Train for 'human remains detection' instead so you can find the dead bodies of the people you don't get that 'call-out' to look for before they died. After all, you can get a title for that.

The pet crowd is to shape up and do Schutzhund or ship out. And if you don't happen to like that reactive dog who wants to bite everyone and everything, it's not the dog's fault, it's the person's! (Never mind that the dog was bred to bite everyone and everything!)

It's all about perception and reality, you see. Reality doesn't count. History doesn't matter. The agreement, the CONSENSUS of what they decide the breed standard is, is what matters. And if that agreement doesn't create the kind of dog pet people, service people, and real live stock working people want, who cares? They don't count anyway, since they aren't towing the right line and don't 'title' their dogs. (Never mind that in the real world type of work they need their dog to do, for practical purposes, there are no 'titles' to be earned, nor that the 'titles' which do exist do not support real work.)

I believe that we should cleave to a breed standard that holds the real-life working character of the German Shepherd dog as sacrosanct. The one where prey drives are sharply modified so the dogs can work livestock safely. The one where dogs aren't 'reactive' or aggressive or 'civil' because they aren't fearful or suspicious, but 'alert', instead. The one which contends that dogs should have energy levels which, while while they will support real-world work (rather than sport) are still appropriate for ordinary family life.

I believe that we should choose (because we, the people, make up breed standards, they are not delivered to us from on high) a breed standard for the German Shepherd dog that provides a healthy and genetically diverse criterion to follow. That criterion should include and welcome a variety of colors and heights and sizes of dogs in order to preserve and protect healthy genetic diversity.

I believe that we should maintain a standard of functional structure that will support the health and longevity and the functional temperament of our dogs. There is no written standard for our breed today which does this. Neither is there any standard by consensus that upholds these values. Too bad. Of course, if we wanted to, we could always go for our own consensus of standards to adhere to. Why not? Everybody else has.

Part IV
The German Shepherd Dog - Health

Jung Tell von der Kriminalpolizei PH

Chapter 7
Genetic Diversity and the Breed Standard

Bernd vom Kallengarten SchHII/AD

Genetic Diversity and the Breed Standard: Health

As we learn more and more about genetics, we are also learning more and more about the challenges breeders of purebred dogs face in the effort to maintain a healthy and healthily varied gene pool while at the same time maintaining breed 'type' (uniformity). Too much insistence on breed type and the line-breeding (dog show/fad/ sport breeding) used to create and maintain it is definitely dangerous both for breed health and soundness and in maintaining a healthy,diverse gene pool.

At the same time, we are learning that the constant narrowing of our breed's (all breeds', really) gene pool is dangerous, we are being bombarded by propaganda by people who urge us to narrow our gene pool ever more tightly by slavishly following an agreed upon breed 'standard' which has, over time, become less and less versatile and less and less genetically diverse.

I know that everyone has heard this, but I believe that 50 years ago German Shepherd dogs simply did not exhibit the bewildering array of infirmities that they do now. Despite arguments which can be fairly made that medical advances in the diagnosis, treatment and care of diseases have made it possible to identify genetic conditions, I still think that dogs then were more healthy and suffered from these conditions far more rarely. Dogs routinely lived long, healthy lives. They worked soundly for 10 years, or more, and were only troubled by hip dysplasia at the end of their lives, if they were troubled by it at all.

I base this perception not only on the words of older dog men and women, but on the experience of my own family. My mother and my grandmother before her worked and lived with German Shepherd dogs, which, I think, gives me a rather unique perspective on the breed. I would suggest that the history of the ever increasing list of alphabet soup genetic conditions parallels the history of the ever narrowing spiral of what is 'acceptable' for the breed as specified in what is agreed upon as the breed standard.

In the beginning, acceptable show ring size for German Shepherd dogs ran from 21 inches at the shoulders to 28 inches at the shoulders and dogs up through 29 inches at the shoulder were acceptable and welcomed into the gene pool. Early Siegers of the breed, notably Luchs van Kalsmunt-Wetzlar, Hettel Uckermark, Tell and Jung Tell von der Kriminal Polizei, 1913's Sieger Arno von der Eichenburg and Siegerin Frigga von Scharrenstetten, Donor Overholzen and Harras von der Juch, son of 29 inch Nores von der Kriminal Polizei and grandson of Horst von Boll measured no less than 27 inches and several of them were 28 inches or more. And all of them were chosen by Stephanitz himself. In the early 1920s, significant numbers of the dogs presented to Stephanitz measured 27 to 29 inches and in 1925 when Stephanitz chose Klodo v Boxberg to be Sieger, Siegerin Seffe v Blasienberg and first runner-up to Klodo, Seffe's litter brother Sultan v Blasienberg were both over 27 inches at the shoulder. Working herding dogs were not merely just as welcome into the pool as those who passed the Schutzhund exams, they were actually more highly thought of, while Schutzhund was merely a secondary test to herding, guide, police and ambulance (search) dogs, which were considered to be first rank in breeding desirability. Schutzhund was merely a pass/fail exam much like the cgc (though physically and mentally much more demanding).

The breed contained all colors of dogs, including dogs from Lower Saxony which exhibited color patterns very like the Panda Shepherds of today and prized red and blue merles as well as liver and tan, grey and tan (blue), and solid white, brindle and sable. Solid black came from Thuringia and their man-hunting dogs. Black and tan was not particularly common and black and red was unknown, or at least extremely rare.

All functional coat types, those which today would correctly be called short stock, stock, long stock and even long coat, were acceptable, as long as the coat did not resemble an Airedale's or a Poodle's. Functional meant the dog could work in all weather. Today's short coats, so lacking in undercoat, would have been considered faulty and excluded because they precluded good working ability in all weather.

Today I see dogs who would barely have been considered a 'long stock' coat under the old standards being excoriated as an 'unacceptable' long coat, according to a modern narrowly defined (and incorrectly interpreted) 'breed standard' from which function has long since been excluded.

The first efforts to limit size from heading into the stratosphere with 30 inch plus dogs were not too troubling. Later attempts to eliminate white and merle were based on the limited genetic knowledge of the time, which indicated that white might be linked with albinism, and through it to deafness and blindness. This proved incorrect, but by the time it was, an unreasoning prejudice had wormed its way into the hierarchy of the breed's governing body and despite the proponents of the color, white was never, as it properly should have been, in light of the new genetic information and in service to genetic diversity, reinstated as an acceptable color.

We now know that merle bred to merle can result in genetic defects, but when bred to other colors is not a problem, and on that basis, at least, an argument could be mounted that merle should also be re-included. Brindle just disappeared except in the Dutchies, by 1950, to be replaced by black and tan. I have no idea why. In the 1960s, livers and blues were arbitrarily excluded by the ruling elite of the breed for no better reason than that they had taken a dislike to those colors and could glean a competitive edge for themselves by excluding them, thus cramping down on genetic diversity once again for no viable reason and doing a grave dis-service to the breed.

It is really no coincidence that the genetic disorders which began to manifest themselves out of the rolling snowball of in-breeding began to force themselves on the notice of an unwilling audience of German Shepherd dog

185

owners a couple of generations after the new 1965 restrictions went into effect. The best thing that could have happened to the breed at that point would have been the widening of the genetic base of the breed. Instead, the German Shepherd Dog Club's deliberate narrowing of acceptable range of colors in service to 'uniformity' proved disastrous for the health of the breed.

Tightening the size down to 25 inches for males and less than 24 inches for females is simply not genetically sound, but that is what many 'working-line' proponents are arguing for under the guise of saying it is the 'breed standard' though it is not at all the breed standard. I would argue that by accepting this incorrect interpretation of the breed standard in conjunction with 'fad' breeding and corrupt dog show standards of structure added to a complete lack of concern over temperament issues, we are going to eventually lose our breed.

The breed appears to be in a downward spiral of ever worsening genetic defect and lack of diversity. I believe that our best hope for our breed lies in welcoming back our breed's original diversity in color and size, in vigilant refusal to increase back-massing in our breeding and in stringent refusals to accept fad breeding in structure and temperament. I believe that we need to work to get our dogs back to being able to stand up again, so that the effects of hip dysplasia can be returned to old age, if they appear at all, and temperaments can return to reliable rather than reactive. In short, to return to the original standards that made our breed so great, before the elitists started eliminating our breed's versatility and diversity in color and size in their heedless drive to enforce their narrow and unhealthy standards of 'uniformity' on their more reasonable and sensible constituency.

I believe that the new genetic tests can be of great help to us in our quest to eliminate the worst of our genetic disorders, but that we need to remember NOT to throw the baby out with the bathwater, and to always, always, keep genetic diversity in mind in making our breeding decisions.

The State of Our Breed

Genetic diversity is said to be the key to long-term breed health for all purebred dogs. After very close to a century of the careful breeding of purebred dogs and dog shows and competitive dog sports, 26 breeds of dogs are said to be on the cusp of extinction and even more are in crisis. Where have we gone wrong?

Every article we read tells us blithely that we need to stop line-breeding and in-breeding (something show people are loathe todo because it is line-breeding and in-breeding that gives them their show champions). They tell us that however successful such practices are in the short run in giving us our show champions and high scoring sport dogs, that however flattering to the ego of the people who use them to get those show and sport champions, in the long run, for the breed (every breed) they are nothing less than a disaster.

In other words, those people who line-breed and in-breed in order to create those show and sport champions are not only NOT 'bettering the breed' they are, in fact, contributing to the long term destruction of the breed (any breed, really) for their own personal ego-satisfaction.

This has resulted in champion lines from the show ring who are fearful, 'working-line' dogs who are reactive and fear aggressive, show dogs with EPI, SIBO, and IBD, sport dogs with Degenerative Myeopathy and plagued both groups with Bloat, Cardiomyopathy, Mega E, Juvenile Renal Dysplasia and Von Wildebrand's (hemophilia). Next to these conditions, hip dysplasia and elbow dysplasia, both of which are caused by environmental issues at least 50% of the time, seem hardly worth mentioning. These days the price of Best in Show is likely to be a spook with EPI and that of a high scoring sport dog an inability to take the dog to a vet, or even to allow anyone to approach their kennel too closely.

Before we can do anything substantive to dig out of the pit we are in (if, indeed, anyone wants to do anything about it) we have to understand how we got to where we are. If we persist in our denial that we're in that pit, and just keep digging it deeper, we will eventually collapse the sides in upon us.

First, we have to recognize that despite our record numbers of dogs world wide, the German Shepherd dog has very little genetic diversity left to preserve, and this despite having started with the materials to have great diversity, with both Swabian and Thuringian dogs going into the mix as well as the Saxony and Brunswick dogs and the Northern 'wolf' dog breed. This is because the breed has lurched from one genetic bottleneck to another throughout the last century as breeders flocked to one popular sire after another without regard for long-term results while breeders sought for that will o' the wisp chimera called 'uniformity'.

It must be admitted that genetic diversity is a new concept, but breeders have always known that when line-breeding was done at least two generations of out breeding ought to follow. Breeders striving towards a goal, either in sport or show, have often ignored what they knew they should be doing in order to reap the rewards of several generations of line-breeding in the short term. We are now paying for that practice.

In German high-line breeding we have the Uran v WildsteigerLand-Palme v WildsteigerLand-Irk v Arminius connection currently running amok, the most recent of our genetic bottlenecks. Back in the '60s, we have the Quanto/Canto v d Wienerau combo causing problems. Canto apparently was Von Wildebrand's affected, and only lived long enough to sire 100 puppies-- all of whom inherited the mutated allele from Dad, making them Von Wildebrand's carriers. At least as bad, Canto was also noted for passing on a shy, fearful temperament unsuited for any real work. Yet people line-bred upon Canto in particular over and over, until there are dogs today which carry twelve lines to Canto in six generations! Think, folks, seriously, about what that means for the proliferation of v Wildebrand's disease! In America we have the Lance of Fran-Jo bottleneck, a perfect example of a good dog who became a disaster for the breed because of extreme in and line-breeding on him. But we're just getting started. The '50s gave us the Lex v Pressenblut/Maja v OsnabruckerLand cork in the bottle and Axel v d DeininghauserHeide collar on the cork. Then there was Ingo v Piastendamm and Sigbert Heidegrund (never heard for him? You will.) Then there as the much touted Utz v Haus Schutting and his sire, Klodo v Boxberg--ok, but that's not all of that particular bottleneck, which is more like a roadblock, with subsidiary blockades named Ferdl v d Secretainerie, Odin v Stolzenfels, and Curt v Herzog Hedan, as well as the aforementioned Sigbert. Klodo leads us directly to another bottleneck, namely Erich v Grafenwerth, who is bad enough on his own but leads us to a bigger problem, and that is a dog named Hettel Uckermark and his sire, the illustrious (maybe) Roland v Starkenburg. Roland was a beautiful dog, but he is also the fountainhead of a lot of the shyness and fearful, unstable temperament which has plagued German Shepherds through the century, particularly those of the show-line persuasion.

Oh, you don't think a dog that lived a hundred years ago could have that much effect on the dogs we are breeding today? Let me give you a clue-- Roland appears 800 times in Quanto v d Wienerau's bloodlines. You can just about count the number of lines that DO NOT go back to Roland in this pedigree on the fingers of one hand. Think about it. That's as if Quanto's grandfather was Roland—on both sides! Still think he isn't affecting today's German high-line breeding?

Ok, you say, but I'm a 'working' dog person and surely we don't have those problems in 'working' lines. That's what I thought (hoped). What I found was a very different matter. Just for kicks and giggles, I looked at Andy Maly Vah. (Cliff got me interested.)

The first 4 generations looked good, a nice open pedigree, no repeated names. But then things started to fall apart. Andy hit the Lex/Maja bottleneck hard, with 132 crosses to this pair, and 6 additional crosses to Lex's sire, Trutz aus der Schwanenstadt just for good measure. Along the way, he collects 23 crosses to Axel v d DeininghauserHeide, which is actually nothing in the great scheme of things, because he also logs 30 crosses to a dog named Utz v Haus Hiller, 25 crosses to Roland v Teglarforst, 34 to Rolf aus dem Urmenkeller, 28 to Iran v d Buchenhohe, 40 to Falk v OsnabruckerLand and 46 to his sire, Dewet Pressenblut (that's 40 thro Falk and 6 more on his own without Falk). Otello v Bergnest appears 25 times, Ingo v Piastendamm 56 times (think he might have had some input into the dog Andy Maly Vah is today? Well, if he did, what about our old friend Sigbert Heidegrund, who shows up a grand total of 69 times?

Now things start to get really interesting. You have the big rats in the snake of Sigbert and Ingo, then, to them, you add Ferdl, an Odin son, Odin v

Stolzenfels, without either Ferdl or Sigbert 21 more times, Curt v Herzog Hedan without his son Odin 45 times, and then you start multiplying. Got your calculators out? You don't even want to know how many times that means that Erich v Grafenwerth appears or even worse, Hettel Uckermark, who is both father and grandfather to the said Erich and that means--you got it, Hettel's sire, Roland v Starkenburg is BACK!!! So much for genetic diversity.

The breed has a problem. In order to solve it, or even to work at improving it, you first have to admit it. Then you have to learn to recognize it. Look beyond that first 4 or 5 apparently open generations to what lies below and take that into consideration in making breeding decisions. Try, whenever possible, to open your pedigrees up even more. Do your homework so you know what's really there (and in what numbers) and use that information when making your breeding decisions. The temptation to use line-breeding to get what we want is always there, but remember, that way lies more Mega E, more EPI, more Cardio, more DM, more Pannus, more von Wildebrand's, and other things we haven't yet been forced to get acquainted with.

Line-breeding

Let's talk line-breeding. Just what is it? There are all kinds of people telling German Shepherd breeders what and how to breed who have no idea what the words mean. Line-breeding means the breeding of what used to be called 'kissin' kin'—cousins. Line-breeding is the breeding of first cousins, second cousins, third cousins and even fourth cousins, and all manner of half-cousins. When this type of breeding is successful in producing the desired results, it is called a 'nick'.

In-breeding, on the other hand, is the breeding of direct relations, mother to son, father to daughter, brother to sister, both full and half, grandmother to grandson, and grandfather to grand-daughter. In the formation of almost all dog breeds existent today, some in-breeding was done to set type and create some uniformity. In-breeding is always problematical genetically, never mind the moral considerations because it sharply and quickly, within a single generation, reduces the gene pool available to successive generations. Repeat generation in-breeding will always get you into trouble, and usually very quickly. Once a breed is formed, it should be quickly and completely stopped, because if it is continued for repeated generations, the breed will very quickly face extinction. A perfect example of this is the Duchess 'breed' of cattle.

Oh, you never heard of Duchess cattle? I'm not surprised. The breed became extinct after only a little more than twenty years as a breed. The Duchess cattle breeders decided to opt for 'uniformity' and 'purity' in their breed, and repeated in-breeding over several generations, and the breed ceased to be able to reproduce as a result.

Line-breeding, on the other hand, if used sparingly, may have its place in good breeding strategies—if it is not repeated in successive generations. Line-breeding has been both misunderstood and misused. It can be a breeder's best friend or his worst nightmare. Used with care and knowledge, it can set a type, and give a breed a strong foundation of great qualities. In the short term, it can make a breeder's reputation, while at the same time, in the long term holding consequences for the breed that weaken the very viability of the breed. Cliff has touched on a generally agreed upon 'rule' for line-breeding—that is, going in for ONE generation to set a desired characteristic, or even to create a pre-potent sire or dam, and then going out again to keep the lines open.

A couple of problems with this practice come to light very quickly upon examination: too many breeders, (including Stephanitz himself) have been seduced by the predictability and the 'control' line-breeding seems to give the breeder into line-breeding for successive generations. The temptation for too many breeders, particularly show breeders, is just irresistible.

Long ago and far away, a very, very good dog by the name of Ingo v Piastendamm reigned very close to supreme. A big, stout dog of sterling character, he was already line-bred on Utz v Haus Schutting. People who wanted more of him line-bred on him. For the first generation it was a roaring success, so they did it again, forgetting (if they ever knew) that they were line-breeding for the third generation on Utz by doing so. In the third generation, they began to hit snags—missing teeth and the occasional cryptorchid. They said, 'well, this isn't too bad, it isn't happening all that often', so off they went to produce another generation, at which point the you-know- what hit the fan.

About the only good thing about this is that at least they knew where they had gone wrong. Problem was, they didn't want to admit to themselves that they had caused the problem themselves—the old blame somebody else syndrome—so they blamed the dogs, NOT their breeding practices. Utz was a good dog. Ingo was a good dog. They brought fine qualities to the table which should be retained and passed on, particularly Ingo, who was both a hip improver and a temperament improver, with good, stout nerve. These are good things.

Did anyone learn anything? No. You've got Lex v Pressenblut and Maja v OsnabruckerLand appearing over a hundred times in pedigrees today. Dogs like Lance of Fran Jo (who was a good dog in and of himself, both a hip improver and a good temperament) was bred on for 10 (TEN!) successive generations!!! With disastrous results. I found Bernd v Kallengarten, a great working dog sire for police, service, stock and SAR dogs appearing 60 times in one pedigree, and for all the great working ability he passed on (Glen Johnson's main pipeline dog was of the lines of Bernd v K) he also occasionally passed on a wonky hip. This is NOT a dog you want to line breed on, particularly NOT for successive generations—but people did it because the dogs won in the show ring.

People talk about not being able to find a pedigree without certain dogs in it and line-breeding certainly contributes to this problem. According to Malcolm Willis, Erich v Grafenwerth, the sire of Klodo v Boxberg, appears in the pedigree of every single German Shepherd dog today. If Willis is right, that means Horand v Grafath and his grandsire Pollux, appears 80 (EIGHTY!) times, rock bottom minimum, in the genetic base of every German Shepherd dog today, because Erich was heavily line-bred on Horand and Horand's grandfather Pollux. And remember, Horand was the originator of both Mega E and EPI and quite possibly JRD as well—meaning that if you can't get away from Horand (which you can't) you can't get away from the possibility of any of those genetic disorders entirely. (And then if you add how many times Erich's son Klodo v Boxberg was doubled up on through his sons and grandsons, things start to get really scary!)

This brings us brings us back around to something Lewie, Chuck and Cliff all touched on—KNOWLEDGE. If you're going to line-breed, you need to KNOW what's back there, and not just for three or four generations. You need to know what's there in the base of the iceberg. For instance, Debbie has had me looking at the lines of some dogs more or less recently, and one of them, I'll call dog C, looked good on the first page of the pedigree, the PDB even said no line-breeding, but you know me, I looked deeper, and I found that every single one of dog C's great grandparents was 4-4 on Hasel v Tannenmeise. EVERY SINGLE ONE! Now, if you also know that Hasel carried 3 lines to Canto v d Wienerau and that Canto was von Wildebrand's affected and had a poor temperament, WHAT kind of a dog do you think you'll get with 12 lines to dear old Canto in EVERY great grandparent? Still think dog C isn't line-bred? And did dog C's owners, who were breeding her, have any idea what was back there?

Now, say, they line-breed dog C (I am happy to report that was not the breeder's plan). I suspect there might be some very nasty surprises in store for the people who buy those puppies, however good they might look in the beginning. (And you wonder where fearful, shy, unstable temperaments come from! And remember, too, that this kind of breeding is almost always done by the so-called 'expert' breeders, the kind of breeders being recommended on the forums, not by the much-maligned 'back-yard' breeders!)

The German Shepherd Dog who can be line-bred on for generations is a myth. Maybe there are dogs in other breeds where repeated line-breeding can be done safely, I don't know, but I really don't think there are any in German Shepherds. (That doesn't mean don't line-breed, that means don't REPEAT generation line-breed.) As Cliff has pointed out, some of the best fountainheads of working ability in the breed had problematic hips. Ingo carried missing teeth and cryptorchidism. If you're going for pretty and movement, you're looking at EPI and von Wildebrand's at the very least, courtesy of Canto v d Wienerau and Irk v Arminius and Uran v

WildsteigerLand adds poor hip construction to the high-line cocktail and these dogs probably have had more line-breeding done on them by the so-called 'expert' breeders than any other modern dogs and if that doesn't give you the willies, nothing will. Many of the good working-line sport dogs come attached to JRD and DM and Bloat as well as problematic hips. AM-line show dogs are starting to show up with Cardiomyeopathy, on top of SIBO and IBD and British dogs add epilepsy and JRD to the mix due to genetic brain chemistry problems.

Bottom line is that line-breeding is a valuable tool in the breeders arsenal and can be used effectively to the benefit of both breeder and breed—IF the breeder does so knowledgeably and with discretion. Problems occur when a lack of discipline cause the breeder to use it generation after generation for short term gains, or when it is used without a thorough knowledge of what genetics the dog contains (the base of the dog's genetic iceberg).

How Did We Lose Genetic Diversity?

In the beginning, when the breed was put together, we had at least 4 disparate types of dog to work with. We had 2 major breeds, the Swabian, so big and strong and stately, with their herding skills and their family-friendly orientation, and we had the Thuringian, small and agile and fierce, always so ready to bite, with their over-the-top prey drive and extreme energy levels. Then the herding dogs of Saxony and Brunswick with their rich variety of colors, added their genes to the blend, and Northern 'wolf' dogs brought their lanky, big-boned height and stout working ability to the mix. They provided the breed with a deep pool of genetic diversity.

What happened to it? Well, line-breeding and in-breeding happened.

The original vision for the breed was for the dogs to be useful and versatile in their utility, but like everyone else, Stephanitz wanted the breed to have a particular 'look'. He, and the men who worked with him, didn't care so much about what color the dog was, or what size it was, as long as it wasn't a Great Dane or a lap dog, but Stephanitz definitely wanted the prick ears and the aquiline head. In fact, he wanted the head of his own pet, Horand v Grafath, replicated in the breed as a whole. To get it, he bred Horand to his daughters and his sisters, and finally to his grand-daughters. And he got what he wanted, Horand's head on most of his progeny.

He also got puppies that died at birth and puppies that died when weaned, sickly dogs who didn't make it to adulthood, and unhealthy dogs which died young. Unfortunately, he never really associated his dogs' illnesses with his breeding practices. He learned however, the hard way, that when he balanced his Horand lines with that of the Swabians and Swabian blends of the Krone kennels, and later with Audifax and Fides Neckarusprung, that his pups quit dying and his dogs were healthier.

Clearly, Horand was carrying some mutated alleles for some bad stuff. What bad stuff it is doubtful we will ever know, since veterinary medicine in the first decade of the 20th century wasprimitive and seriously wanting in knowledge, as well as lacking any really useful scientific tools for diagnosis and Stephanitz himself had no idea what was happening.

We can guess that the puppies that died at birth and weaning might have had Juvenile Renal Dysplasia, or Mega E, or that maybe the pups who lived to adulthood suffered from one (or more) of the digestive conditions, EPI, IBD, or SIBO, but all of that is merelyspeculation. But, while the Captain may have learned to balance his breeding with out-lines, nobody else did. Look at poor Erich v Grafenwerth, with his multiple lines back to Roland v Starkenburg, or the breeding of Klodo v Boxberg, who already carried 4 lines to Roland, to a bitch carrying 5 more.

And many breeders kept right on doing it. Even when they used out-lines, they merely line-bred on the out-lines, with Horst v Boll to Luchs v Kalsmunt to Tell v d Kriminal Polizei, to Jung Tell v d Kriminal Polizei and then back to Horst v Boll again through his son Nores v d Kriminal Polizei. All because they wanted the dogs to have the same 'look'.

This is called 'uniformity'. And, when forming a breed, one does, of course, make some breeding decisions based on ideas about how a breed should 'look'. But, as the Captain learned, uniformity is a chimera with some very, very bad side effects. And, as other groups for other breeds have found, the road to 'uniformity' is a one way road to extinction. It's a highway we have to find some way to get off of right now, if we want healthy dogs in the future. The breeders who came before us have already eliminated too many genetic lines from the breed by running down the uniformity road full speed ahead to preserve good health and sturdy temperaments. Progressively narrowing the breed standard, however debased or genetically unsound that breed standard has become when twisted by the egos and the pocket books of the people in charge is a recipe for disaster.

The whole problem of breeding 'true' is the problem. The dogs already breed too true and to do more line or in-breeding at this time or to narrow the size limits even farther than they have already been narrowed, is both short-sighted, unwise, and far from 'improving' the breed, will eventually bring the breed to smash with its continual drain on the dogs' genetic vigor.

Livestock breeders have used line and in-breeding for decades with catastrophic results for the breeds affected. These days, thanks to line and in-breeding, the Duchess breed is extinct, Herefords now are out-crossed with Angus to create white-faced black cattle, while other ranchers experiment with beefalo, Santa Gertrudis, Charolais and Brahmin. In-breeding in dairy cattle has produced its own problems, such as calving difficulties and mal-absorption of certain nutrients in the digestive tract. (Hummm, the bovine equivalent of SIBO, EPI, or IBD?)

However effective in and line-breeding are in the short term and however satisfying it is to the ego of the show person or the sport person who uses it, for the breed, it is a long term disaster which someone in the future of the breed will pay for in spades, unless, like the cattlemen, they are willing to ditch the breed altogether or to bring in other breeds with which to cross-breed to reacquire the necessary genetic diversity to keep the breed viable. Of course, once we have to do that, it will not quite be a German Shepherd any more, but considering those who are doing the line and in-breeding, I don't believe they will care. It is all about their ego and the uniformity they seek and not about the long term viability of the breed.

To be healthy genetically, the breed needs tall dogs, small dogs, and in-between dogs. The breed doyennes need to embrace diversity, bring back the lost colors and the variations in coatwhich the original breed standard accepted. They also need to stop obsessing about hip dysplasia, which experts in the field calculate is 30% to 70% environmental, rather than hereditary (which means breeders are wasting their time trying to breed it out when their puppy buyers are simply going to give it to their puppies like chicken pox by free feeding them, spaying and neutering them far too young, and injuring them with intense play when they're far too young for it) and which is small potatoes compared to Cardio, DM, EPI, IBD, SIBO, Mega E, von Wildebrand's, Juvenile Renal Dysplasia and the rest--and start doing something about it. Narrowing the gene pool even further is only going to make the problem worse.

Is anybody going to seriously do that? Of course not. People are too selfish and too egotistical to accept or to practice genetic diversity. They are going to keep on with their mantra of uniformity regardless of the price the dogs will pay for their success with their continual line and in-breeding, and just as bad, paid by the people who love the dogs. Uniformity is simply too satisfying on too many levels for people to accept that it is wrong. It is and always has been, an effective marketing strategy. It makes for success on the sport field and for success in the show ring. It makes for great snobbery, too, which is very attractive to some people. For all those reasons, denial is going to continue to be a great deal more than a river in Egypt.

For those rare, few people who want to row against the current and try to raise healthy dogs in spite of the obstacles put in their path, working together is a valuable tool. Few of us can afford to keep the numbers and kinds of dogs it would take to create and preserve genetic diversity in our own dogs. Only by creating breeding circles where we share and exchange dogs so that we can get the out-crosses we need and by using the internet and forums to find each other and to support each other, can we achieve any kind of success in our endeavor to keep at least a slender line of genetically healthy dogs.

How Genetic Conditions are Transmitted

When most people think of Genetic Conditions the first thing they think of is Hip Dysplasia, which is a tremendous misnomer. In actuality, Hip Dysplasia is a condition caused, at least 50% of the time by ENVIRONMENTAL conditions, things such as injuries, malnu-trition (lack of adequate calcium with its necessary satellites) improper feeding, such as 'free feeding' and over-feeding (the reason your puppy doesn't want to eat at supper time is because you fed him too many treats to get him to do what you wanted 'candy' before dinner and because you feed him too much in general!) and early spaying and neutering. Focusing on hip dysplasia (which in many instances is a minor condition which has no symptoms and which can only be diagnosed by x-ray because it does not affect the dog's movement in any way) and ignoring far more important problems is counter productive. There are far scarier things out there than hip dysplasia, and they really ARE passed on genetically.

How are things passed genetically? Well, the answer is complicated. Simply put, each dog possesses a specific number of paired chromosomal strings of genetic material, and each pair of alleles comes with what is called an 'epi-gene' which controls that pair of alleles (an on-off switch). When the female dog's body creates an ovum, one half of each of her chromosomal strings is selected by random chance, and all those halves of her chromosomes collect in the ovum. When male dog's body creates sperm, each sperm gets half of each of the male dog's chromosomal strings, and all those halves collect in the sperm. When the ovum is fertilized by the sperm, each half chromosomal string finds their proper other half and joins it, and a puppy is created.

Dogs affected by a particular genetic condition usually have 2 mutated (damaged) alleles, one from each parent. This is usually expressed as A/A. Dogs which are carriers of a particular genetic condition have received one normal allele from one parent, and one mutated allele from the other. This is usually expressed as A/N. Dogs which have received a normal allele from each parent are referred to as N/N, 'normal' or sometimes, 'clear'.

The breeding of AFFECTED dogs should be discouraged, since these A/A dogs can only contribute a damaged allele to the puppy to be and will create a pool of dogs which are all 'carriers' of the condition.

The breeding of CARRIER dogs is a far more complex issue, as, in most cases CARRIERS are NOT affected by the condition they carry. (There are two very important exceptions to this rule—Juvenile Renal Dysplasia and Cardiomyopathy. In the case of these two conditions, the breeding of carriers is NOT a good idea, as many carriers are affected and these two conditions kill dogs quickly and young.) For all other genetic conditions, the breeding of carriers, even carrier to carrier--if done responsibly--all pups are tested via DNA before any pups are sold, pups affected are culled by euthanasia, carrier pups are sold with limited registration and spay and neuter contracts, while those pups who test normal through DNA can then be reserved for breeding, thus preserving genetic diversity without increasing the numbers of affected dogs--can actually be very valuable to the breed.

Obviously, in cases were NO DNA tests are available, the breeding of carriers is far more problematic.

Juvenile Renal Dysplasia, Degenerative Myeopathy (DM), and von Wildebrand's Disease all have DNA tests available. In the case of Juvenile Renal Dysplasia, affected puppies die, and die young, in most cases, so the DNA test is most valuable for pin-pointing carriers. DM, on the other hand, often does not affect the dog until age 5 or older, and often holds off until the dog is over age 10. (This is because the epi-gene, which in this case controls the expression of the disease, is controlled by environmental factors.) Von Wildebrand's Disease (hemophilia) is also controlled by an epi-gene, which in turn is controlled by environmental factors, which means that an affected dog can live for several years, or even an average life-span without being affected by the disease as long as the dog receives no serious injuries during that lifetime. Thus, for all three of these conditions, a DNA test is valuable and certainly advisable before breeding.

The breeding of DM and von Wildebrand's carriers can be very valuable to the breed (any breed). If breeding a known carrier to a normal (clear) dog, by Mendel's law, half the puppies born will be normal (clear). Using spay/neuter options for the carrier half of the puppies, which would be perfectly healthy, 'normal' or 'clear' dogs could be produced for breeding, thus preserving the genetic inheritance of the parents safely. In this way, affected dogs, which would not be created by this pairing, would be eliminated, and the numbers of carrier dogs would be curtailed.

In von Wildebrand's and DM, it would also be acceptable to breed carrier dog to carrier dog if certain conditions were met. If the dogs possessed a genetic inheritance which it would be valuable to the breed to preserve (particularly any lines representing genetic diversity or outstanding temperament) and stringent DNA testing and the appropriate culling as a result were both done. In any carrier to carrier breeding, by Mendel's law, if eight puppies were born of this mating, then TWO puppies should be Normal (clear), FOUR puppies would be carriers (unaffected by the disease) and only TWO puppies would be affected (and thus should be culled via euthanasia). In fact, far from causing all dogs to be affected by the disease, the breeding of carriers can result in the creation of more NORMAL dogs.

In Genetic Conditions where NO DNA test is available, or in those conditions, such as Cardiomyeopathy (Cardio) or Juvenile Renal Dysplasia (JRD), where carriers are affected by the condition, the breeding of carriers is far more problematic. In the case of conditions where no DNA test is available, the breeder is working in the dark. Carriers of Cardio may seem to be healthy until the condition suddenly claims them at age 5, or 6, or even 7 or 8. By that time they may have had several litters of puppies, in the case of females, or sired many litters, in the case of males. JRD does at least now have a DNA test available. Cardio is a double whammy, in that NO DNA test is available, and Cardio can hit the older dog at any time, even though the dog seemed to be healthy previously, thus passing on the condition before the breeder has any intimation that the dog IS a carrier.

Physical exams can be done which will show whether the dog is NOW affected by Cardio, but these exams are not particularly useful long-term. The dog that exam clears today can be affected 6 monthslater and dead within a year. Therefore, the physical exam is NOT particularly useful for making breeding decisions. The most effective means of preventing the transmission of Cardio is to KNOW the breeding dog's parents, grand-parents, and great grand-parents. Dogs whose ancestors all lived to be 12, 13, or 14 (or older) are highly unlikely to carry Cardio.

EPI, IBD, and SIBO may turn out to be similar in that some dogs may turn out to be affected by the condition even though they are merely carriers, since dogs with these conditions are often not diagnosed until age 5 or 6. On the other hand, as vets become more familiar with the conditions, and better able to diagnose them, we may find that dogs exhibiting the conditions always had them, but just were not getting diagnosed. What information we have on EPI indicates that it is very complex, with four alleles and two epi-genes involved in transmission and expression of the condition and it is entirely possible that IBD and SIBO will turn out to have similarly complex methods of transmission and expression. At this time, given the equivocal nature of the information we have on the transmission of these diseases, it is perhaps better if known carriers are not bred.

Line and In-breeding, by doubling up on certain dogs in the puppy's pedigree, in a form of distillation, double, then triple, then quadruple the chances of a pup winding up with 2 mutated alleles. By the laws of chance, then, we wind up with a greater number of affected dogs. The effect of this line and in-breeding is multiplied by what is called 'the popular sire syndrome'. When a popular sire, such as Canto v d Wienerau, is line bred on by large numbers of people, if that popular sire carries, or worse, is affected by, a genetic condition, then it becomes difficult to find dogs which do NOT carry the mutated allele. Now line breed on this dog, so that every line in a 10 generation pedigree goes back to Canto (there are lots of these lineages out there) then by the laws of chance, half of any given 10 puppy litter will be von Wildebrand's affected, or A/A, just like good old Canto. Not Carriers, AFFECTED.

Conditions for which we need DNA testing: EPI, SIBO, IBD, Mega E and Cardio. While we know that JRD is showing up in this countryin Czech-bred dogs, and that in Great Britain, it appears mostly intheir show-line dogs derived from the German High-lines, thatdoesn't mean it can't show up elsewhere.

EPI is largely transmitted through German High-lines, and anumber of dogs, such as the Uran/Palme WildsteigerLand and Irk v Arminius lines are implicated. It ultimately comes from a dog named Alex v Westfalenheim, who was heavily line-bred on Horand v Grafath.

SIBO and IBD usually are associated with American Show-lines.

Mega E can pop up anywhere, but since few dogs live to breeding age, affected dogs are eliminated from the gene pool by a form of natural selection, keeping the number of carriers down and making it less common. There are some cases where dogs are so mildly affected by the problem that it is not particularly noticeable but these cases are not generally common.

Mega E appears to be a condition in which carriers are generally NOT affected and thus virtually impossible to identify except when a puppy with the condition is born and then dies shortly after weaning. In the past, very few puppies with this condition lived long enough to be sold; those breeders who knowingly sell a puppy with this condition (and it's hard to miss in its acute stage) are not doing the breed any favors. Some owners are now managing to keep such puppies alive longer with modern foods and care; if such a day comes when we are able to keep these dogs alive medically long enough so that they can be used for breeding, then we will see a large increase in carriers and then in affected puppies, because inevitably some of the dogs will be good at some kind of show or sport competition which their owners will then want to perpetuate.

In a rather interesting aside to the Mega E story, a particular breeder who stringently eliminated hip dysplasia in their breeding stock by making hip dysplasia the most important condition in their breeding decisions actually created a line of dogs in which Mega E became commonplace and exhibited itself in a full range of severity, from mild, though troubling, to fatal. It seems highly unlikely that there can be any link between the hips and the esophagus, but it is instructive that making one single condition a litmus test of breed-ability can go so wrong. Other breeds have faced this same dilemma over different conditions—breeding that stringently excludes one condition by making it an over-riding criteria for breeding seems inevitably to lead to the proliferation of an even more serious condition.

Bloat is a sort-of genetic condition. We create it because of a double bias towards 1) anorexic, 'lean' dogs, with the physical structure that gives us the 'lean' appearance so favored and 2) dogs fueled by adrenaline. Comment: I think it interesting that the emergence of 'bloat' as a killer of dogs follows much the same time- line as the emergence of anorexia as a problem for girls who have been urged by society and parents to diet themselves into unhealthy states in order to obtain approval. Just an aside.

These days, both working-line and show breeders are deliberately selecting dogs that are deep-chested and what the old timers would have called 'slab-sided' over the older style of dog with a more rounded barrel, which in the breed standard is described as 'spring of ribs' and which the standard recommends as correct, desired conformation, but which the pundits of today commonly refer to as looking 'fat'. (And by the way, the people who said that we are stuck with bloat as long as we follow the breed standard are, once again, totally wrong. In no way does the breed standard call for a deep, narrow dog. That perception is just another of the 'consensus' breed standards which have nothing to do with the real one.)

Deep-chested, narrow dogs may meet our aesthetic standards for beauty, but they lack adequate space for their internal organs to expand and contract freely, and this condition affects not only the stomach but the lungs and heart as well. (Wonder if this has any bearing on Cardio???) This affects stamina as well and may be one of the reasons why we consider dogs who can merely trot around a smooth track great athletes today when the dogs of yesteryear followed horses twenty and thirty miles at speed over mountains as a matter of course and jumped/climbed six foot walls in Schutzhund tests in the days before it became a competition.

Now, to artificially restricted internal organs, we add a genetically enhanced adrenaline production. One of adrenaline's many effects is to reduce the flow of blood to the extremities and to flood the internal organs, such as the heart and the lungs, with more of the body's blood, in order to allow the heart to pump faster and the lungs to process more air. Blood flow to the stomach and intestines is usually decreased. So if you have one of those highly adrenalized dogs, whether you have a show-line fear-flight adrenaline addict, or a working-line reactive-fight addict, the result is pretty much the same. Your dog's system gets flooded with adrenaline a lot.

Humans get high-blood pressure and have heart attacks when they're put in the same situations. Dogs apparently get bloat, when the adrenaline is combined with the deep, narrow chest. Studies on this are pretty clear about the deep chest/adrenaline-bloat connection, though the percentages they quote differ from study to study. Is it possible that there is a Cardio connection as well? I know of no studies on the matter but it is a question to ponder.

This brings me to a final comment on the proliferation of Genetic Conditions. While the many generations of line and in- breeding are but bearing the unfortunate fruit of our human egoism and arrogance, it is not the ONLY cause of our current crisis state. Modern medicine has made it possible for us to negate much of Mother Nature's bias towards healthy genetic inheritance. In the past, puppies born with internal organs that didn't develop properly, in a manner which supported a healthy, thriving organism, died. Natural selection thus mitigated against the addition of many unhealthily mutated alleles to the gene pool. Carriers did, of course, continue to exist--at

199

least in cases where carriers were not too adversely affected by the mutated allele they carried.

In our own arrogance and pride, we have refused to accept Mother Nature's dictum in these matters, and with science and medicine and extraordinary measures, we have insisted upon saving, and then breeding animals which should not have lived. We have done this because we arrogantly believed we knew better, because we thought they were prettier, because we hoped (or knew) they would have a particular characteristic or talent we wanted to use, and because in our pride, we simply refused to accept something we perceived to be defeat. Sometimes we did it for money. But the end result has always been, and always will be (until we start playing around with the genes themselves) the proliferation of genetically sick animals. And if we do ever start shifting those genes around, we'll muck things up even worse than we already have. Betcha!

Genetic Conditions List

The first of the worst. Here I'm going to list the stuff in Genetic Conditions which I think are the most important, and in need of the most consideration in making decisions in breeding your dog. I'm going to start with a controversial statement--I believe that people who begin such a list with hip dysplasia are profoundly ignorant, since they are making their litmus test in breeding a condition rated by scientists from a low of 30% ENVIRONMENTALLY CAUSED to a high of 70%!!! Trying to breed out a condition thatisn't even genetic to begin with probably 50% of the time is plain,downright STUPID!

One guide dog breeding program which focused on Hip Dysplasia, making it a litmus test for their breeding stock did manage to drastically reduce the incidence of it (but how much of that was due to the education of their fosters and late-juvenile spay and neuter programs rather than to breeding?) instead winding up with a serious problem with Mega E proliferating in their bloodlines. So now, instead of minor hip problems, they have major, life-threatening esophageal abnormalities in their pups. So. Here's the list.

Cardio Myeopathy. No DNA test. Carriers affected, but live long enough to reproduce. Kills your dog. Exams are inconclusive. Six months after exam clears your dog he may be affected by the condition, and he may be (and probably will be!) dead of it within the year.

Juvenile Renal Disease. There is a DNA test. Carriers can be affected, yet live long enough to reproduce. Kills your dog.

Mega E. No DNA test. Kills your puppy in most cases. If puppy lives, life will be short and relatively miserable. Some puppies lucky enough to have 'minor' versions of this condition do live into and through adulthood, but are always at risk of death by asphyxiation or aspiration pneumonia due to abnormal esophageal formation.

Toxic Gut Syndrome: Exocrine Pancreatic Insufficiency (EPI), Inflammatory Bowel Disease (IBD), and Small Intestine Bacterial Overgrowth (SIBO): These conditions affect how your dog digests food. The dog requires Herculean efforts to sustain life, drugs, special food, food additives, and often special routines in order to stay alive. The dog is often miserable, constant digestive upsets and pain can affect the dog's disposition, making them reactive, aggressive, fearful or all three. The dog's life is usually shortened, and the dog is often not able to function well during that shortened life. These conditions can also lead to joint and bone abnormalities due to mal-absorption of calcium and its related constituents.

Degenerative Myeopathy (DM): There is a DNA test, Carriers are not affected by the condition, and depending on when the Epi-gene fails, the dog may have a long life. (Dogs have been known to live as long as to age 15 with this, so it doesn't always shorten the dog's life, it just usually does.) The condition causes a sort of creeping paralysis, beginning in the dog's tail and moving forward. This has been called canine Multiple Sclerosis. Special diets can sometimes slow the advance of the condition, or at least make the dog more comfortable. At the point at which the paralysis makes it impossible for the dog to stand up, most owners opt for euthanasia.

von Wildebrand's (hemophilia): There is a DNA test for this. Carriers are not affected. Even affecteds are often not affected, at least until the Epi-gene fails, and even if it does, there are now clotting agents which can be used in case of injuries and when surgery is done, such as spaying or neutering. That's the good news. The bad news is, the dog is always in jeopardy. Any unexpected injury, however minor, if not promptly and properly treated, can bring on a bleed out, the dog's joints may very well be painful, and internal organs can fail unexpectedly. Some dogs live to a ripe old age, some dogs die young, and some in middle age.

Pannus: Creeping blindness. There is no DNA test for this. Dogs can be tested for it, but the test only provides a reasonable prognosis for about a year. It often accompanies DM, but not always. Dogs may be affected by this while they are young, but most do not present until early middle age, after they have reproduced (if they are not spayed or neutered.) It MAY shorten the dog's life, but does not always. It certainly impacts the quality of the dog's life.

Peri-Anal Fistulas: (a dog's version of hemorrhoids) No DNA test. This is still fortunately pretty rare. If it was more common, it would be up with EPI, IBD, and SIBO, because it makes the dog miserable. It is very painful, and many people who can't stand seeing their dog in pain opt for euthanasia. It requires extraordinary efforts in monitoring and treatment and special diet. It ruins the quality of the dog's life. Any dog whose anal glands are damaged can develop peri-anal fistulas, and for those removal of the anal glands may eliminate the problem. Whether this constitutes true peri-anal

201

fistulas or not remains an unanswered question. Whatever the case, it might be wise to remember that injuries are never transmissible genetically, but that a pre-disposition to be prone to injury can be.

Bloat: This is a disorder which can hit a dog at any time and kill him and for which there is no DNA test. On the other hand, all you have to look at is a dog's structure and behavior and you can tell whether the dog is likely to have problems with bloat. If your dog is deep-chested, slab-sided and highly adrenalized, get his stomach tacked ASAP. And DON'T breed him. Both the structure and the temperament that tends to bloat are inherited so to that degree, it is genetic. Bloat specifically targets the sport, or working-line dog because of the typical slab-sided deep structure this type of dog commonly exhibits, and the highly adrenalized, reactive, driven temperament bred into the dog for high scores in sport. Show dogs which are also highly adrenalized, reactive/fearful in temperament, and deep-chested, with little spring of ribs are also affected. Dogs with moderate drives and a good spring of ribs, such as mandated by the ACTUAL Breed Standard, seldom suffer from bloat, as both the more even temperament and the additional room inside the rib cage for the dog's internal organs seem to mitigate against it.

Elbow and Hip Dysplasia: No DNA test. Dogs are checked by x-ray. Severe cases do result in pain and loss of function, and extreme cases can result in euthanasia, although for dysplastic hips, total hip replacements are often therapeutic, and dogs can live to ripe old ages after having them. Elbow dysplasia is more problematic because there is, as yet, no total elbow replacement. Joint supplements and pain meds can do great things with both of these conditions. Major causes: spaying and neutering young puppies before the growth plates close, obesity in puppies stemming from over-feeding and/or free feeding, malnutrition--a lack of adequate digestible calcium and its satellite nutrients in the growing puppy's diet, and injuries from extreme play, freak accidents, and pounding on hard surfaces when puppies are still quite young. These can create problems with both hips and elbows. (None of that's actually genetic, though.)

Most dogs with mild to moderate hip or elbow dysplasia can live long and healthy lives and even still function adequately. Many military and police dogs have enjoyed long and usefulcareers with hip dysplasia without exhibiting significant discomfort. And, while we're on the subject of hip dysplasia.

Genetic Conditions: Hip Dysplasia

Let's talk hip dysplasia. It is the big bugaboo of our times, and too many people are blaming breeders for something which is only marginally under their control. (Scientists in the field of canine health disorders estimate that 30% to 70% of hip dysplasia is caused by environmental factors.)

Yes, some hip dysplasia is the fault of breeders who have created crippled dogs with their ill-conceived fashions which they force their dogs to conform to. The German Shepherd bred for show is a perfect case in point. These dogs are no longer able to stand up on their feet because they have been bred for such a grotesque stance and bizarre movement.

A veterinary may be excused (slightly) for seeing dollar signs when a German Shepherd staggers into their waiting room with hind legs stuck out so far behind their body that their feet follow their tails, or with hocks wobbling, their back running downhill and their hind legs on the floor. However, if the first words out of that veterinary's mouth are hip dysplasia, and they have no reasonable grounds for saying it (like clear, readable x-rays) it is sheer laziness on their part to make such a diagnosis--if it isn't something worse.

The truth is that hip dysplasia is a condition caused not merely by poor breeding, but even more often by inadequate or over- abundant nutrition, by early spaying and neutering which interferes with the normal growth cycle, and by injuries. Large dogs suffer the most from the condition because they have much higher nutritional needs in puppyhood than smaller dogs, and a much longer puppyhood in which to need that nutrition. Also, they suffer far more from early spaying and neutering because their growth cycle often extends even beyond their second year. Many large dogs actually grow half an inch to a full inch between their second and third birthdays—thus ensuring that if they are spayed or neutered before that point, they WILL suffer from hip dysplasia

All the breeder of your dog can do is to have their dogs certified free of hip dysplasia before they breed them and then feed the female and the puppies properly while they have them. The rest is up to you. Experiments done with dysplastic parents and non-dysplastic parents have proven that nutrition is crucial to the correct development of the puppies' joints. Large puppies who will become large dogs require large amounts of calcium, carefully balanced with phosphorus, vitamin D, magnesium, all the B vitamins, and vitamin C and E, with a wide range of minerals in a form that they can digest.

Your puppy cannot use calcium which is no more nor better than ground up rocks, and calcium requires fats in order to be soluble in your puppy's digestive tract. Milk solids and fats do the job best. If you're feeding your puppy fat free yogurt or no fat cottage cheese, because you've got some kind of prejudice against milk, or are pathological about cholesterol, get over it. You're wasting your money and depriving your puppy. If you are depriving your puppy of adequate nutrition because of some philosophical rant you are on regarding animal foods, forget it. Dogs are carnivores, and they are meant to drink milk and eat meat.

Fat puppies who stress their joints and hips with excess poundage are no exception. Free feeding puppies leads to fat, dysplastic puppies. Remember, kibble is just the beginning, a foundation upon which to build. Add goats' milk, if you can get it, cow's milk, if you can't, and none of that skim stuff, either. Two percent or whole, at least. Cottage cheese is good, if it's the real deal, made with cream, and boiled eggs are great. (Some dogs have difficulties digesting raw eggs, like bloodhounds, and all dogs digest egg white better if it has been boiled. Not to mention that in this day and age, salmonella and e coli are a problem with raw eggs.)

For those who want to feed a 'raw' diet, places like Honest Kitchen provide a steamed dehydrated 'raw' diet which provides all the perks of the raw diet without the fear of salmonella and e coli and can be added to kibble. Or, small amounts of ground beef or chicken or lamb can be added to your pup's diet (NO COOKED BONES!) but pork is usually not a good idea. Don't make abrupt changes in your puppy's menu if you can help it--for many puppies menu changes result in 'accidents' in the house due to upset stomachs.

Stress injuries--you just had to throw that Frisbee one more time, didn't you? And then there was that time you went jogging in the park and your puppy came back lame because your run was just too much for his growing muscles and ligaments. Or what about the time you--but then the vet said the dread words, hip dysplasia, and you thought--it's all the breeder's fault! Sorry Charley. If your pup really does have hip dysplasia, it's three chances out of five that you, you and only you, are responsible.

But--is that vet right? Did he take x-rays before uttering the dread words? If he did, get a second opinion. Send those x-rays to Penn hips or the Orthopedic Foundation for Animals (OFA). And even if he does turn out to be displastic, there are all sorts of vitamins and minerals out there on the market which can make your pet more comfortable without that big bucks hip replacement the vet is touting.

Hip dysplasia doesn't have to be crippling, nor does it have to mean major surgery. You might have to ditch the Frisbee, but that doesn't mean your dog can't chase a tennis ball (don't allow him to keep the ball, as many dogs tear the balls up and then eat the pieces, causing serious blockages in the gut requiring surgery) as long as you don't pretend to be Nolan Ryan and you don't try to pitch nine innings to him. Keep him warm in the winter, give him regular, mild exercise, keep his weight down to a reasonable level (he doesn't have to be anorexic!) and get some of those over the counter supplements to give him some relief when he's sore. A good dog bed might help--orthopedic dog beds are available from dog supply houses (if he doesn't sleep in yours) and all sorts of dog bed warmers are available as well.

Bottom line, there are worse diagnoses for your pet dog than hip dysplasia. With moderation in all things, he may live long and enjoy life with you for many good years to come.

Genetic Conditions: Cancer

A long time ago, in the area in which I live, there was once a chemical plant. In order to make more money, the folks who owned the plant refused employee demands to repair, maintain and replace old, worn and defective machinery. One morning, quite early, some crucial part in the worn, old machinery failed. The result was a chain reaction that resulted in a huge explosion. What few people who had arrived at work early that morning were killed. A huge mushroom shaped cloud of chemicals blossomed over much of the land, moving south and east. Most of the land over which the cloud dropped its lethal load of chemicals was agricultural. A flood of stillbirths, miscarriages and bizarre birth defects among both humans and animals followed in its wake for years.

The owners of the plant were found liable and ordered to pay out money to the families of the workers who were killed and to compensate the farmers and the ranchers for the contamination of their land. The owners of the chemical plant paid out token amounts and then declared bankruptcy and decamped.

Time went on. The rains came and went. The frequency and severity of birth defects and stillbirths and miscarriages declined, although they still happened much more frequently in that area than in healthier places. The people who lived in the area died of health ailments or moved away, if they could afford to. Eventually, the land was sold to developers or broken up into smaller farms and ranches and a few suburban developments. An elementary school now sits right in the middle of the contaminated area.

Today, almost no one remembers either the chemical plant or the explosion and no one seems to know why people who live in that area have more cancer than other places or why it is hard to 'settle' cattle and sheep moms, or why lambs and calves never seem to be quite as healthy in those areas as they ought to be. The people who live there now will never get any restitution from the chemical plant folks, since those responsible are all dead and their wealthy children and grandchildren are all grown up and feel no responsibility for what their parents and grand- parents did to give them their wealth. The people who live there now can't afford, in most cases, to sell out and move away—and who is to say that the place they might move to would be any healthier? Or would it be just another place where no one remembers.

In the 1940s, '50s, and '60s, that same process was repeated over and over again all over this country. I have no doubt it is still going on—the very wealthy are just better at hiding what they are doing now. At least in the earlier years we did not really know what we were doing. These days, unless someone does the research to chart all the health problems of a group of people living in any particular area, we don't even know if they are a 'cancer cluster.' Unless someone keeps track, it is just something that happens, 'just life'. And that is what it is.

We are all the product of our DNA, which pretty much all of us know, these days. Our DNA (and our dogs') is contained in chromosomal strings of genetic material which are sometimes referred to as a 'double helix'. If these double helix straightened out, they would be very long and would resemble a ladder somewhat, with two long bars parallel to each other with

205

rungs between them at regular intervals. These rungs contain what is called an'epi-gene'. This 'epi- gene' is basically a toggle switch that turns 'on' and 'off'.

When people are referring to the 'genetic' component of cancer, this is what they are often unknowingly referring to. And while we do know families in which cancer seems to strike every generation, it is still an open question as to how much of that is encoded in our DNA and how much is the result of shared environment. Families tend to live in the same areas, eat the same foods, participate in the same activities and even share many of the same habits. This is not DNA, people, this is environment. When families of dogs seem to be sharing cancer, people who want to avoid cancer for their dogs would do much better looking to their dog's environment than to their dogs' families. Or if they do look at the other dogs in their dogs' family, they would do well to look at the kind of environment with which those dogs are surrounded.

Most of us organisms, people, dogs, cats, horses all, are born (when we are born healthy) with all our epi-genes firmly positioned in the off position. Then 'environment' happens to us. (Or sometimes it happens to our mothers or our fathers!) And somewhere down the line for us, we get so many environmental toxins dumped on us and into us that one or more of our epi-genes fail and then we get (among other things) cancer. What we get depends upon what epi-gene fails and that depends, in large part, on the admixture and amounts of toxins we get bombarded with.

If cancer treatment succeeds in stopping the cancer and allows the dog or the person to heal and live cancer free, they are said to be in 'remission'. What has happened is that something, the chemo, the diet, the therapy, whatever, has somehow managed to toggle our epi-gene back into the 'off' position. That is what chemo is intended to do.

Dogs are sort of the canaries in the mines of our environments. Stuff shows up in them a lot sooner than it does in us.

Studies are telling us a lot about the things that cause cancer in our dogs, but we need a lot more of them. So far, we have learned that one very common cause of cancer is the spaying and neutering of puppies when they are young and their growth plates are not yet closed. Another is the overuse of vaccinations, and the third biggie is pesticides.

When it comes to spaying and neutering, we are caught between the cleft stick of not wanting to expose our young females to all the dangers of getting lose when in heat (and remember, pregnancy is just one of those dangers!) many of which are life threatening and wanting them to get their full growth before they are spayed or neutered. Male pups are easier because it is easier to keep them safe while they grow, but they are slower to mature and it takes longer for their growth plates to close. The answer for males, delaying neutering until the dog is fully grown, i s easier.

The choice for females is a lot tougher. Some people can keep their female pups safe through their first heat cycles without too great hardship; for others, it is impossible. And, some female pups are a lot more difficult to keep safe than others. The decision of when and whether to spay has to remain completely individual. For some, spaying at 6 months despite the risk of cancer is just the right choice. A female pup who goes out and contracts parvo, or brucellosis, or is hit by a car and dies from it or has her health irretrievably compromised by whelping an early litter when she is just too young would have been better off spayed at 6 months. If she contracts pyrometra, the likelihood is that it will kill her and she would have been better off spayed. And a young female having her first litter of pups (the equivalent of a human girl having a baby at the age of 12) is far more likely to die during whelping or of complications afterwards than an older, healthier, stronger adult female would be. She is also far more likely to wind up with anal fistulas, which are a true misery and which cause many owners to opt for euthanasia because they can't stand their dog's pain. And spaying a pregnant female is a far more complex surgery, with many more possible complications, than a simple pediatric spay. Statistics may tell us that the unspayed or late spayed female lives an average 2 years longer than the early spayed girl, but if she doesn't live to get to that additional 2 years, what's the point?

Both male and female pups who are spayed or neutered before their growth plates close have a far greater rate of cancers, hermangiosarcoma, lymphosarcoma, and mast cell tumors in particular. Males neutered young are prey to the additional cancers of osteosarcoma and prostate cancer. The only cancers which occur with any frequency to intact males and females are testicular and mammary cancers, but the rates for these cancers for intact dogs are much lower than the rates for the cancers spayed and neutered dogs are prone to.

When it comes to vaccinations, this is one of those situations where a little is very, very good but too much of a good thing can do a lot of harm. Puppies need vaccinations for things like parvo-virus and distemper and rabies—though rabies shouldn't be given before 6 months and after the first one year booster not given more than every three years afterwards—and we should be very cautious with other vaccinations. Some vaccinations, like rabies, the snake bite and leptospirosis vaccinations have some very bad side effects and the lepto vaccination can actually do more damage than the goup of diseases it protects against.

We know now that after the early vaccinations, and except for the regular rabies vac, dogs should be 'titered' –that's when the vet checks the dog for immunities instead of just blanket vaccinating and only given additional vaccinations when needed. It is a more expensive proceedure, but it is far better for the dog. If your vet has questions about this protocol, you can refer them to Dr. Jean Dodd's new vaccination protocol. Studies show us that dogs which are 'regularly' vaccinated have a 4 to 6 times greater likelihood of developing hermangiosarcoma, lyphosarcoma, and mast cell tumors than dogs who are sparingly vaccinated.

Next up, we have pesticides. Pesticides are KNOWN carcinogens. Studies implicate just about every pesticide there is, and flea and tick preventatives are among them, along with heart worm toxins.

The problem is that we are inundated with pesticides these days. It isn't just what we put on the dogs, it is the pesticides in the air, in our foods, in the ground, in our water. They can very quickly reach a point of saturation that is dangerous for everyone.

Some pesticides we can eliminate. We can stop using those spot-on products and get rid of the heart worm poisons, at least in places where heart worm is not a scourge. (Here we are, back to decisions about whether we want our dog to die now, or die later. And again, this is an individual decision that depends on each person's and their dog's individual circumstances.) But what do we use in their place?

This is where you start investigating holistic and organic products. For some people in some situations, these products work very well, even better, in some cases, than the pesticides. In other locales, you may never be able to completely divorce yourself or your dog from those pesticides. But then, when your dog is diagnosed with hermangiosarcoma or you start finding lumps, you need to own up to that pesticide you use and make your peace with your choices. At a certain point, it starts to become a race between what you fear the most—heart worm or lyme's disease, or cancer. If you choose to use a pesticide, well, maybe you can make a trade off with other risk factors and achieve a balance of sorts.

Watch the kind of kibble you feed (if you feed kibble). Look at the ingredients for things like corn and blueberries and take note of where your kibble is processed. Both corn and blueberries are found in a variety of kibbles. Corn, in the United States, that is commercially grown (the kind used in kibbles) has been genetically engineered to make its own pesticide, so that it is embedded in the very kernal of the corn as well as the stalks, leaves and silk. When you or your dog eat commercial corn, you're eating pesticides. Not too good for your health. Also, blueberries, which by themselves are powerful anti-oxidents, unfortunately, when commerically grown, are almost uniformlysprayed with pesticides, which blueberries absorb, making them from the little anti-poison pills they are when organically grown, into little poison pills when grown by most commercial concerns.

As for kibbles processed by the Chinese, they've been adding toxins to just about everything they make for years, and dogs have died from the stuff they added to dog kibble to boost the protein content so they could raise the price. Even if you feed raw, these days you have to watch where you get it because the US has just decided to allow the Chinese who poisoned our dogs' and cats' kibble and treats to process and package chicken for people to eat. Apparently somebody decided that there's a lot of money to be made doing this and who cares how many of us the Chinese poison as long as the rich can get richer?

And lastly, without becoming one of those extremist wack-jobs, do try to avoid plastics when you can. Plastics are another KNOWN carcinogen. We can't do much about the plastics that get into the air and soil and ground water. We can, however, keep our own and our dogs' food and water in containers that don't contain plastics. Glass, porcelain and containers free of plastics will be heavier and more fragile, but safer.

In the end, all we can do is to try to minimise how much contamination we are knowingly exposed to and by avoiding actions that disrupt our dogs' immune systems and their hormonal balances. (The point is to be reasonable about it.) We can choose to eat organically and healthily and feed our dogs the same way, using more home/locally grown foods that haven't been irradiated, covered with chemicals or carted all over the world while exposed to who knows what, as much as possible. We can delay spaying and neutering our dogs until their growth plates close, we can vaccinate them moderately and with care, and we can eliminate or at least be more moderate in our use of pesticides. The thing is to be reasonable, moderate, yet mindful, do what we can and then just keep on keeping on. It is all we can really do.

Part V:
The History of the German Shepherd Dog

Beouwulf Rüde

Chapter 8
Origins

Luchs (Sparwasser)

Origins: The 'Old Breed' Swabian, Saxony and Brunswick Herding Dogs

In 1871 German was unified as a single national entity for the first time in its history. Within a decade, people started talking about unifying the various regional types of dogs into one national German dog. Each region (of course) favored their ancestral breed. Some of those breeds had already been around for a very, very long time. The 'Old Breed' also called the 'Old Blood' herding dogs are very ancient. Stephanitz found written records going back eight hundred years when he was researching the origins of these dogs (that would be nine hundred years now) and Master Herder Manfred Heyne indicated that the oral tradition of the shepherds holds that these dogs have been around for a thousand years. The 'Yard' dogs of Thuringia were also an old breed, with written records going back five hundred years at the time Stephanitz researched them (or six hundred years today!). The Northern dogs, whether the 'wolf' dogs or the herding dogs, were less well recorded, but they had been around a while, too.

The 'Old Breed' included two basic types of shepherd dog, those from the Swabian Alps, the Jura Mountains and the Black Forest—Swabia covered an area from lower Bavaria to today's Westphalia, part of which it included, and the dogs from the river valleys of Saxony and Brunswick. (Swabia was the medieval name for what is now Wurttemberg as well as the larger area around modern Wurttemberg—in 1806 it was re-named Wurttemberg after the counts of Wurttemberg were elevated to the rank of prince. The effects of two World Wars since have caused the area to become much smaller than it originally was. The terms Swabian and Wurttemberg both refer to the same dog.) There are some distinct differences in the two types of herding dog in this group—the dogs of Saxony and Brunswick were smaller and more aggressive, handling large numbers of sheep but only sheep, while the mountain dogs of Swabia were larger and more flexible in their ability to handle stock because they handled just about everything.

Thuringian dogs were watch dogs and poacher(man)hunters who primarily did their hunting at night. Thuringian dogs were NOT herding dogs. There was, in fact, considerable controversy surrounding their inclusion in the new breed because of that fact.

Northern breed dogs at least included herding dogs along with their fancy 'wolf' dogs, dogs like the great white dog, Greif, an outstanding herding dog and sire of good herding dogs. Thuringian dogs were small, 'insolent' to use Stephanitz' description, fear-aggressive biters roundly disliked by people who made their livelihoods working with dogs and livestock. Perhaps unfortunately, Thuringian dogs had the pretty face and 'prick' ears most people wanted for their national breed.

Two generations of people inveighed against Thuringian blood being a part of the new breed, but they were rowing against the tide. Well known kennels like Hanau were already using a little Thuringian blood on their Swabians to get that 'touch of class' or at least the 'prick' ears on their dogs.

The Phylax Society was formed, their name taken from their flagship dog, Phylax v Elau, of the Northern breed. Phylax was noted for his strong wolf-like appearance. His hind legs were rather stiff and upright, and his head and face were pronouncedly wolf-like. Herding people were not at all sanguine about his temperament. Some people were tremendously drawn to his aquiline appearance, while others were not so impressed with him. The Northern Breed's inclusion in the new breed was anything but secure. Then someone decided to exhibit a big, white Northern herding dog named Greif.

Greif was not only an outstanding herding dog himself, and a producer of good herding dogs, but he had a somewhat angulated hock and very nice movement. He also had good, upright ears and a rather attractive head and face. A lot of people who had been on the fence about the Northern breed decided, well, all right, if Greif was a good example of what at least some Northern dogs were like, then ok, they should be included.

Schafermadchen, a mottled grey, black and tan working shepherd dog of Saxony, was offered, along with two of her sisters, for exhibition as an example of Saxony herding dogs. Newspaper photos of the time show us that Schafermadchen looked rather like today's Australian Cattle dog. Complaints were heard that she was too small to herd anything but geese, but nobody suggested that Saxony or Brunswick dogs not be included in the new breed.

The Phylax Society foundered, but it wasn't long before the indefatigable Captain Max v Stephanitz had taken up the standard and moved forward into the fray. The truth was, however, that for the rest of the world, a German 'Shepherd' dog already existed.

In 1898, a dog story titled 'Bob, Son of Battle' written by Alfred Ollivant, was published. (Remember, the SV wasn't even formed until 1899 and the German Shepherd Dog wasn't even a recognized breed in Germany yet. Horand v Grafath was alive, but he was still known as Hektor Linkstrom, as he and the Captain hadn't gotten together yet, when Ollivant was writing his story, never mind becoming German Shepherd dog number one in the newly formed SV. And yet, in this the-Scots-collie-is-too-the-best-sheep-dog book, in which the crux of the story is the titanic battle of two supreme sheep herding dogs, each of which has won the local perpetual trophy twice and the one who wins it the third time will retire it for all time, Bob's competitor is a 'German' shepherd dog.

What? A German shepherd dog in Great Britain before the breed was even invented? A dog well enough known outside of Germany, and all the way to England, Wales and Scotland, to serve as the epitome of herding dog excellence for the home grown dog to beat?

Well, he was a 'big' 'red' dog, 'half-again' the size of 'oulde Bob' who was described as 26" and 60-65 pounds. So, maybe 28 or 9 inches at the shoulders and possibly 90 to 100 pounds, allowing for some hyperbole on the part of the author. What 'German' dogs did the author use as his prototypes for his character? Were they from the Krone kennels? Hanau? Or maybe it was a Brenztal dog. Could have been. Both Hanau and Krone kennels were well established long before Stephanitz ever dreamed of the German Shepherd dog. But since he was 'big' one thing was certain, Ollivant clearly intended his big red dog to be the embodiment of a herding dog from Swabia/Wurttemberg, and he equally clearly expected his audience to know the dogs he referred to.

It is impossible to understand the characteristics of the Swabian /Wurttemberger Dog without understanding the people and the land from which they originated. The Swabian Shepherd dog is a very old breed of dog dating back centuries. Stephanitz found written records going back eight hundred years--a hundred years ago. Master Shepherd Heyne spoke of an oral tradition among the shepherds with whom he grew up and worked with which indicated that the dogs had been around for over a thousand years.

The Swabian dog is the sheep, goat, cattle, geese and ducks and horse herding dog of the Celts. They even handled pigs upon occasion. They did this, not in the open grasslands of the river valleys, but in the Jura mountains and the Northern Alps and the Black Forest, some of the harshest and most rugged land, not just in Germany, but in all of Europe itself. They lived in a land that until the middle of the nineteenth century abounded in predatory wolves and bear and even mountain cats.

Food was scarce and hard come by, and winters were long and hard. Life was neither easy nor simple; to be lived at all it had to be lived within a balance and harmony with the seasons, the terrain, and with other people. The Swabian dog was forged in a world where people lived in tightly knit communities that worked together to survive. In these communities the wealthy were not pitted against the poor; there were few, if any filthy rich, and few people who were disenfranchised or grindingly poor.

The Celtic people are a very ancient race. They had already settled Europe when the Greeks built Athens, and they were there when Rome rose on the seven hills. When the Romans came to Great Britain, the Welsh Celts formed alliances with them rather than being overrun by them. Later, in the sixth century, despite the death of half their population from the bubonic plague, Welsh Celts still managed to hold off both Vikings and Saxons. They were the people from which the Arthurian Legend was forged.

The Scots, Pictish Celts, fought the Romans off and held them off with such fierce determination that the Emperor Hadrian built a great wall and posted sentries and armed camps along that wall to defend themselves against them. It was not until the Hanoverian Butcher of Culloden massacred them in 1745, bringing men armed with muskets and artillery and heavy cavalry against their light infantry and claymores, that they were finally defeated.

No one ever conquered the Swabian Celts. The Romans might have said that they never bothered to try and maybe they would have been right. They conquered the Gauls and that pretty much backfired on them. They did take Celtic slaves, when they could get by with it, but that was mostly when they could find a few isolated travelers to take as prisoners. Taking on a group of Celts was something they usually chose not to do. It appears such actions would have been roughly akin to taking a stick to a hornets nest.

The Celts on the other hand, weren't in the business of conquering people. They moved into wild, often thickly forested, sometimes mountainous areas where few people had settled before them and then stayed to make these previously unsettled and harsh, difficult lands their own, simply absorbing any people they found there ahead of them into their own communities. They were the original live and let live people, usually hospitable to travelers but fierce and even savage in their own defense. And that's exactly the way they liked their dogs.

In the mountains of Swabia, permanent winter homes were built to accommodate both livestock and people in a single dwelling to maximize the use of heat and to make it possible to keep stock fed in deep snow conditions. Sometimes the animals occupied the 'ground' floor and the people the floor above, in other arrangements the livestock had one side of the dwelling while the people had the other. Dogs lived in these homes with both people and livestock.

Swabian dogs were expected to deal with the Celts' unusually large sheep, they were expected to deal with goats, cattle, horses, pigs, geese, ducks, and children, all with amity and care. They had to be born with great flexibility of mind so that they could shift quickly and even instinctively between the attitudes and actions necessary to handle such disparate groups of stock. Loose but firm pressure on the horses, tighter, firmer pressure on the cattle, tighter still but much more gentle pressure on the ewes, combined with a willingness to tangle with a ram if he made it necessary, the good Swabian shifted from direction to threat to outright intimidation and back again in the blink of an eye. Automatically changing his body language, even the expression on his face and the look in his eye with no more than the turn of his head, the Swabian's daily routine required him to run a whole gamut of behaviors in response to the stock he was directing and defending.

In spring, the still vigorous older adults took the middling children, not old enough to work in the fields yet, but too old for the aged adults to care for, up to the ancestral summer pastures with them and the dogs, even young pups, went with them. Just as the children learned from their elders, the pups learned from older, mentor dogs. Dogs commonly lived and worked twelve to fifteen and sixteen years, and during that time, middling children grew into young adults who stayed home to work the fields and older adults grew too old to make the trip. Their places were taken by younger adults and children and

218

the dogs had to adjust to new people to work with. Whenever possible, several families made the majority of the journey together, separating only at the end of the trip to travel to their particular pastures. Dogs had to work with the neighbors' dogs and along with the neighbors themselves. Dog aggressive, people aggressive, reactive dogs didn't make the cut.

Swabians had to take on wolves one on one and sometimes even one against two. They had to go up against bears not as a sport, but as a necessity for the survival of their family. They were the only realistic defense their people and livestock had against such predators, when you stop to realize that for most of the dogs' millennia people were armed only with bows and arrows, slings and javelins. Guns were a relatively modern invention which most Celts couldn't have afforded even when they did exist. The dogs did it and they did it well. If they hadn't, neither their people nor their livestock charges would have survived. Because you must remember, that if the mountain cats were seldom seen by 1800 and the wolves pretty much gone by 1850 and the bear by 1900, the dogs were there 800 years before those dates, and more, and for all of those 800 years they did have to cope with them.

On the other hand, they didn't go looking for trouble. It wasn't their job to hunt wolves down, something the Celts didn't often bother to do. Their job was to protect their charges, kids, the elderly, sheep, cattle, ducks and geese, goats and horses, and to keep them together and on the appropriate pasture. They dealt with the wolves in whatever way the wolves made necessary when the wolves came to them.

In the fall, when the harvest was in did some dogs hunt birds and deer for their people to bring down for the table? Sure they did. They had noses, and good ones, noses used to find that bunch-quitting old cow who wandered off to have her calf, the neighbor's straying mare, another neighbor's runaway goat. They used those noses to locate lost children. Being willing, even eager, to track whatever and whoever their person wanted them to track and then sticking to that track, whatever adversity they came up against, were qualities the Celts required in their dogs--any lack in the dogs meant certain death for either livestock or child.

Strong genetic obedience meant survival, not only of the dog, but of the dog's family. I'm not sure the word necessity is strong enough to express how important it was. If there is anything beyond necessity, that is what genetic obedience was to the people of Swabia. Dogs were sent out with young boys and girls (pre-teens and young teens) to look after the stock because the adult men and women were needed to bring in the crops and preserve and store them for the winter. The dogs had to take responsibility if everyone was to survive and they had to have self-discipline and even restraint in dealing with the younger kids who didn't yet know what to do or how to do it and stock who were sometimes contrary and sometimes just generally out of sorts.

Everybody, kids and dogs alike learned on the job; the price of not learning on the job was injury and death for one or all of them. Every heard the phrase 'failure is not an option'? Both kids and pups learned from the older dogs and kids, mostly by observation, or else. And or else tended to be pretty extreme. Imagine a kid who messed up having to watch his entire family die. Don't think it didn't happen. It did, and more often than we'd like to contemplate.

Swabian dogs were either resilient or dead. Resilience was not something anyone paid any attention to unless it wasn't present. A dog lacking resilience couldn't stand up to the rigors of life in the mountains, but, like everything else, had to exist in balance. The dog who didn't quit when told to had better have a pretty good reason or they wouldn't last.

Swabian dogs did not have an over-abundance of prey drive. A dog's prey drive was either sharply modified to serve herding aims or the dog died. Dogs who harried or killed stock were in their turn killed, and quickly. Good stockmen don't tolerate dogs who are hard on stock because they can't afford to tolerate them. Bites mean infections, lost calves and lambs and in the age before penicillin and lockjaw vaccinations, could be a death sentence, for man or beast. Bites mean lame animals with torn ligaments and tendons and broken bones. Bites mean wool ripped and torn so that it can't be spun into thread or woven into cloth. Ruined wool means fleece that can't be sold, so you can't get the money you need to buy what you can't produce. It means going hungry or cold or just without.

In the kind of society the Celts lived in, if you didn't kill the dog with too much prey drive, or prey drive without sharp enough limits, then your neighbors would kill the dog for you. They might be very unhappy with you for forcing them to do it, but they would do it. It was merely considered a person's civic duty to kill a dog that bit either children or livestock.

Dogs that didn't learn quickly, while still young, to keep their teeth in their mouths did not live to grow up. Dogs had to learn to handle stock more with moral authority than with their teeth in order to get into the gene pool. High bite thresholds were a necessity and dogs that bit people and worse, livestock, simply were not tolerated.

Because Swabian dogs were often outside working in all weather in the mountains and some of the most difficult and cold conditions in Germany, Swabian dogs tended to be heavily coated. The long-stock and stock coat come from the Swabians, the coats deep and heavily doubled, with both outer and undercoat strongly water resistant.

Swabian dogs come in all colors, as long as they were predominantly light or variegated, white and grey and tan (blue) and red and tan (liver) were commonplace, and 'wolf' grey sable and grey and tan predominated. They were light-colored, white and grey because the summer sunlight at high elevation can be harsh, and sun off snow in the winter can be even harsher.

220

Light colored dogs can work in such conditions long after dark colored dogs would either quit or suffer heat exhaustion. (Think of other Alpine and mountain sheepherding/guarding dogs—the Pyrenees Sheepdog and Great Pyrenees, the Greek Tatra, the Hungarian Kuvasz, and the Italian Maremma, all of whom have a light/white base color.)

The variety of colors welcomed in these old breeds provided a rich source of genetic diversity which kept the Swabian breed strong and healthy over a thousand years, in contrast to most modern breeds, which humans have managed to ruin in a mere hundred years--or less. The Swabian people did not discriminate against colors, believing that any good working dog was a good 'color' but dark colored dogs would not have held up under harsh daytime working conditions so would be very uncommon.

Swabian dogs were big dogs, their size and bone an evolutionary necessity for the conservation of heat in cold climes, males running from 26" to 29" most of the time, with ample substance, but dogs could be either bigger or smaller and as long as they could work, were considered just fine. They tended to large, broad, rounded heads, with strong muzzles, which some people considered 'plain'. Their ears sometimes 'tulip' or wavered a little at the tip. Some of the variation in their ears was from the bumps and bangs inevitably suffered by dogs who worked for a living, and Stephanitz even commented upon this in his book. Some of the looseness was caused by a little softness in the ear cartilage. 'Prick' ears were considered, among those people who actually worked for a living, the ultimate in insignificance, completely unimportant in their scheme of things.

And while some dogs tended to be tall, leggy and lanky (and some Swabian dogs who did police work were later called Swabian Service dogs) most were compact, powerful, and heavy boned. They had to be for any number of reasons having to do with the stock they tended, sheep literally double the size of most of the rest of sheep in, not only Germany but Europe, and cattle, horses, and geese as well as goats and pigs. They were big because they had to match up against mountain wolves. They were big because they had to stand between their livestock and bears.

And they were big because they lived in the mountains. If you look at mountain wolves and coyotes, you will find that they are almost always larger than the wolves and coyotes of the prairies and the river valleys, and often double the size of those from the desert. Whether it is to withstand cold, or the terrain they have to travel, or something else, the mountains breed bigger, whether it is animals or men. It is simple natural selection at work.

Big Swabians worked all day every day. They took a workman-like manner to their jobs; they were professionals. The modern penchant for dogs that dance around, all happy-happy, with zest and verve and DRIVE would have been considered idiots and probably found worthless by people who worked stock for a living. These dogs waste energy and effort burning off the calories in the food they eat with extravagant profligacy. Since every bite of food a dog ate was food not available for the children of the family, the less wasteful a dog was of energy, the less food he would have to consume to work, making the profligate bouncy-bouncy, happy-happy dog with his high caloric needs an anathema.

A dog was expected to be serious about what he was doing, to take a measured, stable, balanced attitude towards their work, and expected to get the job done despite adversity. Dogs worked in rain and snow, in cold and wind, tracking and herding as necessary so that everyone could eat. A stoic attitude was virtually required. They tolerated discomfort and even pain to get the job done. They learned quickly to put out as little energy as possible to get each specific task done so there will be enough energy left to keep working at the end of the day, and tomorrow, and tomorrow after that. Call it either natural or artificial selection, Swabian dogs were selected for those qualities for a millennia. That practical working, common-sense attitude is characteristic of the Swabian as is the stoicism that carries a dog through when the job isn't fun, or easy, or a game.

The unreasoning prejudice among some German Shepherd people today and their assertions that big dogs can't work is just that, unreasoning prejudice. All the history of the Swabian breed, and more than a thousand years of it at that, makes those who espouse this modern cant, ignorant at least. Poorly structured big dogs, fat big dogs, and big dogs who have never had to work and therefore are not conditioned to work may not do well. Little dogs in the same circumstances would probably not do any better.

Conservation of energy meant that big dogs were able to survive and work on minimal amounts of food. The small, eager, zesty, drive-y dog burns more calories to stay warm and more calories when they work because of their profligate energy use, and that means they must consume more calories. In today's modern world that doesn't mean much. In a day when feeding the dog meant food taken from your children's mouths, dogs that required more calories to work than the dog who used less calories to do the same or a better job meant hungry children. Spread that survival strategy over a thousand years and you get the Swabian, using just enough energy to get the job done and not a smidgen the more, thus not only getting the job done but keeping the kids fed as well. If that's dull or boring, well, sobeit.

Today, when buying kibble is easy, we don't value energy conservation, unfortunately. People today want Whee! dogs, running around, jumping around and generally spewing energy everywhere with profligacy. Such dogs are appealing, attractive. Serious dogs are out of favor, and the Swabians with them. Too bad.

The 'Old Breed' Shepherd dogs of Saxony and Brunswick were significantly different from those of Swabia for a wide variety of reasons, beginning with the people. The rootstock of the people who lived in the rich river valleys of Central Germany was largely Saxon, and the Saxon were very different people from the Celts. Far from egalitarian, they considered all people but a small ruling class to be vassals. People who didn't belong to the rigid hierarchy of the ruling class existed on the same legal plane as the livestock they tended. When land was bought and sold among Saxon landowners, people were bought and sold with it just like their livestock. What few 'freemen' there were congregated, first in villages, and then in cities, having become tradesmen and artisans. This put dogs in a very different position.

Here, they were no longer contributing family members with their own responsibilities and their own place, they were vassal companions to their fellow slaves. Ok, by 1900 they were not 'owned' along with the land any longer—that status had begun to change in the eighteenth century, but again, the weight of centuries of tradition should not be ignored. For these dogs, the common goal was survival for themselves and their partners in the keeping of the flocks which were the means of their survival. This was one or two dogs and one person, usually a man, but not always, tightly bonded to each other for the lifetime of the dog, struggling together to keep the flocks. In order to manage the keeping of these huge flocks, both dogs and people had to be completely dedicated to the task. It was not an easy one.

Swabian peoples, even when they moved into cities and abandoned their semi-nomadic lifestyle, were noted for their devotion to their dogs. Indeed, it was said of the people of the city of Wurttemberg that they were 'dog-dotty'. Herding dogs in Central Germany tended to share the status of their sheep herding handlers and that was not a high one. The humans in these situations did not often possess much in the way of worldly status or possessions; they were not all that far removed from the vassals they had been.

The lush river valleys of Saxony and Brunswick were pretty much always devoted to croplands, with grazing land relegated to the margins of the fields, woods and orchards, village commons and the stubble-fields after harvest. At the beginning of the nineteenth century, the large landowners started taking over the village commons, 'enclosing' them and squeezing the small-holders out. Herds of sheep in the river valleys had always tended to large numbers, but now those numbers grew even larger as the land the sheep were allowed to graze grew even more marginal. Profit was to be found in a high turnover of animals and in the sale of fleece.

By the turn of the twentieth century, in Britain, an undamaged ewe's fleece might bring as much as three shillings. It would take 20 shillings to make a pound and a hundred pounds at the least to keep a roof over a person's head and food in their belly and in the belly of a dog. That translates to the fleece of seven hundred sheep to support one shepherd and their dog. The price of whatever meat the sheep provided would have to pay the rest of the expenses, taxes and rents on the grazing land that supported the sheep and the profit necessary for the support of the sheep owner. The ratio in Germany would have been very similar. By 1900 it was commonplace for the Saxony and Brunswick herding dogs to handle flocks numbering from 600 animals to 1000.

The pressure on the dogs and the men herding those vast numbers of animals was intense. The penalties for the destruction of crops in a world in which crop insurance didn't exist and government subsidies didn't either could be catastrophic. Sheepherders had to pay, not only for any damage any sheep did to any crops out of their pitiful wages, they also had to pay the value of the sheep to the owner of the flock for any injury their dog did to the sheep. The price of a sheep might be a month's pay. The price of a field of corn might take years to pay off. Dogs and men alike had to walk a very fine line between those two realities. It took very tough men and very tough dogs to do it.

It might not be as bitterly cold in the river valleys as it was in the mountains, but it was still cold, it still snowed, and here it rained as well, which was quite possibly worse, when dogs and people had to work a full day out in the elements. Hungry sheep were no respecters of wet and cold; they still had to eat. That was survival for them.

Six hundred sheep had to keep moving; no single area could support a flock that size for long. Generally speaking, an acre of ground that bears well may keep three or four sheep for a year. If one has not more than a hundred acres all in one place to dedicate to keep sheep, and one is trying to keep a flock of six hundred or more, the sheep will have to move constantly from one smaller area to another. Sheep moving along the verges between the roads and the fields grazed as they moved in order to scrounge every possible twig and blade of grass.

The area through which the flock moved would not be fenced. No barrier protected the fields from the sheep or the sheep from the carriages, wagons and horsemen on the road. At least, no barrier but the dog's body and the dog's will.

Consider the dog's situation. Biting the sheep, which would result in the shepherd losing a huge chunk of his wages, money desperately needed to feed both dog and person and quite possibly person's family, or tearing fleece which would result in a fine, albeit perhaps not a very stringent one, or allowing the sheep to get run over on the road, which would be more costly than merely biting them, or worst of all, allowing the sheep to get into a field and decimate the crops growing there. Depending on how bad the damages here, a man could be ruined. The cost of damage to a ruined crop might mean the shepherd's children, if he had them, would starve. If he did not have them, it could mean that the shepherd and his dog were out on the road with no wages to sustain them, a situation which could very well mean a long, cold, hard death for both.

I'm not sure the modern mind can even imagine the kind of pressure 600 hungry sheep would exert. And they would be hungry, some of them more than others, as their relative position in the flock gave them better or lesser access to the available grazing. Oh, they'd have enough food upon which to live, and to reproduce, but they would never have been satisfied, would never have had quite enough. They'd have always been just the least little bit desperate for another mouthful of grass.

Think of the cohesion of the flock giving it somewhat the properties of water, more particularly, the water of a river in flood. The dog and Shepherd are the levies holding the river between its banks. If there is a break in the levy, the water will pour through the gap in a heartbeat, widening the gap as it pours, and in seconds, the field will be inundated.

With the bite a last resort, and no real time to grab a particular ewe by the fleece and really do much of anything with her, the dog and Shepherd have to govern by sheer force of will effectively utilized.

Today when we think of a dog's energy, we think of a dog madly running from one end of the flock to another; in fact, this is the least effective use of the dog. The most effective demonstration of force of will is made by the dog deliberately sweeping along the flanks of the flock and up the sides with a powerful gaze focused on the sheep. As he passes, he meets the eyes of the sheep and they flinch away from that gaze as if struck, even though the dog may have passed six feet away from them. Such is the power of the dog's will, focused through his gaze, that they watch for him, move away from the very suggestion that he might come their way. It is as if he carries a visible force field along with him, a field of power that forces the sheep back away from the barrier he's created with his own body and that force.

They are not afraid of his predation. The ewes do not fear for their lambs, they are not inclined to warn him away from their young. He is force itself, like a hard wind buffeting them, a wind they move away from, as it presses against them. This is aggression, brought to the surface and forged to an invisible force by a will of iron.

A long time ago I worked with the nephew of the famous outlaw Cole Younger, helping him to arrange his retirement, and he told me about his uncle. A Civil War veteran, Cole Younger had killed men both in the war and afterwards, in his bank robbing career. For years, he lived at large with a price on his head yet no one of the many men who knew him quite dared to attempt to collect it even though they, themselves, were Civil War veterans and no strangers to firearms or killing. He walked into group after group of men for whom that money would have been a boon—the equivalent of winning a million dollars in a lottery today—without the taxes. Yet no man ever dared to try him. Why? Because the man who did KNEW he would die if he did. Men believed that the first three men who tried to take Cole Younger would die in the attempt. Sheer numbers could, of course, eventually overwhelm him, but the men who started it all wouldn't be alive to enjoy it—and nobody wanted to die. The money was literally meaningless to those men, because they didn't believe, viscerally, that they would ever live to spend it.

That's the force, without the words, that the Saxony and Brunswick dogs had to find within themselves and wield, if they were to be able to control those huge flocks of hungry sheep. It wouldn't do to bite the sheep and have the ewe find out that she could survive being bitten—she might be less afraid next time. And all right, being grabbed by the fleece and thrown down and having the air knocked out of her would be a lot scarier and a lot more effective as a detriment to that particular ewe ever trying the dog again, but it took time—time during which the rest of the sheep could get out into the road or the field—and they'd be a lot harder to get back than they ever were to keep together and in line and moving in the first place.

The selection that created these dogs came perilously close to being natural selection because it was, in a very real sense, a matter of survival. People didn't begin with hundreds of sheep, they began, over millennia, with a couple of dozen and as the centuries passed, the flocks got progressively larger and the dogs got progressively more forceful and intense and their genetic obedience grew stronger. In the beginning, like the Swabian dogs, they handled a range of livestock, sheep and cattle and goats and whatever, but as the centuries rolled on dogs that handled more than the ever larger flocks of sheep became less and less common.

Saxony and Brunswick dogs were not often planted in the middle of families. Shepherds and their dogs often went for weeks with little outside human contact. Unlike the groups who traveled to summer pasture in the mountains, consisting of a couple of adults and a scattering of kids, they were fortunate if there was more one other person with them, and sometimes it was just one person and a pair of dogs. Once they reached areas where the sheep had enough graze to stay for a while, shepherds often were forced to leave the dogs in charge of the flock in order to travel to the nearest village or town for supplies. Dogs had to keep the flock to their grazing area and keep them safe even from themselves (especially from themselves!) with no Shepherd present to enforce good behavior.

Saxony and Brunswick dogs came in a rich variety of colors, among which the lighter shades predominated. Stephanitz tells us that the tiger-striped brindles, featuring an orange and black stippling as well as silver and black was a big favorite among some of the Saxony folk, and that blue and red merle as well as grey and tan and red and tan were commonplace, as well as, of course, the ever popular 'wolf' grey and the always useful white. Blacks and black and tans were not much seen and would not have been considered useful if they had been. Dark colors could not stand up to the hard sunlit days of summer, never mind the glare of sun off snow, so were not much considered in the realm of real working dogs. Dark colors in dogs is a real tip-off that the dogs are more for show or sport than for real work.

People who can indulge their preferences for dark colors are people who work in some kind of police, military or para-military capacity where

226

intimidation is important and dogs do as much or more night work as they do day work. Either that, or these folks don't really work at all, but just train for sport if they train for anything at all and have the money to indulge their whims.

In Swabia, dogs ate with their people. If the winter was long and hard and food got scarce, dogs went short just like the people did. When people ate well, dogs ate well. Summers might be spent in a lean-to on a mountain side, but winters were spent in a good, sound house. Shepherds in Saxony and Brunswick didn't always have that luxury. Saxony and Brunswick dogs ate with their people as well, but the shepherds they lived and worked with were already marginalized, with a diet less than optimum to begin with, and their ability to supplement that diet was limited, both for the shepherds and the dogs. Dogs tended to be smaller and lighter framed than the big mountain dogs, but they were often a little stocky, the better to support their power. They had to make up for their lack of size by their greater force of personality to get the job done.

Swabian Character:	**Saxony and Brunswick Character:**
Solid nerve, serotonin based	Solid nerve, with both adrenaline
Highly reliable	and serotonin at base
Highly reliable	Still quite reliable
Strong genetic obedience	Strong genetic obience
Handler sensitivity	Handler sensiivity
Sharply Moderated prey drive	Sharply Moderate prey drive
Tracking	Tracking
supported by	supported by
Hunt drive (tracking)	little Hunt drive (not needed)
Focus/Concentration	Focus/Concentration: strong
High biddability	High biddability
Resilience	Very strong resilience
Softness/Patience	Little softness, less patience
(herding)	
Flexibility	Very little flexibility
High bite threshold	High bite threshold

Defensive Aggression only	Great force of will; very close to naked aggression
Some Sociability (for community living-good with kids)	Little sociability (not needed)
Large size, tall, big-boned	Smaller size, often stocky
Rich variety of colors	Rich variety of colors
Workman-like attitude	Intense working attitude
Strong work ethic supported by Commonsense Energy conservation Serious intent Stoicism/patience	Strong work ethic supported by Commonsense focused use of energy Very serious intent Stoicism-not a lot of patience

Swabian dogs can tend to a very heavy frame in combination with such height that some people consider it a fault. Others consider their high bite thresholds a fault and confuse their unwillingness to bite when not DIRECTLY attacked, a lack of nerve. Stoicism in the face of adversity is no longer considered a virtue--modern German Shepherd owners consider dogs that bark and whine and scream in their crates for attention to be the norm.

Neither is the high intensity of the Saxony and Brunswick dogs considered much of a positive. People find that high level of focus less than comfortable to live with and the nearly naked aggression that fueled the dogs' ability to keep huge numbers of sheep in line plain scares some people. It should. Unless it is accompanied by the high thresholds of the truly working livestock dog, it can be dangerous. Too many people like the idea of it in the abstract, but find out that once they have the dog it is a lot more than they bargained for.

Since few people do actual physical labor any more themselves, they neither recognize nor appreciate a workman-like attitude in their dogs. Happy-go-lucky dogs who care little what their people want and pay little attention to them are desired in place of serious dogs. People adore dogs who have to be kept on 'Nothing In Life Is Free' regimens in order to get any obedience out of them at all.

New training techniques make genetic obedience boring. Trainers want dogs with which they can show off their skill in training over artificial courses doing meaningless and impractical made-up tasks, not dogs who come genetically programmed with basic abilities aimed at practical labor. The energy conserving Swabian is excoriated as a 'couch potato' because he fails to service some people's need for a sycophant instead of a companion. Too bad.

The old Swabian breed dogs are ideal SAR dogs because of their genetic obedience and strong hunt drive. They make excellent aide dogs for the disabled because of their herding instincts, their high bite thresholds, their genetic obedience, their stoicism, their sociability, their commonsense, their balance and stability, their flexibility and ability to adjust to differing circumstances and dispositions, and even for their much despised larger size. Their softness, patience, stoicism, and biddability which often amounts to actual empathy allows them to make excellent Therapy dogs.

The Saxony and Brunswick character can make a great alert dog for people with health problems, when its original high thresholds are preserved, because their intense, channeled focus and concentration can allow them to stay on the job day and night, alert for sounds, scents or even more subtle clues as to their person's state of health. The heritage of the Saxony and Brunswick dog to bind themselves tightly to one person and one person only means that they will not be distracted from their appointed tasks easily, if at all. And, because of their biddability, if raised and socialized and trained properly, they can even achieve public access status, if, and only if, they have the high thresholds to support that training.

The old Swabian is also an excellent choice for a family dog with small children and an excellent deterrent dog for people who want a mild element of 'protection' without the liability of a dog that bites inappropriately. Because of their large size they are often seen as imposing and even intimidating. Well socialized, the old Swabian only needs a bit of basic obedience training to make an excellent companion dog under most circumstances. They are wonderful on small farms where they interact well with the livestock.

The old Saxony and Brunswick dogs can also do well on small farms, with a little training to modify their handling of smaller groups of sheep and other livestock. They would do better with smaller families who do not have a lot of friends or relatives coming in and out and they MUST have their original HIGH thresholds intact, but for the small farmer who wants to do some competitive trialing with their dog on sheep, they would be IDEAL.

The old Swabian dogs are NOT appropriate choices for modern bite sport work. Their high bite thresholds and everything that goes into making them good with stock unfits them for running down a football field and biting the first person they see as hard as they can, even though that person is minding their own business and threatening nothing and no one. They do NOT belong in Schutzhund, Ring Sport, or any of the alphabet soup of the myriad so-called 'protection' sports. Swabians are very good at protecting their people in real life when those people are actually, physically attacked. They don't really 'get' the purpose of biting some stranger merely for existing.

If you want to do bite sports, get a Thuringian, or add Thuringian blood to that of the Saxony and Brunswick dog to lower the bite threshold and the other thresholds along with it. If you do that, however, you had better be ready to deal with a dog which is going to be 'too much' dog for most handlers. The power of the Saxony and Brunswick genetics, when de-stabilized by the low thresholds of the Thuringian can be downright dangerous in the wrong hands.

Origins: The Northern Breed Dogs

It all started with the Northern dogs. That aquiline wolf-like profile, the prick ears, the wolf-grey color, they all just appealed to people. And then, of course, there was Phylax, touring the country, being exhibited here and there. People didn't seem to care much that his temperament left a good bit to be desired, at least for people whose livelihoods depended on their dogs.

Then again, what kind of Northern dog was desired? Dogs like Greif, and one of the breed's early herding champions, the Lady of Arizona, with good, dependable temperaments able to do a day's work? Or dogs like Phylax, pretty to look at, if you liked that sort, but not good for much else?

The Phylax Society foundered on just that controversy.

Northern dogs, it must be admitted, had a wide variety of talents. Some of them pulled carts for their semi-nomadic people, carts on which their people's supplies and household goods were packed. Others, sometimes even the same dogs, earned their keep as hunting dogs as well, tracking game for their people.

There were also, clearly, some very good herding dogs among the Northern breed; Grief and Max v d Krone, who was a mix of Northern breed and Thuringian, and first Sieger Jorg v d Krone who was also a champion herding dog, and, of course, the aforementioned Lady of Arizona, another of the first herding champions. So there's no doubt that SOME of the Northern breed partook of herding characteristics and the even more common use of the dogs in tracking wild game would mean that tracking characteristics would be strong in these dogs.

Whether the dogs were herding dogs, hunting dogs, carting dogs, or a little of all three, Northern dogs were uniformly large, not just tall, but big-boned as well. Again, that seems to have been an adaptation to extreme cold. Northern dogs needed their larger body-size in order to retain their body heat when working in frigid environments.

The rootstock of the people of Northern Germany was yet again different from the rest of the country. The people here were neither Celts nor Saxon, but they perhaps resembled the Celts more closely than they did the Saxons. Their environment was very harsh and did not lend itself to large landowners or rich fields of crops. Land that could support sheep year around tended to come in small areas, and instead of wide fields, food was grown in small, private gardens. Many of the people lived between summer camps and winter homes like the Celts. Others merely moved from one seasonal encampment to another. Meat would have been a major staple of their diet and dogs could subsist on meat and help to put it on the table as well.

Despite their impact on the beginning of the breed, after Stephanitz took over, the Northern dogs very quickly became marginalized, as the Captain, situated in Southern Germany and under constant pressure from the Herding folk of Swabia and Saxony and Brunswick, seemed to pretty much forget about them. Northern blood might produce herding champions, but Stephanitz was not a working dog man when it came right down to it; his own personal preference lay with the pretty faces and bright manner of the Thuringian dogs and their dark colors. So while early pillars of the German Shepherd were dogs like Max and Jorg v d Krone, Stephanitz very quickly left them behind for dogs like double Sieger Roland v Starkenburg, with his heavy infusion of Thuringian blood through grandmother Lucie.

In part, this may have been because Northern dogs were so very variable both in structure and in character. They might be uniformly big-boned and large, but within those limits they could be harmoniously put together and gently angulated strong, graceful movers, or very straight-legged and stiff, awkward, ungainly movers. They might have strong herding dog character, with all the attributes that went with it, or they might be feral characters leading to a suspicion that some actual wolf blood was involved in their ancestry and that to attempt to use them on sheep would be tantamount to killing said sheep. Northern dogs simply had no consistency of type. Perhaps that was why the use of them after the formation of the breed became so infrequent.

Northern dogs were not to make their mark upon the breed again until World War II and its aftermath. They came back into use at the end of the war when the Germans were out of almost everything else and the Swabian, Saxony and Brunswick and Thuringian dogs were beginning to wear thin. Because like the old Swabians, they were big dogs, they could fill in with the old ambulance litters, getting wounded men off the fields of battle and saving their lives, both as search dogs and as cart dogs when their was no petrol left for the new, mechanized ambulances.

After World War II, when Communist Czechoslovakia was isolated by the Iron Curtain, native dogs of the Northern breed kept the German Shepherd dog alive and even thriving, when, if the folks trying to maintain the breed for border patrol had been limited to the dogs they could get from East Germany, the breed would have perished due to in-breeding. Selective breeding by humans, both in the native dogs they chose to add to their German Shepherds, and in selecting which pups to breed on from those matings, was responsible for the development of the unique character of the Czech German Shepherd.

Northern dogs originally came predominantly in shades of grey, grey sable, grey and tan, and white, but light colored dogs were a target and made their handlers a target. Handlers who made their living keeping Czech citizens behind the Iron Curtain and catching smugglers trying to make a living bringing in goods Czech factories couldn't produce needed dark colored dogs more difficult to spot at night and in the deep shadows of the forest. The light colored dogs had to go.

The change wasn't difficult to make; the dogs brought in from East Germany carried significant infusions of Thuringian blood with its black/dark colors, black, black sable and black and tan. Add the dark colors to the grey dogs, eliminate the white dogs and cull the light colors from the resulting litters and it didn't take long before the Czech dogs, even with their heavy infusions of Northern 'native' dog blood were pretty uniformly dark.

The Czechs didn't need to make much of any effort to bring the large size of the Northern 'native' dogs down—the addition of Thuringian blood did that for them, at least to the levels they preferred. Czech dogs do tend to be larger and more heavily boned than most of the so-called 'working-line' dogs of West Germany, and even than many of the East German dogs from which they came. The observation that a good many Czech dogs are inclined to use the greater strength they have and to power through situations with it seems to be a characteristic they gain from the Northern blood they carry. They tend, also, to exhibit an intensity rather like that of the old Saxony and Brunswick dogs, so that, if they are inclined to be sociable, for instance, they will be intensely sociable, and not particularly amenable to efforts to get them to moderate their behavior in that area.

The Northern blood also seems to bring with it a high degree of persistence, that is, persistence with intensity, probably the result of having developed in a very harsh climate. Whether carting, herding or hunting, dogs had to bring an intense work ethic to the job in order to be able to accomplish it successfully.

Northern Dog Character:
>Solid nerve, adrenaline based, generally reliable
>Strong Genetic Obedience in the herding dogs
>Not a lot of handler sensitivity
>Distinct prey drive, variably moderated
>Herding dog: sharply moderated
>Hunting dog: not much moderated, if at all

Tracking:
>Supported by
>Strong Hunt drive
>Strong Focus/concentration

232

Strong Persistence
Sheer Intensity, often overmastering intensity
Not a lot of flexibility
Variable thresholds in general, bite thresholds in particular
Strong Aggression
Variable Sociability—to the point of extreme variability
Some biddability, variable
Big-boned, large, sometimes angular construction
Originally light in color, white, and variations of grey
Variable work ethic

Just not a lot of consistency over all. Dogs could be great or not much use, or very good at one particular thing. People had to do a lot of picking and choosing to get the dog they wanted out of this group.

Today's descendants of the Northern dog are the Czech dogs and people tend to either love them or dislike them. For those they suit, they obviously do very well. They are often found in the military, the police, and in personal protection (security work). Czech dogs tend to require some physical strength in their handlers. They tend to be a very BAD choice for Assistance dogs for the disabled. They are seldom used for herding.

Some people like them for sport, some people don't. It depends on the sport and on the temperament of the handler. Czech dogs are often hard and dominant, characteristics which may come from the Northern blood they contain, or may not. It's hard to tell, now, a century later, after so many combinations of the originating breeds have occurred.

Some statements can be made with a fair amount of accuracy. Czech dogs do tend to be different from the other 'lines' of German Shepherd dogs. Czech dogs do contain more Northern breed, or 'native' dogs in their bloodlines than most other types of German Shepherd dog. You can make of that what you will.

Origins: Thuringian "Yard" Dog

The nature of the Thuringian is inherently an unbalanced, and therefore unstable one, suspended, as it is, on the point of adrenaline, between flight or fight. It is meant to be.

Historically, the written records of the Thuringian 'Yard' dog (stable-yard) go back six hundred years. They belong to a society diametrically opposed to that of the Swabian, so it is no wonder the temperament of the dog they created is diametrically opposed to that of the Swabian.

Thuringian dogs were the invention of gamekeepers and stable-masters entrusted with the management and protection of valued property. Stables contained horses and equipment and the supplies necessary to the horses' maintenance and use. Gamekeepers were in charge of sometimes

233

massive tracts of wooded land in which game, from rabbits and wild birds to deer and boar lived. Both stables and wooded lands were constantly under a sort of attack by people kept in starving, oppressed conditions by the wealthy landowners who owned the woods and the stables.

Leather and buckles brought a premium price on what amounted to a black market, spurs could be sold to be melted down, even used horse shoes were of value. And horses ate corn and oats or barley, any of which could be used to enrich a poor man's family's fare enormously. A handful of grain thrown into soup or bread could add much needed nutrition, and make two meals out of a pot which would previously only stretch to one. The taking of the occasional rabbit or game bird could make the difference between starvation and survival. And the bit of twigs and branches gleaned in the woods could make a difference between freezing to death of a long winter's night, and making it through.

The wealthy Landowner's attitude, of course, was that all these things belonged to him, and the poor were a form of vermin anyway, and the more they were fed, the more they would reproduce so better they starve, they were valueless anyway. Such words are harsh, but that is pretty much the attitude of the great landowners in the centuries prior to 1900, particularly those of Saxon origin. (Try reading a little Dickens, some time!)

The Thuringian is not a stock dog in any herding sense of the word unless they were mixed, as they often were, with the herding dogs of Saxony or Swabia to create a Thuringian dog capable of herding. Today, some residue of herding instinct may remain from those crosses, but the likelihood is, for the dog predominantly Thuringian, that such residue is made up only of rags and tatters of whatever herding instinct those other breeds of dogs possessed.

Yard dogs chased stock, when they had anything to do with them at all. Their job was, first and last and foremost, to attack people. Their entire raison d'etre was to allow the wealthy men who owned them to enforce oppressive laws against the poor. They were bred, raised and trained to be agents of terror so that the people they were directed against could be better controlled. This type of use is not protection, and has never been protection though that misnomer is used as a euphemism in place of the kinds of words which would accurately describe their employment.

In the 1930s the Nazis used Thuringian dogs crossed with Saxony and Brunswick very effectively to control the people they put in concentration camps. In WWII, the Nazis expanded their use to POW camps. After WWII, the Communists adapted them to Border Patrol, in order to terrorize people and keep them from attempting to escape the oppression of Communist East Germany and Czechoslovakia. They were used to guard the no man's land between fences and take down anyone trying to escape exactly the same way they had been used to bring down poachers in earlier ages and their use against smugglers trying to bring in goods not available for sale in their countries goes back decades. They have always been used by dictators and tyrants to force their will on other people.

They are NOT good family dogs, they have never been good family dogs, but some people find their prick ears, pointed nose and triangular head very appealing and decide to make them family dogs. Strung up on adrenaline as they are, they are apt to be very alert and very active. Fearfulness, suspicion and timidity are common attributes, the other side of the adrenaline coin from their fierce aggressiveness. Sociability in a dog of predominantly Thuringian blood would be an anomaly. Aloofness is about the best you can hope for but they often enjoy life intensely. They are not dull and never boring.

Though often described by such words as incorrigible, disobedient and intractable, they can be very sycophantic, and certain human personalities find that very attractive. They were not bred to be biddable because they didn't need to be. The only time they were off leash was when they were on the attack. The rest of the time they were on a chain or shut up in a stall. They were never intended to be friendly.

In the beginning, they protected stable-yards from thieves who would seek to steal brass or silver harness fittings for a quick re-sale. They protected feed bins from grooms and others who would scoop out a handful of oats or barley or corn to take home and feed their children if given the slightest opportunity. They lived mostly on chains in the stable-yard, under cover during the day and inside the warm stable at night. They first barked an alert, and, when loosed from their chain, launched themselves at any intruder with the single-minded determination to bite. Calling them off was seldom an option, they usually had to be dragged off their victims by main force.

Aggressiveness was a key ingredient of their characters. Their owners and handlers required a lot of it and they didn't want it modified by much of anything. These dogs were bred to run on adrenaline, and lots of it. Matched with their aggressiveness, it provided them with all the fight their handlers wanted. Even when matched with fear, it was useful to them. Frightened dogs can be very aggressive and fear can be used to channel that aggression very effectively. Yard dogs were trained, as much as they were trained, to be more afraid of their armed gamekeeper/handlers than they were of the sometimes armed poachers they were hunting.

A mix of over-the-top prey drive fueled by adrenaline often laced with fear and a touch of hunt drive made these dogs truly terrifying night hunters. A frightened dog can feed off the fear of his prey and who needs nerve if you've got enough adrenaline to go around?

Thuringian dogs were owned by the wealthy landowner and handled by an employee of his, usually the gamekeeper, men who were often rough and brutal. Dogs that were not hard (uncaring) enough to tolerate their rough handling seldom survived. Biting the hand that fed them might get them a kick in the ribs, but showing fear was more likely to get them a real brutal beating, and both gamekeepers and their employers had a tendency to decide that a fearful dog wasn't worth feeding. (An attitude that still finds a following today.)

The dogs were deployed, often at night, to hunt poachers. The word poachers meant anyone who gathered leaves and twigs and branches off the ground to burn in their fires to keep warm and to cook what little food they had. It included anyone who snared rabbits to eat to keep from starving, and anyone who snared birds like pheasant or quail for their table as well. It could even stretch to simple trespass--anyone found on any portion of the wealthy man's land at any time of the day or night could be taken up as a poacher and whipped or even hung, at the land-owner's whim. That was the law of the wealthy for at least five hundred years (up until WWI) in not just Germany, but most of Europe.

Poachers defended themselves, of course, and used dogs as well, spaniels and dogs we would call pit bulls today. The Yard dogs had to be willing to take on anyone, man or beast, in an all out offensive attack. Gamekeepers and their yard dogs acted as if they believed a good defense was a good offense. They didn't wait to be attacked; they attacked on sight, and if it turned out that the victim was innocent, well, too bad. Nobody cried much over spilt milk of that sort. If the dog crippled somebody, well, so what?

Very little has changed in the attitude of people who 'like' this kind of dog today, actually. Recently, when a 'working-line' dog belonging to a member of one of the 'working-line' German Shepherd dog forums charged out of his yard and across the street to attack and pull down an innocent jogger going by, the various people of the forum wrote five pages to say that the dog was innocent, the jogger was at fault--apparently merely for existing. No one on the forum expressed the concept that she might have a right to use a public thoroughfare free of the danger of being attacked by a loose dog. Forum members hurried to excuse the dog of wrong-doing despite his infliction of serious bites on the woman and a badly broken wrist requiring several surgeries to put right--if it ever could be--in a completely unprovoked attack. Bite sport aficionados rallied to support the attacking dog. Unfortunately for the dog and his owner, the court didn't share the forum's attitude—the dog was put to sleep.

Because of their frequent use at night and their deployment in the woods where game was maintained for the landowner's sporting pleasure, Thuringian dogs were bred in dark 'pigments' to be dark colors. Black dogs, black sables, bi-colors and blanket-backed black and tans were preferred. Not only could they disappear in the shadows of the trees during the day, the better to stalk their human prey, dark colors are more intimidating to most people, quite possibly directly because of this historical use of dark colored dogs over millennia.

When weather was bad, cold, wet, icy, raining or snowing, poachers stayed home, so game-keepers and their dogs did as well. And since Thuringian dogs were almost always under cover and slept warm tucked up in thick straw nests in stables heated by the bodies of many large animals, they didn't need rich undercoats, or indeed, a double coat at all. As a result, Thuringian dogs have a short, tight, slick coat that sheds water reasonably well, but has little undercoat. Often, at most, they sport a bit of soft fluff in the spring. They are not well suited to extremes of weather, either heat or cold.

Thuringian dogs are vocal. They were intended to be. Chained in the stable-yard as they were, barking was their job. They were there to intimidate. Barking, howling, and screaming were all acceptable. Whimpering and whining were less acceptable, but dogs with a lot of adrenaline in their systems are going to make a lot of noise.

Thuringian dogs, like terriers, are also going to do a lot of digging. Some of it may be an expression of their over the top prey drive, as they may be hearing or smelling gophers, mice, rats and moles underground, but some of it is also just a function of their over-abundance of adrenaline.

Physically, Thuringian dogs are smallish, wiry, active dogs driven by adrenaline. Some, the occasional few, can be stocky, though they are never tall. A 24" dog is considered a large Thuringian, and the dogs were compact and agile, with narrow chests and rather flat rib cages (called slab-sided, in old-timer parlance) making them a little weak in the back and prone to bloat on today's rich diets. (Yard dogs were often kept short on rations in order to make them more aggressive. Sort of the historic version of 'Nothing in Life is Free (NILF.)

The use of German Shepherd dogs containing more than 30% Thuringian blood during WWI was found to be problematical. Thuringian dogs proved not to be entirely dedicated to their people's purposes, particularly when the going got tough. For dispatch work, the trick was to get the smaller size and darker colors in a dog of around 40/40/20 Swabian/Saxony/Thuringian so that the dog would have the dedication to the human purpose to carry dispatches through shot and shell yet still be small enough to fit through tight places and dark enough not to be seen.

According to an article by Stephanitz, written not long after WWI, ambulance dogs used to locate the wounded and get medics to them needed to be at least 75-80% Swabian in order to do the job reliably. Dogs with high concentrations of Thuringian blood did not work well on their own recognizance. And dogs with too much Thuringian blood bit the medics and ambulance drivers and litter carriers working with them and often refused to even look for the wounded, instead using the 'bring-sell' fastened on their collar to indicate a find they had not made. Some dogs carrying high percentages of Thuringian blood looked for and found wounded men, only to attack them when they found them. Altogether, they did not prove very satisfactory at the work.

Stephanitz was less specific about mine detection work. Presumably, since the dogs could work in close proximity to their handlers, they were more effective than they were at other early military tasks.

At sentry work however, largely Thuringian blood dogs come into their own. Sentry work, after all, is essentially what they did in stable-yards for six hundred years. With an armed handler to back them up, and their abundance of adrenaline to make them excruciatingly alert, predominantly Thuringian dogs would have been right back in their element again.

Today, almost all bite sport and military/police dogs are based on the Thuringian foundation with Saxony and Brunswick blood for nerve and aggression that can be controlled. The DDR used some Swabian blood to give their dogs some size and substance, the Czech dogs using the old Northern wolf-dog blood for the same purpose. The Northern influence provides the Czech dogs with their big heads and their substance, and the Swabian the DDR with their slow maturation and what little substance that remains to them, but both these groups of dogs have been carefully bred to maintain the essential Thuringian character despite the infusion of other blood to give them their size.

The native 'Northern' breed Czech dogs used to balance the Thuringian adds intensity and detracts, somewhat, from the dogs' intelligence--Czech dogs are noted for their preference for the use of brute force to get things done rather than their brains, and sometimes DDR dogs get a bit too soft for their Thuringian/Saxony base, but both are mostly just scaled up Thuringians.

Thuringian 'Yard' Dog Character:

Nerve based on adrenaline, making it variable
      Dogs either ferocious, or Fearful
Zero (or close to it) genetic obedience
Very Low bite thresholds
Very Sharp and quick to bite
High Aggression
High to very high prey/play drive
Some hunt drive
Intensity rather than Focus or Concentration
Dark colors, slick coat, little or no undercoat
Small size, wiry, either light-framed or stocky, prick ears, smallish,
      triangular head
Little or no sociability
Little or no softness
Little or no biddability
Lots of hardness
Very bright, alert, engaging

Highly distractible, often fractious
No patience
High activity levels easily channeled into work, at least unti the going
    gets tough
Always ready for a game of fetch

Dogs with a high percentage of Thuringian blood are the premier bite sport dogs of today. Their willingness to bite anybody for no good reason at all, their high prey drive and affinity for games, their need for high levels of activity and their ability to fixate on balls and tugs all suit the modern mind-set and new way of doing things. Whether it's Schutzhund, Mondio, Ring Sport, PSA, personal protection, Service Dogs of America, KNPV, or any other sport men can invent featuring dogs biting other men, dogs containing high percentages of Thuringian blood excel.

The Malinois breed is built predominantly from the Thuringian, and Dutch Shepherds carry a good jolt of this blood along with Brunswick/Saxony blood. Thuringians influence the breeding of Belgium (German) Shepherds and what are often referred to as West German 'working-line' dogs as well as form the foundation of the DDR and Czech German Shepherd. Breeders simply genetically engineer variables of size and temperament depending on the type of outside stock available and the desired goals for the dog.

Ever since the Iron Curtain came down, the heavily Thuringian dogs of the Czech and East German Border Patrols have had an outsize influence on the German Shepherds of the world. They have pulled the German 'High-line' show dogs back towards the middle in terms of lowering the camel-humped roach backs so popular in the 1980s and '90s, and even had some influence on the character of the German show dogs.

Though often touted as 'family' dogs by their breeders, few families do well with these dogs. Mixing them with friends, extended family and children should only be done with the utmost care and attention to avoid unfortunate incidents such as the dog who attacked her owner's eight-year-old nephew on the stairs merely for being there. People who persist in taking these dogs into their home without a clear understanding of their low bite threshold and their willingness to bite quickly and hard without the slightest provocation are people asking for trouble.

These dogs are noted for their dramatic 'long bites' and their 'full, hard, grips', and people who ignore those words can get into trouble with them quickly. These dogs are adrenaline based, and any excitement at all will set them off--like the dog who bit the car pooling Mom he knew perfectly well, merely because he got excited. Or the dog who bit both his owner and the owner's neighbor because they got between him and his ball. Or the dog who dragged his owner across the street to bite a perfectly innocuous stranger walking along a public sidewalk and minding his own business.

Dog Aggression, Reactivity (which is just a euphemism for excited aggression) and Fear Aggression are more remarkable in their absence than they are in their presence in these dogs. Most Thuringian-based dogs have some form of 'Reactivity', the only question is whether their owner/ handler is honest about it or not. People struggling to fit these dogs into what are--if they were honest about it--'pet' homes, pay thousands of dollars during the dog's lifetime in 'training' fees and for equipment to help them control the dogs and still have to 'manage' the dogs for life to avoid unprovoked bites and the resulting liability. Total hip replacements for a good dog would be cheaper, in more ways than one.

Thuringian dogs belong in sport homes where they will be kept tired, on military bases, and in cop cars. That is their true milieu. They have no place working stock except in such sports as 'extreme sheep herding'. If crossed with enough Saxony/Brunswick Shepherd blood or Swabian/ Wurttemberg Shepherd blood, they may be excellent competition dogs, but should never be left with the sheep on their own recognizance the way dogs of very high percentages of Swabian or Saxony Shepherd blood can be. (It would be a good way to lose a lot of sheep very quickly.)

When dogs with a lot of Thuringian blood are trained (if they can be--they often can't) and used as aide dogs for the disabled, they are prone to 'meltdowns', as they lack the equanimity to handle the public over long periods of time (or at all). Few of them could pass a public access test if it were properly administered. In fact, many could not even pass a correctly conducted Canine Good Citizen test. They are a very poor choice for this kind of work.

Dogs with too much Thuringian blood tend to make poor Therapy dogs, and those who are used for therapy work often have or create problems when doing the work. Some of these dogs might be able to do Hearing Ear work or Alert work, but they are likely to lack the Focus and the Patience for the long haul. Their intensity may look appealing, but it doesn't wear particularly well, and it is Not reliable.

Thuringian based dogs would be a good choice for a competitive Agility dog, however, particularly the small, light-framed type. They'd also be a good choice for made-up sports like fly-ball and dock-diving, though not so good a choice for obedience—unless, of course, their person likes a challenge.

For some reason, certain human personalities are drawn to these dogs and become utterly devoted to them despite the dogs' lack of suitability for the tasks asked of them. I know of a sight-impaired person devoted to her reactive Czech-Thuringian/Northern breed dog despite his repeated failures to work for her. Though he has let her down time after time and even gotten her hurt a time or two, she remains loyal to him no matter how often he has failed in loyalty to her through his total lack of self-discipline.

People whose particular type of character draw them to the Thuringian -based dog and find him pleasing tend to become fiercely and unreasoningly devoted to this type of dog. They will cleave blindly to dogs whose behavior is hardly less than feral, deny to their last breath that the dog's behavior is anything less than exemplary, and recommend them to friends and family in terms that are hardly less than outright lies. They will excuse every kind of misbehavior with fond indulgence and rationalize every unprovoked attack away as somehow acceptable, when they don't deny it happened altogether-- even as they relate what happened! For the kind of people who are drawn to this kind of dog, if it came down to a choice between their kid and the dog, I truly believe they would choose the dog.

Why such people become so attached to such ill-tempered dogs who will bite virtually everyone, including them, can't be walked on a leash without an electronic collar or a prong collar or some kind of head collar, can't be trusted with kids, can't be trusted with stock, and who have to be put on management programs which amount to 'if you won't mind me I won't feed you' is a mystery to me. But anyone who cares to browse the several public Internet forums available and read the material posted there by people about their 'working-line' German Shepherd dogs, can examine the phenomenon on a daily basis.

Captain Max v Stephanitz was the first to exhibit this unreasoning and illogical behavior more than a hundred years ago, undoubtedly confounding his friends and family, and from that day forward, literally millions of people have followed in his foot-steps. If you are one of them, you can console yourself that you have plenty of company.

Today's 'working-line' dogs are heavily based in Thuringian blood. Most of them have the short, slick, tight coat with little or no undercoat and very little weather resistance now being touted as the 'standard' coat. The use of the word 'standard' as the label for the coat implies that this type of coat is correct according to the breed standard. It is NOT. It is, in fact, faulty. The correct coat according to the breed standard is fully double, with a distinct, thick undercoat. This is correctly called a 'stock' coat, not a 'standard' coat.

Today's 'working-line' dogs have the typical Thuringian type of structure, complete with their flat rib cages and narrow, deep chests so prone to bloat. They carry the dark Thuringian colors and pigment, and have the Thuringian's wiry, agile bodies, light frames and small stature (with the exception of some Czech and DDR dogs, some of which are larger). Most of all, today's 'working-line' dogs carry their forebears' aggression, low bite thresholds, sharp readiness to bite, and high prey drive.

Today's 'working-line' dogs also possess their ancestors' propensity for adrenaline production, with the reactivity it creates. If they are lucky (well, at least the bite sport people would call it lucky) they get the fight version. If they're not so lucky, they get the unstable excitement version, and if they're really unlucky, they get the fearful/flight version. This has little or nothing to do with the 'quality' of the breeder. The so-called 'reputable' breeder of 'titled'

241

dogs is just as apt to turn out fearful, unstable aggressive dogs using this genetic material as the much maligned 'back-yard' breeder because the fearful, unstable elements are embedded in the genes themselves. The 'fault' of the breeder for the production of these fearful, unstable dogs actually lies with the 'reputable' and supposedly knowledgeable breeder deliberately and knowingly using these genes in order to create dogs to compete in the dog sport world.

People who are considering whether they want a German Shepherd of Thuringian ancestry should think long and hard about the history of these dogs and what they were used for before getting one. It has been said and is considered something of a truism that people who refuse to learn from history are condemned to repeat it. If you are not going to use the dog you choose in the military, police, or bite sports, it is very important that you know what you are getting into before you bring your 'working-line' pup or dog home. These dogs require a great deal of exercise, and a couple of walks around the neighborhood a day just doesn't get it done for them. They need to be tired out, every day, with long ball playing sessions and regular DAILY training work-outs.

If you find yourself with a dog inappropriate for you or your living situation, you need to bear in mind that these dogs are very difficult to re-home successfully. Dogs with reactivity issues or worse yet, bite histories seldom have much of a chance in the world of dog shelters and rescues and dogs with undisclosed bite histories are a liability. You may be condemning yourself and your dog to 12 to 14 years of misery or a short life that ends on a vet's table, leaving you with a sense of failure and guilt.

For those who know and love this kind of dog, getting another is a no-brainer. But if this is your first German Shepherd, or you have had German Shepherd dogs before but you aren't very active these days, well, a Thuringian-based dog might NOT be the dog for you. When these dogs are successful in a 'pet' home, it is usually a very active pet home with a lot going on and people who give the dog a lot of exercise and a lot of training and time and attention.

Few people find a middle ground when it comes to 'working-line' Thuringian-based dogs. They either love them, or, like Horand v Grafath's first owner, consider them useless and worthless. Until you know which camp you're going to be in, DON'T GET ONE!

Origins: The Blend/The Split

The German Shepherd Dog was originally supposed to be a blend of the predominant strains of shepherd and 'yard' and 'service' dogs working in Germany at the turn of the twentieth century. Dogs from the north, such as Phylax v Elau, were to be combined with the Thuringian dogs and Swabian/Wurttemberger shepherd dogs and the best of the shepherd dogs of Saxony and Brunswick. The idea was to create a national dog of varying size and flexibility of mind and body, with a weather resistant, fully 'double' coat and

242

wide variety of colors. By using all these differing types and sizes and colors of dogs, they hoped to create a versatile dog which could be used for a variety of military and civilian tasks.

From the very beginning, there were disagreements. The supporters of the Thuringian dogs thought both the Swabian dogs and the Northern dogs too big. The Thuringian crowd thought the Northern dogs, in addition to being too big, not pretty enough and at least some of them stiff moving and the Swabian/Saxony crowd thought both some of the Northern dogs and most of the Thuringians were too wolf-like and didn't trust either type of dog with stock (often for good reasons).

They complained, in particular, that the Thuringians were too small to manage mountain-bred sheep successfully, that they were too likely to savage them rather than manage them. They objected to the Thuringian dogs' prey drive which they said was way too much for the dogs to be reliable with stock. They argued that Thuringian dogs had too little genetic obedience and most of all that their bite threshold was W-A-Y too low.

The Thuringian crowd countered that the Swabian dogs and the Northern dogs were too big, the Swabians, Saxony and Brunswick dogs' ears too soft (they did have a tendency to tulip, or fly a little at the tips) and that both Swabian and Northern dogs were too heavily boned. They complained that the Swabian dogs' heads were heavy and coarse and just not pretty enough. (Just the way today's Czech crowd likes them!) And that the dogs weren't quick enough to bite.

The Swabian, Saxony and Brunswick group argued that it was ability and usefulness that mattered and not pretty heads or faces and that they'd rather have a dog who could handle stock than dogs that killed stock. As far as they were concerned any good working dog was a pretty dog and the Swabian/Wurttember folks added that their dogs were NOT too big, nor too heavy, they were MAJESTIC and so there!

The first attempt at a national German Shepherd dog failed, along with the Phylax Society.

Then Captain von Stephanitz stepped in. An aristocrat, with a great deal of money at his disposal, a great deal of arrogance, and the political power to make things happen, he aligned himself with the great Krone Kennels (Herr Eiselen), Artur Meyer, and a couple other dog breeders of the time, and pretty much told them what was going to happen and how. For literally thirty years, Stephanitz decided which dogs would be named champions and of what they would be champions of and so out of different, old, and distinct breeds, he formed the German Shepherd dog, a dog that was always intended to be a blend of all these ancestral types of dog.

Schutzhund, begun in 1899, was a breed test, a simple pass-fail, with remarks to help in selecting breeding stock, NOT a competition, and not 'scored'. It was invented, not to supersede herding dogs, police dogs, search dogs, or the dogs who were later to become guide dogs, but to provide a secondary test for dogs whose owners had not been able to place them in that first rank of preferred breeding dogs. The 'long bite' was as yet undreamed of, and dogs biting men were a peripheral and not very important part of a test that featured an obstacle course, obedience and tracking. Dogs who actually worked sheep for a living were designated HGHs and considered to have passed the equivalent of the Schutzhund test and to belong to a higher echelon of the breed. Dogs who had been called Swabian Service Dogs for nearly half a century already by working with the police, were designated PH, for police dog. FHs delineated dogs used for Search work, such as the ambulance service dogs did. Later, dogs would be 'tested' to achieve these designations, but in the beginning, the designations were merely a recognition of what already existed.

With the ancient Swabian Shepherd dogs, the off-shoot Swabian Service Dogs, the Saxony and Brunswick Shepherd dogs, somewhat smaller but fairly close in type to the old Swabian, the Northern type, also known as either the wolf-dog, or the Northern Herding breed, and the Thuringian, at the onset, the new breed had the elements of great genetic diversity. In essence, the breed was split into two main types, the Swabian-Saxony and Brunswick Shepherd group, often referred to as 'Old Breed' or 'Old Blood' and the Thuringian show dog type Stephanitz so loved, with the Northern wolf-type group a sort of red-headed step-child while the Northern herding dogs were naturally aligned with the Swabian/Wurttemberger and Saxony and Brunswick dogs.

The Thuringian and some of the Northern wolf-dog representatives had a great deal in common, once you disregarded their size differences. Both types of dog often had low bite thresholds and unreliable temperaments. Some of the Northern dogs, such as the white dog Grief and his daughters, and an early stock working champion, the Lady of Arizona, were very good stock dogs with excellent and strongly reliable temperaments. The Northern breed blood in both Jorg and Max v d Krone was of this type, but many other Northern dogs were not so good on stock, and both types of dog were used for hunting, though the Northern dogs were used to hunt game and the eastern Thuringian was used to hunt men. The Northern dogs tended to be a lot taller and leggier than the Thuringian, as well as much heavier boned, and often pulled sleds or worked in harness. Both the Northern wolf-dogs and the Thuringians had prick ears and wolf-ish heads.

Stephanitz (and a good many other people) considered the Thuringian the prettier, and called them 'show' type dogs, or 'fancy' dogs, but the Captain constantly inveighed against allowing that preference to be used to make breeding choices as he believed that other shepherd dog breeds, most notably the Scots Collie, had been ruined by breeding for looks instead of working ability.

Swabian/Wurttemberger and Saxony and Brunswick dogs were all herding dogs, though the Swabians were bigger and more flexible of mind. Dogs of Saxony and Brunswick only herded sheep, animals far smaller than those the big Swabian dogs handled, but they herded a lot of them, in flocks sometimes numbering as many as six to eight hundred animals. It was the Saxony and Brunswick dogs which perfected the tending style of herding where the dog kept the sheep on designated grazing land by trotting along 'furrows' that marked out the land where the sheep were allowed from the land where they were not allowed.

Swabian dogs did something similar, but their boundaries were less well marked, and their herds contained a great many animals other than sheep, though the numbers were fewer. If Saxony andBrunswick dogs were specialists, Swabian dogs were generalists. Both dogs braved the elements day in and out, and though the Swabians had more extreme weather to deal with, both breeds possessed rich, deep coats, genetic obedience in abundance, with high bite thresholds, strong serotonin-based nerve, and stable, balanced temperaments. The Swabian and Saxony and Brunswick dogs were the fount of much of the versatility the German Shepherd Dog enjoyed into the 1960s. Today, the red and blue merle colors so prized in Saxony and Brunswick have been long lost to us, along with the brindle preserved in the Dutch Shepherd, but the livers, grey sables and grey and tan dogs of the Swabian and Saxony and Brunswick dogs remain, although they have been marginalized along with the genetic heredity from which they came.

In the beginning, these various types of dogs provided the German Shepherd breed with a rich cornucopia of genetic diversity, which, unfortunately, began to be immediately eroded by egotistical and self-indulgent breeding practices, among them those of Stephanitz himself in his irresponsible in-breeding on Horand v Grafath. The overuse of Horst v Boll, however, was hardly any better, though he, at least, had a sound temperament. The repeated in-breeding on Roland v Starkenburg, however beautiful, with his faulty temperament, was an abomination, and was largely responsible for the poor nerve in show dogs to this day.

The disqualification of white dogs in the 1930s due to a misunderstanding of genetics was excusable under the circumstances, and the difficulties with the merles--breeding merle to merle can result in deafness, and sometimes even blindness--was certainly reason enough to suspend the breeding of them until the mechanics of those color genetics were better understood. However, the refusal to re-include the colors, particularly solid white, which is no problem at all, is INexcusable and has been and continues to be damaging to the long-term genetic health of the breed.

The loss of brindle might have been a simple matter of basic preference, as it is a dominant color, but it should be repatriated into the breed, along with the lost genetic diversity it represents. The later loss of liver and grey and tan in the 1970s through nothing more nor better than prejudice and a desire to cut out competitors in the show ring, is downright disgusting, thoroughly dishonorable and a loss of genetic diversity which the breed, as it presently stands, simply cannot afford. The continuing exclusion of these colors out of nothing more than uninformed prejudice calls into question the validity of the entire breed standard. It is no coincidence that the proliferation of genetic disorder began with the loss of the 'Old Breed' herding dog colors, as eliminating the colors of the 'Old Breed' has taken much of the genetic diversity of the 'Old Breed' dogs with them.

The further erosion of genetic diversity which the current and apparently successful narrowing of the height ranges (in an effort to further weed out Swabian/Wurttemberger and Northern breed influences) and to further 'standardize' the breed, brought about by the so-called 'working-line' people is nothing less than disastrous for a breed already struggling with its lack of diversity.

The selection of Klodo v Boxberg, with his multiple crosses to Roland v Starkenburg as Sieger in the 1920s was another devastating blow to genetic diversity which seriously harmed the long-term health of the breed. A far better choice would have been either of the two Blasienberg dogs, Seffe, Siegerin to Klodo, or her litter brother, Sultan, who went second to Klodo that fateful day. Both Seffe and Sultan brought strong nerve, reliable temperaments and well-balanced, open pedigrees to the breed, along with great genetic obedience and outstanding herding talent and general good health. In contrast, Klodo, with his heavy in-breeding on Alex v Westfalenheim and Horand and his grandfather Pollux, suffered from digestive problems which were probably EPI from age 6 on. But then, Seffe and Sultan were largely Swabian/Wurttemberger in type and ancestry, with only a nod to Horand, while Klodo v Boxberg was heavily in-bred on Horand.

In choosing Klodo v Boxberg as Sieger that day in 1925, Stephanitz serviced his agenda to keep the dogs of the breed from heading into height realms upwards of 30 inches superbly. That may, perhaps, have needed to be done, but his choice of Utz v Haus Schutting, a son of Klodo out of a line-bred descendant of Horand-Roland, and then Utz' son Hussan v Haus Schutting, to be followed by Klodo's other grandson Odin v Stolzenfels, by son Curt v Herzog-Hedan, also out of an in-bred Horand mother, created a devastating bottleneck which would adversely affect the genetic health and the working nerve of the breed for the next hundred years and perhaps for all time.

Klodo was of the line of Roland v Starkenburg, and therefore Horand, he was the same size as Horand had been, and brought the breed back around to Horand again, to dogs of unsteady nerve and poor genetic health. Every one of Klodo's multiple lines to Roland was two lines to Horand and five more to Horand's grandsire, Pollux, for a sum of 152 lines to Horand's lack of genetic obedience, unreliable nerve, his reactivity and low bite threshold, lines that carried his Juvenile Renal Dysplasia, his Mega E, and his EPI (which Klodo, with his poor digestion, undoubtedly suffered from).

It also signaled the end of the blend in Germany as a viable reality. Though some dogs, like the Blasienbergs, remained to carry on the Swabian heritage, and America would preserve the Swabian blend dogs into the 1960s, Klodo's choice as Sieger rang the death knell of any real genetic diversity in the breed. Klodo's most outstanding sons, Curt v Herzog Hedan and Utz v Haus Schutting, were out of mothers who merely added more crosses to Roland to add to the 152 Klodo had, which meant more lines to Horand and all his genetic health and temperament problems.

For a time Communist East Germany kept some Swabian blood in some of their dogs in order to maintain the larger size they wanted. They were successful in maintaining greater height and superior substance in some of their dogs--at least until the fall of the Iron Curtain--along with slower maturation rates, both physically and mentally and a trace or two of softness here and there. By and large, however, they bred well away from the typical Swabian temperament in order to get a more heavily adrenalized dog with more sharpness and a much lower bite threshold. Today, the big old DDR dog has almost disappeared due to out-crossing with the West German 'working-line' dogs.

The Czech dogs, another of the Iron Curtain dogs which had until recently at least retained the head of the Northern Wolf-dog and some of the big Northern dog's bone structure, will soon be losing what minimal traces of that ancient heritage they still have. With State support for their breeding a thing of the past, they will soon be so inundated with 'working-line' blood from West Germany and Belgium and Holland that the repeated infusion of Thuringian blood will eventually overwhelm the qualities that have made the Czech dog a distinct type of their own.

It is not that the Czech dog does not need outcross blood, it does, it is that without the substance and strength of either the Northern dogs or the Swabians, that strength and substance cannot long continue in the face of constant infusions of the blood of lighter framed, smaller dogs. Had a font of either Northern or Swabian blood remained to add back to the blend, now and again, the Czech type could be preserved--without it, the preservation of the Czech type dog with its strength and substance will not be possible and without maintaining significant quantities of the old Northern breed blood, the unique character of the Czech temperament will be impossible to preserve. Thus we reap the results of our short-sightedness in not valuing the sources of the qualities we desire in our dogs.

Today we see a three-way split in the breed, though most show and 'working-line' folks only acknowledge two of the split's constituents. The first, the so-called 'working-line' dogs which do little work but which are mainly sport dogs with a few dogs still in the military (a precious few!) and a few dogs doing police work (not many) constitute one branch of the split. The show dog which is for all practical purposes a functional cripple beset by health problems and temperament issues is the second, and the 'old-fashioned' dog carrying the last of the 'Old Breed' Saxony and Brunswick and Swabian (aka Wurttemberger) Shepherd and Service dog blood is the third. Essentially, the German Shepherd dog is being returned to his component parts. Only a representative branch of the old Northern dog is missing but it could be argued that the remaining old Czech type represents at least one branch of that type.

Neither of the three branches have any use for each other, or each other's dogs. The Thuringian crowd, now calling themselves 'working-line' still hate the Swabian/Wurttemberger dogs for the same reasons they always have. According to them, the Wurttemberger/Swabian Shepherd dogs are too big, not pretty enough, and worst of all, from their point of view, don't like to bite people for fun. The Swabian/Wurttemberger-Saxony and Brunswick dog crowd, now calling themselves 'old-fashioned' don't like the 'working-line' dogs because they're too small, not reliable on stock, too quick to bite inappropriately, reactive, and have WAY too much prey drive to be reliable stock dogs. Both groups think the other's choice in dogs is a poor excuse for a German Shepherd and the show crowd pretty much ignores them both from their perch way out there in Fantasy-land where they dwell.

The 'old-fashioned' people point to the history of the breed in their claims to legitimacy, and that claim is valid, though the 'working-line' folk pooh-pooh it and deny that the history even happened--or, they aver, if it really did happen, well, it doesn't matter anyway, their dog is the right one and no other no-how and na, na, na on you. This stance is indicative of the 'working-line' people's attitude in general but doesn't have much else in the way of validity to support it.

The 'working-line' people's argument that the 'old-fashioned' group does too little with their dogs IS valid, though fewer 'working-line' people actually do Schutzhund--or other bite sports--than they like to admit. 'Old-fashioned' dog fanciers SHOULD do more with their dogs than they do, although it must be admitted that at least a part of the reason they aren't out training their dogs constantly and paying big bucks in training fees is because their dogs have far fewer behavior problems needing work than the 'working-line' crowd's reactive dogs do.

Another consideration regarding 'old-fashioned' dogs is that those dogs who are working, on small family farms, in herding, in assistance work, in SAR and the occasional police dog tend to be invisible to the 'working-line' crowd because the people working with them don't spend their time on dog forums bragging about it. Also, 'working-line' dog people tend not to give 'old-fashioned' dog people credit for the work their dogs do is because it tends to be real work, rather than the kind of sports that generate 'titles'. For the 'working-line' crowd, since real work doesn't generate 'titles' it doesn't exist, and anyone telling them that their dogs work is lying.

The 'old-fashioned' people spend very little time bashing the 'working-line' dogs or their owners. They tend to go their own way and mind their own business. The same, unfortunately, cannot be said of the 'working-line' group, who froth at the mouth when 'old-fashioned' dogs are mentioned and manufacture thirty pages of diatribe against them full of half-truths, out-right untruths, innuendo, blatant rudeness and character assassination at the drop of the very label.

The 'working-line' people go ballistic at the 'old-fashioned' people's generally accurate portrayal of their dogs as the dogs 'your grand-parents knew'. This is a pretty valid description of their dogs (modern pictures of 'old-fashioned' dogs match up quite well with the photos of German Shepherds from WWI to approximately 1965). Neither 'working-line' dogs nor current 'show' line dogs, either German or American much resemble the dogs of the past—in fact, it is often difficult to even tell they're the same breed. It is also an excellent, and far and away the best, marketing tool the 'old-fashioned' people have.

People remember those old, largely Swabian dogs of the past fondly. This is what makes it such a hot button for the 'working-line' people and a large part of why they are so rabidly against 'old-fashioned' dogs. Essentially, this generally true statement made by the 'old-fashioned' crowd keeps people from buying 'working-line' dogs, which takes money out of the pockets of 'working-line' dog breeders. 'Working-line' people will try to counter by denying history yet again 'you were a kid,' they say, 'and the dog wasn't really as big as you remember', or they try on the lie 'you were a kid, the dog wasn't really a pure-bred' to see if they can convince you to doubt your own memories--or your grand-parents' veracity. 'Working-line' folk tend to be very ready to call anyone they don't agree with liars. They don't value people's experiences or their memories or their stories—unless those experiences and memories and stories verify their prejudices. They want everything written down in black and white and stamped as official and if it doesn't please them or verify their prejudices, they still won't believe it.

'Old-fashioned' dogs make better stock dogs and better family pets because of their higher bite thresholds, more moderate prey drive, and greater levels of genetic obedience than 'working-line' dogs, something the 'working-line' people do NOT want the pet buying public to ever understand. Since the family pet market is far and away the largest in the world, easily larger than all the stock-working, military and police, tracking and bite-sport working venues put together, it is THE great reservoir of money which dog breeders can tap into.

Since the 'working-line' people cannot admit that it is the competition for that money that disturbs them (without admitting they're in the business of dogs for the money, a big no-no in the dog culture of pretty much all breeds) they have to find other reasons for their diatribes against 'old-fashioned' dogs. The arguments they find have a grain of truth to them, which does make them sting.

One, too many 'old-fashioned' dog breeders ARE too hung up on their dogs' size. They want 'em big, and brag about pushing 'em up over 30 inches whenever they can. This is nothing new. Stephanitz' choice of both Klodo and Utz as Siegers in the 1920s was fueled by breeders in Germany and American and even Great Britain who had all gotten carried away breeding big dogs. A pre-occupation with big dogs merely because they are big has been a part of the breed since its inception. It started with Phylax and the Phylax Society before Stephanitz even got into the game. That the practice of breeding for large size has a historical foundation in the breed doesn't make it good practice, however, and breeding specifically for large size, or giving it priority over matters of character or health or functional structure does not tend to preserve the best attributes of the breed.

The best attitude for the best interests of the breed, would be to breed the dog to be functional and to welcome a wide range of sizes for varying tasks for their genetic diversity and the richness and good health they can bring to the breed. The 'working-line' crowd doesn't do this any better than the 'old-fashioned' crowd, opting for a height limit that is far too narrow in scope for the genetic health of the breed.

The second objection is also serious, that 'old-fashioned' people tend to stand on their historical laurels and not to do much with the dogs they have today. That they neither work them in real jobs or to test them against real strictures, such as those in tracking tests and obedience trials, never mind Schutzhund or other bite sports. They ignore, even if they understand it, which most do not, that as they are done today, the so-called 'protection' sports, absent as they are of any threat other than artificial and largely symbolic to the dog or handler whatsoever, are offensive to 'old-fashioned' people.

The number of dogs of any breed except possibly Border Collies and Queensland Blue Heelers who actually still work stock are few and while some 'old-fashioned' dogs are to be found in SAR, their handlers seldom insist on making them known as such. Those in the know are fully aware that the 'working-line' people currently taking over SAR groups would drum them out of the corps if they realized what the dogs were. And 'old-fashioned' dogs working as aide dogs for the disabled tend to be so far out of the mainstream of the breed as to be ignored completely.

There is, however, another truth, and that is that those people still using their 'old-fashioned' German Shepherds on stock tend to be invisible to the breed mavens and too busy working their dogs in real life to bother bringing themselves to the attention of people they consider to be (pretty accurately) largely a bunch of snobbish, elitist idiots. The occasional stock dog working 'old-fashioned' person attempting to join any 'working-line' group under the mistaken assumption that 'working' actually means work, quickly finds out how unwelcome they are in that group and how very rude, over-bearing and nasty the 'working-line' in-crowd can be to someone working an 'old-fashioned' dog. While it is impossible to tell for certain, the probability is that the 'old-fashioned' have about the same number of dogs doing SAR, working stock, and taking care of the disabled that the 'working-line' crowd have dogs working on real jobs with the military, police and SAR. And both groups have dogs working with police in one capacity or another.

The third objection the 'working-line' crowd make to the 'old-fashioned' dogs is that the 'old-fashioned' group actually accepts and cherishes the original historical pantheon of colors in their dogs. Red and tans, grey and tans (the so-called blues), black and tans, blacks, bi-colors, whites and sables are all welcome in the 'old-fashioned' fold. Far from being the great transgression the narrow-minded, inflexible 'working-line' mavens make it out to be, the inclusion of all these colors by the 'old-fashioned' group has not only a firm foundation in the history of the breed, but is one of the 'old-fashioned' group's greatest strengths. The genetic diversity thus preserved may be their dogs' salvation.

It may be that even though the 'old-fashioned' is the smallest group in actual numbers of dogs, because of the wider range of sizes accepted into the group and the greater numbers of colors, as well as the lack of competition, with its popular sires which everyone has to breed to (for all sorts of reasons, including marketing) this group has the most genetic diversity left in the breed. Presently, though 'old-fashioned' people do as much or more genetic testing than any other group, 'show' or 'working-line', their dogs test out to have significantly fewer percentages of dogs with genetic disorders such as von Wildebrand's and DM. They also have the lowest incidence of bloat, SIBO, IBD, EPI and JRD. This may be because 'old-fashioned' dogs' lines contain far less in-breeding than either 'working-line' or 'show-line' dogs and avoid the worst of the 'back-massing' to be seen in both those groups.

On the other hand, the objections of the 'old-fashioned' group to the 'working-line' dogs are equally valid. Schutzhund, the be-all and end-all of the 'working-line' group is now no longer anything at all like the Schutzhund of Stephanitz' time. The fierce competition, the changes in the rules, the shift in purpose from that of a test to bring out the inner qualities of the dog in order to make better assessments for breeding purposes to one of marketing and competition and the featuring of the 'long bite' attacks on the decoy, have made a drastic change in the character of the dogs bred for the sport. The intensity of the competition now inherent in all 'bite sports' drives the creation of dogs ever more extremely prey-driven, ever sharper, with lower bite thresholds generation after generation, while 'hardness' is prized more and more and genetic obedience for anything other than eagerness to bite people gets thrown out the window to service the egos of the dogs' trainers.

Concerns about the effect of these changes on the character of the breed are all legitimate. The placement of dogs with extreme prey drive, high reactivity, low bite thresholds and hardness appropriate only for professional handlers as well as dogs needing to live on 'Nothing in Life is Free' programs in pet homes is a disaster for the breed. Shelters and rescues are now crowded with dogs they can't legitimately place and bite statistics have been driven upwards to the detriment of everyone.

Dogs from 'titled' parents, far from 'protecting' their homes, are now running across streets and into other people's yards to bite completely innocuous strangers minding their own business. This sort of thing does nobody any good, and is far more serious than a few over-size dogs, though the 'working-line' people will never admit it.

The entire corruption of the language so that 'working-line' dog means nothing more nor better than a dog whose 'work' is to run down a football field and bite a complete stranger threatening no one is a problem itself. Breeding a dog to readily and rapidly bite the first person the dog sees that isn't his own handler is not conducive to creating a dog that fits well into the world as it is today. This is an era when breeding dogs to RAISE their bite threshold and to wait for a clear and present danger to occur before biting someone, is appropriate, not the other way around.

Stephanitz could get away with a dog that chased his tenant farmers' stock because they were his tenant farmers and were dependant upon his good-will--whether they liked it or not. His dogs could bite his servants and the tradesmen, delivery boys and people from the middle and lower echelons of society with impunity because those people could do nothing about it. They couldn't sue him and they had no recourse when his dog bit them. Stephanitz could get away with bragging that his dog knew by a man's clothing whether or not he could bite that man with impunity. Today, Stephanitz would get sued and Horand, with all his delight in provoking strife and his joy in biting anyone not wealthy enough to afford expensive clothing would not live long enough to be the father of a breed—he'd be put to sleep in short order.

We are no longer the rich aristocrat living in the big house on the hill to whom everyone else has kow-tow whether they like it or not, though many 'working-line' people take an on-line attitude towards their beloved Fido's behavior that certainly makes them appear to think they are. We can be sued. If our dog bites the mail-carrier, we can lose our mail delivery. When he attacks the meter reader, our power can be cut off. Animal control CAN take our dog and we CAN find ourselves in front of a judge if our dogs harm people, and our dogs CAN be put-to-sleep, whether we like it or not.

Few of us have a sister who would allow our dog to attack her eight-year-old on the stair while we were baby-sitting him without serious ill-feeling

252

and perhaps even a family rift. When our dog bites someone minding his own business these days, there are consequences, not merely for us, as the owner of the dog, and not merely for the dog who bites, but for whatever breed our dog belongs to and for all dogs in general. When we allow our dogs to menace other dogs and people, when we make egregious excuses for them, their behavior and ours reflects badly on all the dogs and dog-owners in our breed and by extension, on all dogs and dog owners.

Sharp, hard, dominant, reactive, extreme prey drive, aggressive, low bite threshold dogs belong in the military, they belong on police forces and they can belong to folks who enjoy bite sports--but they do not belong in families as pets. 'Working-line' folks who market their pups to families so they can sell the pups for whom they are unable to find sport homes are doing the families to whom they sell these puppies no favors, they are contributing to breed specific legislation and insurance company bans and playing into the hands of PETA and the Animal Rightists. Worst of all, they are hurting the breed.

The 'working-line' dog, already in genetic difficulties due to its heavy back-massing on Lex v Pressenblut and Maja v OsnabruckerLand, and on Horand through Klodo and Roland v Starkenburg with Cardio, DM, Pannus, Mega E, JRD and bloat, is living on borrowed time lent it by the fragile remaining thread of its Northern blood, and the infusion of native Czech dogs from the Border Patrol and Slovakia. The determination of the 'working-line' breeders to keep their dogs sacrosanct while at the same time breeding on a very small minority of podium climbing Schutzhund winners will soon narrow their gene pool beyond redemption despite their record numbers of dogs registered.

The show lines are already defunct, and just haven't admitted it yet. Bottlenecks on Lance of Fran-Jo here in the United States are pernicious, but cannot compare to those on the WildsteigerLand/Arminius lines in the German High-lines, never mind Quanto and Canto v d Wienerau, which lead directly back to Klodo, Roland and Horand with a short stop at Lex and Maja on the way. It's no wonder that the German High-lines are steeped in EPI, bloat, DM, JRD, Mega E, Pannus, and vonWilldebrand's disease. In Great Britain you can add Epilepsy to the list, and in American show-lines, SIBO and IBD take the place of EPI with Cardio killing dogs as early as two and three years of age. And they all may suffer with Hip and Elbow dysplasia, though since those are about fifty percent environmental, they're a pretty minor matter genetically. Additionally, most of the show-lines suffer, if you can call it that, from unreliable temperaments, with shyness and timidity to downright fearfulness commonplace.

German High-line dogs who are supposed to qualify through at least Schutzhund 1 have a dozen ways to get around it, from simply greasing the palm to back door arrangements and all kinds of creative chicanery. And with many of the dogs possessing roach backs that make them look like camels, along with hind legs that stick out behind them, often as much as a foot to eighteen inches, it isn't to be wondered at that back problems, stifle joint problems, hock and hip problems have become commonplace in their lines.

American show people don't bother to make elaborate claims about their dogs' temperaments other than to assure anyone who asks that their dogs' temperaments are good. Good for what? One might ask. They aren't interested in specifying and they don't, for the most part, pretend to care much. They don't delude themselves that their championships are for anything other than a beauty contest. Their gene pool is in only slightly less trouble than the Germans', with no relief in sight. About the only good thing you can say about them is that the American show dog is declining rapidly, as fewer and fewer people can stomach either the faulty temperament or the crippled hindquarters that characterize most of the successful dogs.

The white German Shepherd people have two separate registries and two separate groups in America and another in Switzerland which doesn't help anything when it comes to genetic diversity. They occasionally throw 'colored' dogs into the mix in a token attempt to create some genetic diversity but since those dogs are almost always American show-lines, that's pretty much a joke. On the other hand, they seem to be the only group aware of the crash waiting for them if they don't mind their gene pool, and they are at least acknowledging the problem. No one else is.

Then you come to the 'old-fashioned' group. So far, they have the least back-massing on their dogs of any other group. They're not prejudiced against traditional colors the way the 'working-line' and show-line groups are, welcoming all the old original colors into their fold (which is one of the reasons they're called old-fashioned) and they don't compete, so they aren't troubled with the popular sire syndrome. Because they aren't competing, they aren't tempted to in-breed as irresponsibly as the other groups do, and they're basically sensible. They do a lot of health testing in an effort to avoid the problems the other groups have had, and they're the last group that does actual work in the real world with their dogs besides the rare few 'working-line' dogs doing police work and military service.

'Old-fashioned' dogs work stock on family farms all over America, and their variety in size and color helps to keep their gene pool healthy. Since the people using them tend not to be sophisticated in dog world matters, they often still train in old ways, depending on their dogs' genetic obedience, and thus preserving it. This is the best group of dogs from which to find dogs which can do service work for the disabled, and for therapy dogs.

Some 'old-fashioned' breeders are still producing SAR dogs and stock dogs for ranch use, but because of their lack of sophistication in dog matters, many of these breeders have no eye for functional conformation and no vocabulary for matters of temperament. Too few of them work with their dogs, too few of them test their dogs' temperaments, and too few of them understand the value of working with and testing their dogs. Even fewer of them know the danger in which their dogs stand, or anything about genetic matters.

This is a very small group, probably not as large in sheer numbers as the white dogs alone, and that is frightening. The number of dogs that carry strong genetic inheritances from Swabian Shepherd dogs can probably be numbered on all your fingers and toes and still leave some to spare. If some pretty heroic efforts aren't made soon, the last of the genetic inheritance of the Swabian Shepherds, that most ancient of breeds, will be lost forever—and once those Swabians are gone, any hope for the preservation of the blend which is the true German Shepherd dog will go with them. Only Thuringians with slight variations will be left.

That will suit the 'working-line' folks just fine. Or at least, it will until the only way left to keep their dogs from spiraling down into complete genetic collapse is to inter-breed with Malinois. In the end, of course, all that will do is take the Malinois down with them since the Malinois have their own working vs. show-line split.

So there you have it. The eventual dissolution of the German shepherd dog as a blend of the ancient breeds of Germany will happen, and probably sooner, rather than later, the way things are going, as the breed splits back into its constituent parts. The Blend may not be defunct just yet, but it is very close to being moribund. How long it will actually take to go is anybody's guess, but the end is in sight.

Chapter 9
The Pioneers

Fig. 123. Audifax von Grafrath, SZ 368 HGH.

Audifax von Grafrath

The Pioneers: The Original Dogs

    Despite being formed from four relatively old breeds of dogs (Swabia/Wurttemberg herding dogs; Saxony & Brunswick herding dogs; Thuringian 'Yard" dogs; and Northern 'wolf' and herding dogs) used for various useful purposes, the German shepherd breed was actually formed from a rather small group of individuals. Below are those I've been able to locate and identify:

Horand v Grafath
  (aka Hektor v Linkstrom from v Sparwasser)
  By Kastor Rude
    By Pollux v Hanau   Swabian/Wurttemberger
  Out of Schafermadchen   Saxony herding dog
      Out of Lene Sparwasser
        By Greif   Northern herding Dog
          Out of Lotte Sparwasser   Thuringian
And his full brother: Luchs Sparwasser
Madel Sparwasser   Thuringian
Lene II Sparwasser   Thuringian
Pollux v Hanau   Swabian/Wurttemberger
    by Roland
    out of Courage
Prima v Hanau   Thuringian & Swabian/Wurttemberger
Schafermadchen v Hanau   Saxony
Phylax v Eulau   Northern
Galle v Eulau   Northern
Phylax v Waldenreut   probably Swabian/Wurttemberger
    (from Brenztal & v d Krone)
Jorg v d Krone, HGH
      by Luchs Sparwasser   Swabian-Saxony-Northern-Thuringian
      out of Nelly Hundin   Swabian/Wurttemberger
Phylax v d Krone, HGH   Swabian/Wurttemberger
Madame v d Krone the Elder HGH Swabian/Wurttemberger
Neckar Rude (v d Krone), HGH   Swabian/Wurttemberger
Werra (v d Krone)   probably Swabian/Wurttemberger
Nelly Hundin (v d Krone)   probably Swabian/Wurttemberger
Butz v d Krone   probably Swabian/Wurttemberger
Irma v d Krone   probably Swabian/Wurttemberger
Lena v d Krone HGH   Swabian/Wurttmberger
  By Russ Rude HG
   By Russ Rude HGH
    Out of Molli Hundin HGH
  Out of Fanny Hundin HGH

By Woerro Rude HGH
    Out of Fanny Hundin HGH
Lippert v d Krone   probably Swabian/Wurttemberger
  By Russ Rude
    By Libbert HGH
    Out of Elsa v Hinterofen
  Out of Fanny Hundin
Luchs v d Krone HGH   probably Swabian/Wurttemberger
Max v d Krone, HGH   Thuringian with Northern herding
  By Wolf 990698   and probably some Swabian as well
  Out of Madel
Loni v d Krone   Swabian/Wurttemberger
Sali v d Krone   mainly Thuringian
Audifax(v d Krone)Grafath, HGH   Swabian/Wurttemberger
  by Russ Ruede HGH
    by Russ Ruede HGH
    out of Molli Hundin HGH
    out of Fanny Hundin HGH
  by Woerro Ruede HGH
    out of Fanny Hundin HGH
Mores Pleiningen HGH(v Schwaben)   Swabian/Wurttemberger
  By Franz HGH
      Out of Werra HGH
Carex Pleiningen HGH(v Schwaben)   Swabian/Wurttemberger
  By Prinz Libbert HGH   Mores and Carex were NOT
  Out of Sibylle Hundin HGH   closely related
Dora v Schwaben HGH   Swabian/Wurttemberger
Fides Neckarusprung   Swabian/Wurttemberger
  By Caro Rude HGH
    by Stromer Ruede HGH
    out of Rassa Hundin HGH
  Out of Ceres Hundin HGH
      by Lump Ruede HGH
      out of Fanny Hundin HGH
Loria v Brenztal HGH   Swabian/Wurttemberger
Peter Schlemihl v Brenztal HGH   Swabian/Wurttemberger
  by Neckar Rude   Swabian/Wurttemberger
Cilli Hundin(v Brenztal)HGH   Swabian/Wurttemberger
Elsa Hundin   Swabian/Wurttemberger
Minka Hundin(v Brenztal)HGH   Swabian/Wurttemberger
Schuft(v Brenztal)HGH   Swabian/Wurttemberger
  by Busche Rude   Swabian/Wurttemberger
    out of Selke Hundin   Swabian/Wurttemberger

Wachtel(v Brenztal)HGH	Swabian/Wurttemberger
Rex Rude(v Bergedorf)	Swabian/Wurttemberger
by Luchs Rude	
out of Flora Hundin	
Elsa Hundin (v Bergedorf)	probably Swabian/Wurttemberger
Wanda Hundin (v Bergedorf)	Swabian/Wurttemberger
out of Lene Hundin	
Liese v Geussnitz HGH	Swabian/Wurttemberger
By Luchs v Geussnitz HGH	Swabian/Wurttemberger
Out of Lotte v Roden(v Geussnitz)HGH	
by Wolf Zeitz	Swabian/Wurttemberger
out of Wanda v Roden	Swabian/Wurttemberger
(v Geussnitz)	
Lene v Roden (990351)	Swabian/Wurttemberger
Wanda v Gramont	???
by Prinz Hardisleben	???
out of Gloria v Gramont	???
by Prinz Rude	???
out of Lora v Gramont	???
by Persie Rude	???
out of Marta v Gramont	???
Hella v Burg Fasanental	Saxony & Brunswick
by Marko Rude (990561)	Saxony & Brunswick
out of Lena Hundin (990350)	Saxony & Brunswick
Siegfried v Burg Fasanental	Saxony & Brunswick
out of Lena Hundin (990350)	Saxony & Brunswick
Grete v d Hurde	Swabian/Wurttemberger
Lotta v d Hurde	Swabian/Wurttemberger
Luchs Rude (v d Hurde)	probably Swabian/Wurttemberger
Mande (v d Hurde)	probably Swabian/Wurttemberger
Amanda v Roden(St Ingebert)	probably Swabian/Wurttemberger
Fritz Rude (St Ingebert)	???
Hella Hundin (St Ingebert)	???
Prinz Wolf (St Ingebert)	???
Fichte v Park	Swabian/Wurttemberger
Lexe v Park	Swabian/Wurttemberger
Schaefa v Park	Swabian/Wurttemberger
by Luchs Rude	
out of Grete Hundin	
Betha v Brotzingen	???
Fanny v Brotzingen	???
Luchs v Brotzingen	???
Prinz v Brotzinge	???

Leo v Weste(r)nholz	???
by Moritz v Lietzenburg	???
out of Minka v Betzgenrieth	???
Lora v Weste(r)nholz	???
Grete Thorigen	Thuringian
Pan Torigen	Thuringian
Dohne v Klostermansfeld	Thuringian herding mix
Lotte v Klostermansfeld	Thuringian herding mix
by Wolf Rude	
out of Dame Hundin	
Alice v d Wandse	Swabian/Wurttemberger
Ajax Rude	Swabian/Wurttemberger
Elsa Hundin	Swabian/Wurttemberger
Allie	Swabian/Wurttemberger
Karo	Swabian/Wurttemberger
Barry Hundin	Swabian/Wurttemberger
Basco Rude 990026	???
Bella v Gelterkindern	???
Bella v Herbrechtingen	???
Bella Schwenningen	probably Swabian/Wurttemberger
Bethli v Rubiland	???
Betty v Wallwitzberg	???
Bilstrud Hundin	probably Saxony/Brunswick
Canna 1900 Siegerin	???
Chausseur Rude	???
Lori Hundin	???
Cilla Hundin	???
Daisy Mannheim	???
Dewet v St Georgian	???
Dora	???
Flink Rude	???
Flora Agrippina	???
Flora v Brandenburg	Brandenburger
Flora v Basel (v Habsburg)	Swabian/Wurttemberger
Flora v Habsburg	Swabian/Wurttemberger
Out of Flora v Burgin(v Habsburg)	
by Prinz Rude	
Flora Hundin	???
Flora v Kirchheim	???
Flora 1 v Oberschwaben	Swabian/Wurttemberger
Flopi Hundin	probably Swabian/Wurttemberger
Formosa Hundin	???
Grete Hundin	???

Gretli v Memmingen	Thuringian herding mix (?)
Gretel Oberwaldhof	???
Gretle v Schatten	Swabian/Wurttemberger
Gretschen Krissler	???
Hektor v Ebersbach	???
Hektor Spaag	???
Minka Spaag	???
Harras Rude	???
Herta Hundin	???
Herta v Langensalza	???
Hertika Hundin	???
Hetta Hundin	???
Hexe	???
Ingo v Burghalde	possibly Thuringian herding mix
Juno (Knecht)	???
Kitty (kurzhaariger collie)	Collie
Kora v Luzern	???
Krimhild v Hoheluft	???
Kuropatin Muller	???
Laura v Wellingen (990342)	???
Lena v Saarbrucken	???
by Wolf v Volklingen	
out of Jule v Dudweiler	
Leo Rude	Swabian/Wurttemberger
Liese v Holzheim	???
Loni Hundin	???
Lola Hundin	???
Lore (Willenberg)	???
Lotte Hundin	???
Lotte v Mohs	???
Lotti v Klosterhof	???
Luchs v Ebersdorf	???
Luchs v Gommesheim	???
Luchs v Unstut	???
Lucie Hundin (99048)	???
By Tell (990673)	???
Out of Rosa v Klostermansfeld	probably Thuringen herding mix
Max v Holstein	Northern
Helmchen stets Getreu(fr Holstein)	Northern
Max v Busch	???
Max v d Alp	probably Swabian/Wurttemberger
Melaxie v Schwarzwald	Swabian/Wurttemberger
Meno (male)	???

261

Mino (fem)	???
Merry	???
Minka v Betzgenrieth	???
Minna v Langenau	probably Swabian/Wurttemberger
Miss II Hundin	Swabian/Wurttemberer
Nelly Boll	probably Swabian/Wurttemberger
Nelly Hundin 990521	???
Nelly Hundin 990523	???
by Lord Rude	
out of Dame Hundin	???
Nelly v Grimminghausen	???
Nero Rude 990535	
Persie Hundin	???
By Donau (990102)	
Out of Siene (99066)	
Prinz (v Gamstadt)	???
Prinz Rude (bred to)	???
Russ	???
Saale	Thuringian
Rosel v Goetal	???
Schama v Reussenstein	probably Swabian/Wurttemberger
Scharsch Uckermark	Swabian/Wurttemberger
Schmusse v Trossingen	???
Selma v Altfeld	probably Saxony/Brunswick
Senta v d Augustahohe	???
Sibylle v Tautenburg	Swabian/Wurttemberger
by Merko Rude	
by Dux Rude	
out of Rose Hundin	
Out of Alte Lotte	
Strom Rude (990667)	Herding mix
Schnippe Hundin (889648)	Herding mix
by Dux Rude (990107)	Herding mix
out of Saale Hundin	Thuringian
Therese Hundin	probably Swabian/Wurttemberger
Tyrann Rude	Swabian/Wurttemberger
Tillie Hundin	Swabian/Wurttemberger
Ulla Hundin	???
Udo v Ravensberg	???
Wali Hundin (990703)	???
Wanda Thuringen	Thuringian
Wolf v Forstheide	???
Wolf v Gerlach	???

So, that's 200 dogs I've been able to identify (so far) upon which to found a breed. Undoubtedly there are others I haven't found yet, but I do not believe there are a great many remaining to be discovered and many of these dogs appear only once, limiting the genetic diversity they might have provided. So far, even though Canna was declared the Siegerin for 1900, I have been unable to find a pedigree in which she even appears once, and no pedigree for her appears in any of my books or the pedigree data base. (By which we can tell she wasn't of Horand or Pollux lineage. Stephanitz never passed up a chance to brag on them!) Jorg v d Krone, Sieger in 1899 and a herding champion as well, according to Stephanitz, was used only rarely (unfortunately).

In actuality, only a small coterie of these dogs forms the majority of the foundation of the breed. Beginning with Grief and Pollux and Prima of v Hanau, their son Fritz, aka Wolf v Schwenningen, their daughter Lucie v Starkenburg (grandmother of Roland) Horand v Grafath (of course) Mores and Carex Pleiningen, Madame v d Krone the Elder, Fides Neckarusprung, Horand's full brother Luchs Sparwasser, Audifax v d Krone v Grafath, Neckar Rude, the founding father of both v d Krone and v Brenztal lines, and, of course, Max and Sali v d Krone. Liese Geussnitz and the v Roden girls, Lotte and Lene appear now and again, and Loria Brenztal made a major contribution through her great grandson Horst v Boll, without whom the breed would have been very, very different. (Loria's loose ligamentation is still with us today!) Sibylle v Tautenburg and Schuft and Wachtel made hefty contributions, and the Karlsruhe dogs, Prinz and Flora were seminal. The v Park dogs, Rose and Roland were important, and so were the Nahegau and Kohlwald dogs, who came a little later.

All of our dogs today carry these dogs and they carry them many times over. Our dogs aren't just line-bred on these dogs, they're in-bred on them and even back-massed upon them, particularly on Horand v Grafath and his grandsire Pollux, most notably through Roland v Starkenburg. Pollux was there at the beginning with Phylax and Grief, traveling around the country, going head to head with his rival in exhibitions and spearheading the effort to create a national breed of shepherd dog. Those 3 dogs, Grief, Pollux and Phylax got it all started.

The three seminal kennels, v Hanau, v d Krone and v Brenztal didn't just spring up with the Phylax Society; they were there, breeding, training and selling premier herding dogs long before the Phylax Society was created. They and their dogs were already known all over Europe long before somebody got the bright idea of a blending the existing regional herding dogs into one national breed. Without their whole-hearted participation, the German

Shepherd would have been a very different breed—if it had ever come together to be a breed in the first place, which is doubtful.

The v Burg Fasanental dogs were there at the beginning, too, but didn't have much impact on the main line until the 1930s, though they were an important source of military dogs during World War I. Their bloodline, still running through our West German Working-lines today, remains one of the strongest resources of the old Saxony/Brunswick herding blood.

Outside dogs were added along the line, particularly after World War I and World War II to keep the dogs from becoming extinct due to a lack of genetic diversity, but basically, these dogs are it. Unfortunately, given the limited number of these dogs, many of these dogs were only used once or twice, while others, such as Pollux or Horand and their line-bred off-spring, such as Hektor v Schwaben, Beowulf Sonnenberg and Roland v Starkenburg, were used over and over again in repeated line-breedings, and even in close in-breeding, to the detriment of the genetic base of the breed as a whole. Even as long ago as 1904, Stephanitz was forced to add the outside line of Audifax (from v d Krone kennels) because his repeated in-breeding on Horand had already gotten him into trouble.

The history of the German shepherd breed is a history of repeated, multiple generation line-breeding, often close line-breeding, beginning with Horand. Only the heavily Swabian base with which the breed was endowed has allowed it to endure this long, but now, as we breed more and more to the Thuringian elements in the breed to get our show dogs and our bite dogs we erode that base further and further and the day will come when there are not enough of those diverse Swabian elements to hold. When that day comes, the end will not only be in sight, it will have arrived.

The first truly great sire of the breed was not Horand at all, but Hektor v Schwaben, the son of Horand and Mores Pleiningen. Mated to his own half sister, Thekla v d Krone by Horand and out of Madame v d Krone the Elder, he produced Beowulf Sonnenberg, Wolf and Pilot. The beautiful black but temperamentally challenged double German Sieger Roland v Starkenburg was produced by breeding Heinz v Starkenburg, the son of Hektor v Schwaben and Lucie v Starkenburg to Bella v Starkenburg, the daughter of Beowulf out of Lucie v Starkenburg. Lucie v Starkenburg was the daughter of Pollux and Prima v Hanau. Thus, Roland v Starkenburg carried 5 lines to Pollux v Hanau, 3 lines to Horand v Grafath and 2 lines to Prima v Hanau. No wonder poor Roland was mentally unsound.

Hettel Uckermark, Sieger, 1909

By 1907 Guntar and Hettel Uckermark, Roland v Starkenburg sons who appear at least once, and usually multiple times in virtually all German Shepherd pedigrees, carried their sire Roland's 5 lines to Horand/Pollux as well as their mother Gretel Uckermark's 2 lines to Horand/Pollux through her sire, Beowulf Sonnenberg. Beowulf Sonnenberg was Guntar's and Hettel's grandfather on their mother's side and their great grandfather on their father's and so we add yet another level of in-breeding to that which produced Roland. So now 7 lines back to Pollux have been loaded into the breeding in five generations. The 1909 Sieger Hettel Uckermark who appears in bloodlines at least as often as his full brother Guntar, was produced from the same pairing.

Alex vom Westfalenheim, 1914

Next we reach Alex v Westfalenheim, 1914, the first German shepherd dog in which EPI was identified. Alex was the son of Hettel out of a grand-daughter of Guntar, Bella v d Leine, an uncle to niece breeding on one side. And though the names were not exactly the same on Bella's maternal side, the in-breeding on Horand and Pollux on Bella's maternal grandfather, Frack v d Limpurg, was pretty extreme. Every one of Frack's great grandparents except one carried Horand and Pollux. Bella's maternal grandmother, Asta v d Warmenau, wasn't quite as bad, with only 9 lines to Horand and Pollux through the usual suspects, Beowulf Sonnenberg and his full brother Pilot, just to begin. But if you were to look for different bloodlines in her sire, you'd be disappointed. Not only was her sire, Ajax v Hohenstein the son of Guntar Uckermark, the full brother of Hettel, but Ajax's dam, Cilly v d Maikammer, was a daughter of Roland v Starkenburg as well.

Thus, on Ajax v Hohenstein, Bella's sire's side, she carried 13 lines to Horand-Pollux, while on her mother, Ilse v d Warmenau's side, she carried 31. Ilse's sire, Frack v d Limperg, was highly in-bred on Horand and Pollux through his sire, Hektor v Rinderfeld, who carried Horand through every one of his great grandfathers and through all but one of his great grandmothers, as well. The main culprits? Roland v Starkenburg to Beowulf Sonnenberg and

Pollux, Hektor v Schwaben to Horand and Pollux, Horand's full brother Luchs v Sparwasser to Pollux. Given that degree of in-breeding on Horand and Pollux, 7 lines on top through Guntar Uckermark and 44 lines from his mother, Bella v d Leine, for a total of 51, is it any wonder poor, sick, shy Alex was unhealthy and short-lived?

Erich von Grafenwerth, Sieger, 1920

Erich v Grafenwerth, the son of Alex brings us to the next generation. A Sieger in 1920 and then imported into America to become a champion there, ostensibly because of the new 'courage' test being instituted for dogs considered candidates for the Sieger show which pundits of the time asserted Erich could not have passed, but probably also because of the big money available for him, Malcolm Willis posited that every German Shepherd dog in the breed contains at least one line to Erich. If he is right and that is true, that means that every dog carries Erich's 51 lines to Horand and Pollux through his sire, Alex v Westfalenheim, as well as 29 additional lines to Horand and Pollux through his dam, Bianka v Riedekenberg for a total of 80 lines to Horand and Pollux.

Erich was a tall, leggy dog very much in the Swabian style, although he certainly carried plenty of Thuringian blood. He was only somewhat longer than he was tall, with long stifles and long thighs. A very beautiful dog, he appears to have been a modern style blanket back black and tan, a color which seems to have entered the main line through Erich's grandmother, Flora Berkemeyer.

Erich's mother, Bianka v Riedekenburg was his father, Alex v Westfalenheim's half sister, as they both shared the same sire, Hettel

Uckermark, doubling up on the in-breeding for yet another generation. Unfortunately, Bianka's dam, Flora Berkemeyer, was not noted for her fine temperament, but rather for the shyness that accompanied her rare refinement of face and figure so prized at the time. Bianka's temperament was described as dubious at best, and reports of Erich's temperament are little better. While it is said that he was police trained, other reports have him running out of the ring in 1921 either at the sound of a gunshot or backfire (depending on who is telling the story) along with most of the other dogs Stephanitz was judging that year, leading to his sale to the American market.

Klodo v Boxberg, Sieger, 1925

But, if you think that's bad, lets look at Erich v Grafenwerth's celebrated son, Klodo v Boxberg. To his sire's 80 lines to Horand and Pollux, add 72 more lines through his mother, Elfe v Boxberg. Can you say Back-Massing? At this point we have gone beyond line-breeding, and have passed in-breeding, leaving it behind us in the dust. Main line breeders of show dogs, however, paid no attention to this creation of theirs, and charged right ahead into another generation of line-breeding/back-massing.

268

Utz vom Haus Schutting Sieger 1929

Shall we go yet another generation, to 1929 Sieger Utz v Haus Schutting? Utz' sire was, of course, Klodo v Boxberg, so we start right out with Klodo's one hundred and fifty-two (152) lines to Horand and Pollux— yes, that's right, 152 lines! You think that's bad, consider the two hundred and forty-nine (249) lines to Horand and Pollux carried by Donna zum Reuerer, to whom Klodo was bred to create Utz v Haus Schutting!

Now, let's look at how this was done. Klodo was the son of Erich v Grafenwerth. Donna was Erich's granddaughter, making Donna Klodo's niece. But that was not the only way in which she was related to Klodo. Klodo's maternal grandmother, Doni v Wyhratal was also Donna's paternal great grandmother. And Jung Tell v d Kriminal Polizei not only appears in Klodo's maternal line, he also appears in Donna's maternal line. And Donna's sire, Falko v Indetal, was not only sired by Erich v Grafenwerth, but his dam, Donna v Grunatal was sired by Billo v Riedekenberg, the litter brother of Bianka v Riedekenberg who was Klodo's paternal grandmother. And just to add to the in-breeding, Utz' maternal grandmother, Donna v Ludwigskai, was sired by Diethelm v Riedekenburg, the half brother of both Bianka and Billo. So not only do these dogs go back to Horand and Pollux way, Way, W-A-A-Y too many times, 301 times, in fact, they go back to Horand and Pollux through too many of the same dogs.

Utz v Haus Schutting was the German's Sieger in 1929 and there are few dogs today that do not carry Utz. Those who don't, few as they are, may go back to Klodo through a different route, that of Utz' nephew, 1933 Sieger

Odin v Stolzenfels. Let's see if he does any better than Utz' 301 lines back to Horand and Pollux.

Odin v Stolzenfels Sieger 1933

Odin was sired by Curt v Herzog Hedan, a son of Klodo out of Barbel v d Halskappe and Barbel was by Rex v Frieseck and out of Astana v Birkental. Oh, goodie, different names, at least. Rex was by Billo v Riedekenburg, and here we are right back again where we started from, with a badly in-bred dog of poor temperament. Rats. Well, let's see if Rex's mother fares any the better. Her name was Aster v d Horstburg and she was by Nores v d Kriminal Polizei and out of Freia v Fallerslebertorwall.

Billo we know is a problem, with 29 lines to Horand and Pollux and a poor temperament to go with those lines. What about Nores? Well, he's by Horst v Boll, a bulwark of great temperament, but unfortunately Horst carries 17 lines to Horand and Pollux. Not so awful in the grand scheme of things we're seeing in the other dogs, considering all the great Brenztal blood he carried, and the lines to Mores Pleiningen and Madame v d Krone the Elder. He certainly wasn't hurt, either, by Carex Pleiningen, a fortress of great temperament. But what about Nores' mother? Who was she and how many lines to Horand and Pollux did she carry?

Well, her name was Giza v d Kriminal Polizei, and she was kind of an oops when it comes to lines to Horand and Pollux. Her sire was Jung Tell v d

270

Kriminal Polizei, and he was by Tell v d Kriminal Polizei and out of Gerta v Boll. Tell, who was by Luchs v Kalsmunt-Wetzlar, carried 24 lines to Horand and Pollux, 13 from Luchs and 11 from his mother, Herta v d Kriminal Polizei. Giza's mother, Rezia v d Kriminal Polizei, was also by Tell v d Kriminal Polizei—that is, she was the half sister of Jung Tell, carrying Tell's 24 lines to Horand and Pollux as well as her mother, Fanny v d Kriminal Polizei's 5 lines to Horand and Pollux through her mother Tillie v Goldsteintal and one through her father, Tell v Goldsteintal.

Oh, but we're not done yet. Now we have to figure out how many lines to Horand and Pollux Giza's father's (Jung Tell) mother, Gerta v Boll carried. In one way, that's easy, since she's the litter sister of Horst v Boll, so we know she had 17 lines to Horand and Pollux, but in the sense of in-breeding, Horst was being bred to his grand-niece. Not horribly close, but considering how close every other dog in this pedigree is . . . well, not so great.

So, ok, let's start doing the arithmetic. Tell's 24 lines added to Gerta's 17 lines give Jung Tell 41 lines to Horand and Pollux. Ouch! But then, since he was bred to his half sister, Rezia, who had her father Tell's 24 lines added to her mother Fanny's 6 lines, that makes 30 for Rezia. So now we add Jung Tell's 41 lines to Rezia's 30 lines and that gives us 71 lines to Horand and Pollux through Nores' mother to add to the 17 he got from Horst v Boll his father, for a grand total of 88 lines to Horand and Pollux for Nores alone! Whew! No wonder he didn't have the greatest disposition.

Nores, in his turn, was bred to Freia v Fallerslebertorwall (whew! Take a breath). Freia's father was Arno v d Eichenburg, German Sieger in 1913. Arno's father was—wait for it—Tell v d Kriminal Polizei. So, back we are with Tell's 24 lines to Horand and Pollux all over again. Arno's mother was Diana v d Blossenburg, whose father was Roland v Starkenburg who had 5 lines to Horand and Pollux (those lines are starting to look pretty mild, now aren't they? Just remember those 5 lines to Horand and Pollux were packed into 3 generations, though.) Diana's mother was Christel v Jena-Paradise, and her father was Siegfried v Jena-Paradise, who carried 7 lines to Horand and Pollex, and those lines were almost as tightly bound and close up as those Roland carried. The result was that good old Arno carried 36 lines to Horand and Pollex.

But what about Freya's mother, Lotte v d Harzberg? Well, her father was Wolf II v d Alp, who was by Graf Eberhard v Hohen Esp in his turn, and out of Fanny v d Alp. Fanny had good Swabian blood on top without a single taint of Horand or Pollux, but her mother, Fritigild v Lindenhof carried 2 lines to Horand and Pollux. Graf Eberhard v Hohen Esp was by Wolf Balingen, the son of Beowulf's full brother Pilot, and his mother was Nelly II Eislingen. Wolf Balingen carried 4 lines to Horand and Pollux and Nelly 2 more, so that makes 6 lines for Graf Eberhard. Add Fanny's 2 for 8 for Wolf II to the 7 Lotte's mother, Julie v Eckertal carried through her father, Roland v Park and

271

her mother Liese v Eckertal whose father was Hussan v Park (a son of Roland v Park out of his half sister Rose v Park) and you get 15.

That means that Freia gets 15 lines to Horand and Pollux from her mother and 36 from her father for a total of 51. And we're going to add that to Nores' 88? Boy, howdy! Poor old Aster v d Horstburg carries 139 lines to Horand and Pollux. So then we add poor Billo's 29 lines to get Rex's total of 168, and that's the number of lines to Horand and Pollux carried by Barbel's sire, Rex v Friesbeck. What about her mother, Astana v Birkenal? Let's look at her.

Well, Astana's father was Claus v Flugel, and his father was Ajax v Huhenstein, and Ajax was by Guntar Uckermark and out of Cilly Maikammer. We've done Guntar and Cilly before—Guntar carried 7 lines to Horand and Pollux and Cilly 8. Cilly and Guntar were half brother and sister, both sired by Roland v Starkenburg. So Ajax carried 15 lines to Horand and Pollux and he carried them the worst way, through in-breeding. What about Claus' mother, Fricka v d Unfehlbarkeit? Well, her father, Odin v Nord Albingen could almost be considered an out line, with only 3 lines to Horand and Pollux and some good Swabian blood on the top and bottom from Audifax v d Krone v Grafath and the Geussnitz bunch.

Fricka's mother, Mira v d Niedersachsen carried 2 lines from her sire, Wolf v Niedersachsen and 6 more from her mother, Lola v Niedersachsen, for a total of 8. Added to Odin's 3 and you get 11 scattered over 4 to 6 generations. Could be worse. At least Swabian blood here and there, with Leo v Niedersachsen, Wolf's sire going back to Carex Pleiningen through his mother, Elsa v Schwaben.

So now we have 26 lines to Horand and Pollux through Claus. What about Astana's mother, Adda v Geotal? Well, Adda's father was Olaf v d Kriminal Polizei, so we're right back to Jung Tell and Tell v d Kriminal Polizei, because Olaf was by Ito v d Kriminal Polizei who was by Jung Tell who was by Tell. In addition, Olaf's mother was Jung Fanny v d Kriminal

Polizei, and young Freia's father was Chlodwig v d Kriminal Polizei, and his father was Jung Tell and 'round we go again. Chlodwig's mother was Fanny v d Kriminal Polizei—yes, the same Fanny we encountered in Nores' family tree and Jung Fanny's mother was Minka v d Kriminal Polizei whose father was whoops! Roland v Starkenburg, and Minka's mother was hey, Fanny again. Whoo! Can we say IN-BRED??? So don't be surprised when you find that Olaf carries 120 lines to Horand and Pollux.

But hey, what about Adda's mother, Ella v Greifberg, what about her? Well, Ella was sired by Hettel Uckermark (Roland v Starkenburg again) for 7 more lines to Horand and Pollux again (2 through Hettel's mother, Gretel, remember?) and her mother was Afra Jena-Ost. Afra's father was Arno v Starkenburg who was by, no surprise by now, Roland v Starkenburg. (That makes Hettel and Afra half brother and sister, by the way!) Afra's mother was

Elfriede v Geussnitz. Now, Geussnitz, we know by now, means a good grounding in Swabian blood, but in this case, it also means Elfriede's father, Siegfried v Jena Paradies and his 7 lines to Horand and Pollux. Elfriede's mother, Irma Geussnitz, was by Baron v Haus Tautenburg, with only 1 single, solitary line to Horand on the top and good old solid Swabian on the bottom with Liese v Geussnitz. So, Ella's total? 21 lines to Horand and Pollux. Doesn't sound like much after 120, does it? But that gives Adda 141 lines in all to Horand and Pollux.

We add Claus' 26 lines to Horand and Pollux to Adda's 141 and we get, hey, presto! 167 lines to Horand and Pollux. But that's just for Astana. We have to add Rex' 168 to Astana's lines to get the sum of Barbel's lines to Horand and Pollux, and the grand total is—335.

But wait a minute! We're not done yet. In order to obtain the number of lines to Horand and Pollux that the sire of Odin v Stolzenfels, Curt v Herzog-Hedan carried, we have to add the lines that his sire, Klodo v Boxberg carried to those Barbel carried, and to do that, we add Klodo's 131 lines to Barbel's 335 lines, and that gives us a total of 466 lines to Horand and Pollux for Curt.

Now, we have to add up the lines carried by Odin's mother, Bella v Jagdschloss Platte. Bella's father was Mohr v d Secretainerie, and Mohr's father was Sieger of 1921 Harras v d Juch, a Nores son. That's right—we're right back to Nores again, and his 88 lines to Horand and Pollux. But what about Harras' mother, Lora Hildenia? What's her breeding? Well, to begin, she's a granddaughter of Arno v d Eichenburg, and we know that's 36 lines to Horand and Pollux right there. Then there's her father's mother, Hilde Agrippina, with 12 more lines to Pollux and Horand. (Twelve? Humm, not bad in the scheme of things we're seeing so far.) So now we add 66 to 88 for Harras v d Juch, which gives him 154 lines to Pollux and Horand. But that's just Mohr's topline. What about his mother, Flora v d Secretainerie? Well, her father is Edi v Herkules Park and her mother is Chrimhilde v d Secretainerie.

Edi v Herkules Park is by Jung Tell v d Kriminal Polizei (again) with his 41 lines to Horand and Pollux and Edi's mother was Hexe v Mundtsdorf whose father is—here he is again! Hettel Uckermark with his 7 lines to Horand and Pollux, mostly through Roland v Starkenburg. Hexe's mother was Asta v Mundtsdorf who added 33 more lines to Horand and Pollux to the mix, through more of those usual suspects, Hussan v Park, Beowulf Sonnenberg and Dewet Barbarossa.

Chrimhilde is just a repeat, with her maternal grandfather Norbert v Kohlwald bringing back Beowulf Sonnenberg and Hella Memmingen, and her maternal great grandmother leading to Luchs v Kalsmunt-Wetzlar, sire of Tell and grandsire of Jung Tell. Her maternal grandmother, Krimhilde Hildenia doubles up on Norbert v Kohlwald for a total of 58 lines to Horand and Pollux for Chrimhilde. This brings us up to 293 lines to Horand and Pollux for Mohr v d Secretainerie, the sire of Bella.

On to Bella's mother, Nora v Stolzenfels. Her sire, Arno v d Villa Hugel is a new name, but if you were hoping for new bloodlines, you're out of luck. Arno actually carries 505 lines to Horand and Pollux. That's right. FIVE HUNDRED AND FIVE! His father, Bodo v Alfreds Park carries 366 lines to Horand and Pollux and Bodo's father, Cito Ischeland carries 226 lines to them. Cito's sire might be another new name, Arno v Furstenberg, but his grandsire, Alex v Westfalenheim isn't. Arno's mother, Clara v Herkules Park was by Jung Tell v d Kriminal Polizei and Clara's mother, Hexe v Mundtsdorf, adds another 40 lines all by herself.

Cito's mother, Cleo v Grafenwerth, half sister to Erich, was by Ito v d Kriminal Polizei, adding another 68 lines to the total, and Cleo's mother, the infamous Bianka v Riedekenburg, holds up her end with the same 26 lines she donated to Erich's cause. It ought to be noted that Cleo's father, Ito v d Kriminal Polizei, was the son of Jung Tell v d Kriminal Polizei. In fact, while Jung Tell might appear twice in this family tree, Hettel Uckermark appears 3 times and never mind how many times Roland v Starkenburg and dear old Beowulf Sonnenberg show up.

But we're not done yet. Oh, no, we're not even close to done. Bodo's mother, Regina v Steinfurter Schloss, carries 141 lines to Horand and Pollux. We start right out with a familiar name—Regina's father is Arno v d Eichenburg (oh, no!) and his 36 lines to Horand and Pollux (which are starting to look like small potatoes at this point!) Regina's mother, Hella v Steinfurter Schloss carries 105 more because, oh, hey! Hella's father was Jung Tell v d Kriminal Polizei. Hella's mother Anita Steinfurter Schloss was by (guess who?) Arno v d Eichenburg (AGAIN!) and her mother was Tantieme v Sandberg. Another new name! But not really. Because Tantieme's father was Guntar Uckermark, and her mother, Gretel v Kormannsburg was by Luchs v Kalsmunt-Wetzlar, and Gretel's mother was Nellie Roten Berge. Nellie's father was Siegfried v Jena-Paradies and Siegfried, as we know by now, was by Dewet Barbarossa and out of Hella Memmingen (same old-same old). The only slightly positive note in all of this is Nellie's mother, Wally v Geussnitz, but even she carried one line to good old Horand through her father Baron Hans v Tautenberg. So there we are, with 28 lines to Horand and Pollux through Tantieme alone.

But all those lines are just those Arno v d Villa Hugel got through his father. What about his mother, Blanka v Mathildenhof? Well, her father was— oh, no - here he is again! Erich v Grafenwerth! With his 80 lines to Horand and Pollux. Blanka's mother is a new name (thank goodness) Zira Mercedes. Kind of a neat name. So what about Zira? Well, her father was Arno v d Eichenburg (AGAIN!!) and her mother was Ada v Bockerhof.

Ada v Bockerhof? Hummm. Her father was Gregor v Osterdeich, a new name. Unfortunately, his father was the by now very familiar Guntar Uckermark. Her mother, Lola v Osterdeich was by Aribert v Grafath and out of Prima v Sandhof. Prima's father was—ta da! Beowulf Sonnenberg. Prima's mother, Cora v Enztal, was by Fritz v Schwenningen, whose father was Pollux himself. So there we are, 22 more lines to Horand and Pollux, just through Ada alone. So much for Arno v d Villa Hugel.

Let's try Nora's mother Wega v d Kriminal Polizei. Starts out ok, with another new name, Aribert v Saarland, but things go downhill fast when we encounter his sire, Erich v Grafenwerth. Aribert's mother, Maya v Erlenbrunnen was a granddaughter of Jung tell v d Kriminal Polizei on the top, with Horst v Boll the sire of her paternal grandmother, Frigga v Schulberg. Frigga piles up even more lines to Horand and Pollux with Harras v d Kriminal Polizei and Christel v d Hofwache, 27 to be precise, for a total of 44.

Maya's mother, Ella v d Welle doesn't help, as she is a daughter of Arno v d Eichenberg (popular sire syndrome, anyone?) and Freia Schortautal, herself a daughter of Roland v Starkenburg and a granddaughter of Siegfried v Jena-Paradies as well as a great granddaughter of Beowulf on the bottom. Total lines to Horand and Pollux for Ella? 51, allowing Maya to rack up 136 lines to Horand and Pollux altogether.

And now we find ourselves facing Nora's grandmother on the bottom, Irma v Nassau. Sounds good—until you see that her father is again! Ito v d Kriminal Polizei with his 68 lines to Horand and Pollux. Irma's mother is Cora v Horstein and her father is—oh, heck! Jung Tell v d Kriminal Polizei. But there is hope. Cora's mother is Helma Jagerslust—or is there? Guess not. Her paternal grandfather was Roland v Starkenburg (him again!) and her maternal grandfather was Beowulf v Nahegau, the son of Beowulf Sonnenberg. (Here we go again.) And last of all, Tillie Barbarossa takes us back to Hella Memmingen with her 3 lines to Horand and Pollux and then up through Jorg v d Krone on the top back to Pollux again for 13 more lines in all for Helma Jagerslust.

This gives us 338 lines to Horand and Pollux through Nora's mother Wega v d Kriminal Polizei, together with 505 lines for Arno v d Villa Hugel for a grand total of 843. It seems impossible that that much in-breeding could be crammed into 30 years, but it was. And so, Odin v Stolzenfels, German Sieger of 1933, carried 843 lines to Horand and Pollux. Those lines came, time and again, through the same individuals. By now, you can recite the names with me: Hektor v Schwaben, Beowulf Sonnenberg, Roland v Starkenburg, Hettel and Guntar Uckermark, the Riedekenbergs, Bianka and Billo, Dewet Barbarossa and Siegfried v Jena-Paradies, Hella v Memmingen, Arno v d Eichenburg and Luchs v Kalsmunt-Wetzlar, the Kriminal Polizei dogs, Ito and Nores, Fanny and Jung Tell and Tell, Erich v Grafenwerth and Alex Westfalenheim. Basically 20 dogs.

Look at the Siegers. Jorg v d Krone, in 1899, was a grandson of Pollux. Then Hektor v Schwaben the next 2 years, a son of Horand and great grandson of Pollux. Then Peter v Pritschen, another son of Horand, in 1902 (and thus another great grandson of Pollux). Roland v Park followed him, a Hektor v Schwaben son with 3 lines to Horand and Pollux, and then Stephanitz' own Aribert v Grafath in 1904—aha, Max picked his own dog!! Can we say conflict of interest? Then Beowulf Nahegau, son of Beowulf Sonnenberg, carrying Horand and Pollux twice through him. Then in 1906 and 1907 Roland v Starkenburg, with his 5 in-bred lines to Horand and Pollux was chosen Sieger in consecutive years, poor temperament and all. After him came big, stout Luchs v Kalsmunt-Wetzlar with 13 lines to Horand and Pollux.

After Luchs, Hettel Uckermark, an actual herding dog from a mother with heavily Swabian blood and only 7 lines to Horand and Pollux almost seems a breath of fresh air, though he was sired by Roland v Starkenburg. Hettel was followed by Tell v d Kriminal Polizei, a son of Luchs v Kalsmunt-Wetzlar, with his 24 lines to Horand and Pollux. Tell was followed by Norbert of Kohlwald, a son of Beowulf v Nahegau and grand-son of Beowulf Sonnenberg, in 1911 and 12, with his 16 lines to Horand and Pollux. He was followed by Arno v d Eichenburg, a half brother to Luchs v Kalsmunt-Wetzlar, in 1913 with his 36 lines to Horand and Pollux.

Alex v Westfalenheim would almost certainly have followed Arno, but he was born in 1914 and World War I derailed the Horand train until 1919, when Dolf v Durstenbrook took the title. Dolf wasn't really much of an alternative. He was in-bred on Guntar and Hettel Uckermark on top and Riedekenburg on the bottom with more Guntar Uckermark there as well. About all you can say is that he wasn't the direct son or grandson of another Sieger since he was a great grandson of Hettel Uckermark, albeit on the topside. Dolf was followed by Erich v Grafenwerth, another grandson of Hettel Uckermark, in 1920 with his 80 lines to Horand and Pollux and the main line was back on track again and roaring full speed ahead, regardless of Erich's doubtful temperament.

After Erich came Harras v d Juch, the Nores son and great grandson of Tell v d Kriminal Polizei and double great grandson of Luchs v Kalsmunt-Wetzlar, with 88 lines to Horand and Pollux just through Nores alone. He may have been an aberration—it is said he was the only dog left in the ring after a loud backfire interrupted the Sieger show of 1921, when all the other dogs, (Erich v Grafenwerth among them, according to the story) ran away. According to what by now is more a legend than a verifiable fact, the next year Stephanitz introduced the first 'courage test' by firing a gun into the air.

Cito Bergerslust and Donor v Overstolzen followed Harras, perhaps because they too, could pass the new 'courage' test? but they were barely steps to the side before Klodo v Boxberg, with his 152 lines to Horand and Pollux was chosen to be Sieger in a closed door session before he ever set foot on the show grounds.

Erich v Glockenbrink followed Klodo, a great grandson of both Erich v Grafenwerth and his sister Cleo v Grafenwerth, and while Arko v Sadowaberg may have temporarily interrupted the Horand line (although not by much!) Erich v Glockenbrink was chosen to be Sieger by Stephanitz a second time, in 1928, before he happily turned to Utz v Haus Schutting in 1929. Then he chose Herold aus der Niederlausitz in 1930 and 1931 before going back to the Utz son, Hussan v Haus Schutting in 1932. Hussan was followed in 1933 by his own first cousin, Klodo grandson Odin v Stolzenfels. Sensing a pattern here? You should be.

Every generation in Alex Wesfalenhein's family tree is a line or in-breeding, half-brother to half-sister and cousin to cousin, with 8 lines to Lucie Starkenburg alone. This amounts to a form of distillation performed on genetics. When one asks oneself why such a distillation was performed, the obvious answers present themselves. In the formation of a breed of dogs created by rich men—and v Stephanitz was certainly that! line-breeding is done to create a 'look' to the dogs which is desired to be passed on down through the generations with a certain uniformity. There is no doubt that was a consideration in the line breeding used in dogs like Alex v Westfalenheim. It is just too bad that v Stephanitz, who talked a good game, didn't put his ego where his mouth was, but from the beginning v Stephanitz's sentimental attachment to Horand impaired his judgment. He didn't care that his multiple-generation line-bred Horand dogs weren't mentally or physically healthy; his ego and his sentimental attachment to Horand were more important to him than healthy, mentally sound dogs.

Time after time, Stephanitz faced choices between mentally and physically sound dogs ready, willing and able to do useful work and dogs of Horand's lineage. With very few exceptions, he turned away from the healthy, sound dogs to the unsound, unhealthy dogs, dogs like Alex v Westfalenheim and the closely related Riedekenburg dogs. (And you wonder why we have fearful, temperamentally unsound dogs riddled with genetic disorders today? Look no farther than the breeding decisions and the choice of Siegers Stephanitz made!)

Stephanitz declared, from the very beginning, that he wanted the new German Shepherd dog to be a breed established for real work in the real world. He inveighed, time and again, that 'his' dogs were to be true working dogs and not 'fancy' (show) dogs—yet what did he do? He founded the whole breed on a dog whose temperament was so faulty that he WOULD not and COULD not work! A dog who by his own admission was 'incorrigible' and 'untrainable'. A dog who was 'impudent' 'an incurable provoker of strife' and who his friend Herr Eiselen said contemptuously needed to be 'put on a leading string'—one of the most profound insults a working dog man of the era could utter. Far from having the 'good' character Stephanitz ascribed to him, Horand v Grafath had an appalling temperament. Even his doting master once conceded that Horand was so dog aggressive that he could not see another dog without attacking it and he could not be around stock without chasing them hither and yon for his own enjoyment to the detriment of the stock, the fury of the stockmen and Stephanitz's chagrin.

Stephanitz' beloved pet was so lacking in obedience that he would have to be driven off the stock by staff wielding shepherds—the reason Stephanitz had been able to purchase the dog in the first place. Horand's proclivities for biting Stephanitz' servants, tenants, and any chance met stranger would be a liability today and a one way ticket to being 'put to sleep'. Can you say 'kennel blind'?

Instead of using just enough Thuringian to get the ears up and keep them there, Stephanitz kept encouraging people to add more and more of it, mostly through Lucie v Starkenburg, but also through the 2 Nelly Eislingens and their mother/grandmother Ella Gmund and the Sparwasser dogs, which he loved. The result was that dogs bred in on this blood turned ever more fearful and shy—they went from Horand's lack of balance and stability to outright and downright unstable, with extremes from hostile, angry dogs good for nothing, to fearful, anxious dogs good for even less. Because this is the foundation of the 'main' line of the breed, whenever dogs today are line-bred for more than a single generation, these characteristics are those which will emerge from the distillation, whether in just a few of the pups or in the entire litter.

The idea that a breeder can somehow, by force of will alone, repeat line breed for generations and yet avoid these results is a fantasy. You cannot change what is there in the genes of the dogs, put there, into the very chromosomes, by a kennel blind Stephanitz and the breeders who curried his favor in order to do well in the breed and make money selling their dogs. The so-called 'split' we have today is the very creation of the dichotomy between what Stephanitz said he wanted his breed to be, and what he actually made of it by his own breeding decisions and the breeding decisions he forced upon others as they attempted to make their way in the new breed.

Some people stuck with the 'country' dogs, the dogs of Saxony and Brunswick, the herding dogs of the North, and the Swabian dogs from the Wurttemberg region, so they could continue to breed useful, mentally stable dogs with strong genetic obedience and good nerve. Their dogs languished in obscurity, as Stephanitz focused his attention and his care on the show dogs of Thuringian ancestry, dogs heavily in-bred on Horand and Pollux. According to Stephanitz, dogs like Baron v d Krone were all but 'lost' to the breed, because they were mated to true working dogs, rather than to the fancy dogs he preferred, but were they really? Or has the diversity of the Baron's mother, Madame v d Krone the Elder, of Mores and Carex Pleiningen, of Audifax and

278

Max v d Krone, of Fides Neckarusprung, of Gretel Uckermark and Sibylle v Tautenburg, brought down to us through the supposedly 'mis-mated' country dogs, gifted us with what little diversity and good health remains to our breed today?

What we do with that little dab of diversity that remains will rest largely upon our understanding of the situation the breed is in. If we persist in burying our heads in the sand and refusing to take to heart the ever proliferating list of genetic disorders our perpetual back-massing on Horand and Pollux have created, insisting that those people finding fault with the breed's state are merely 'trolls' and crack-pots nobody should listen to, then there really isn't any hope for improvement. If, instead, we take a clear-eyed look at where the breed is today, we might be able to make reasoned actions in order to improve it.

Some people are talking about out-crossing with other breeds, such as the Malinois and Dutch Shepherds, which really are merely out-growths of the Thuringian and Saxony and Brunswick elements of our own breed, while others are ridiculing the very idea by tossing out possibilities of out-crossing the German shepherd with breeds to which it has no relationship at all. Why not take a more logical, but less drastic step and repatriate the original colors as much as possible back into the breed and stretch the size limits back to their original generous spread between 21 and 29 inches? Stop harping on 'titles' which drive the breed to unhealthy extremes and start emphasizing real, genuine, honest work instead, thus pulling the breed back towards stability and soundness and moderation, both in temperament and structure?

These are reasoned, logical, and practical ways to repair the breed's damaged genetic diversity. They would work, albeit gradually. For these very reasons I don't expect anyone to attempt them. The outcry against them by the 'title' hounds of the sport world and the show world is sure to drown out any voices of reason that might be found. But when you consider their arguments that we ought to ignore the breed's problems and focus instead on the 'good' dogs we have—the argument favored by the bite sport/ 'working-line' crowd, or the show people's defensive pleas that they're trying to do better, perhaps we ought to remember the colloquial definition of insanity: doing the same thing over and over and expecting a different result.

If we are merely going to continue back-massing over and over on the same dogs, snow-balling the effects of in-breeding by repeating the same breeding over and over, it is certain that no improvement can be made in the dogs we turn out by such methods. If things do not change, if we do not dedicate ourselves to at least bringing back what diversity the breed possessed to begin with, we must resign ourselves to ever increasing genetic disorder and greater and greater numbers of fearful dogs as the back-massing on the unhealthy and fearful elements Stephanitz glorified in the beginning of our breed continue to multiply with every breeding of the limited approved and 'titled' dogs who created the problem in the first place.

What happens to the German Shepherd dog, whether the breed continues to roll downhill, back-massing on Horand and Pollux in increasing numbers with every generation, or whether we try to make some changes, bring in the old colors and sizes and repair to some extent, the breed's genetic diversity, or whether we allow the breed to continue on its current path until large changes, such as out-crossing with other breeds becomes necessary to stave off extinction, does not depend entirely upon the people who breed the dogs. It depends, just as largely, with the people who buy the dogs the breeders produce.

Breeders cannot breed their dogs in a vacuum if they intend to make any money with their pups. The few breeders who turn out a litter of puppies every three or four or five years for their own use and the use of a few of their friends and neighbors can and do continue to turn out great, healthy, sound, genetically diverse dogs, but in the greater scheme of things, they matter very little to the breed. You might love to have one of their herding, search and rescue, guide/aide/alert service dogs, with their rich veins of genetic obedience and solid nerve, but the odds that you could even find such a breeder are slender. The odds of your managing to get one of their dogs, even if you could find them are even more miniscule. You probably wouldn't want one of their moderate, serviceable, soundly structured, stable dogs anyway—after all, the person producing them would undoubtedly fall under the forum label of 'back-yard' breeder.

But here's the thing. If you want a good, stable, sound, moderate family dog to act as a deterrent to malefactors yet still be able to behave courteously towards family, friends and neighbors without misplaced aggression or fearful 'natural suspicion' with good health, you, the buyer, are going to have to turn away from the 'title' crowd and their insane back-massing on all the same old lines in the same old ways. You're going to have to ignore the hype, search out the back-yard breeders whose dogs vary in size and color and even embrace the larger dogs and the white dogs and the grey dogs and the red dogs and all the rest and encourage the kind of diversity that all the pundits on the forums love to hate. Because in the final analysis, what will happen to the breed will happen where the money is spent.

Spend your money on cookie cutter show dogs of all the same color and all the same size, or on a puppy whose parents have all those sport 'titles' to prove how good they were, and you will continue to get dogs with one genetic disorder after another and eventually you will wind up with pups whose diversity consists of which disorder you find least disruptive. Do you want a dog who is fearful but otherwise healthy? Or a great temperament with Degenerative Myopathy? Or how about a nice blind dog, thanks to Pannus?

And after all, that pretty black/red dog only has to have a hundred dollars worth of enzymes added to his kibble every month to stay alive.

Or what about that drivey, flat-ribbed sport dog who just never gives up chasing his ball? He's so much fun, when he's not driving you nuts because he won't settle down until he's had a ton of hard exercise. Too bad bloat will carry him off at nine or ten, if he manages to live that long.

Then again, there's that gorgeous puppy that was everything you always wanted—unfortunately, he died before his fifth birthday, courtesy of Cardiomyeopathy. And ooh, what about that dog with the perfect hips? Of course, he's got a mild case of Mega E, meaning that his esophagus hasn't developed properly and he'll die of aspiration pneumonia sooner or later, probably long before he reaches the ripe old age of 8, but hey! His hips are perfect! (As long as you don't spay or neuter him too young!)

And give us a few generations to catch up with the British—their show dogs now have a heredity form of epilepsy, where the dogs have seizures, some of them pretty severe. Am-line show dogs have already set their feet upon that path. How many generations do those dogs have left before we start seeing the people on the forums assuring puppy buyers that those little seizures their puppy is having are 'normal'?

Stephanitz put his money in one place and his mouth in another. He talked a good game about wanting his dogs to be 'useful' but when it came down to backing up his statements, he encouraged illness, poor and fearful dispositions and the proliferation of dogs good for nothing but to look at. Where will your dog buying dollar go? Will you back the people struggling to create genetic diversity with their dogs of different colors and sizes? Or will you be like Stephanitz, continually saying you want healthy, stable dogs, but forever putting your money into unstable, fearful, unhealthy dogs because they're the 'right' color, and the 'right' size and they were bred by the 'right' people?

Chapter 10
The Dogs Who Started It All

Hecktor von Schwaben

The Paradox of Horand von Grafath

Hektor Linksrhein gen. Horand von Grafrath 1.

Horand von Grafath was the first dog to be registered as a German Shepherd Dog. It is no coincidence that he was Captain von Stephanitz's beloved pet. But there is a great deal more to Horand's choice as the number one German Shepherd dog than just the fact that he was Stephanitz' pet. Horand was deliberately chosen for the role for some very specific reasons.

When Stephanitz bought Horand on January 15, 1898, he was buying a dog with a known pedigree which combined Swabian, Saxony, Northern and Thuringian dogs all in one individual. Further, four of the dogs in Horand's immediate ancestry were dogs which had been exhibited as examples of the finest of Germany's working shepherd dogs and two of them were at least noted in the circles of German dog fanciers, and one of them, Pollux v Hanau, the Swabian dog, was outright famous.

Horand's sire, Kastor was exhibited at Heidelberg in 1896, as an example of a shepherd dog of Germany, while Kastor's sire, Pollux, had been exhibited a number of times and declared, on more than one occasion, an ideal example of a shepherd dog of Germany. Upon at least one occasion he was adjudged much superior to the Phlax Society's poster dog, Phylax von Eulau. Pollux was well known, as were the Hanau Kennels he came from, a kennel highly regarded for producing working shepherd dogs.

Kastor's dam, Schafermadchen v Hanau, had also been exhibited, in Frankfurt in 1891. A 'grey spotted' (blue merle) bitch of Brunswick/Saxony's favored type, she was smaller than the Swabian Pollux and found scant courtesy among those who preferred the larger, Swabian type for their herding. Even though Schafermadchen (translation, sheep herding girl, or shepherdess) was an actual working dog in the real world, her detractors said she was too

283

small to herd anything but geese. (A hundred and twenty years and nothing has changed--people are still hung up on size, only now it's the smaller dog that's in favor!)

Horand's dam, Lene, was bred by the well known Thuringian Sparwasser Kennels, and her sire was the proto-type (at the time) dog of the Northern breed herding type, Greif, a white dog exhibited in Hanover in 1882 as one of the standard bearers of the Phylax Society's 'ideal' German Shepherd dog. Not only was Greif himself exhibited as an ideal of the shepherd dogs of Germany, but so were two of his daughters. In Hamburg in 1888, these two bitches were chosen first and second respectively, in the shepherd dog class. (All three dogs, Greif and both of his two daughters, were white and all three were working herding dogs.)

Lene's dam, Lotte, wasn't famous, but she had been bred out of one of the well-known Sparwasser Kennel's Thuringian dogs. Did she carry Saxony or Swabian or even Northern shepherd dog blood as well as Thuringian? Quite possibly she did. Most Thuringian dogs who worked stock did have some other blood in them, most notably Brunswick/Saxony blood, since the Saxony dogs were primarily sheep herding dogs, while the Northern dogs were used as often for hunting and pulling sleds and small carts as they were for herding. Swabian dogs would have been less convenient to add, as the areas of the country where they were most common were farther away from Thuringia and the Sparwasser Kennels than Saxony.

So, Hektor v Linksrhein, as Horand v Grafath was originally named, was the ideal dog with which to begin a new organization for the founding of the German shepherd dog, bringing together, as he did, all four of the main original types of shepherd dog in Germany into one body. Greif and Pollux had both come out of the Phylax Society beginnings, with Greif a far less controversial dog than Phylax himself (Greif actually worked as a shepherd dog and lacked Phylax's strongly wolf-like appearance, being much more shepherd-like in look). Lene brought in the Sparwasser Kennels, the standard bearer of Thuringia, and Schafermadchen included Saxony into the fold.

Politically, he was perfect. Just finding a dog containing in one body not only the blood of all four types of regional dogs, Wurttemberger/Swabian and Thuringian and also including Northern and Brunswick/Saxony blood must have seemed fortuitous in the extreme. Finding one with a pedigree which had been recorded, and which included such illustrious names as Pollux and Grief must have seemed a Godsend. Of course the Captain had to have him. Making him the SV's number one dog was a no-brainer.

In looks, he had the prick ears and wolf-like head so preferred by the Captain and the still influential members of the disbanded Phylax Society, so that was good. In form, he was over-built and in pictures, a little awkward appearing, but Stephanitz found him quick and agile and strong for his size, which was thoroughly medium. Horand was not as big as the Swabians and

284

the big, tall, Northern dogs, he was lighter framed and generally smaller, at a little over 24 inches in height than either of the fountainheads of the large type shepherd dogs. He was, on the other hand, bigger than some of the smallest of the Brunswick/Saxony dogs and much of a size with the main group of them.

In color, he was what we would today call blue, and which was then mostly referred to as grey and tan. His grandmother, Schafermadchen, was what we would now call a blue merle though in her time she was called grey spotted. Horand appears to be more patterned, rather like a blanket-back black and tan, though he was not at all black and tan--Stephanitz and others clearly refer to him as grey. It is perhaps important to remember that though we are now prejudiced against these colors, and may not wish to admit that the very founder of the breed was a color we no longer consider 'breed-worthy' at the turn of the century, both grey and tans and merles were perfectly acceptable and the grey and tans were even more than acceptable, they were preferred.

Personally--well, in a day when the media was limited to newspapers and word of mouth and travel was difficult, uncomfortable and expensive, Horand's personal attributes probably didn't matter much. Stephanitz, who was devoted to Horand, called him 'intractable' and 'incorrigible' and complained that his first owner didn't train him. Horand was 'the maddest rascal' and a constant 'provoker of strife'. The Captain complained that Horand 'suffered from a superfluity of unemployed energy.' Stephanitz often mused that if only someone could train the dog, he might be able to accomplish great things, but unfortunately, with the methods of the time, he was not 'trainable' at all.

In Stephanitz' day, one trained a dog by working with the dog's own 'genetic obedience'. Dogs learned by watching other dogs (they had to watch them work, instead of picking fights with them) and by working with people 'on the job'. Given Horand's lack of 'genetic obedience', and his proclivities for picking fights with other dogs, the training methods of the day were ineffective. Had Stephanitz had the training methods of today, the 'Nothing in Life is Free' program and behavioral techniques, along with a good electronic collar, he might have been able to train Horand to be useful at something, tracking, perhaps, if stock-work was out of the question. If, of course, the Captain had been willing to put in the time and the effort to do it.

In fact, the dog only became available for purchase because he was 'worthless' on stock, as Herr Eiselen reports, and his previous owner had given up on him in frustration. Although the Captain stated unequivocally that Horand never killed a chicken, it may not have been for want of trying ('provoker of strife'). The Captain also insisted that he never bit a child. Apparently, Horand knew where his master drew the line, as he bit servants, tradesmen and strangers whose mode of dress indicated they were not of the Captain's social status with abandon.

285

From the day he came to live with the Captain as the first German shepherd rescue, Horand became a pet and a pet only. He was 'unemployed' in any productive endeavor other than following the Captain around and entertaining him--in fact, he was not useful in any way, nor did he do anything even approaching work. All the Captain asked was that his dog be 'loyal' and 'devoted' to him, and he was satisfied that Horand was. Overall, he was satisfied, even happy with the dog, and determined that the new breed should carry 'his' dog's stamp. Certainly in that Stephanitz was successful.

Horand's use as a stud dog might have been justified by his pedigree and the need to bring the supporters of each disparate type of shepherd dog together in order to forge the new breed, but repeated line and in-breeding on Horand amounted to nothing more nor better than self-indulgence in sentimentality and pride on Stephanitz' part. But line-breed and in-breed on Horand, the Captain did, generation after generation.

It is from Horand that our modern shepherds get their lack of biddability, their reactivity and their low bite threshold and many of the genetic disorders with which we deal today. According to Willis, (in The German Shepherd Dog) every German shepherd dog today carries Erich v Grafenwerth in their lineage at least once. If so, that means that every modern German shepherd dog today carries at the very least Erich v Grafenwerth's 80 lines to Horand v Grafath. Erich's sire, Alex v Westfalenheim, who is said to be the originator of EPI carried 51 lines to Horand in the first six generations.

What little data we have about the early breeding on Horand indicates that Alex might not actually have been the first dog in Horand's line to exhibit symptoms of what appeared to be EPI. Along about the second generation of line-breeding on Horand (and in-breeding, father to daughter and brother to sister) problems started cropping up among the puppies. The third generation puppies started dying outright. Some of them died at birth (most likely Juvenile Renal Dysplasia) and some at weaning (again, probably Juvenile Renal Dysplasia, and likely Mega E as well). Of the second generation, a number of those pups who had attained young adulthood, many began sickening and dying of no apparent reason, starving despite seemingly good appetites and plenty of quality food. We now recognize such symptoms as those of EPI.

Be that as it may, it was clear, right from the beginning, that if you wanted to get anywhere in the new breed, you had to breed to the Captain's Horand and you had to line-breed on him. Every year for nearly thirty years, the Captain picked the top dogs of the new breed, and with very little exception, he chose dogs that carried line-breeding on his beloved pet, Horand.

It was a clear case of do as I say, not do as I do, when it came to the Captain. His own breeding program had only the most limited of successes-- it was left to others, like Herr Eiselen of the Krone kennels and Tobias Ott of the Blasienberg Kennels, to make champion working dogs of the new breed. Largely, that was because the Captain bred with his heart instead of his head, and the clearest and most cogent example of that was his insistence on in-breeding and line-breeding on Horand.

Stephanitz' repeated avowal was that his breed of dogs was not to be bred for a 'fancy' appearance, but to be 'useful'. He encouraged the use of the new German Shepherd dogs for police work, formalized the training of 'ambulance' dogs to search for and find the wounded on battlefields, and he helped to pioneer the use of his dogs as guide dogs for the blind. He laid out the foundation for stock dogs to be classed on the same level as police and military dogs with Schutzhund dogs of a second rank to dogs doing truly useful work (a stricture which has been pretty much forgotten) and he inveighed over and over again against the use of 'artificial' means to judge dogs.

His fear was always and ever that the German shepherd dog might fall afoul of the same beauty contest mentality that had ruined the Scots collie, which was already in decline at the turn of the twentieth century, due to breeding for what was called a 'fancy' appearance. He even placed a statement in the first breed standard which said that nothing should be done in the breeding of the dog to detract from the 'usefulness' of the dog, no matter how much someone thought it might improve the appearance of his dogs. Yet even as he inveighed time and again against these abuses, he chose Roland v Starkenburg, with his unstable temperament and his in-breeding on Horand to be twice Germany's Sieger and Erich v Grafenwerth, who was elegant, but unsteady, after him because of their great beauty.

At the end of his life he fought ceaselessly against the use the Nazis made of his dogs to attack people indiscriminately and to terrorize them, he decried the low bite thresholds and the high prey drive they used to turn his beloved dogs into dogs who would bite women and children at the will of their despicable handlers. In fact, his daughter blamed his death on that very battle, saying that it exhausted him and brought on his final illness. Captain von Stephanitz' daughter reports that on his deathbed, his last words were for the breed he had established by main strength and determination. He begged that his dogs be kept strong and bred for usefulness, never for looks. So much for today's show dog.

The paradox of Horand was that he was never anything more than a pet, yet he was the progenitor of a breed which was to become known for its ability to work at, and be trained for, a wide variety of tasks, while he, himself, remained useless for anything but to amuse his master, and virtually untrainable. His character, his aggression, reactivity and low bite threshold, high prey drive and extreme energy levels supported best the use for his dogs which Stephanitz hated the most, as concentration and POW camp guards and Border Patrol dogs whose sole purpose was to attack and do great bodily harm to people, and not merely men, but women and children as well, which horrified Stephanitz. And it is Horand's energetic character, which Stephanitz so hoped to find a positive and worth-while use for, which today finds its most popular outlet in a 'bite sport' which is the epitome of the 'artificial' strictures he so hated. A sport that features, as its most treasured component, an unprovoked attack by the dog on a human.

Stephanitz chose Horand because of his looks and his pedigree, completely ignoring the dog's inability to work at anything constructive or useful. He adored the dog's zest and joie d'vivre, disregarding the dogs instability and penchant for biting, and his propensity for creating chaos wherever he went. Only the death of litter after litter of puppies and young adults kept him from in-breeding on Horand for a fourth generation. The seeds of the destruction of the German Shepherd Dog were all present in the body of the very dog Stephanitz chose to create it; in his reactivity, aggression, sharpness, low bite threshold, high prey drive, limited biddability, scant genetic obedience, instability and genetic disorder. All of those qualities were there, in that single, cherished pet.

Today as show breeders and working-line breeders flock to popular sires over and over again, creating one genetic bottleneck after another and rolling up enormous back-masses of breeding on relatively few individuals, the genetic disorders that felled Horand's descendants have returned to plague us. Now, we not only struggle with Jrd, Epi, and Mega E, we find ourselves facing Cardio, von Wildebrand's, Sibo, Ibd, Pannus, Epilepsy (in Great Britain) and Dm in a downward spiral where the odds favor the inheritance of affected genes over healthy in ever increasing numbers. At the same time, our very right to dog ownership has been put under siege by the forces of Animal Rightists and PETA people and to be called a breeder has become a label to be avoided. Breed specific legislation hovers over all our heads. Every dog bite resulting from the irresponsible breeding of reactive dogs by working-line breeders from 'titled' bite sport dogs and 'fear aggressive' dogs by show-line breeders who care little about their dogs' temperaments brings us that much closer to losing our dogs altogether. The stupidity of the people who buy dogs bred to bite people and then just can't believe their dog would actually bite someone just adds to the problem.

It's a toss up which end will come first--whether the short-sighted and self-indulgent popular sire/in-breeding for competition will destroy the breed with genetic defect first, or whether the breed will be legislated out of existence before the breed's genetics tank completely thanks to the 'bite sport' breeding of high prey drive, high aggression, low bite threshold, reactive dogs chomping down on an innocent public. Either way, the German Shepherd dog is on the way out, and the end of the breed we're facing all started with the breed's first registered dog, Horand v Grafath.

Did better dogs exist upon which to found the breed? Possibly. But there is no getting around the fact that the choice of Horand was politically correct. Was there another dog available who carried all four basic types of Germany's regional dogs in equal parts? Who could trace his lineage back, in so few generations, to a noted dog of each faction of the country? (Beyond Horand's own brother, Luchs v Sparwasser?) Doubtful. Could the breed have been founded on any other dog? We will never know. The fact is that the breed was founded upon Horand for good or ill. Whatever went before, with Phylax and all the rest, Horand v Grafath was officially the first German Shepherd Dog.

The Dogs Who Started It All The Mothers of the Breed: Madame v d Krone the Elder and Mores Pleiningen

Horand v Grafath may have been the father of the modern German Shepherd dog, but in order for there to be a breed, there had to be mothers, too. For the German Shepherd dog, that was Madame von der Krone the Elder and Mores Pleiningen, both of them herding dogs with the coveted (at the time) HGH attached to their name, designating that they were the crème de la crème of herding dogs. Both Madame and Mores were of Swabian/Wurttemberger type, big, stout, reliable girls, tall and sturdy and strong. They would both have been only slightly longer than they were tall, with good breath of body and well-rounded, broad hind-quarters of what was then referred to as pronounced herding type.

It is possible to guess about Madame v d Krone's color, as both Horand and his son Hektor v Schwaben were grey and tan, and pictures of Beowulf Sonnenberg, Madame's grandson, who was sired by Hektor, show a dog that looks to be what we would now call a 'black sable' with lighter undercoat hair showing through at the forearm and haunches in particular, with lighter hair showing around the shoulders and the neck under the black overcoat. Sable is a dominant color, requiring at least one sable parent. Since Beowulf's father, Hektor, was grey and tan, his mother, Thekla v d Krone must have been sable. By the same quirk of color genetics, that makes Madame v d Krone the Elder sable as well, since Horand, Thekla's father, was grey and tan as well.

Certainly Beowulf Sonnenberg had the most impact on the breed in the main line, doubtless because of the combination of Madame with Mores Pleiningen, thus strengthening the strain of Swabian/Wurttemberger blood, but Madame's impact through her son by Horand, Baron v d Krone, was far from negligible and grandsons Pilot and Wolf (full brothers of Beowulf Sonnenberg) were hugely important. That great reservoir of genuine country working ability that was Horst v Boll, carried 6 lines to Madame v d Krone the Elder through not only Beowulf but through Pilot and Baron v d Krone as well. Nor was the breeder of Horst the only breeder to pick up on Madame and to line breed on her in order to reach the fountainhead of working ability she represented. Even before World War I, American breeders were reaching out to Madame to produce dogs for work in the real world.

We have no way, unfortunately, to tell what color Mores Pleiningen was since Stephanitz does not give us a picture of her to look at, and her son, Hektor v Schwaben, was grey and tan like his father, Horand. About all we know about Mores is that she was the mother of Hektor v Schwaben and that she was an HGH level herding dog of Wurttemberg. We know her parentage, at least for a single generation; she was by Franz and out of Werra. We do know one more thing about her, and that is that she was defamed by the report that she was the great granddaughter of a wolf. Stephanitz himself investigated the calumny and found it without validity. And however we might feel about Stephanitz' integrity regarding such a matter touching on one of the founding mothers of his beloved breed, the testimony of her use on sheep to the point at which she was awarded the HGH must be regarded much more seriously. The idea that men whose livelihood was invested in their sheep would allow a part-bred wolf into any kind of proximity with them, never mind entrusted their sheep to their care, is ludicrous.

In structure, if one looks at the pictures of Horand, a dog of rather uneven type, somewhat angular and only marginally of what the herding people of the time called the 'herding type' and of his son Hektor, a dog of much more pleasing harmony, with the rounded hindquarters of the herding dog, greater breadth and the more smooth construction of a working herding dog, one can deduce that Mores was of distinctly herding type, with good breadth of body from chest to tail. She would have been round behind and smooth throughout, slightly longer than she was tall, and of probably sable color. Given her grandson Beowulf's dark sable, it is likely that Mores herself was a dark sable, since Hektor looks a markedly darker grey in his pictures than his sire, Horand, did in his.

In temperament, Mores must have been sound and stable; given Horand's temperament, which might best be described as that of a 'holy terror', Hektor's great working temperament had to come from somewhere. Horand had no biddability at all, neither the desire nor the ability to work stock, and no willingness to learn anything, so who was left to provide Hektor with his excellent biddability and working ability?

Mores' claim to fame rests almost entirely on her son, Hektor v Schwaben, but he is more than enough to anchor that claim. Though she had other get, none equaled Hektor's accomplishments. Sieger in both 1900 and 1901, he carried the HGH designation as well as his honors as a double Sieger. Additionally, he is present at least once, and most often a great deal more than once, in every pedigree of every German Shepherd dog today. Bred to his half sister, the Madame v d Krone daughter Thekla, he sired Beowulf Sonnenberg, Wolf and Pilot. While they are not the only foundation stones upon which Hektor's influence on the breed rests, they may be the most important. It was the combination with his own son, Beowulf, that gave us Roland v Starkenburg (no recommendation, that!) and to name just a few of his get, there was Nero v Blumenhaus, Roland and Rose v Park, Lady Wenden, Sara v Siegestor, Leo v Niedersachsen, and others too numerous to mention.

Without Mores and Madame's contributions to the breed, there is considerable doubt that there would even be a German shepherd breed; the likelihood is that the attempts to create a breed out of the disparate herding dogs of Germany would have been as unsuccessful as the Phylax Society's efforts for the two decades before Stephanitz took over the struggle. Stephanitz never gave these two great ladies the credit they earned and deserved; he never acknowledged their contribution to the effort, preferring to focus on his beloved Horand at their expense, but the plain fact of the matter is that without the sound nerve, solid work ethic and rich fount of genetic obedience that Mores and Madame brought to the breed, the German Shepherd dog would have been doomed from the beginning.

Horand was deeply unpopular with the country people who depended upon their dogs to work; he was a 'fancy' dog pet and only a 'fancy' dog pet. He was worthless on stock, a noted troublemaker, he was too small for the majority of the stockmen of the time to take seriously, and was known to bite without provocation and with little discretion. The Mores son, Hektor v Schwaben, put an entirely different complexion on the matter, with his proven ability to work stock, his attitude and appearance as a herding dog, and his stable, sound temperament. Enough larger than his sire to be taken seriously as a stock dog to be reckoned with, the 'country' people were willing to put aside any reservations they had on that head and accept him for his working ability.

In combination with Baron v d Krone, the blood of Mores, through her son, Hektor, was mixed with the good herding Brenztal dogs to create Horst v Boll. And it was by crossing the multiple great grandson Luchs v Kalsmunt-Wetzlar with the Boll blood that created the Kriminal Polizei line, and the Kriminal Polizei line which, in turn, formed the Secretainerie lines, while Luchs, himself was created by the blending of the brothers Pilot and Beowulf Sonnenberg, thus bringing the lines of Mores and Madame to the fore.

Horand v Grafath was, in size and temperament and type, very much the prototype of the modern bite sport dog, with his low bite threshold, his low thresholds in general, his aggression, his superfluity of unemployed (and largely unemployable!) energy, his scarce biddability and his over-abundance of prey drive. Mores Pleiningen and Madame v d Krone the Elder were, on the other hand, the quintessence of the 'old-fashioned' values of the breed, its heart and soul. From them we have sound nerve (when we have it) and they were the fountainhead of genetic obedience, stability and biddability. For all the people who have ever put in a day's work with a German Shepherd partner and companion, these ladies embodied the essence of the breed, they gave us the qualities that make a German Shepherd, well, a German Shepherd, not just a bite sport dog. We owe them a great deal, not least of all our thanks and our remembrance of their names.

So, to Madame and to Mores, without whom we would not have a German Shepherd dog—at least not as they once were. As to whether they will ever be again, well, that is another story.

The Dogs Who Started It All

The Dichotomy of Horst v Boll

Today we have something in the German shepherd breed we refer to as the 'split'. Most people who give the existence of this gap between dogs capable of doing real work and dogs not capable of doing real work credence assume that it appeared out of the ether some time in the late 1960s or early 1970s. It did not. With the exception of a 'golden' age for the breed that occurred between the late 1940s and the late 1960s, the German Shepherd dog has been profoundly split between the camps of the people who want dogs for real work in the real world, herding, tracking/scent work (search and rescue and detection) police work and service (alert dogs, guide dogs, brace/balance dogs and wheel-chair aide dogs) and dogs whose only use is to be found in the show ring or as pets (like Horand v Grafath) or as attack dogs as the Nazis and the later Communists used them. For that mere 20 years of time out of time from the '40s to the '60s, before the bite sports emerged as competition sports, when show dogs worked and working dogs showed and war dogs turned into service dogs, the breed was one, and that one entity listed heavily towards the Swabian side of the blend. Thuringian characteristics were minimized and even disregarded, genetic obedience and strong nerves were valued and given strong consideration in breeding decisions made by 'back-yard' breeders, and the German Shepherd gained the icon status it still, to some degree, enjoys today.

Then the show ring breeders, in Germany, in Britain and in America, all three, with their self-indulgent repetitive generation in-breeding ruined it all, breeding unhealthy, temperamentally unsound dogs for their pretty looks and artificial way of going and forcing them onto the reluctant, German Shepherd dog buying public to the disgust of most of the people who had a real use for their dogs, even including many of the pet people. Then the Iron Curtain opened up and suddenly the market was flooded with Czech border patrol dogs and East German border patrol and prison camp dogs, and people had a choice again. The West German sport dog breeders jumped into the mix, and hey, presto! We had a major split in the breed again. Not quite the same 'split' we started with, but a 'split' none-the-less, albeit a three-way, this time, instead of the two-way 'split' we started with.

The more things change, the more they stay the same. So how did it all begin?

The beginning, of course, came with Stephanitz and Horand. Stephanitz started the breed with the oft-stated determination to create a 'useful' national breed of shepherd dog by preserving and blending four of the traditional, regional breeds of German dogs, three of them shepherd breeds and one of them the 'yard' dog breed. A distinct sub-set of people argued that the Thuringian 'yard' breed didn't even belong in the mix because it wasn't a shepherd dog at all, but the 'yard' dogs were Stephanitz' personal favorites of the four breeds, so they got included regardless of what anybody else wanted or thought. It could equally well have been argued that if he truly wanted a 'useful' shepherd dog, adding Thuringian wasn't the way to get one, but for Stephanitz, personal preference always got in the way of fact and logic.

The 'split' originated with Stephanitz himself, and it was comprised of the difference between what he said he wanted the breed to be, and the dogs he chose for himself and for the breed. For, given a choice, Stephanitz would always choose the useless, worthless, impudent, insolent, incorrigible, untrainable provokers of strife—I use his own words here—over dogs of proven value and usefulness. Stephanitz found reliable, good working dogs 'dull'. He said he wanted his breed to be 'useful' but when it came right down to it, he found the truly useful dogs boring, so he was continually suspended between the dichotomy of what he said he wanted and what he actually 'liked'. The dogs he 'liked' always won out over the good working dogs and until 1909, when Horst v Boll was born, the rest of the people trying to get in on the ground floor of the breed were stuck with Horand and the equally despised (among working dog people) Roland v Starkenburg.

Then came Horst v Boll. Horst was the epitome of everything that Stephanitz said he wanted for his breed; he was supremely useful, trainable and versatile and he was correspondingly popular among the group Gordon Garrett calls the 'country' people. Formally trained for police work, he was to prove himself in stock work and tracking as well, and even more to the point, he produced highly trainable dogs able to work in any number of arenas. He provided the people who wanted a good working dog with a viable alternative to the hated Horand and the beautiful but timid, fearful and useless Roland v Starkenburg. Country people flocked to breed their dogs to him and he was to sire over 800 puppies during his lifetime.

According to Goldbecker and Hart, Horst was used more frequently than any other sire of his era. Even his son Nores, a dog far inferior to his father, was used so heavily in the hopes of replicating his father that he sired 180 litters comprising 877 puppies.

Horst's progeny, crossed with that of Luchs v Kalsmunt Wetzlar, produced the Kriminal Polizei and Secretainerie lines, and were instrumental in the creation of the Berliner Polizei lines. Innumerable working stock dogs and many 'ambulance' dogs who proved their worth many times over in World War I came from Horst. Indeed, today we understand that much of the true 'working' temperament, nerve and genetic obedience of the breed that remains to us does so courtesy of Horst v Boll.

So who was Horst v Boll? Beyond a big dog whelped a mere ten years after the formation of the SV? The answer may perhaps confound the folks whose 'working-line' dogs owe what decent nerve they have (when they have it) to Horst. What pictures we have of Horst show us a big, heavy boned, rather light grey and tan dog with plenty of breadth and a nice spring of ribs. He was koered at two years of age at just over 28 inches in height and with what we know today about maturation rates among dogs of his predominately Swabian heritage almost surely topped 29 inches when fully grown. Just as certainly he would have weighed in at 105 to 110 pounds, if his owners managed to keep him lean and fit.

In color, he met the preference of the working dog people of the time for a grey base coat with a washy yellow tan on his legs which is the commonplace for tan today but which considered rather unusual then. He was, in fact, the quintessence of what the country people wanted the breed to be; a dog rich in solid nerve and genetic obedience with the size and in the color they believed appropriate for the jobs they had for the dogs they wanted. Finally, country people sighed, they had a dog who fit their idea of what a German Shepherd ought to be. They flocked to him in droves.

Perhaps predictably, Stephanitz clearly disliked Horst. Undoubtedly, the dog put his nose out of joint. One of those dull, boring working dogs more popular than his beloved Horand? In vain did he inveigh against the use of Horst—the country people ignored his prejudice. The popularity of this dog among the people who had so reluctantly been forced, proverbially kicking and screaming, to breed to Horand, and even more reluctantly, to Roland v

Starkenburg must have really amounted to rubbing his nose in the difference between what working people wanted and what Stephanitz deigned to give them. He may have consoled himself with the idea that the 'country people' who so preferred Horst to his beloved pet, Horand, and Horand's heavily in-bred progeny, Roland, didn't count.

Certainly books which celebrate the show dogs of the breed tend to ignore him, but the 'country' people persevered, preserving that good Swabian heritage of nerve and genetic obedience through the decades so that people who never heard of Horst and who would spit on any dog that resembled him either in size or color could at least have halfway decent nerves in their sport dogs. Those of us who have real jobs in the real world for our dogs, instead of those made-up busy work exercises the pet people invent and call jobs have Horst to thank for the dogs we have today who can do something more and better than the dog version of video games.

Horst was sired by Munko v Boll, a dog in his turn sired by Graf Eberhard v Hohen Esp out of Nelly II Eislingen. Graf Eberhard was by Wolf Balingen. Wolf was sired by Pilot, a full brother to Beowulf (the grand-sire of Roland v Starkenburg). Pilot, like Beowulf, was by HGH Hektor v Schwaben and out of Thekla v d Krone. Both Hektor and Thekla were by Horand v Grafath, with Hektor out of the Swabian HGH Mores Pleiningen and Thekla out of the Swabian HGH Madame v d Krone the Elder, thus providing good underpinnings of Swabian herding blood.

Wolf Balingen was out of Nelly II Eislingen, who was also by HGH Hektor v Schwaben, which brings back both Horand and Mores v Pleiningen. Yes, that's right, Wolf Balingen was bred back to his own mother, making Nelly II both Graf Eberhard's mother and grandmother at the same time. Nelly Eislingen, the mother of Nelly II, was by Horand and out of Ella Gmund. Ella, in her turn, was by HGH Max v d Krone, a Thuringian crossed with Northern breed herding dogs (at one point Stephanitz refers to his Mira v d Krone v Grafath as a mix of Northern and Southern Swabian blood without mentioning Thuringian blood at all, even though Mira was line-bred upon Max on the top and out of Lida I v d Krone, who in her turn was by Max and out of Sali v d Krone, who both Stephanitz and Herr Eiselen agreed was fully Thuringian. So where the Swabian was supposed to be in this line I couldn't tell you, but it makes sense that Max was something other than full Thuringian, as Stephanitz says over and over that to get good herding dogs out of Thuringian blood you have to mix it with something else, and Max was obviously a good herding dog, since he had the HGH (and since Herr Eiselen obviously liked him and used him heavily in his breeding program).

Munko v Boll's dam was the Swabian herding dog Lori v Brenztal, and it was from Lori that Horst received the long thighs and stifles and loose ligaments which today provide the artificial 'flying' trot so beloved in the show world. (Remember Lori when deciding whether to consider the merits of great

295

grandparents and beyond in assessing your dog's heritage—that the characteristics, bad as well as good, can and do transmit through the decades and the generations, as we look at the 'flying' trot and the loose, long thighs, stifle joints and ligaments of today's show dogs.) Lori was by Rigo v Brenztal and out of Loria Brenztal. Rigo takes us right back to Hektor v Schwaben and Horand, Mores and Madame through his sire, Beowulf Sonnenberg, full brother to Wolf and Pilot. Rigo was out of Grete v Algaeu who was by Fritz v Schwenningen by the Swabian Pollux and out of Prima (Pollux was the grandsire of Horand, so we don't get too far from him, do we?) Grete v Algaeu carried at least one strong outline through her dam, the Phylax Society's Flora, who was sired by Ajax and out of Elsa. Possibly Northern breed?

The Swabian Loria Brenztal, long thighs and stifles, loose ligaments and all, is a breath of fresh air, sired by the Phylax Society's Swabian HGH dog Karo and out of the Swabian Madam. (Not, apparently, Madame v d Krone the Elder—at least as far as we know.)

Horst v Boll's dam, Hella v Boll, was by Achim v Tautenburg by Baron Hans v Tautenburg by Graf v d Grube who in his turn was by Baron v d Krone, a son of Horand and Madame v d Krone the Elder, the Swabian HGH lady. (One could ask how it is possible to fit 7 generations into a mere 10 years!) The dam of Graf v d Grube was Freia Wandsbeck, who was by the Swabian HGH dog Carex v Pleiningen (not a brother to Mores, but the same breed, HGH Swabian/Wurttemberger) and the Swabian Alice v d Wandse. Though heavily Swabian, Graf v d Grube represents lovely, open lines, without a single line breeding in sight.

The dam of Baron Hans v Tautenburg represented more lovely, open lines, with Sibylle v Tautenburg by the Phylax Society's Merko Rude, by Dux Rude and out of Rose Hundin. (Almost certainly Swabian/Wurttemberger dogs.) Sibylle was out of Alte Lotte Ulrich.

The dam of Hella's sire Achim, Kriemhild v Tautenburg returns to the main line, sired, as she was, by Beowulf, which brings back Hektor, Horand, Mores Pleiningen and Madame v d Krone the Elder again. Kriemhild was out of the largely Swabian HGH Hexe v Hohen Esp, who was by the highly in-bred HGH Luchs v Schatten, who in his turn by the Swabian HGH Wolf v Postdorfle and out of Bella Eislingen. This Wolf was by HGH Max v d Krone and out of Bella Eislingen, making Bella both Luchs' mother and grand-mother. Bella was by Swabian HGH Phylax v d Krone and out of Thuringian Sali v d Krone. Hexe's dam was Gretle v Schatten, whom Stephanitz identifies both as HGH and a Swabian.

Horst's dam, Hella v Boll was out of Minka v Boll who was by Pascha zum Bach and out of Eva v d Hardt. Pascha was by the almost entirely Swabian HGH Pax v Brenztal, who was sired by Fritz v Schwenningen who was sired in his turn by Pollux. Pax was out of Schmuck v Engen (from Schura) and

Pascha was out of Flora Neckarusprung, who was by Horand and out of the Swabian HGH Fides v Neckarusprung.

Pascha was clearly heavily Swabian, but Eva v d Hardt, to whom he was bred, was a far more mixed bag. Eva was sired by Tell Bipontius who was by the first Sieger, Jorg v d Krone. Jorg was by Luchs Sparwasser, a full brother of Horand's, and out of the Phylax Society's Nelly Hundin. Given Herr Eiselen's preference for herding dogs, we can guess that Nelly was either of his favorite Swabian blood, or Northern herding breed, probably his next preference, but it is only a guess. What is not a guess is that whatever his desire to be at the cutting edge of the new breed to be (which he certainly was!) Herr Eiselen was always dedicated to real world working dogs. Virtually every HGH dog Stephanitz ever had was bred by Herr Eiselen and trained and worked to that HGH before Stephanitz got the dog.

Tell Bipontius was out of Schmuck v Zewibrucken (who would name their dog Schmuck??) and Schmuck v Z was out of Schmuck v Engen. (Two generations of Schmucks!!)

With Eva v d Hardt's dam we go right back to the main line again, as Cora Schwarzwald was by Beowulf Sonnenberg, which puts us right back to Hektor v Schwaben and Thekla to Mores Pleiningen and Madame v d Krone the Elder again. On the positive side, Cora was out of Swabian HGH Elsa v Schwaben by Swabian HGH Carex Pleiningen and out of Swabian HGH Fides Neckarusprung. Elsa to Fides and Carex was a VERY strong line for working values.

The strong working values in these lines come through Madame v d Krone the Elder, Max v d Krone, Mores and Carex Pleiningen, Fides Neckarusprung and the Brenztal girls, Lori and Loria. You might notice that all but the Brenztal girls are repeated several times. Madame v d Krone the Elder appears 6 times, Mores nearly as often, Fides Neckarusprung twice and Carex and Max twice. As often as Horand appears and as heavily line bred on Horand and his grandsire Pollux as this line is, Horand and Pollux are always balanced by good, strong working dogs.

The only dog missing from this line-up of strength and stability and working value is the Swabian HGH dog Audifax (v d Krone) v Grafath. Also note that all the working dogs except Max are Swabian/Wurttemberger dogs. These dogs, Madame, Mores and Max, Carex and Fides and the Brenztals are the recipe for success in real world working dogs. It is out of these dogs that solid nerve and genetic obedience come. There may be others of great nerve and genetic obedience but this small group, with Audifax, comprise the main foundation of the breed's working ability—and it is through Horst v Boll that working ability is most often and most reliably transmitted down through the last hundred years to our dogs today.

Ironic, isn't it? That this big, solid, strong dog, the compendium of all the physical attributes 'working-line' people love to hate, a dog of the 'wrong' size and the 'wrong' color, is the progenitor of all the qualities of character, stability, strength of purpose and balance they purport to desire for their dogs. Until the breeders of 'working-line' dogs understand this, they will be cursed by the regular appearance of fearful, unstable and unbalanced temperaments in their dogs that are genetically linked to their small dark dogs through the Thuringian blood from which those qualities of character come. Like Stephanitz, the 'working-line' people say they want one thing, but make all the wrong choices to get what they say they want.

The Dogs Who Started It All

The Anatomy of Fear: Roland v Starkenburg

On November 1st, 1903, a black pup was born to Bella v Starkenburg in a litter sired by Heinz v Starkenburg. He grew up black, beautiful, and full of fear. Some people called him a mutant; Stephanitz called him Sieger, in both 1906 and 1907. Some people said he changed everything.

His pedigree has been called a classic example of the kind of in-breeding used to establish a breed. It is the same kind of in-breeding going on today in virtually all show breeding establishments for almost all breeds of 'fancy' dogs (meaning dogs not bred for any purpose other than walking and trotting around a show ring for people to look at and ooh and aah over). The sire of Heinz was Hektor v Schwaben, by Horand and out of Mores, while the sire of Bella was Beowulf Sonnenberg, who was by Hektor and out of Thekla v d Krone, who was in her turn by Horand and out of Madame.

The problem of this pedigree, in it's consequences for Roland's character, is not so much in the in-breeding on Horand through Hektor—in those cases Mores Pleiningen appears twice to anchor good character to the

298

line, and Madame appears once, but in the double appearance of the Pollux/Prima daughter Lucie v Starkenburg. For you see, not only were Heinz and Bella related through their sires, Hektor and Hektor's son Beowulf, but both Heinz and Bella were out of the same mother—Lucie. In essence, double in-breeding. But the in-breeding doesn't stop there! For you see, Pollux is not only the sire of Lucie, appearing twice in the third generation, he is also the grandsire of Horand and therefore the great grandsire of Hektor and the great, great grandsire of Beowulf.

Now, if you know that at best, Pollux was noted for his unstable, unbalanced temperament, it might be considered a poor idea to compound that temperament repeatedly. Double it up with the beautiful but equally unevenly temperamented Prima, with her significant infusions of Thuringian blood, and you have a recipe for disaster, at least in terms of temperament.

Stephanitz was very good about talking about wanting his breed to be 'useful'. He spent all kinds of time and exerted all kinds of political pressure to get his dogs into both police service and the 'ambulance' service (the search and rescue dogs of the time). He even helped to get Fortunate Fields off the ground, where both guide dogs for the blind and police dogs were bred, raised and trained. But when it came time to put his money, so to speak, where his mouth was, Stephanitz failed over and over again. Inveigh as he might against 'fancy' dogs, and swear up and down as he would that 'his' breed would never, should never, become a 'fancy' dog, that's all Roland v Starkenburg ever was, and all his breeding ever could have made him.

Roland v Starkenburg was beautiful. Lucie Starkenburg was beautiful. Prima was beautiful. And they were joyous, with the insolence and insouciance that Stephanitz loved, but they were also fearful, untrainable and 'useless'. Stephanitz made excuses for them. He called Roland 'spoiled'. He complained that he had been raised as a 'lapdog' rather the same way that he had complained that Horand had not been trained (by someone else—Stephanitz apparently never took the responsibility for training him and asserted that he was untrainable). Pollux was certainly never trained for any kind of real world work, either. Maybe he was 'untrainable' too. No wonder Roland was 'spoiled'.

Stephanitz adored Horand; when Herr Eiselen told him not to in-breed on Horand, Stephanitz did it anyway. He made a point, in choosing his Siegers, to return to dogs in-bred upon Horand, what he called 'the Horand family', over and over again, and there was no surer way to success in the new breed than to make certain that Stephanitz knew how many generations one had in-bred upon his dog. He knew what he was doing, too. He talked about the problem of popular sire breeding and he knew that any dog he chose as Sieger would be badly used and over-used and so affect the breed he so loved adversely (but not enough to discipline himself to do the right thing for it!). What Stephanitz knew didn't matter. Given a choice between a useless, mentally unsound 'fancy' dog in-bred on Horand and a stout, physically and

299

mentally healthy working dog of proven ability, Stephanitz proved, over and over again, that he would put the 'fancy' dog up over the good working dog, no matter what he said he wanted 'his' breed to be.

Today we'd call that a 'conflict of interest', and when it came to Stephanitz' attachment to Horand and all dogs issuing forth from Horand, sentimentality would always win out in the end when it came time for the Captain to choose a Sieger. Even in referring to the line of Horand and Pollux, he attributed Pollux to Horand, not Horand to Pollux, as if Pollux had issued forth from Horand, and not the other way around.

Hettel Uckermark, Roland's best son, crowned Sieger in 1909, was out of the good, predominately Swabian Gretel Uckermark. When additional Swabian blood was added to Hettel, good working dogs could be produced. When Hettel was bred back into the Horand line (as he was) dogs like Alex v Westfalenheim, the first known EPI affected dog, were produced, as well as the Riedekenberg B litter, renowned for their unstable, timid, shy, fearful temperaments. Alex was no prize, either. He, too, was noted for his fearful, shy temperament, as well as for his ill-health and short life.

Nor is it any coincidence that Roland was black; dark color is a Thuringian inheritance, right along with the small stature, the fearful temperament, the instability and the imbalance of character. It may be that if one wants the 'joy' that adrenaline produces, the inexhaustible energy (drive), the 'beauty' and the small size, one will have to take the fearful temperament that comes attached to all those desired qualities. To, as it is said, take the good with the bad.

Today, the presences of strong Thuringian lines, particularly lines carrying Roland v Starkenburg, produce fearful, unstable, unbalanced dogs if not balanced by a strong presence of the good working/herding Swabian lines. The problem for the breed is the same problem Stephanitz faced and failed; the big, stout Swabians carry the versatility, the good character, genetic obedience and the strong nerve people say they want in the breed, but the Thuringian dogs are the progenitors of the prick ears, the small size, and the adrenaline fueled 'joy' and 'insolence' that the 'working-line' folks, at least, choose (like Stephanitz) every time. No wonder they find themselves complaining, ever and over, about their fearful dogs and constantly dealing with dog aggressive and reactive dogs.

Today's German High-line show dogs carry, on average, 800 lines to Roland v Starkenburg. Is it any wonder that they are plagued with shy, fearful temperaments?

Gordon Garrett said to go back to the pedigrees, to start from the beginning and to work forward and you would see, and he was right. The lessons those early pedigrees have to teach us are right there in the names and the letters attached to them. Load up on Roland v Starkenburg and you get show dogs and ONLY show dogs. Balance him with good Swabian blood, and

300

the possibility at least exists for herding dogs, tracking dogs and police dogs. Follow the temperaments down the lines—add more Horand to Roland and you get fearful, unhealthy show dogs. You get Alex v Westfalenheim, and the B litter Riedekenberg. You get Erich v Grafenwerth, German Sieger of 1920 running away at the sound of gunfire in 1921 and subsequently being sold off to the United States. You get Geri Oberklamm following him to the U. S. because he couldn't pass the newly instituted 'courage' test.

Breed on Roland, double up on Roland, and you WILL get beautiful dogs who WILL do well in the show ring. That truth has remained the same down through German Siegers and American champions, from Hettel Uckermark to the Erich son Klodo v Boxberg, to the Klodo son Utz v Haus Schutting, to Klodo's grandsons Hussan v Haus Schutting and Odin v Stolzenfels (all 4 awarded Siegers) down all the way to Quanto and Canto v d Wienerau and right on through Palme and Uran v WildsteigerLand and the rest. For every Utz, a dog of good character, you will get Erich and Geri and Canto and Palme and the rest with a character which is less than sterling.

But there is one thing you should understand—all German Shepherd dogs carry at least one line to Erich v Grafenwerth, and that means 80 lines to Horand v Grafath and Pollux v Hanau, including 2 lines to Roland v Starkenburg through Hettel Uckermark. So, whether you will or no, every German Shepherd dog carries at the very least 2 lines to Roland. Most, to be frank, carry a great many more. That fearful temperament everyone loves to hate? It's not some odd aberration brought to us courtesy of some off the wall 'back-yard' breeder—it is an integral element in the main line of the sine qua non of German shepherd breeding from the very beginnings of the breed. It was brought to us, not from some much maligned and largely innocent 'back-yard' breeder, but courtesy of the 'best' breeders of the 'greatest' champions, and by the very progenitor of the breed himself, Max v Stephanitz, embodied in the closely in-bred offspring of his beloved Horand.

And this is why, sooner or later, if line-breeding (really, in-breeding, at this point) is featured in your dog, regardless of what line your dog belongs to, fearfulness will raise its ugly head. Because the bottom line is, line-breeding, ALL line-breeding, is doubling up on Roland v Starkenburg, and line-breeding on Roland is how fear became intertwined with the German Shepherd breed.

The Dogs Who Started It All

Beauty, the Silent Deception: Flora Berkemeyer

If Roland v Starkenburg was the father of fear for German shepherd dogs, Flora Berkemeyer was the mother of it. Born in March, 1911, like Roland, Flora was of exceptional beauty. Tall, graceful, elegant, and black and tan in color in a day when black and tan dogs were rare, she had the refinement of the great champions of the 1940s, '50s and '60s and was without doubt the progenitor of it. Celebrated for her beauty during most of her life, by the end of it, Stephanitz was complaining about her 'rabbit-like fecundity' and he wasn't making that complaint because her puppies grew up lacking in acceptable structure.

Poor Flora had 7 litters of puppies, each from a different sire, in a largely futile effort to find a male who would complement her structurally and still correct her unfortunately fearful temperament. None of the 7 males to whom she was bred ever really satisfactorily achieved that goal.

Kuno Edelweiss, the father of Flora's A litter, had good, stout Swabian herding blood through his sire, Jockel Schwetzingen, a son of Beowulf Sonnenberg and Krone v Park. Had Kuno had a bottom-line to match, Flora's pups might have turned out less beautiful, but better in temperament. Unfortunately, Kuno's dam, Grete v Nahetal, was sired by Roland v Starkenburg. Grete, herself, out of a stong herding line mother, achieved both an HGH and a PH (herding and police) designation, so she clearly had both good nerve and genetic obedience, but when the genetic fear of Roland v

Starkenburg was combined with the genetic fear of Flora, the results were not good. Ajax, Aeko and Armin (particularly Armin) would provide a conduit through which Flora's fear could travel for years and generations of German Shepherd dogs to come.

Perhaps if someone had realized just how prepotent Roland v Starkenburg and Flora, herself, were going to turn out to be for the transmission of a fearful temperament, something might have been done. Roland's breeder figured out that if he bred Roland on to heavily Swabian lines for at least 2 generations, that Roland's transmission of fear could be mitigated by the steady nerve of Swabian/Wurttemberger herding dogs. The problem, for the Starkenburg lines, and for the breed itself, ultimately, is that Stephanitz did not support this type of breeding.

Stephanitz picked all the Siegers, and was the author of much of the breeding advice handed out for literally 30 years and he did not 'like' steady-nerved, reliable dogs. He found them 'dull'. They bored him. He much prefered the 'impudent' Thuringians, with their unsteady nerve and unstable temperaments. 'Insolent', 'impudent' 'provokers of strife' amused him. He never trained a dog, and he never worked a dog, in his life. He had no understanding of the exigencies of work nor of the kind of temperament necessary to a dog that worked an 8, 10, 12 hour day, all day, every day. When he wanted a trained dog, he bought a dog bred, raised and trained by his friend, Herr Eiselen, dropped the v d Krone name and slapped v Grafath in its place and happily took the credit for the dog's achievements. He was not the man to support the kind of breeding necessary to balance dogs like Roland and Flora.

For her second litter, Flora was put to 1909 Sieger, Hettel Uckermark. The son of a largely Swabian mother, (Gretel Uckermark) Hettel was a large, stout, strong dog of good nerve, ready, willing and able to put in a day's work with stock. Flora's B litter contained some very important dogs who contributed significantly to the looks of the German shepherd breed. From Bella, Bianka, Billo and Bendix come the large, upstanding, wide set ears we so love today, the aquiline head, large eyes and a distinctly elegant, athletic form. Unfortunately, right along with their beautiful heads and faces, their athletic and graceful forms, the B litter brought fear. People who met the dogs from the B litter were inevitably impressed with their great beauty and then just as impressed by their fearfulness. They were called everything from 'spooks' to 'shy' to frightened out of whatever wits they might have had (if any).

By this time it ought to have been clear that Flora and Roland were a bad combination, to put it mildly. One could have called them a toxic cross without exaggeration. With 20/20 hindsight, we can say she ought not to have continued to be bred, but she was so beautiful that her owners struggled on in the search for a 'good' cross for her which would mitigate her pitiful fearfulness.

303

Apollo Huhnenstein came next, the sire of Flora's D litter. This litter included Diethelm, Diana, Dolli, Dora and Dorte, dogs who would all appear in the main line leading to Siegers and Siegerins for decades to come (especially Diethelm and Dorte). Sired by Ajax v Hohenstein, a double grandson of Roland through Guntar Uckermark, Hettel's full brother, and Cilly v d Maikammer, Apollo himself was of a good, steady nerve, thanks to a mother, Liselotte Hannover, a police trained grand-daughter of Adalo v Grafath through her father and a grand-daughter of Jorg v d Krone on the bottom through Rassa Hannover, also police trained. Police trained himself, Apollo was a perfect example of how Roland could be used to effectively improve the looks of dogs yet still keep good nerve by constantly balancing Roland with strong Swabian and Northern herding influences.

While he would later be sold to the United States and become one of America's greatest early champions, he had little better success with Flora than Hettel had in improving the temperament of her offspring.

The next of Flora's litters was a lot more successful as far as temperament was concerned. Elfe, Erna, Elsa and Erda were all sired by Falko v Scharenstetten, litter brother of 1913 Siegerin Frigga v Scharenstetten, and a son of Horst v Boll. Falko, however, like his sire, Horst v Boll, was a big dog, and while his structure was nicer than that of his sire, the results of the cross, however successful in correcting Flora's fearful temperament were bigger and stouter than Stephanitz and his 'fancy' dog people really liked, in spite of their beauty. The girls from this litter were used very little, unfortunately, and not always wisely. Elfe was bred back to her own half brother, creating more disastrous temperaments, and Erna into the Kriminal Polizei, which was probably the best use which could be made of her at the time.

Flora's next litter was by Marc v Hohen Esp, a double grandson of Horst v Boll. An obvious attempt to repeat Falko's success in correcting Flora's temperament through Horst again—after all, it had worked once, why not try again with a smaller, lighter dog--this time it was the structure of the pups that took the hit. Marc had the stiff, wide-set, upright ears so sought after, and a refined, almost feminine head and face. He was also small-bodied, narrow, lacking in breadth, depth, or a decent spring of ribs and very leggy with Loria Brenztal's long thighs. Of this group, the I litter, Inge was the most often used. The I pups were narrow and a little leggy, with long thighs and low stifles and some of old Loria Brenztal's loose ligamentation, but their temperaments were generally all right. Of course, the moment you took them back to Roland, they were going to go into the dumper again, but as long as you stayed away from Roland or the Thuringian bunch, which didn't often happen, they were of reasonable nerve strength.

Riedekenburg should have called it quits with Marc, but oh, no, they kept trying. (Poor Flora.) Next came Edi v HerkulesPark and the O litter. Edi was sired by Jung Tell v d Kriminal Polizei (1913 Champion of Holland) and

Jung Tell in his turn was by Tell v d Kriminal Polizei (German Sieger,1910). Tell was by Luchs v Kalsmunt-Wetzlar (German Sieger, 1908). Edi's bottom-line, through Hexe v Mundtsdorf, carried both Hettel and Guntar Uckermark, and therefore 2 lines back to Roland. Edi was a tall, leggy, racy dog with little breadth or depth of body or spring of ribs and not a lot of substance. The O litter was not a success in either structure or temperament.

But poor Flora wasn't through yet. After Edi, Harras v d Juch and the U litter arrived. Harras, a Nores v d Kriminal Polizei son and Horst v Boll grandson, was chosen Sieger in 1921. Police trained, the story goes that he became Sieger by default—either a gunshot or a car backfiring (depending on the story you hear) some distance outside the show ring put most of the contestants to route, leaving Harras and a handful of others to finish the competition. The next year Stephanitz, disgusted by this exhibition, instituted the 'courage' test.

Harras himself had good nerve, but the problem was that his sire, Nores, did not, and with that background, however stout Harras had proven, he was not the best choice for Flora. The U litter disappeared into the same obscurity which had claimed the O litter.

There is a quote by one of those old Greek philosophers which says that beauty is a silent deception. That old Greek might have had Flora in mind when he said it. On the face of it, Flora had no reason to be prepotent for fear. She should not have been fearful herself, and she should not have passed it on so consistently. Her family tree contained numerous police trained dogs. And ok, yes, she carried one line through her mother, Cilla v Distelbruch, to Sali v d Krone, who was known to pass on unstable temperaments. But Cilla was the daughter of Dewet Barbarossa, who in addition to the lines he carried to Horand and his brother Luchs Sparwasser, carried Fides Neckarusprung and Madam v d Krone the Elder through Baron v d Krone. And Cilla's mother, Minka, was sired by Fritz Schwenningen, son of Pollux with some certainty. Fritz may have been a son of Prima as well, but that is not so certain. Was Prima combined with Sali v d Krone the source of the fear that Flora suffered from and passed on so freely? She certainly was one of the dogs pinpointed as being the cause of the fear Roland exhibited and passed on with such regularity. If Prima was and if she, indeed, was Fritz' mother, it would certainly explain why Roland and Flora were such a bad combination, doubling up on Prima as they did. On the other hand, Fritz was not noted for passing on poor temperaments, indeed, he sired a number of HGH (herding) and PH (police trained) dogs. Quite possibly a touch of Prima was not a problem, but doubling up on her, or matching a dog carrying Prima in their lineage with a dog carrying Sali v d Krone may have been the triggering factor.

Minka's mother, Wachtel v Birken, was good herding blood on the bottom, going back through Selke v Birken to Schuft and Wachtel, which, in combination with the dogs on top, Madam and Fides, SHOULD have provided good, steady nerve, but somehow didn't. Possibly the answer lies in Flora's sire.

Harras v Lippestrand was sired by Mohr v Burghalde, a son of Roland out of Rosa v Burghalde. Roland of course carried Lucie v Starkenburg, a Prima daughter, in a double dose, while Rosa, a daughter of Beowulf Sonnenberg, carried Nelly Eislingen on the bottom. Nelly Eislingen was a daughter of Ella Gmund, who in her turn was the daughter of Sali v d Krone. The combination of Lucie and Sali seems to have overpowered the sources of better nerve in Harras' family tree. Harras himself should have been solid. He was police trained, his sire, Mohr, was police trained, and his dam, Flora v d Kirchheim was police trained as well, Flora despite carrying more of Pollux and Prima through her dam. Perhaps the blood of Fides and the good Swabian Dora v Schwaben carried her through, but when the Prima and Sali blood was doubled up on again, through Cilla, the snowball effect took over.

If there is one thing studying these pedigrees teaches, it is that whenever fear sources are doubled up, they take over. A touch of the Thuringian here and there works well, but to maintain strong nerve, high thresholds and good genetic obedience, good, solid herding sources have to be continually reintegrated into the bloodlines, preferably from Swabian /Wurttemberger sources. This may (and will) push the size of the dogs up, as the Falko v Scharenstetten E litter, BUT it will keep the nerve base strong. When (if) the size starts getting too far up there again, another touch of Thuringian can be added back again to bring back the refinement and to bring the size of the dogs back down a little. If the breeder allows for the range of size to be wide, expects it and uses it to advantage, the diversity thus created will strengthen the dogs and preseve the breed.

The breeder who cannot accept the larger dogs, who will not use them, whether out of ignorance or prejudice, will be fated to fight against fear and unstable aggression cropping up in their dogs when they least expect it. When the Swabian/Wurttemberger influences are eliminated from the genetic base, sooner or later the temperament of the pups produced will fail. (And more often sooner rather than later.)

Chapter 11
The 1930s:
The Era of Hitler and the Nazis: Utz v Haus Schutting, Nester v Wiegerfelsen, and Cherusker von Burg Fasanental

Cherusker von Berg Fasanental

By 1933 the dogs of Stephanitz, Eiselen and Tobias Ott had reached an apex. Stephanitz' main line dogs were so in-bred at this time that they were riddled with digestive disorders and early deaths from unexplained bleeding were no longer uncommon. Eiselen, older than Stephanitz, was no longer able to provide him with well-bred, well-balanced real world working dogs with which to correct his breeding mistakes. Tobias Ott, no longer young and discouraged by Stephanitz' choice of Klodo v Boxberg over his far healthier and stronger temperamented Blasienberg dogs, was ready to lay down the standard. Many of his best dogs had been sold to either the United States or to Great Britain—those who had stayed in Germany were mostly to be found at Fortunate Fields in the breeding program there, producing guide dogs for the blind and police dogs. He was in no position to take up the struggle anew against the Nazis.

In 1933, when Stephanitz named Odin v Stolzenfels, grandson of Klodo v Boxberg, as German Sieger, the country's national champion German shepherd dog, the sale of siegers and their get to other countries, most notably the United States, had become a major source of income, not just for a few individuals, but for the entire country. Since 1920, all sieger hopefuls in the main line were heavily used for breeding while still young (like Geri v Oberklamm) and then turned over for export as soon as they won the title (or failed to pass the courage test) with the same process being repeated with their sons and grandsons. In such manner Erich v Grafenwerth, Geri v Oberklamm (who was exported before he could be 'courage' tested, as it was known he could not pass) Klodo v Boxberg (leaving behind more than 600 pups) Pfeffer and Gockel v Bern, and eventually, Odin himself, along with Odin v Busecker Schloss and finally even Utz v Haus Schutting, made the trip across the pond. This had the effect of bringing the dogs the Germans themselves considered their best to the rest of the world, where they collected in Great Britain and the United States, in particular.

Meanwhile, back in the Fatherland, political changes were occuring which would affect everything in the country, not least of all the German shepherd dog. Specifically, in 1933, the National Socialist Workers' Party, under the leadership of Adolf Hitler, gained control of Germany. Hitler promptly began a program of suppression of all opposition and absolute control over all cultural, political, and economic activities of the German people. That included the breeding of the German's national dog, the German shepherd.

(It may be a little known footnote in history, but Hitler was a great aficionado of the German shepherd dog. Of course, in this, as in everything else, he wanted his own particular kind of German shepherd.)

The great old herding dog, the family dog, the farm dog, the 'useful' dog that Stephanitz promoted everywhere but in the show ring, was of no use to the Nazis and the SS. They needed, not the rural police dog who spent as much of his time finding lost items and children as he did chasing malefactors and who kept 'order' by his mere presence, but something much more fierce, something not merely ready to bite in case their handler was actively threatened, but a dog who would bite without provocation, a dog who would bite women and children at the drop of a hat, regardless of what they did or did not do, a dog who, when loosed, would bite anyone at which they were pointed. Stephanitz' 'useful' dogs, with their high thresholds, their open, approachable temperaments, and their prey drives moderated to support that usefulness, particularly in herding livestock, were no longer the kind of dog wanted. The Nazis had something entirely else in mind.

Continuing to breed a little bit of Thuringian onto a strong Swabian/ Wurttemberger base that maintained good genetic obedience and stock working ability and good, high thresholds while getting the prick ears and pretty faces wasn't the way to get it, and they knew it. They had to find another way. So they did. It can't be said that Stephanitz' dogs didn't need new blood. They were, in fact, desperately in need of out-crossing. By now, the Saxony and Brunswick dogs out working sheep in the country-side, just as they had been doing for centuries, had pretty much been forgotten, as far as the main-line breeding was concerned, and the blood of the Northern dogs, who had produced so many early herding champions such as Greif, Max v d Krone, Jorg v d Krone and the Lady of Arizona had long been marginalized in the new breed.

The Nazis didn't want just any new blood, they wanted aggression in their new blood, and lots of it and they wanted it close to the surface and ready to use. They wanted thresholds lowered, and lowered drastically, they wanted prey drive heightened and intensified far beyond herding levels for good stock handling, and they wanted dogs that would bite often, bite hard and readily, and bite anybody they were pointed at, without any provocation necessary. (Can anybody hear the echoes of the bite sport voices today in this catalog of qualities developed for the Nazis? Did the Nazis ask the same question first on the minds of all bite sport folk? Did they, too, ask first and foremost, 'Can he bite'? Of course they did.)

All they had to do was look around them. The country dogs of Saxony and Brunswick were still out there, still handling sheep by the hundred, and even sometimes by the thousand, and if they weren't all registered in Stephanitz' SV because the country people who bred and worked them had not accepted his 'fancy' dogs' qualities, well, so what? They had aggression aplenty, and close to the surface, too, and if they had good high bite thresholds to go with it, well, what could be easier to get rid of? All they had to do was to add their intense, aggressive new dogs to the old, in-bred Thuringian dogs with their low to non-existant bite thresholds, and hey, presto! They got the dog they wanted, and in only one or two generations, too.

They did it with two dogs, basically, Nestor v Wiegerfelsen, a dog of the old lines, with strong Thuringian underpinnings, and Cherusker v Burg Fasanental, a dog of the 'new' 'Old Blood', of predominantly Saxony and Brunswick herding lines building on the foundation of a third dog, Utz v Haus Schutting, as their base for their new breeding. Nestor v Wiegerfelsen on the Hohen Ficte daughters of Cherusker v Burg Fasanental produced the Meisterreiche dogs, most notably Gotz v Meisterreiche, and Hitler had the dogs he wanted, dogs that would bite indescriminantly, 'hard' dogs of intense aggression, dogs who would not hesitate to bite a woman or a child. Mix this combination with the blood of Utz v Haus Schutting, to hold what little nerve was wanted—fear aggression is always a good source for ready biting, particularly when you want a dog to bite women and children—and there you have it. The Nazi version of the German Shepherd dog.

Utz v Haus Schutting was of the old 'main' line. Born in 1926, he was made sieger in 1929. A short (24 inch) dog, Utz was anything but small, with a stout frame, very correct, with excellent breadth throughout. Though it would be the Utz structure which would account for many a siegership through the next thirty years, it would be the ability of the blood of Utz to hold the nerve-base, to be the bedrock of the temperament of many a dog to come which would be his most enduring legacy.

We know that Utz, himself, was quintessentially main-line, with 401 lines to Horand and Pollux, but the line-breeding to Doni Wyhratal in Utz' dam, Donna Reuerer, matched to the presence of Doni Wyhratal in Klodo's lineage, was in its turn, a line-breeding on Werra Heinrichsruhe and Falko v Sharenstetten. For her part, Werra was a conduit to the strength of Dewet Barbarossa, and the great v d Krone dogs, especially Audifax v Grafath v d Krone and Falko, litter brother to 1913's siegerin, Frigga v Scharenstetten, was sired by Horst v Boll out of the Swabian herding girl Adelheid v Scharenstetten, who lined back to Audifax. That combination, of Horst v Boll, Audifax, Dewet Barbarossa and the rest of the largely Swabian Krone dogs and the Swabian Scharenstetten dogs, is one of the great foundation stones of good nerve-base in the German Shepherd dog. It can be and has been de-stablized with Thuringian blood, time after time, but if it is returned to, regenerated and buttressed with the blood of the great Swabians, Fides Neckarusprung, Mores and Carex Pleiningen and Madam v d Krone, yet again, it will return solid nerve-base to the dogs that carry it.

Nestor v Wiegerfelsen was the de-stablizing agent. When you look at a four generation pedigree of Nestor, you see both a bunch of new names and some old familiar names, Starkenburg, Secretainerie and Grafenwerth. The old names all end up in the same old places, and so do many of the new names, but some of the ways they end up there are interesting, to say the least, and some of them are even rather novel.

Nestor v Wiegerfelsen carried a lot of really great elements. The old stand-by of good to great nerve, Horst v Boll appears often enough to be reassuring (although perhaps it should not!) along with strong elements of 'Old Blood' both from familiar Swabian sources, such as the Scharenstettens, the Brenztals, the v d Krones and the Blasienberg dogs, and from the less familiar dogs such as Jockel v Schwetzingen, the Otzbergs and the Melibokus dogs along with less common Saxony and Brunswick dogs. In fact, Nestor v Wiegerfelsen is a perfect example of what are usually strong elements for good in a pedigree used in such an unbalanced manner that when they are combined with the usual Thuringian elements (along with a few unusual Thuringian elements) they result in creating the kind of catalyst for change that Nestor epitomied.

Too many of the sources of Horst v Boll in this lineage come through his son Nores v d Kriminal Polizei, perhaps the only Horst v Boll son known to carry and pass on fearful temperaments. A touch of Nores could be perhaps excused, but the repeated presence of Nores in line after line going forward to Nestor has to be considered, at the very least, suspect.

Beowulf Sonnenberg, one of the breed's strongest pillars, is in-bred upon in this lineage (something not in the least unusual) in repeated generations way beyond the in-breeding on him that was commonplace. Both Beowulf Kohlwald and Beowulf Nahegau are repeated to a degree seldom found in a pedigree of this era, bringing in strong Thuringian sources which do not always serve the dogs in which they are found, well.

Roland v Starkenburg, himself heavily in-bred, is in-bred upon in successive generations. Practical experience of the time found that the best (for working purposes) over-all use of Roland was to immediately out-breed him to strongly Swabian sources, as both Hettel and Guntar Uckermark proved, and as many very successful generations of Starkenburg breeding showed. Instead, in Nestor, the out-crossing to strong Swabian sources only occurred after Roland had been distilled by additional in-breeding to an intense (and toxic?) brew.

The same rather odd pattern could be found in the in-breeding on Dewet Barbarossa, usually through the old Stephanitz favorite, Siegfried v Jena-Paradies, but also through Tillie Barbarossa and even Cilla Distelbruch, the mother of Flora Berkemeyer and therefore a potent source of fear as well. Dewet Barbarossa, founded on the addition of Thuringian blood to strong v d Krone lines, was usually used sparingly. In Nestor, he was not only a strong presence, but a strong presence distilled to its essence. These intensified elements, juxtaposed, even set against each other in opposition, rather than balance, created a dog set to detonate in the old breeding rather as nitro is refined by the chemist.

If Nestor was the nitro, then a dog by the name of Cherusker v Burg Fasanental was the glycerin.

311

One of the first things you notice, when you run this pedigree out is that Cherusker v Burg Fasanental was not likely to have been an accident. Counting the generations, you will find that on top of what might be termed 'the usual suspects' this dog is the result of EIGHT generations of v Burg Fasanental breeding. You won't see that in very many pedigrees, particularly today. These days you're lucky to see two generations of the same kennel's breeding in a pedigree, never mind three and even in the early days it is not common to see more than three generations of a single kennel's breeding behind a dog but in this lineage, the v Burg Fasanental dogs span the entire time period from 1934 to 1900. That's remarkable.

Eight generations of one single kennel's breeding is highly unusual but that's far from the only unusual feature here. Along with a clear effort to use a good deal more than the bare minimum of the 'real deal' herding dogs to shape the kind of dogs they were breeding, it looks as if the people of v Burg Fasanental made a concerted effort to include every war dog they could in their breeding. Going back over the pedigree it sometimes seemed as if a deliberate attempt was made to include every sentry dog and every dog who ever carried a messenger pack in World War I that they could possibly reach in this lineage and more than a couple of them were v Burg Fasanental dogs themselves which tells one a good deal about the v Burg Fasanental dogs.

Even when they used 'the usual suspects' Hettel and Guntar Uckermark, the dogs from the B litter Riedekenburg, and the rest, instead of the usual line-breeding you would normally see, you find this breeding followed in the next generation by a balancing with lines to Horst v Boll (Bella to Horst grandson Marc v Hohen-Esp, Billo to Horst grand-daughter Doni v Wyhratal) and Jung Tell Kriminal Polizei as well as the much less dependable Horst son, Nores v d Kriminal Polizei. (When Erich v Grafenwerth is used, he is balanced by being matched to a Horst grand-daughter bolstered by a bottom-line heavy in the old herding v Park dogs or an Arno v d Eichenburg daughter carrying Osterdeich and v Boll blood on the bottom.) And always, particularly in the middle of the pedigree, the Saxony/Brunswick dogs of v Burg Fasanental dogs maintain a strong presence.

So it becomes very clear very quickly that the folks of v Burg Fasanental were following their own path. They used Stephanitz' sieger dogs when it suited them, Hettel Uckermark especially (and Guntar as well), quite possibly because Hettel was such a stout fellow and such a great herding dog (hgh) but otherwise minimized Roland v Starkenburg about as much as possible. Instead they went with Arno v d Eichenburg to Tell v d Kriminal Polizei to Luchs v Kalsmunt-Wetzlar, Jung Tell to Tell and, of course, Utz to Klodo. The Scharenstettens, the Heinrichsruhe and Siegfried v Jena-Paradies appear repeatedly, particularly in the bottom-lines, making it clear that these dogs were regarded as foundation stones of the dogs they wanted to produce.

(Siegfried v Jena-Paradies, a Dewet Barbarossa son, was one of the war dogs they used, and used repeatedly.)

In combination with Nestor v Wiegerfelsen, Stephanitz' thirty years of in-bred champions was pretty much exploded. The in-breeding on Siegfried v Jena-Paradies in Nestor locked into the foundation line breeding on the same dog in Cherusker, while the Nores breeding in both dogs' lineage added to Cilla Distelbruch served to destablize the aggression provided by the Saxony/ Brunswick v Burg Fasanental dogs. Roland v Starkenburg provided the fear and low thresholds from both sides of the equation through myriad sources, ably assisted by the sons and daughters of Flora Berkemeyer, and the threads of the Thuringian blood from Sali v d Krone and Lotte Thorigen and Prima provided the-over-the-top prey drive to go along with the fear, and the rest, one may say, is history.

Almost immediately, this 'new' German shepherd was put to 'work'. At book burnings, the intelligentsia who might have objected to the burnings had they only men they thought they could reason with to contend with might have been able to mount a successful protest against the book burnings, or at least action to stall the burnings to give more rational arguments a chance to be heard. Hitler couldn't have that, and his 'new' German shepherd dogs were enormously successful in stifling dissent. Reasonable men might object to Hitler's policies, they might deplore his actions, but they could not reason with his dogs. Anyone trying to protest his policies or his actions could and would soon find themselves under attack by Hitler's beloved dogs. (And Hitler did love his German Shepherds!)

Hitler's deployment of his 'new' German Shepherds as a weapon of terror was only too effective. Anyone disagreeing with his policies or his actions might dare a beating at men's hands. They did not dare a mauling at the teeth of one of his dogs. A man might be able to heal from a beating, if not delivered too brutally. Bumps and bruises and even a broken bone or two could heal. The deep puncture wounds and the ripping and tearing of muscles and tendons and the crushing of bones was a far different story. In a day when antibiotics did not yet exist and medical expertise did not even approach today's levels, when lockjaw was common-place and vaccines and serums to combat it were uncommonly found and not always efficacious anyway, dog bites could cause life-long crippling or outright death.

When Hitler began to round up the Jews for transport to Concentration Camps to be exterminated, his 'new' German shepherd dogs were of inestimable value. It may not be too strong a statement to say that the roundup of the Jewish people could not have been accomplished without the help and the over-the-top aggression of Hitler's new line of German Shepherd dogs. And once the Jews, the Gypsies, and anyone else who disagreed with Hitler's policies had wound up in the Concentration Camps, it was Hitler's German Shepherd dogs who allowed a few men, often not many more than a hundred, to terrorize and murder thousands. Later, during the war, they were used to terrorize prisoners of war and to keep them from successfully escaping the Germans' prison camps. Still later, after the war, the Communists used them to great effect to keep people from escaping the brutality of their totalitarian regimes.

It is with these dogs that the love-hate dichotomy of the German Shepherd dog originated. Prior to the Nazis, German Shepherd dogs consisted of show dogs who were largely extraneous to the dog world at large, and the working farm and ranch and movie dogs, like the original Rin Tin Tin that dog people knew and loved. These dogs were renowned, often quite justly, for their 'intelligence' as it was called then, what we now term, quite as erroneously, as 'genetic obedience.' People who lived with them loved them, and they were a byword with their families, friends and neighbors as great dogs for real world work with stock and people.

It wasn't until we met the people who had escaped from Prisoner of War camps and Concentration Camps and the Communist countries, who had their own horror stories to tell of the dogs' indiscriminant maulings of children and women and men while German soldiers watched and laughed until death by a merciful bullet truly was an act of compassion, that the fear and hatred of the German Shepherd became commonly known. This behavior among World War II era Germans, was, unfortunately,commonplace. It happened more often than people today, sharing a far different sensibility, want to admit.

During World War II, British Intelligence conducted an experiment in information gathering with their German prisoners of war. (Maybe American Intelligence of today might have a look at their methods!) Beginning with a few high ranking officers, including generals, and by the end of the war also including a good many common soldiers who had been captured from troops and places about which they wanted more information, the British followed a counter-intuitive plan of action during which they surrounded their prisoners with comfort (and lots and lots of listening devices) and then simply allowed them to talk. To say that they did, and that what they talked about among themselves in their own language, when they thought no one could hear or understand them, was horrifying, would be an under-statement. The Brits gathered more than 85,000 pages of information by so doing, and the picture they created, not just of the avowed Nazis, but of the common German soldier as a whole, was chilling.

German officers and enlisted men recounted, in the most horrifyingly casual fashion, endless tales of brutality, rape, murder and the deliberate application of extreme terror, all for the amusement of the common German soldiers engaged in these pursuits. One soldier recounted the casual gang rape of any pretty girl that was unlucky enough to cross the path of his tank battalion. German pilots gleefully reported strafing and murdering British civilians, often women and children, in the streets and country-side of Britain, for sport. Obviously, the concept of non-combatants did not exist for these men. Pilots competed to see how many murders of women and children they could score and there were German pilots who bragged of literally hundreds of these murders. By contrast, British and American pilots only counted as 'kills' the downing of other pilots and their planes, while agonizing over possible civililan casualties in their attempts to bomb German munitions factories and weapons sites.

A German general reported, in the most mundane of fashions, during a game of patience, that he had been forced to order the common German soldiers (not Nazis) under his command, to quit stripping young girls naked, raping and murdering them in the streets of the town they occupied in front of their families before they and their buddies murdered the girls and their families by mowing them down with machine gun fire. The general didn't care if they did it, he only cared that they did it in front of everyone and he was tired of streets made impassible by the bodies of the people his troops had murdered for fun. He ordered them to take the people out into the forest to rape and murder. He added as an aside that he had told them it would be more fun if their victims tried to escape so that they could chase them like wild game (since there wasn't any wild game left to chase).

Another German soldier related, in the most conversational of fashions, that he had been once billeted for a short time with a unit who, during his stay, gunned down a thousand men, women and children. He saw nothing wrong in taking part in the mass slaughter; he called it good sport.

The development of the German Shepherd dog as a weapon of terror by the Germans at this time has to be understood within the context of what was going on in the country. Brutality, rape and murder were the German currency of the time. The men handling these dogs were not any different from those whose words were captured by British listening devices. Dogs had to not only stand up to brutal handling by their German soldier masters, they had to dish out brutality as well. Any dog unwilling to rip into innocent victims with or without command by his handler to do so would not survive long. This is what the German Shepherd dog of Nazi Germany had to be, and this is what he was. It is from this dog that the bite sport dogs of today come from, and anyone who doesn't like the facts of the matter is free to run the pedigrees back and to examine the history themselves. They may not like what they find.

Anyone who might think that Stephanitz bowed to this type of breeding or even approved of it would be far from correct. In fact, to his dying breath, the old man fought to keep his breed more moderate, more useful and a good family dog renowned for its versatility and solid good nature. His daughter credited his battle with the Nazi breeders with bringing on ill-health and his final demise through the strain and disappointment he felt at this degradation of his beloved breed. She was convinced that this final battle of his for the preservation of his breed as a useful dog of value to families in particular and all people in general caused his death.

One cannot fault the old man for a lack of courage. Disagreeing with the Nazis and Hitler meant Concentration Camps and a hard death for most people either brave enough, or stupid enough, to do it. To his credit, Stephanitz did stand up to them. Unfortunately, this was one battle he was fated to lose.

Chapter 12
The Post-War 1940s: Lex v Preußenblut and Maja v Osnabrucker Land

Lex Preußenblut SchHIII/FH

The end of World War II for Germany was an unthinkable disaster. Some high ranking Germans, faced with the reality of what their country had become, turned their faces to the wall and died. Others committed outright suicide, while others tried to survive by simply denying everything and blaming it all on Hitler and the Nazis. Locked in a struggle with the Communists that became known as the 'Cold War' the west tacitly supported the group that denied everything by soft pedaling the war crimes trials. Only the worst of the Concentration Camp Commanders and a few of the SS were indicted, and to be convicted, their crimes had to be so horrifying and abominable that they were almost literally unspeakable.

The dog that had made these crimes possible obviously had to go underground, or at least as far away as Communist East Germany and Czechoslovakia. The Nazi dog, a combination of the fear aggressive Thuringian and the intense, sheep-herding aggression of the Saxony and Brunswick dogs, was tailor-made for the Communists. They were almost immediately pressed into service.

Border patrols, ostensibly to keep out smugglers wanting to make a fortune on goods that could not be produced cheaply enough or in adequate quantities or qualities to satisfy the demand for them, were formed in order to protect the local businesses. But even more, the dogs were used to find, terrorize and murder people seeking to escape totalitarian Communist regimes. Once again, the dogs developed by the Nazis were used to make oppression possible. Dogs ready, willing and able to deliver an Unprovoked bite against unarmed victims, for the most part, served Communist dictators very well. They could move faster than the soldiers they partnered, they could find both smugglers and innocent escapees who would otherwise have managed to avoid detection and flush them out like a covey of quail to the hunters' guns. They effectively closed the borders of the countries wishing to prevent their people from leaving.

Historically, when people find the government of the area in which they live unacceptable, or natural disaster has made the land untenable, they vote with their feet. Celts left the inhospitable Alps and Jura Mountains for the wild hills and lush valleys of Wales, just as in Ireland, men and women emigrated to America to escape the potato famines. In the eighteenth century French men and women emigrated across the channel to escape 'Madame La Guillotine', while Americans traveled west to escape the tyranny and the thefts of the wealthy. At the end of World War II, a great many people voted with their feet as well. Some wound up in England or Canada. Russian Jews emigrated to Israel, joining Polish, German, and French Jews to the disgust of the Arabs. Nazis who no longer found Germany welcoming settled in South America. Countries claimed by Communist governments started to lose their populations at an alarming rate.

Communist leaders had two choices. Change their form of government, or stop the exodus. Well, dictators don't change their politics just because the governed don't like them. If they did, they wouldn't be dictators. The Communist governments closed their borders, ratcheting down their controls and killing people who attempted to leave. Building fences to enclose an open stretch of ground along their borders, often mining the land to make it even more difficult to cross, they stationed soldiers with dogs along the fences to hunt down and kill anyone found attempting to escape. This was called 'the Iron Curtain'.

Germany, divided into East and West, suffered greatly. The city of Berlin was encircled, and for a hundred days supplies had to be airlifted in to keep the people from starving. Eventually a compromise was made, but those compromises were all the more remarkable for their rarity. People who stayed in their countries and tried open protest in an attempt to improve matters were mowed down in the streets by soldiers with tanks and machine guns. People who tried to strike for better working conditions were massacred. Stalin cut a swath of murder through his own people and Mao Tse Tung used the same method in China in order to stifle dissent. For decades, the fences grew ever more impenetrable and the murder of those trying to escape ever more inevitable, and yet still, people kept trying.

People who did manage to escape inevitably linked their success to either their ability to evade the dogs or their ingenuity in effecting their escape in such a manner that the dogs were not involved. One group sewed up a hot air baloon and sailed over the border at night, thus avoiding the dogs altogether. There were very good reasons why people chose to face dangers which, on the face of it, might seem far more perilous than dogs.

The dogs the Nazis created out of the genetic base of the old Thuringian, Saxony and Brunswick breeds were lethal and they were terrifying. They might not be overlarge dogs but the sheer intensity of the aggression they could focus on a person could make people's blood run cold. Once upon a time that aggression had kept hundreds of hungry sheep from challenging the single dog standing between them and the crops that would have filled their empty stomachs. Focused on a single person, that person had to know that the mauling they were going to suffer would be crippling, if it didn't kill them outright, in the most agonizing of fashions. The dogs were truly a 'weapon of terror'.

What obedience these dogs possessed to their handler was minimal. They MIGHT 'out' promptly on command. They might not. They lived on short rations (much as their ancestors, the poacher hunting Thuringian 'yard' dogs had) a pretty stern version of the newer, kinder, 'Nothing In Life Is Free' program, and they worked in collars that would make our modern 'prong' collars look whimpy. If they disobeyed their soldier handlers, 'corrections' were brutal. Dogs that couldn't stand up to this kind of treatment and learn

319

what they needed to do not only didn't get into the gene pool, they didn't survive.

These dogs were 'tough' and often what we could call 'dominant'. A few of them worked solely with one handler for the most of their working lives, but the majority of them did not, being passed from handler to handler as convenient for the military service to which they belonged. Dogs that 'came up the leash' at their handlers were severely beaten, and those who didn't learn not to do it again got shot. Genetic obedience, that partnership between species in which the dog, as well as the human, dedicated themselves to the task at hand degenerated to a dog who did what he had to do to keep from being beaten senseless and to get fed at night. Dogs intelligent enough to out-think their handlers need not apply.

Outside of the Iron Curtain countries, in West Germany, most dog people were hurriedly scrambling to get back to the main line dogs the West found acceptable. They couldn't repudiate the dogs of the Nazis quickly enough. For them, the party line meant going back to the blood lines of the dogs Stephanitz had approved.

Some Germans, of course, clung to their bite machines, to dogs with low bite thresholds and high levels of aggression, dogs which could be pointed at anyone and told to bite and who would, regardless of whether they were being asked to bite women or children or not, but in the aftermath of the war, these folks had to pretty much go underground along with the rest of the Nazi sympatherizers. They might, in their heart of hearts, be convinced that they had the only true German Shepherd dogs. They might, and certainly did! revere these 'hard', 'dominant', 'nasty' dogs, but in the '40s and early '50s, it wasn't a good idea to flaunt them.

Lines like those of Utz v Haus Schutting could be easily repatriated into 'new' bloodlines from 'country' dogs to re-establish the main line of the old Siegers, and one pair of dogs, Maja v Osnabrucker Land and Lex v Preussenblut, led the way. Their son, Rolf, of their famous R litter, (Rolf, Rosel, Reina, Rena, Racker, Roland and Ina of their I litter) was chosen VA1 (the equivalent of Sieger) in 1951 in Ludwigshafen while Reina went VA1 for bitches in 1949 and litter sister Rena was chosen VA1 in 1950. The dogs of the R litter, with Ina, became intrinsically entwined in the 'main' line of German Shepherd dogs, influencing both show line and the so-called 'working'-line breeding for the next 50 years.

Lex was tightly in-bred to the 'main' line of Siegers chosen by Stephanitz, a tight weave of the lines of Roland v Starkenburg, Flora Berkemeyer, and Horst v Boll, with significant infusions of the Hohen-Esp dogs through Hexe and Graf Eberhard, and of Audifax and Dewet Barbarossa, with Madame v d Krone the Elder through Horst and the Hohen-Esps, with everybody winding up at Beowulf Sonnenberg sooner or later. He, of course, brings in Mores Pleiningen and yet more Madame. Nestor v Wiegerfelsen and

Cherusker v Burg Fasanental are notable more for their exclusion, than otherwise. Nothing could make it more clear than this pedigree that the main-line breeders in Germany were turning away from the dogs of the Nazis.

The line-breeding in Lex v Preussenblut is so tight that it becomes difficult to call it line- breeding. In-breeding is what it really is with most dogs related to every other dog in the pedigree to some degree and most of those degrees rather close. Uncles are bred to nieces, and first cousins to each other, and half-brother to half-sister breedings are common.

Just to begin, there is the matter of lines. In an eight generation pedigree, the eighth generation should be made up of the names of two hundred fifty-six dogs (256). In Lex's eighth generation, one hundred twelve (112) of those names are repeats. Roland v Starkenburg, for instance, appears 4 times in the eighth generation spot, while his sons Hettel and Guntar Uckermark appear 11 times in the eighth generation spot. Add the number of times Hettel and Guntar appear in the 6th generation (or less) spot (3) and you may begin to get an idea of the magnitude of the problem. Now add that Roland v Starkenburg appears 278 times altogether in a 12 generation pedigree, and you begin to see the full impact of the in-breeding. That isn't line- breeding any more, it isn't even in-breeding, it's back massing. Add the fact that every line to Roland v Starkenburg is 5 lines to Horand and his grand-sire, Pollux, and the sheer numbers involved in the in-breeding start to snowball to unimaginable heights.

At this point some folks start talking about something called a co-efficient of in-breeding, which is a complex and rather bloodless way of referring to the degree of in-breeding present in such lines. Using jargon like this has a way of distancing the problem, and making it both incomprehensible and less significant to most people—and therefore easier to justify compounding through continued line-breeding and even in-breeding. That's unfortunate, because it is exactly this kind of in-breeding which is causing the number and frequency of the genetic 'disorders' our dogs are experiencing today.

To regard the simple arithmetic of Roland v Starkenburg alone is not to really grasp the true nettle of the in-breeding involved here. The Hohen-Esp dogs, mainly through Graf Eberhard and Hexe, mother of Gretel Uckermark, who in her turn is the mother of both Hettel and Guntar Uckermark, the Roland v Starkenburg sons, are strong warp threads in the genetic fabric of Lex v Preussenblut's pedigree. Graf Eberhard sired two dogs, Munko v Boll, who in his turn sired Horst v Boll, and Luchs v Kalsmunt-Wetzlar, who sired Tell v d Kriminal Polizei out of a Roland daughter. Horst and Tell became the out-lines of choice for the Roland v Starkenburg line, despite the fact that Tell wasn't an out-line at all, being a Roland grandson, and that Horst had strong Horand v Grafath affiliations through Graf Eberhard to

Pilot, the full brother of Beowulf Sonnenberg and through Madame v d Krone the Elder's son, Baron v d Krone. (Both Pilot and Baron carried Madame.)

Tell in his turn sired Jung Tell v d Kriminal Polizei and Arno v d Eichenburg, Jung Tell being Holland's champion in 1913 and Arno Germany's sieger the same year. The bottom line on Arno comes as close to an out-line as we get, going back, as it does, to the Karlsruhe dogs through Diana Blossenburg to Dewet Barbarossa and the v d Krones again. (Her topline is Roland v Starkenburg—again!) Tell's bottom line, as we have already seen, brings Roland back, and only his grandmother carries any kind of out-line in Tell and Tillie Goldsteintal, with both Tell and Tillie re-occuring in the bottom-line of the Kriminal Polizei girls, Herta, Rezia, Gisa, Fanny and Jung Fanny.

Then again, Tell and Tillie Goldsteintal are not exactly a breath of fresh air, since they are half brother and sister through Mom Rassy Goldsteintal and cousins through Beowulf Sonnenberg and Roland v Park, both sons of Hektor v Schwaben. Add Lucie v Starkenburg, double grandmother of Tell v d Kriminal Polizei's sire, Roland, also a daughter of Pollux on Tell Goldsteintal's topline to the relationship, with Pollux the grandfather of Horand v Grafath, Hektor's father as well as the sire of Lucie, and you have the kind of in-bred line people giggle behind their hands over. And as far as Tell v d Kriminal Polizei is concerned, Tillie and Tell Goldsteintal are related to him through Hektor v Schwaben and to Arno v d Eichenburg through Flora 1 v Karlsruhe as well. So calling them an out-line is a bit of an exaggeration.

Perhaps it shouldn't be so surprising, then, that Tell v d Kriminal Polizei was the first German Shepherd dog we know to have died at the age of four from an unexplained bleed-out. He may not have been diagnosed with canine haemophilia, otherwise known as vWildebrand's disorder, (I doubt such a diagnosis was possible in 1912) but the similarities to Canto v d Wienerau's death at age four of the same cause are undeniable. Bad enough to use an unhealthy dog in breeding, even if he was structurally sound and of excellent character, but to have line-bred upon him, even in pursuit of the dream of producing siegers was poor practice. In-breeding on him was worse, with long-term consequences for the breed we're just now coming to understand fully. Lex v Preussenblut was more than in-bred upon Tell v d Kriminal Polizei, he was back-massed on him, to the point where he carried 104 lines to Tell. (Every one of which was a line to Roland v Starkenburg, as well!) And Lex, too, died young, supposedly poisoned, or at least that was the story spread to cover his death at such a young age.

Twist and turn as you will through Lex's genetic heritage, and no matter if you encounter a new name here and there, they always seem to wind up in the same place. Even worse, the farther back you go, the fewer the places you wind up. Tell v d Kriminal Polizei may have been the source of vWildebrand's disorder (canine haemophilia) but it was Lex (and Lex's sons and daughters) who were the conduit through which the disorder has been passed to our modern dogs.

Falko and 1913 Siegerin Frigga v Scharenstetten both lead through Horst v Boll to Graf Eberhard to Pilot on the top and through Mom Adelhaid Scharenstetten on the bottom to Audifax and Beowulf. Pilot and Beowulf were full brothers. Audifax winds up being the only real out- line in the mix. But the folks who liked the heavy Swabian lines of Falko and Frigga generally seemed to like the Wierra Heinrichsruhe lines as well, and they were often matched with her, sometimes directly, with Falko, sometimes indirectly, through Frigga. Wierra brings in Audifax twice, and Dewet Barbarossa through Sigfried v Jena-Paradies twice. Dewet Barbarossa takes us right back to Madame and Horand through Sara v d Krone on the bottom and to the Karlsruhes again on the top.

This is not really all that bad. Good nerve comes from the Pleiningen pair, Mores and Carex, and from Madame v d Krone, Fides Neckarusprung, and from Audifax and the Sigfried v Jena- Paradies/Dewet Barbarossa connection built on the good v d Krone foundation. We get those connections from the Horst v Boll and Graf Eberhard v Hohen-Esp, through the Heinrichsruhe and Scharenstetten conduits, as well as from the Kriminal Polizei lines to Luchs v Kalsmunt- Wetzlar.

Ever since the 1930s, one of the best ways to get to the good nerve-base of these dogs has been through Utz v Haus Schutting, and Lex travels that path 5 times in the first 6 generations. Perhaps unfortunately, he also carries 7 lines to Alex v Westfalenheim through Erich v Grafenwerth in those 6 generations and through Billo, Bianca, and Bendix Riedekenburg 3 more times not including the lines to Bianca through Erich. This means a lot more fearful lines appear than good nerve lines, because, as we know by now (right?) both Erich and the Riedekenburg dogs were most notable for both their beauty and their fearful temperaments. It is never a good thing for the fear sources to outnumber the good nerve sources. Additionally, Alex was the first dog to be identified with EPI. Doubling up on Alex was bad news on the health front as well as for fear issues but virtually all main-line dogs do it. No wonder show dogs are noted for their issues with fear and their re-occuring health problems. Given the in-breeding on dogs noted for their fearfulness and their ill-health in the drive for that coveted VA1 or that championship, it could hardly be otherwise.

This takes us to Maja v Osnabrucker Land. Maja represents a main-line dog bred for strong character without the kind of extremes produced by the Nazis. Neither Cherusker v Burg Fasanental and Nestor v Wiegerfelsen appear in this pedigree. Instead, the strength is produced by returning, over and over, to Horst v Boll, Dewet Barbarossa, Audifax and the strong herding blood of the Brenztals, the v Parks, and the v d Krones.

323

Theoretically, a 12 generation pedigree, reproduced with four generations appearing on each page should produce 256 pages of pedigrees. (Start with one 4 generation pedigree. Take each of the 16 names that appear in the last row of the pedigree—if there are 16, any name that appears twice—or more, only to be charted out once—and do a 4 generation spread for each of them. Then take the last row of names, which may very well—and usually does—contain repeated names, and do another 4 generation pedigree for each of them. 16 times 16 is 256. Every page less than 256 represents in-breeding.)

By not reproducing the same pedigree for any dog that appears in the last row of names more than once, and then counting the pages left, the in-breeding becomes numerically obvious. When the pedigrees that duplicate those that appear in Lex v Preussenblut's are eliminated as well, Maja is left with only 59 pages of pedigree. In other words, 198 of the pedigrees that appear in Lex v Preussenblut's genealogy also appear in Maja v Osnabrucker Land's genealogy.

That means that just about 78% of Maja's genetic inheritace is identical to Lex's. A half sister to half brother mating would contain LESS commonly held genetic material. This is roughly equivalent to the breeding that produced Roland v Starkenburg—a brother/sister pair through their mother who were also related through their fathers as well. One could liken Ina and the R litter to pups produced by breeding a half brother/sister pair who were first cousins as well.

That would be just about the same amount of like genetic material as that in this mating of Lex v Preussenblut to Maja v Osnabrucker Land.

Even worse, the same names, Tell v d Kriminal Polizei, Roland v Starkenburg, Horst v Boll, and Dewet Barbarossa reappear over and over again through the same dogs, Nores and Jung Tell v d Kriminal Polizei, Arno v d Eichenburg, the Scharenstettens, Hettel and Guntar Uckermark appear on those 59 pages of pedigrees that are different—slightly--from those 198 that are identical to Lex's pedigree. The main difference between Maja's pedigree and Lex's are not in the difference in the names that appear, but in the numbers of times they appear. In those 59 different pages of pedigree, Horst v Boll, Audifax, and Dewet Barbarossa appear 79 times to Roland v Starkenburg's 80 (without Tell v d Kriminal Polizei). When you add the times the Brenztal, v Park and v d Krone dogs appear, the Swabian foundation upon which Maja v Osnabrucker Land was built becomes quickly apparent.

Just to begin, compared to Lex v Preussenblut, Maja carries a lot more Horst v Boll—he appears no less than 35 times on these 59 pages of pedigree in addition to the times he appears in the identical pages of pedigree. Audifax appears no less than 17 times, and Dewet Barbarossa appears no less than 27 times. This is the real difference between these generational pedigrees-- the heavy weight of Swabian herding blood that appears in Maja through the Brenztal lines, the v Park lines, and Audifax and the rest of the v d Krone dogs.

324

(No wonder the Lex/Maja son Rolf was known to throw 'oversize' and Rosel produced the very large Troll v Richterbach when combined with the Swabian inheritance of Onyx Forellenbach and Arras v d Stadt Velbert blood in Axel v Deininghauser Heide.)

Besides the 35 times the Brenztals appear through Horst v Boll, they show up 15 more times, mostly through Pax v Brenztal, but not always. Julie and Irene v Brenztal are there as well. The v Park dogs appear 25 times, mostly through Rose and Roland (brother and sister—we just can't get away from all that in-breeding!) and Schaefa v Park. Only the v d Krone dogs that appear on these pages present much of a change and that's not as much of one as you might expect, since 27 of those appearances are through Dewet Barbarossa's dam, Sara v d Krone and 17 more come through Audifax, who was bred and trained in the v d Krone kennels before he was sold to Stephanitz and had his name changed to v Grafath.

On the other hand, the v d Krones represent some real diversity, including, as they do, Jorg and Max v d Krone, Sali v d Krone through Ella Gmund and Lida v d Krone, Madame the Elder through both Baron and Thekla, Perle, Tyras, Satan (I don't even want to think about what kind of temperament he had!) the aforementioned Sara and Audifax, and yet others who did not appear more than once. Neckar Rude, one of the v d Krone foundation sires, appears several times, through Adalo v Grafath along with Phylax Waldenreut, another of the dogs used by Herr Eiselen of v d Krone.

And those dogs are the answer to the question as to why these dogs could be in-bred in much the same way Roland v Starkenburg was in-bred, yet still bring solid nerve to their descendants —they are the Swabian base, those Brental and v d Krone dogs, who bring the reliability and the stout character and the strong nerve needed too produce good working dogs for work in the real world. These are not the dogs to run down a football field and to bite the first person they see as hard as they can for no reason at all. These are dogs with 'genetic obedience', dog commited to the dog/human relationship, dogs who can and do internalize human goals for their own, dogs with moderate to high bite thresholds, dogs with moderate to high thresholds over all and prey drive commensurate with good stock working ability rather than extremes, and aggression disciplined and controlled to be appropriate to the task.

Can such dogs be trained for attack work in police work and schutzhund and other bite sports? Yes, of course they can, if you are skilled ehough and know how to first desensitize them to the bite and then add the right obedience and training mechanisms. But first you have to get them past the idea that when you ask them to bite somebody who poses no threat whatsoever to either of you that you, the handler ought to perhaps take a chill pill and go lie down until you get over this strange idea, which is this kind of dog's first response to the concept of biting strangers who are no threat whatsoever for no good reason. These are not dogs geared   for the indescriminate bite, nor are they geared to bite women and children. Bring a REAL threat against one of these dogs, a REAL rapist, a REAL burglar, a REAL kidnapper, and they are utter monsters in defence of their person but fake threats won't raise an eyebrow and todays' decoy/helpers who stand around lackadaisically and still expect the dog to come in like gangbusters, well, these dogs just aren't going to take them seriously.

Why, and how, with the use of many of the same dogs, were Hitler's breeders able to produce dogs eager to take a bite without the slightest breath of threat, dogs eager to bite women and children indescriminately, dogs who only had to see a sleeve to take a bite out of it? The answer, very simply, is in the genetic base.

Hitler's dogs were based in the Saxony and Brunswick herding dogs with their over-the-top aggression honed on flocks of sheep that numbered literally hundreds of animals that had to be very tightly controlled, most particularly the v Burg Fasanental dogs. Both types of German Shepherd had Thuringian added. In the case of the bite dog the Thuringian blood was added to destablize the aggression of the Saxony and Brunswick dogs and make it more readily accessible. Remember Herr Eiselen of v d Krone kennels? He once said that the only thing a Thuringian dog needed in order to bite something or someone, was for that Thuringian dog to SEE something or someone. Add aggression to that base, and you get Hitler's concentration camp weapons of terror and todays bite sport champions.

It's not a simple recipe. One of the qualities that drives the Thuringian's over-abundant desire to bite is fear. Get the ingredients of the recipe a little bit off, and you can get a ferocious fear aggressive monster or a dog that's just plain angry all the time. Then again, maybe that's what you want. On the other hand, you can get a dog with fear-flight response just as easily (remember the Riedekenburgs!) Hitler's Nazis and the later Communist border patrol didn't care because it didn't bother them in the slightest to kill the fearful, spooky, timid dogs and the angry and fear aggressive dogs served their purposes very well indeed. Re-label that touch of fear 'natural suspicion' and there you are, good to go, with a dog that believes the best defense is a no- holds-barred offense. Vigilance 'r' us with a vengence and everybody's a threat so there is no such thing as an unprovoked bite for these dogs. Just existing is provocation enough for them.

If you were a lone sentry on a frontier, and your dog was your only back-up against violent smugglers, if you had to cover a big stretch of the Iron Curtain and you had to prevent anyone from getting across that stretch of ground alive, one of these dogs might very well mean the difference between your living and your dying. Even today, on the sport field, these dogs can put up high marks, if drilled skillfully enough. But put them in your neighborhood and try to make them a pet, and you are just asking for trouble. That is NOT what these dogs are.

In the case of the main-line dogs, they were built on a largely Swabian base with some of the best Northern herding blood thrown in for good measure. Here, the Thuringian blood was added for purely cosmetic purposes. Stephanitz liked the Sparwasser dogs' prick ears and pretty faces and he wanted them on 'his' breed, and he was willing to put up with fearful dogs to get those pretty faces and prick ears. The best breeders of 'main-line' dogs tried to work around the fear, struggling to preserve the 'genetic obedience' of the Swabian herding dogs and their reliability and versatility while attempting to turn out dogs with the prick ears and pretty faces Stephanitz and so many folks wanted.

Some of them, Herr Eiselen of v d Krone, and the Blasienberg and v Haus Schutting folks, managed it pretty darn well, turning out dogs for police work, 'ambulance' (search and rescue) work, and guide dogs for the blind. Indeed, v Haus Schutting produced Utz, who was to be the foundation of versatile real world working dogs of good character and good nerve for closing in now, on a hundred years. It is no accident that both Lex v Preussenblut and Maja v Osnabrucker Land carried multiple infusions of Utz, nor that the destabilizing Nestor v Wiegerfelsen was almost entirely left out of their make-up and the influences of Cherusker v Burg Fasanental were completely shunned.

Lex and Maja's R litter (and Ina!) in-bred as they were, were to become the foundation of all the German Shepherd dogs to come after them, whether they were show dogs, or whether they were bite sport dogs. Their influence would be felt not just in Germany, but in the United Kingdom, in Japan and in the United States. Through Rolf, Rosel, Rena, Reina and the rest, they would produce German siegers, American, British, and Canadian show champions, police and military dogs, bite sport dogs, and even guide dogs for the blind. Very, very few of the world's German Shepherds today do not carry at least one line to these dogs, and many, many dogs carry well over a hundred lines to this pair. Therefore, understanding the breeding that produced them and the characteristics that breeding carries is of paramount importance in understanding modern German Shepherd breeding.

It is imperative that breeders understand that their literally hundreds of lines to Roland v Starkenburg and to Flora Berkemeyer through the Riedekenburg dogs in all German Shepherd dogs means that fear will always be lurking in the background, ready to break out whenever the lines go too far to the Thuringian side of things. And the many, many lines to Tell v d Kriminal Polizei in both Lex and Maja mean that Rolf, Rosel, Reina, Rena, Racker, Roland and Ina will always be conduits to Tell's haemophilia, while the equally numerous lines to Alex v Westfalenheim mean that EPI and toxic gut syndrome will always be waiting in the wings to crop up whenever the back-massing on Lex and Maja starts to snow-ball. Breeders who insist on close line-breeding and outright in-breeding for competition, whether it is dog show competition or bite sport competition without understanding these genetic

327

facts are the reasons we have so many genetic disorders in German Shepherd dogs today.

Chapter 13
The Golden Age: The 1950s and '60s

Axel von der Deininghauser Heide
SchH III/DPH/FH

The Golden Age 1950s: Bernd and Bodo v Lierberg, Axel v d Deininghauser Heide, and Claudius v Hain

The Golden Age of the German Shepherd dog came into being because, 'for one brief, shining hour' to cadge the words of Camelot, the breed came together as one type of dog. The extreme dogs of Hitler still existed in the Communist countries where their use as weapons of terror to prop up totalitarian and dictatorial governments continued unabated but they had been marginalized in number as well as in character. For about twenty years, the German Shepherd dog reigned as a supremely useful dog, the sine qua non of working dogs, and working meant work in the real sense of the word, rather than running down a field and biting the first person they saw as hard as they could. Show dogs could work and working dogs could win in the show ring.

Built largely on the blood of Utz v Haus Schutting infused into dogs of heavily Swabian/ Wurttemberger foundation, these dogs were big in every sense of the word, big-framed, broad and strong, agile and athletic. They were often tall as well, the football players of the dog world. In-breeding and a lack of genetic diversity had yet to take its toll, and most of the alphabet soup of genetic disorders so common today were as yet undreamed of. Post World War II additions of mostly Swabian/Wurttemberger herding blood along with some Saxony, Brunswick and Northern dogs pushed the size of the dogs back up to post World War I levels. And while Hitler and the SV might have disqualified the white dogs, in most of the rest of the world they were still working and still used in breeding, enriching the breed and adding great genetic diversity to prop up the breed's overall good health. Disney even featured a white German Shepherd in their 'White Shadow' series.

Axel v d Deininghauser Heide was added to the blood of Lex v Preussenblut and Maja v Osnabrucker Land while Bernd and Bodo v Lierberg, to some extent, grew out of them; but these three dogs were the go-to dogs in the creation of the type of real-world working dog of the 1950s and '60s. Axel was essentially the out-line. The combination of Axel with the progency of Lex and Maja, often through Bernd and Bodo v Lierberg, pretty much set the underpinnings of today's modern dogs. American show lines came through Axel son Troll v Richterbach, who was also a Rosel (Lex/Maja daughter, litter sister to Rolf) grandson, to Lance of Fran-Jo and Bernd v Kallengarten. Through Bernd v Kallengarten and Troll v Richterbach son Ulk v Wikingerblut come the great real-world working dogs for herding, guide dogs, Search and Rescue dog and Police dogs. Many of the so-called 'working' bite line dogs come from Mutz v Peltzerfarm through Axel son Alf v Nordfelsen. East German (DDR) 'working'-line dog Don v Rolandsteich also came down from Axel.

Axel was a great fount of versatility in real world work, as opposed to bite sports. (The bite sport people have appropriated the label of 'working'-line for their dogs, but their dogs do not work. They perform complex routines predicated upon a dog biting a person in a situation where no genuine threat to the dog's handler exists. While the routines performed are complicated, they do not, for the most part, last much longer than ten minutes at a time. This is in no way comparable to a dog performing actual labor for hours at a time and day after day!)

Guide dogs for the blind breeding programs around the world were founded on Axel. Want a SAR dog? One who doesn't have to play ball to run a track? One who will stay on the track from dawn to dark and then track all night until you find who or what you're looking for? Go back to Axel. Want a dog to handle stock? Axel. Looking to get back some 'genetic obedience'? Try Axel.

In combination with dogs descended from Arras aus der Stadt-Velbert, Onyx v Forellenbach and the Bernd and Bodo v Lierberg brothers, as well as with any of the dogs from the Lex-Maja R litter, Axel tended to produce dogs we would call 'over-size' today. He was clearly a conduit to Swabian genetics. Though Axel himself was 25 inches tall (today's 'ideal' height) today's pundits would call him 'fat' because he was a dog with very good breadth carried from front to back, including the good spring of ribs so unfashionable today. He was a big-framed dog with a lot of bone under him, and weighed more for his height than most dogs today would because of that breadth and bone.

In fact, overall, dogs of the 1950s and '60s were much heavier dogs than dogs of today for those very reasons. Dogs then were broader from front to back, had a much broader spring of ribs and more substance overall in addition to greater height. Dogs in the Golden Era tended to be big dogs as well as tall. Dogs of 27, 28 and 29 inches in height were not at all unusual and nobody got bent out of shape because those dogs were bigger and taller than some 'ideal' somebody declared all dogs ought to emulate and dogs didn't all have to be the same size and the same color to be approved by some self-elected elite.

Bernd and Bodo v Lierberg had yet to become icons, but people used them to get good working dogs for police work, herding, and guide dogs. Bodo, in particular, was known to be a good foundation for guide dog breeding. The first Sar dog I ever worked with was mildly line bred on both Bernd and Bodo v L as well as Axel. And like Axel, they were founded themselves in real world working dogs, not just for one generation, but for generation after generation, and all three dogs were noted for putting good hips on their progeny, even through the generations, all the way from Alf v Nordfelsen to Mutz v Peltzerfarm to Jupp v Hallerfarm and Don v Rolandsteich for Axel. (The only exception to this is Bernd v Kallengarten. For while Bernd v K threw wonderfully athletic herding, tracking and police dogs, he also threw the occasional incomplete hip socket.)

331

Another go to dog of the era was Claudius v Hain, both as an outline to Rolf v Osnabrucker Land and Bernd and Bodo v Lierberg and as a source of old herding blood. Highly in-bred upon Jockel v Schwetzingen through Rolf v Karolingen, the in-breeding, most particularly in Claudius' topline through a series of half brothers and sisters, concentrated the early herding resources of the Guessnitz girls, Krone v Park, Audifax, and Hektor v Schwaben. Although Claudius did carry some of the usual mainline dogs, Roland v Starkenburg made few appearances, Klodo v Boxberg and all his progeny, including Utz v Haus Schutting are excluded and Tell v d Kriminal Polizei was minimized in favor of Jockel v Schwetzingen and Horst v Boll and his forebears.

Like the other dogs of his era, particularly Axel v d Deininghauser Heide, Claudius v Hain was a big dog without being tall. He had the kind of balance throughout not often seen today, with breath from front to back, good spring of ribs and very good substance. And also like Axel, he was the classic black and tan 'saddle' pattern. Axel, Bernd and Bodo v Lierberg and Claudius were the dogs who transmitted herding genetics down to the rare and few dogs we have today who still carry the capacity to herd and do public access work. The bloodlines of these dogs built those of our modern dogs, not only in West Germany, America and Great Britian but in East Germany, and even Czechoslovakia.

Up until 1965, the good old herding lines of grey and tans upon which the breed was quite literally founded were still common and adding their genetic richness to the healthy stew of genetic diversity along with the great old red and tans of the Hohenwartes and the Scharenstettens and Siegestors. The decision in 1965 to go hard line on the disqualification of the whites and the additional disqualification of the grey and tans (with the re-labelling of them as 'blues' in an effective smear tactic to associate them with unhealthy genetics found in other breeds) and the red and tans (they were re-labelled 'livers', for the same reason the grey and tans were re-labelled 'blues') was devastating to the overall genetic health of the breed, but the effects of that decision were not to be felt for another decade.

Generally, the 1950s and the first half of the '60s were a time when the great old herding blood of the Swabians made a comeback into the breed, bringing great health and vigor and superb trainability with it along with their hefty size. Dogs like Rolf v OsnabruckerLand, son of Lex and Maja, Bernd and Bodo (litter brothers) v Lierberg, Axel v d Deininghauser Heide and Claudius v Hain produced several generations of big dogs who did not merely win beauty contests in the show ring, but who could go out and do the 'job', whatever that job might be. These dogs invented a new form of search and rescue in the wilderness, guided the blind, made police dogs a commonplace around the world, fought two more major wars, in Korea and Viet Nam, and served as invaluable 'hired' hands on small farms everywhere, handling livestock and baby-sitting children. They even proofed the Alaskan pipeline for oil leaks through dogs carrying the blood of Bernd v Kallengarten.

The dogs of the 1950s and '60s were really large dogs. Utz v Haus Schutting was, himself, a short (24") dog, but NOT a small one. Though more compact than his sire, Klodo v Boxberg, he was big framed, with excellent breadth throughout. His broad chest provided ample room for his lungs and heart and his great spring of ribs added more room for the rest of his internal organs, and supported his spine strongly. Nor did he narrow down in his hindquarters as so many modern dogs do, he was as broad behind as he was in front, giving him a superb and secure platform from which he could wheel, pivot and spin at will. When the blood of Horst v Boll was added back to Utz through the Scharenstettens, Onyx Forellenbach and Arras v Stadt Velbert, just to name a few of the dogs still carrying heavy infusions of Swabian blood, the size of the dogs with heavy inheritances of Utz' blood was springboarded upwards. It is no accident that the large Vello zu den Sieben Falen produced dogs we would now call 'oversize' in Bernd and Bodo v Lierberg, or that Rolf v Osnabrucker Land and Axel v d Deininghauser Heide and Bernd and Bodo themselves were all noted for producing large dogs.

The 'oversized' Troll v Richterbach, who himself sired so many big dogs, was the result of mixing Rolf's litter sister Rosel v Osnabrucker Land with Axel v d Deininghauser Heide, a cross that was 'the' premier go to bloodline for the '50s. These large dogs that we now label 'oversize' happened both because of what is called 'hybrid vigor' (Axel came as close to being an 'out-line' to the main-line of Lex and Maja as the German Shepherd breed could provide) and even more simply because the old Swabian dogs were big, and when you load up on Swabian blood, you get bigger dogs. More importantly, for the future of the breed, as well as the past, the reason the 1950s and '60s were the Golden Age of the breed was because in that era we accepted, even expected, more diversity in our dogs. We didn't make the color judgments so common today, and nobody in the mainstream seriously discriminated against larger dogs (or smaller dogs, either, for that matter) nor did people toss dogs out of the gene pool for being the 'wrong' color.

Dogs were judged on their temperament, their working ability (and working ability did NOT mean biting! It meant actual, real work!) their health and their longevity. Breeding dogs to be 'good pets' was a priority, and any nitwit mouthing the platitude that dogs should not be bred to be a pet would have been regarded as an idiot. People knew that breeding dogs to be 'good pets' meant breeding for strong, healthy dogs of good character, long life and general utility. It was 'good pets' who made the great military dogs of World War II, the Korean conflict and the Viet Nam war. It was 'good pet' breeding that supplied our police with their dogs, and such good dogs that police dogs became de rigueur for police departments over the entire country and much of the world. 'Good pets' made good farm dogs and good guide dogs for the blind and it was 'good pet' dogs who went out into the wilderness and taught us that they could find lost people and save lives and that they could alert on health issues and help the disabled to live richer, better lives. It is no coincidence that the show dog and the bite dog folks sneering at good pet dogs and good pet dog breeding do not value these dogs.

In the 1950s and '60s most folks did not much value show breeding because they knew that show breeding meant in-breeding and they knew, perhaps more instinctively than otherwise, that in-breeding was bad for dogs' health and longevity. (They were right!) Competition bite sport breeding did not really exist; Schutzhund, on the rare occasions it was practiced in America, was done mostly as a way of training police and military dogs. Even more rarely, it was used as a breed test to help decide who to breed. Scoring and competition in bite sport did not arrive here in the United States until the 1970s.

What people didn't consider, but which was made all too clear in 1965, was that show breeding and competition drives the desire for uniformity, and uniformity, as the now extinct Duchess cattle so amply demonstrate, leads to death. When dogs—or cattle or horses or people or anything else—become too uniform, too standardized, too pure, they first lose their vigor and then their health and finally their ability to breed. Too many German Shepherd show dogs are so in-bred that they're well on into the health issues already with cryptorchids and monorchids beginning to appear here and there and everywhere. When those cryptorchids and issues of missing teeth raised their ugly heads in the 1950s and '60s, people addressed the issues with out- breeding (which had the effect of creating bigger dogs, which people accepted as natural and even welcomed!) in order to eliminate them. Unfortunately, today's dog show and competition bite sport folks bury themselves in denial instead, and keep right on keeping on, on their ruinous path of in-breeding for unformity and denial that their actions are creating any problem.

Today, Bernd and Bodo v Lierberg are icons for people 'in the know' in German Shepherd dogs, although often they don't quite know why. Axel is mostly forgotten, except among the American show crowd, who mostly remember grandson Bernd v Kallengarten and great grandson Lance of Fran Jo. Utz v Haus Schutting is a name lost in the mists of time, and Claudius v Hain is known only to a rare few folks who know a little bit about herding dogs and what bloodlines to go to in order to get dogs to work on stock.

Today, instead of realizing that they have latched onto some old herding genetics when the colors of their dogs start to lighten, people are supposed to be mortified that 'color paling' has occurred (because of all the in-breeding being done) and the first things the folks who know just enough to be dangerous do is start yammering on about 'pet' breeding. No wonder the 'Golden Age' of the German Shepherd is gone and almost forgotten, more mythical than real these day, to the few folks who have parents and grandparents who try to tell them about the dogs we knew then.

The Golden Age The 1960s: Lance of Fran-Jo and Canto and Quanto v d Wienerau

The decision in 1965 to disqualify the grey and tans and the red and tans from the show ring was a turning point for the breed. It took the breed away from the old herding blood and genetic diversity and towards more uniformity. The plethora of genetic disorders with which we are dealing now are the direct result of that decision and of the drive towards uniformity and the in- breeding which fueled it. At the same time that short-sighted decisions by the ruling bodies of the breed, both in Germany and the United States were being made, decisions were being made in the show rings in Germany and the United States which would have their own resounding consequences.

In the United States, Lance of Fran Jo became both an American and Canadian Champion, and in 1967 Grand Victor. A few years later, Canto v d Wienerau would become celebrated in Germany, and Quanto v d Wienerau would be named VA2. In-breeding on all three dogs immediately began throughout both show worlds, not that in-breeding in the show world was anything new. For the seventy years the breed had existed up to that point, German Siegers and American champions had been produced by in-breeding on dogs who had achieved championship and Sieger status. A short list of not just popular, but for all practical purposes, required sires dominated the show scene. Judges knew the sons and grandsons of Siegers and champions when they saw them and put them up over dogs which may have possessed better substance, greater soundness of body and temperament, dogs which might very well have been better for the long-term health of the breed. They did this, not merely because the dogs they turned away from were not of the same old bloodlines, but also because no one would have accepted either the dogs or the judges who put them up and anyone with any real knowledge of the show world would realize that, even if they refused to admit it. The die was cast.

People have a vested interest in the status quo. Money and ego invested in breeding and in showing, the cost of travel, the expenses involved in hiring the 'right' handlers, the ego involved in owning the 'right' dogs and winning the 'right' shows are all powerful ties that simply get stronger and tighter as the years roll on. The more power and prestige a person accrues in such a situation, the more important it is to them to retain and support the status quo, and the more difficult it becomes to make any kind of substantive change in the situation.

In the middle of the 1960s, the stewards of the breed all around the world started pushing for greater uniformity in the breed. Throughout the Stephanitz era, Max's personal preferences for dark-colored dogs heavily line-bred on his beloved Horand ruled in Germany, while in the United States, and

335

to a lesser extent, Great Britain, greater diversity was tolerated. Home grown lines of champions vied with champions imported from Germany and dogs spread through a wide range of regions over a land area larger than Stephanitz could even imagine retained a wide range of colors and sizes and genetic backgrounds. Both Great Britain and America had grey and tan and sable champions, as well as the occasional red and tan, black, bi-colored and the more classic black and tan champions. They didn't need Hitler to take the breed in a whole other direction to keep from being mired in a swamp of ill-health and fearful temperaments, though they certainly had their share of the latter, given that they started with dogs like Erich v Grafenwerth and Geri v Oberklamm.

The post-war recovery didn't change that for the United States. While in Germany, the breed mavens merely went back to the old genetics of Stephanitz' time, America's dogs were blossoming, aided by the bloodlines of the best of the German dogs they could get. Poor Britain had no such blossoming; they lost too many dogs during the war to rationing and bombs and the military. They were entirely dependent on what dogs they could get out of Germany to rebuild their bloodlines, and since Germany was also rebuilding, Britain could only get whatever dogs they could outbid the deep-pocketed Americans for.

The Germans made a killing; they were operating in a sellers' market. It would not be exaggerating to say that German Shepherd dogs played a significant role in re-building Germany after the war, just as they had in the 1920s after World War I. Bodo v Lierberg wound up here in America, founding a guide dog program, while Americans sought the blood of Rolf v Osnabrucker Land, Axel v d Deininghauser Heide, Bernd v Lierberg and all the rest to add to their own home grown champions. But time marches on, and nothing stays the same. Change is inevitable and world-wide, the push was towards uniformity (and sometimes more than just in dogs!)

Did people then know what the price of uniformity for our dogs would be? Probably not. Despite the fact that Darwin's work had been around for a century, people were just beginning to explore his discoveries in depth and really, very little was known about genetics. Even today, with all that we have learned about genetics since the 1960s, we know that there is a great deal we yet do not know. Still, breeders knew that in-breeding for generation after generation was not a good idea. They did it anyway. Sometimes they lied to themselves about what they were doing (just as we continue to do today) by ignoring all the in-breeding that underlies the 'line' breeding that they are doing, that in fact, takes it beyond line-breeding, beyond even in-breeding and into back-massing. In-breeding was simply too successful a way to achieve the ego status of producing a champion dog to turn away from. (It still is.)

Further, people forgot, if they ever knew, how many health problems some of those early sieger/champions had. They forgot that Alex v Westfalenheim suffered from EPI, that Klodo v Boxberg became a 'reluctant' breeder after the age of six, due to his digestive difficulties, that Tell v d Kriminal Polizei died young, at the age of four (the same age at which Canto v d Wienerau, who struggled with haemophilia as well, died) of what we would probably label vWildebrand's, today. They forgot, if they ever knew, that Flora Berkemeyer and Roland v Starkenburg had both been prepotent for fear, and that they passed it on, both alone and in combination, and only remembered that they had been beautiful. It's perfectly possible that they didn't understand how doubling up on those genetics would affect the dogs they were breeding.

Their dogs were healthy, diverse, strong. The idea that in-breeding on those healthy, diverse, strong dogs would bring them ill-health, weak, unsound physical structures and equally weak, unsound mental structures would probably never have occurred to them. If someone had proposed such an idea, they would have undoubtedly scoffed at it. And so they started down the uniformity road we're treading today.

In the United States, Lance of Fran-Jo was frequently combined with his cousin, Champion Bernd v Kallengarten. In fact, Bernd v K was Lance's cousin through Bernd's grandsire Axel, who was also Lance's great grandsire, as well as through Rosel v Osnabrucker Land. Rosel, whose litter brother Rolf appears in Bernd v K's sire's line, appears not once, but twice in Lance's family tree. Rosel, Reina and Rolf, all of the Lex-Maja R litter, are the conduits to the toxic gut syndrome (SIBO and IBD) that occur so often in American show-line dogs.

Lance himself was not a bad dog. A little over-angulated (as Denlinger forecast in 1952 with his remarks about ignorant people finding the flashy action produced by over-angulated but weak hocks), but otherwise pretty nice overall. At least there was nothing wrong with his character. Unfortunately, twenty years and ten generations of in-breeding between the descendants of the already related Lance and Bernd v K, quite often with every single dog in the pedigree going back to one or the other of those two, left many of the dogs in the American show world severely over-angulated and sickly, with the deficits in character that naturally result from a sickly constitution and a weak structure.

The German High-line state of affairs was not unlike the American situation, with one difference--Canto v d Wienerau was in no way as good a dog as Lance. In fact, Canto was a sickly dog who died at the age of four of vWildebrand's (haemophilia). In addition to his ill- health, his character was poor and his structure unsound. Longer of thigh and stifle than most other dogs of his age, he pioneered the peculiar type of flying trot so popular in the High-line show ring today, not just in Germany but in Britain and America and Canada as well, while at the same time making cow hocks, fragile stifle joints prone to ligament, tendon and cartilage injury, poor hip construction and weak hind legs the new norm for dogs that conformed to the type he set.

Combined with the better temperamented and better structured Quanto v d Wienerau, with whom his descendants were interbred much the same way that Lance of Fran-Jo's and Bernd v Kallengarten's descendants were interbred, Canto seeded his haemophilia, his poor temperment and his weak hindquarters throughout the German High-line with the same profligacy he stamped his red and black color upon them. Unfortunately the judges loved these dogs. The drive towards uniformity, the red and black color, the so-called 'flying trot' and roach-backs picked up momentum and quickly became a juggernaut that took the German Shepherd of the German High-line for a ride the dogs are still on.

Thanks to generations of in-breeding on Canto v d Wienerau, the German High-line dogs are often as noted now for their shyness as Flora Bermeyer and her Riedekenburg sons and daughters once were. As to whether they are as beautiful, well, beauty, as has been said, is in the eye of the beholder. Few dogs have a more beautiful head and face than the typical German High-line dog, and there is no doubt that many people love their characteristic red-tan and black coat. And if that beauty comes with weak, wobbly hind legs that have the dog staggering along at something that resembles a hobble more than a walk, a back humped like a camel's and ill- health, well, folks on the forums don't seem to much mind paying that price for those pretty heads and faces. Just don't ask these dogs to do any useful work. And when it comes to biting a sleeve, well, maybe they might be able to, as long as you held the sleeve down where they can reach it.

Forget asking the dog to jump up to take the sleeve—the dog's hind legs are simply unequal to the task of providing the kind of upwards thrust that action requires. When it comes to bite sports, it doesn't matter if the dogs' spirits are willing or not—their bodies aren't capable of supporting any spirit they might have and asking them to achieve what is for them physically impossible and then criticizing their temperments for actions their bodies can't perform is simply futile. No wonder some people started looking for a more athletic dog.

Chapter 14

The Modern Age: Held v Ritterberg, Mink v Haus Wittfeld, Fero v Zeuterner Himmelreich, Troll v Arminius Palme and Uran WildsteigerLand

Held vom Ritterberg

The Modern Age: Held v Ritterberg, Mink v Haus Wittfeld, Fero v Zeuterner Himmelreich, Troll v d Bosen Nachbarshaft, Irk v Arminius and the WildsteigerLands - Palme and Uran

Today we have something we call the 'split' in the breed between people who long for the old 'useful' classic, old-fashioned German Shepherd of the early days of the breed, people who have found their own 'true' German Shepherd in the descendents of Hitler's Meisterreiche dogs, and the folks who think that today's show dogs, whether German High-line or American (or British) show lines are just about perfect. The second group doesn't care about irrelevancies like Degenerative Myeopathy, Pannus, Juvenile Renal Dysplasia, or any other genetic disorder as long as the dogs bite quickly and easily in the complete absence of any threat and have a good, hard grip when they bite. The show group simply doesn't admit any of the disorders mentioned above actually exist in their dogs and furthermore they don't admit the rest of the pantheon of disorders they've created over a hundred years of in-breeding exist either; as far as they are concerned, vWildebrand's, cardiomyeopathy, EPI ('you just add enzymes') SIBO and IBD are minor issues not worth mentioning, and as for the dogs having seizures from genetic brain anomolies brought on by a century of in-breeding or puppies dying at birth or within short weeks or months because of Juvenile Renal Dysplasia (both of which are becoming common in Great Britain and starting to appear here in the United States) well we aren't supposed to talk about them. Maybe if we just close our eyes while we in-breed another generation on the same old bloodlines, they'll just go away. And the old-fashioned folks? They care, they just aren't sure what to do about it all.

Then again, people in the outer world have something very similar to 'the split' in the attitudes they have about dogs in general. On the one hand the German Shepherd dog is high up on the list of breeds of dogs some people want to ban. On the other, the German Shepherd dog has spent the last decade occupying one or the other of the top five positions on the AKCs list of most popular breeds of purebred dog. Go figure.

Back in the mid '70s the old TV show Emergency! featured a story in which a German Shepherd dog of what the elitists of today would sneeringly call 'pet breeding' metaphorically flagged down the firemen on a back road and led them to where his boy lay broken after a fall into rocks. The dog further helped the firemen, when, needing parental authority to treat the injured boy, they were able to locate the boy's parents by catching the dog and reading the tags attached to his collar. The dog was shown as being quintessentially breed standard in temperament. Approachable by friendly strangers and capable of being handled safely by them while not making friendly overtures himself—besides leading the firemen to his boy. Somehow I have a hard time seeing anyone try to do that story on a T V show today.

That story was fiction. In the 1980s, my mother's brace-balance dog pulled the leash out of her unconscious hand, where she had collapsed on the sidewalk, and ran the two blocks to the emergency entrance to the local hospital. Abby managed the hospital's electronic door somehow, found one

340

of the local paramedics (a man she knew) and convinced him to follow her back to my mother. This story is fact. (No doubt today's elitists would also scoffingly refer to Abby's guide dog, herding dog, and Sar dog breeding as 'pet breeding' and sneer at her as being 'watered down'.)

Today we live in an age of specialization and professionalization. Search and rescue work grew out of the herding dogs' abilities to track down lost livestock, but today's SAR folks would blow a gasket at the very idea of where their dogs' abilities came from. Even though they are volunteers, they have become 'professionals' in their own minds, highly trained and by that very training, sharply limited in their outlook and their attitudes. They consider themselves an 'elite' group, and as an 'elite' group, they have no need to be courteous to others, or to welcome them into their groups or to teach them, never mind be good neighbors. Service to their community according to their talents and skills is the farthest thing from their minds in too many cases. They jealously guard their law enforcement affiliations and scorn anyone not satisfactorily 'qualified' according to their lights. The result is that they get few call-outs, and mostly spend their time in rigorous training for certifications they can use to prove how much better they are than anyone else.

Given the state of the German Shepherd dog of today, guide and assistance dog trainers have no idea how or even whether to use German shepherds, and as a result, mostly they don't. A good German Shepherd may be one of the best dogs to do the work, whether it's alert work, guide work, pulling a wheelchair or helping someone to stay on their feet so they can get the chores of life done, but whose good German Shepherd are we talking about? Then again, finding a good German Shepherd for real work is not the easiest thing for someone to do. German Shepherd dogs truly suitable both mentally and physically for real work in the real world are not thick upon the ground, and are not usually to be found with either of the two mainstream branches of the split—the show dogs or the 'titled' bite dogs.

The show folks are sure their dogs are the best, of course. After all, they have the championships, the best in breed and best in show trophies to prove it, trophies they've given each other to bolster their egos and their claims for their dogs. And the aficionados of the bite dogs are equally certain that their dogs are the best. After all, their dogs have 'proved' their quality since the bite dog folks give each other 'titles' for their dogs, awarded for their dogs' willingness, even eagerness, to engage and bite people who don't threaten their handlers in any substantive way. Group think as to how the qualities they breed into their dogs in their respective venues actually impact the dogs' abilities to do real work tends more to myth and magical thinking than to reality.

In fact, neither group has the slightest respect for real work or for any of the qualities it takes to enable a dog to do any real work. Nor do they care, in any genuine way, about the health of their dogs. Like the people who denied that tobacco smoke was unhealthy, and paid generations of dishonorable Mds

341

to deny the dangers of cigarette smoking, they talk a lot about testing for health conditions, which, when examined, devolves into discussions about hip dysplasia and what kind of 'guarantee' each breeder provides.

Few breeders, guarantee or not, actually test their dogs for any of the very few genetic disorders which can be tested for, such as vWildebrand's, Juvenile Renal Dysplasia (which if your puppy has will probably kill him before he reaches six months of age, if he even lives that long) or Degenerative Myeopathy. Pernicious conditions like Mega E, EPI, SIBO, IBD, and Cardiomyeopathy as yet cannot be tested for genetically, but only diagnosed when they manifest themselves, as is the case with thyroid deficiencies as well. The dog is usually well beyond that two year limit on the buyer's 'guarantee' before any of these conditions become so acute the buyer actually realizes that something is truly wrong with their dog, making the whole issue of 'guarantees' for puppies inherently dishonest, something the breeder uses to convince the buyer that the puppy they are buying is healthy, when, indeed, the breeder's belief in the pup's putative health is more a superstition than a verifiable reality.

In fact, many a vet takes months or even years to manage to diagnose these problems, since few of these things show up on a routine blood panel or urinalysis and the vet has a long list of things to exclude before he is finally stumped and can't think of anything else. The vet, in the meantime, will be worming the pup/dog, giving the pup/dog courses of antibiotics and steroids and other nostrums mostly just to see if the condition will clear up, which it very well may, temporarily, at least, since antibiotics help with the bacterial overgrowth of SIBO and steroids are the main staple of treatmeant, along with diet, for IBD. As soon, of course, as the pup/dog is taken off the antibiotics or steroids, if dietary measures aren't taken, and even sometimes if they are, in time the pup/dog will become sick again. And around and around we go until the pup/dog dies, often early, of either ill-health or an old age which shouldn't have arrived so soon.

Mega E may show up early in its more more acute manifestations, as may EPI, SIBO, and IBD, but if the condition is less severe it may take take weeks or even months or years to become evident, if ever and, sooner or later, the poor dog dies of aspiration pneumonia. Many times such conditions trouble the dog for years without becoming so acute that the vet is able to diagnose them. Dogs with one of the digestive conditions may merely be labelled 'picky eaters' for years, may even simply fail to ever have a truly robust constitution and die young of what is becoming increasingly acceptable premature 'old age'.

Talk about health testing makes a great smokescreen with which to gull buyers and lull the breeders and competitors who swear by them to make them think they are doing something about the genetic disorders their decades of in-breeding has distilled out of the genetic stew. The concept of health testing allows them to continue doing that very in-breeding so that they can keep right on producing the same old dogs the same old ways for the same old reasons and awarding themselves the same old silver trophies for the same old criteria. The problem is, of course, that health testing changes nothing. Health tests merely illuminate, upon the few instances where we have them, the genetic anomolies which are present in the dogs tested. As long as 'health testing' is merely marketing hype for hip and elbow x-rays, which are largely environmental in origin, they'll continue to be meaningless in the greater scheme of things.

See, here's how the testing works. The breeder x-rays his or her intact animals, which are four times as likely as spayed or neutered animals to x-ray sound, merely by the fact that they are intact, and if the breeder is fortunate, that animal's x-rays are read as normal by whichever of the assessing agencies the breeder chooses. Puppies from said 'normal' parents are then sold with a two year guarantee for hips and elbows. What the seller doesn't tell the buyer is that they will have to x-ray the pup/dog at the age of two, pay for the x-rays, and then for one of the assessing agencies to read them—and by then, if the pup/dog does, indeed, turn out to be dysplastic in either hips or elbows, well, too bad—the guarantee doesn't cover the pup/dog after the age of two! Gotcha!

And nobody tells the buyer that if he spays or neuters his pup at six months of age or before, he is virtually guaranteeing that his pup/dog will develop some degree of hip or elbow dysplasia merely because of the extended growth of the pup/dog's long bones caused by that early spay or neutering. Usually what happens in these cases is that the dog starts to show some discomfort sometime after his or her third birthday, the vet offers a diagnosis of dysplasia right off the bat, does several hundred dollars of x-rays and then assures the buyer that yes, indeedy, his dog does have hip dysplasia and will need a total hip replacement toute suite and to the tune of several thousand bucks, thank you very much.

Then again, if your pup does come up lame in the rear before age two, and it doesn't turn out to be pano (old-fashioned 'growing pains' in puppies, for which you cut down on the protein the pup gets, and maybe the calories as well, if he's getting a bit pudgy and get him to rest a little and the next thing you know he's outgrown it and rushing along on his merry way) you have him x- rayed, send the x-rays to OFA for a second opinion after your vet has his innings at them, only to find out that your pup does, indeed, have hip dysplasia, what are you going to do? Scrap the pup? A good many of the guarantees out there require the buyer to return the pup to the breeder so he can be put to sleep. Dead puppies don't sully the breeder's reputation the way live, dysplastic puppies do! And they can't give the lie to the breeder's claim not to put out dysplastic puppies.

What about the guarantee of those breeders who know very well that under those circumstances you won't send the pup back? Will they still give the buyer his money back? Do they pro-rate the amount they refund according to the age of the puppy when diagnosed? What about if they tell you they'll replace the pup with another one? What kind of breeder trusts you with a second one of their pups after you've broken the first one? Or do they simply change their e-mail address and stop answering their 'phone? So much for guarantees and health testing.

Bite dog ('working-line') folks would rather jettison the breed itself by out-crossing to Dutch Shepherds and Malinois than to diversify their own bloodlines by accepting black and tan dogs into their folds. Never mind add in good, healthy, genetically well-diversified 'pet' bred dogs, or Dog forbid, some of the old bloodlines the white dogs have preserved. And we really, really don't want to hear their opinions about adding show bloodlines to their dogs (for which it is difficult to blame them!) And the show dog folks really, really are working on improving things, truly they are—though how they plan to manage this while in-breeding for another generation on Lance of Fran-Jo or Reno, or Sundance, or Caralon's Hein or, well, whichever bloodline is their choice for that ride on the ego train of championships, champagne and over-angulated hocks, long, unstable thighs, frail stifle joints and unsound minds. What's that old definition of insanity? Doing the same thing the same way and expecting different results? As my grandmother used to say, if the shoe fits. . . .So let's start with Held v Ritterberg. By now we all know that the beginning of the split was the beginning of the breed itself, a reflection of the dictomy between what Max v Stephanitz said he wanted 'his' breed to be, and the results created by the choices he made because of his personal preferences when he named which dogs were to become Siegers. Stephanitz did make some good chioices for the breed, particularly when he chose the big dogs the country people liked, like Hektor v Schwaben and Jorg v d Krone and Luchs v Kalsmunt-Wetzlar and dogs of that stripe, but there were also Horand v Grafath, Roland v Starkenburg, Flora Berkemeyer and Alex v Westfalenheim, all of whom created some real problems for the breed in terms of both health and temperament. Certainly some of the folks Gordon Garrett calls 'country' people went their own way with their own breeding in order to get the dogs they needed to do the jobs they had for them. The biggest example of this would be the hugely popular Horst v Boll, the dog the 'country' people used so often that he became the most used stud dog of his time, a major thumb in the eye for Stephanitz.

When Hitler started mandating the breeding of his Meisterreiche dogs, the country people avoided his extreme attack dogs the same way they'd avoided Stephanitz' fearful, unhealthy show dogs—quietly and without fanfare, they qualified their dogs for breeding in the most minimal ways they could get by with, and then they went their own way, just as Hitler's foundation kennel, v Burg Fasanental had before them. After the war, Stephanitz' mainline dogs rebounded strongly, and for a while the breed had a golden age when the dogs were what Stephanitz had always said he'd wanted them to be, but after 1965, the in-breeding and the creeping extremes of dog show competition started to catch up with German Shepherd dogs. Something had to give. Something did.

In 1978, a decade after sick, shy Canto v d Wienerau was born (and lived just long enough to ensure that he would be followed by a lot more sick, shy dogs) Held v Ritterberg was born. Quintessentially of the main line, he was heavily line- bred on that intensely in-bred pair, Lex v Preussenblut and Maja v Osnabrucker Land. In fact, Held packs thirty-one (31) lines to Lex and Maja in ten (10) generations and another thirty-one (31) to Nestor v Wiegerfelsen and Cherusker v Burg Fasanental. And if that isn't enough to give you the colly-wobbles, think about this - Held carries more than two hundred and fifty (250) lines to Utz v Haus Schutting, another hundred and fifty (150) to Utz' half brother, Curt v Herzog Hedan, and in addition to those lines, another hundred lines to the sire of both Utz and Curt, Klodo v Boxberg, through dogs other than Curt or Utz, for a grand total of over 600 lines to Klodo. Considering how many lines Klodo carried Roland v Starkenburg and finally to Horand v Grafath and Pollux v Hanau, is it little wonder that the 'working' (bite) line dogs that came from these lines have their own unique DNA patterns?

Held v Ritterberg carried just about 75% of the same dogs over and over and over again. In other words, another dog who was in-bred so tightly his mother and father might as well have been half brother and sister on one side and first cousins on the other. In fact, if you look at the 31 lines to Lex and Maja, through Ina and the R litter dogs, mainly Rolf, and then look at Nestor and Cherusker, with another 31 lines, you can see that Held was a dog balanced between the unfettered aggression of Hitler's attack dogs and the old main line of Stephanitz' dogs.

As the mainline dogs grew more and more unbalanced and awkward through the 1970s and '80s, with their long thighs, long, fragile stifle joints and weak, over-angulated hocks, a distinct subset of German Shepherd fanciers began to evolve as well, people seeking more athletic dogs. Schutzhund provided those folks an alternate venue for competition. They saw the way the show world was going, with ever increasingly grotesque stances and bizarre aberrations in structure, and they balked at breeding their dogs to conform to such extremes. For those folks whose measure was actual work in the real world, the show world simply became extraneous. They had their own measures in actual work, so they pretty much just went their own way. Other folks wanted to compete and if they couldn't compete in the show ring because they refused to breed such UNfunctional dogs, well, there was Schutzhund, just waiting for them to take it up and make it more than it had ever been before (and else, too, in time but nothing stays the same—it either evolves or it dies).

345

Decades passed, and Schutzhund did, indeed, evolve, and as it did, the dogs and the people who involved themselves in it evolved with it. Mink v Haus Wittfeld, Crok v Erlenbusch, Fero v Zeuterner Himmelreich and Troll v d Bosen Nachbarshaft each in their time became important dogs in the evolution of the world they helped to create, the world of the 'working' (bite)-line dog. Rare is the dog in the bite sport world who does not carry one of these dogs in its ancestry and more often than not, the dog carries more than one of them. When people talk bite sport dog breeding they often mention how difficult it is to find a dog that does not 'carry' Fero, or how common it is to see dogs that 'carry' Crok. And, since Crok was sired by Mink, and Troll by Fero, the in-breeding just keeps on coming.

If you look back at Quanto v d Wienerau (and Canto, too, to some extent) you will see the same dogs appearing that you will see in all of the pedigrees, those of Crok and Mink, Troll and Fero as well as Quanto. Condor and Volker v Zollgrenzschutz Haus, Condor v Hohenstamm, Jalk v Fohlenbrunnen, Arno v Haus Schwingel and, of course, Bernd v Lierberg, Vello zu den Sieben-Faulen and Alf v Nordfelsen are all there to be found, and repeatedly. Alf leads to Axel v d Deininghauser Heide, and you will find Rolf and the rest of the R litter OsnabruckerLand (and Ina) along with Claudius v Hain, with Rolf and Rosel repeated quite a lot, Rosel mainly through the Richterbach connenction—mostly Hein, rather than Troll.

The Richterbach line is particularly interesting because Hein v Richterbach was a son of Rosel v OsnabruckerLand (back to Lex and Maja again) and the brother of Lende v Richterbach who was the mother of Troll v Richterbach who was the grandsire of Lance of Fran-Jo, just to give you an idea of the inter-connectedness of German Shepherd breeding, world wide. Hein appears eight times in Mink v Haus Wittfeld, the sire of Crok v Erlenbusch, while he appears seven more times in the bloodlines of Tanja v Sudmuhlenkolk, Crok's mother. The Troll-Fero group add eight more lines to Hein, so if you're thinking to use the Troll-Fero as an outline to Crok-Mink, well, it isn't much of one. If you consider, for instance, Bernd v Lierberg and his sire Vello zu den Sieben-Faulen, well, Mink carries four lines to Vello and Crok, through his mother, Tanja, eight more, some through Bernd, and some without Bernd. Troll and Fero, between the two of them, log twelve lines to Vello in all, four through Fero and eight more through Troll's mother, Askia v Froschgraben.

To carry this further, Mink carries twelve additional lines to Rolf, Roland and Racker v OsnabruckerLand, while Crok adds six more through his mother. That makes thirty-three lines to Lex and Maja in all. Mainline dogs like Casar v d Malmannsheide and Ajax v Haus Dexel appear over and over again and if you add in the number of times Axel v d Deininghauser Heide and Claudius v Hain appear and do the math, you will quickly find that Mink and Tanja carry just about fifty percent of the same genetics. Do the same thing with Troll-Fero and you will get just about the same result. In fact, the bottoms of the iceberg on all four dogs, Crok, Mink, Troll and Fero are all pretty much the same, and Quanto v d Wienerau does not vary as much from the big four as you might think. Canto v d Wienerau, yes, there are some major differences there, but given Canto's temperament and his early death from vWildebrand's I'm not sure that's a good difference.

So where do the mainline German Highline dogs and the sport dogs vary? They vary the same way Held v Ritterberg does, in that they balance the mainline bloodlines they carry with the blood of Hitler's dogs, with Nestor Wiegerfelsen and Cherusker v Berg Fasanental, and the Holtzheimer-Eichwald dogs. That's it. Quite simply, the mainline dogs carry Swabian genetics for balance, and the sport dogs, the West German 'Working' lines, carry the genetics of Saxony and Brunswick dogs to provide the aggression to add to the over the top prey drive of the Thuringians. Czech dogs add distinct thread of out-lines from old Northern breed dogs to this mix.

The addition of these out-line genetics was an absolute necessity for the Czech dogs as the percentages of their in-breeding without these additions would have risen far over the 75% the German showlines routinely run. A lack of vigor and some pretty severe health problems would certainly have resulted, putting the survival of the breed in Czechoslovakia at risk. It is no accident that it is the Czech dogs and the German High-line dogs which carry the highest incidences of Juvenile Renal Dysplasia.

This brings us around to Irk v Arminius and the WildsteigerLand pair, Palme and their son Uran. This triad holds down the center of today's German High-line, largely due to the choice of Uran v d WildsteigerLand as German Sieger two years running, in 1984 and '85 and that fact alone means that he will continue to be a linchpin of German High-line breeding for some time to come. On paper it seems a logical pairing, Palme with her two lines to Canto v d Wienerau, with one additional line to Quanto v d Wienerau and Irk with his two lines to Quanto v d Wienerau. They both carry the usual suspects, Rosel through Hein v Richterbach and Rolf here and there, Jalk v Fohlenbrunnen to Vello zu den Sieben-Faulen, Alf v Nordfelsen, Sieger son of Sieger Axel v d Deininghauser Heide and even Claudius v Hain appears once or twice. But Palme carried Canto's lesser attributes along with his better talents, she had a less than steller temperament and didn't pass on the best hips, either, and Irk v Arminius carried EPI to add to the mess.

Under those circumstances, you would think that people with the best interests of the breed at heart wouldn't line or in-breed on Uran v WildsteigerLand. But people certainly did and do. Uran's two years as Sieger guarantee that. Particularly since, as pundits tell us whenever they speak of Canto or Quanto v d Wienerau or Uran v WildsteigerLand, they produced the much desired red and black color consistently in their progeny.

One of the first reasons people give for decrying the breeding of white German Shepherds is that when people breed for color they are likely to compromise the health and the general integrity of the dogs in structure and in temperament in order to more consistently produce the desired color, whatever it should be. Nowhere is that process more obvious than it is in the German High-line; it is doubtful that the white dog people have ever come close to the degree of disregard for the soundness of structure, temperament and health of their dogs as that displayed by the German High-line breeders. The use of Canto v d Wienerau at all has to be questioned; Canto's short, miserable life due to vWildebrand's, his unfortunate temperament and his poor hips should have precluded his being used for breeding. In fact, any one of those conditions, never mind all of them, should have made NOT breeding him a no-brainer. But in fact, he is line bred upon to the point where there are dogs in the German High-line being awarded high ranking who carry as many as 12 lines to Canto. And Canto only achieved Sieger status once. Imagine, if you will, the effect Uran v Wildsteiger Land is having on the German High-line today with two years as Sieger to boast of, given that he's passing on all the attributes of Canto with the EPI of his sire, Irk, to add to the mix. But hey, those wobbly, cow-hocked, roach-backed, long frail stifle-jointed, bloat, EPI, and vWildebrand's prone, soft, shy, timid and sometimes downright fearful dogs are RED and BLACK! Just the way so many people want them.

So that's pretty much where we find the modern German Shepherd today, a dog suspsended between the extremes of the aggressive, highly prey driven temperament that fuels bite sport competition and breed bans, and the various show lines, with their myriad health and temperament issues and their extreme structure. The two main groups of German Shepherd dogs, the bite sport so called 'working'-line dogs and the show dogs, whether German High-line or American show-line are more a construct of smoke and mirrors and exceedingly slick marketing than substance. The breeders of both groups are working with heavily in-bred dogs and they don't intend to change their breeding strategies any time soon. The bite sport people would rather vitiate the breed itself than change what they're doing, and the show folks are so deeply immersed in the fantasy-land they've created for themselves that they won't make any changes until the day they wake up to the nightmare of the out and out extinction of their dogs. In fact, given the science available now, I expect that in twenty years or so when their dogs are all sterile and can't breed, they'll just start cloning the poor things.

When they do, you can expect them to award championships to the clones and then follow those championships up with marketing which will explain to puppy buyers why clones are better than naturally produced dogs. And just as a puppy from show parents adjudged not good enough to follow in Mom or Dad's footsteps will cost you just about twice as much as puppies from most other breeders, you can be sure that the clones will cost a pretty penny when they arrive. And some people will buy them, just as some people will always continue to purchase puppies bred to bite people and bring them into their homes. When the bite sport folks face off with the breed banners, I'll put my money on the bite sport folks. The breed banners may have the money and the politicians in their back pockets (well, politicians will always follow the money!) but the bite sport folks have guns and they are a lot meaner.

As far as the future goes, well, there's nothing really good on the horizon for any of the so- called 'pure' breeds of dogs. People have put their egos ahead of their dogs' health for too many years, have done too much in-breeding for too much 'uniformity' for too long, and pursued too many specialized preferences, whether 'good, hard grips' or red and black color, or grotesque motion and bizarre stances, while forgetting the work out of which their dogs originated and what made it possible for the dogs to do that work. Some pure-breds are looking extinction in the face right now, while others are watching it approach with wary eyes. Folks of other breeds, like those of German Shepherds, keep themselves steadfastly turned away, too busy with their so far highly successful marketing to admit that it's coming for them, too. Those folks it will catch unaware.

By that time, it may be that few people will care, busy as they will be with their variety of oodles and doodles the pure-breed folks are so busy denouncing now. After all, if the German Shepherd people (and the rest of the pure-bred dog breeders) continue to insist that no good German Shepherd (or any other pure-bred) dog breeder should make the attempt to breed good pet dogs regardless of the fact that 98% of the market for all dogs is the much despised 'pet' market, why shouldn't people go to breeders who will make the attempt to provide them with a physically and mentally sound dog of good health and long life? We may quibble with their way of going about it, but at least they're making the attempt to provide people with good pet dogs of nice, high thresholds and decent sociability. German Shepherd breeders of the two main groups apparently have no real intention of doing it.

The modern German Shepherd dog show people and bite sport people are producing and fully intend to continue to produce is a specialized dog of and for extremes, mental extremes, physical extremes, and even in extremes in color. Bite dogs have to be black/dark, and preferably sable at that, German High-line will accept red and black and only red and black and no other color of dog should even bother to step into the ring, and the American show scene is nearly as constrained to black and tan. Bite dogs are now so extreme that most of them aren't even of use in the police and military venues for which they were developed in the first place. Show dogs have become so extreme in structure that their use of their hind legs has been compromised, while the contempt of the show people for real work and the kind of temperament that supports real work has vitiated the temperament of so many show dogs that they're not much good for anything.

No one apparently cares that the German Shepherd was created for the express purpose of being the exact opposite of specialized. The German Shepherd dog was created to be the antithesis of what it has become in the hands of the show people and the bite sport crowd. The German Shepherd dog was supposed to be a useful dog, a herding dog, a search and rescue dog, a guide dog for the blind, a helpful dog and a faithful companion, a community police officer, agile and athletic and strong and noble, not a weapon of terror or a cripple with a pretty face. The German Shepherd dog was supposed to be a good pet—in fact, good pets were all that Max v Stephanitz' dogs ever were (except for Horand v Grafath, who didn't even manage that!) and they were supposed to come in a rainbow of colors and a wide range of sizes out of which individual people could pick their favorite, of course, but people were supposed to understand that no good dog is a bad color, all of which people seem to have forgotten.

Right now, the German Shepherd dog is living off the reputation the breed has built on the backs of the good pet dogs of earlier generations, but the handwriting is on the wall. People are starting to notice the breed's unfriendly disposition and unhealthy constitution. How long people will cling to the last remnant of the breed's good looks when the hostility and aggression over- taking the breed makes the dogs a liability to own is an open question? How long will they keep to the breed when the fearfulness which has always been present in some dogs makes them difficult to own? And how many folks will turn away from the breed when dogs with poor health produced by snowballing in-breeding create such a financial hardship for their families are questions no one can answer, but already people are deciding German Shepherd dogs are not for them because of these conditions.

If people can turn over in their graves because of what goes on in this world, then poor Stephanitz must be turning cartwheels. 'His' dogs have turned into everything he inveighed against and even fought to the death to prevent—the bite sport dogs have become the extreme hostile, aggressive weapons he fought Hitler to prevent them from becoming, and the show dogs with their extreme structure have become the 'fancy' dogs he feared from the very beginning of his first attempts to form the new breed. And perhaps most ironical of all, where the breed goes from here depends upon the group most bite sport and show people despise most of all—the pet people. The future of the breed rests in the hands of those both the bite people and the dog show people insist no one should breed for—the pet people.

Pet people will choose whose dogs they are willing to buy, how much they are willing to pay for those dogs, and, in the final analysis, whether or not they will allow breed bans to exist. How long they will be content to purchase, for those very dear prices, the cast-offs of the bite sport and dog show world is anyone's guess. P. T. Barnum did say there was a sucker born every minute. Will enough of them be born in the years to come who part with their money to keep the show and bite sport worlds going? Or will people wise up, turn their backs on the slick marketing ploys of 'titles' and 'championships' and choose other dogs? Only time will tell.

Part VI:
Final Thoughts

Marko vom Cellerland

Chapter 15

Reflections from the Dog House

Uran vom Weststeiger Land

Reflections from the Dog House: Competition Breeding

Captain Max v Stephanitz had some very cogent remarks to make about the use of successful competition dogs in breeding. He considered them a poor choice overall and declared that using competition as a breeding test would result in the degradation of the breed. Specifically, he stated that, "breeding worth and exhibition worth are fundamentally different things." He also said, "Exhibition awards must never be taken as a judgment of breeding value." And "The over- appreciation of exhibition awards, which is connected with all kinds of considerations apart from the dog, can become a real danger for the breed." He observed that breeders "will compete blindly for the services of a prize-winner, who is then over-used." He added that, "In the case of bitches, the qualities [needed] for Exhibition and those for breeding are nearly as far apart as the poles." And, "there have always been quite a number of unreasonable people who will always forget that for a mother substance is of far greater importance than beauty." He declared flatly that "It is not to be doubted for a minute that emphasis on exhibition requirements is a danger to our breed."

Stephanitz may have gotten into trouble with his own breeding program because he had a tendency to lead from his heart and make sentimental decisions, but when he started talking about breeding in general, he was usually right. Certainly he was in his statements above. The idea that dogs should have 'titles' gained in exhibition of one type or another in order to be breed- worthy is absolutely and categorically wrong and not only because Stephanitz said so.

'Title' breeding is wrong for many reasons. One, 'titles' are gained, as Stephanitz noted, by considerations apart from the dog, considerations such as the skill of the trainer, the skill of the person handling the dog in the ring, the amount and quality of nutrition the dog receives, the subjective personal prejudices 'likes and dislikes' of the judge, the artificiality or utter uselessness of the pursuit in which the dog is exhibited, and the effect on the breed of the very act of judging in itself (last but far from least in its deleterious effects). In Schutzhund and the rest of the bite sports, while 'nerve' is a consideration which can be genetically transmitted, the training without which the dog cannot compete, never mind even excel, is NOT genetically transferable. And in the show ring, Jimmy Moses' reputation may make an otherwise marginal dog into a champion, but it cannot be transmitted genetically. Neither can being 'owned' by the 'right' person ready, willing and able to pump a fountain of money into a dog's competitive career.

The world is full of dogs who, with the 'right' training and the same amount of money spent on their competitive careers could and would be just as successful. Are their genetics less worthy of being passed on because they didn't have the luck of the draw to be placed in those circumstances? Who owns them and who trains them and whether they compete or not does not change their genetics.

Then again, the bite sport folks are not the only people saying that only their dogs are 'breed- worthy'. Of course, the show folks are saying the same thing about their dogs. Why? Because they don't want to share the pet market dollar. Stephanitz said that "Efficiency for work must count more with the Shepherd dog breder than the honors of the show ring." He was right again, of course. When it came to what he said, he usually was. So let's look at the effects of judging.

Both bite sports and show ring dogs are judged. Those judgments are based solely on subjective and artificial standards invented for purposes of competition. That is, for the express purpose of choosing a number one dog. For those who have heard that Schutzhund was once upon a time a breed test invented specifically for the German Shepherd dog, that is true. In the beginning, Schutzhund was started to provide a substitute test for dogs who were not actually working. It was intended as a secondary, and lesser breed test, invented to confer distinction upon dogs who did no actual work, the first rank of distinction being reserved for herding dogs, guide dogs and police dogs.

Dogs judged in Schutzhund were granted a mere pass or fail. No scoring was done, although comments were added to help make complementary pairings. Schutzhund dogs were ranked one, two and three, according to the level of their obedience, primarily, but also according to their ability to navigate an obstacle course and do some basic tracking. Courage tests consisted of fending off an attack on their handler and the sound of a gunshot close by. Unprovoked biting remained, at that time, undreamed of, and probably would have been considered egregiously reprehensible. Tracking titles (also done pass-fail) separate from Schutzhund, carried a distinction of rank at least as high as designated for dogs whose only distinction came from Schutzhund.

The first problems started in the show ring (of course) with Roland v Starkenburg. An unusually beautiful black dog, Stephanitz picked him as Sieger for two years running, a mistake that still reverberates in the breed today. Appearance is only a part of what makes up a dog. His temperament, his heart and soul, are what infuse his body and make him either a good dog, a great dog, or a failure as a dog. Roland was a failure as a dog, he was fearful, lacking in genetic obedience and useless but in the early years of the breed, those 2 years as Sieger gave him an impact on the genetics of the breed that has been little diffused by the hundred years that have passed since his death. We are still fighting the effects of the fear he imprinted on the genetics of the breed because of Stephanitz' judgment making him twice a Sieger. (And in choosing his son, grandson and great grandson to follow him!)

Whenever a dog is picked number one in any contest, either in the show ring, or in bite sports, the people involved with those venues are going to take their females to that male in the hope that she will give them the next number one dog. The effects are multiplied, when, as so often happens, the son or grandson or both, of the winning dog are also declared winners themselves. All of a sudden half brothers and half sisters are being bred to each other, grand-daughters are being brought back to grandfathers, and even, in some cases, sons to mothers and fathers to daughters. When this is done for a single generation, it is called in-breeding. When it happens for multiple generations, it is called back-massing. Picking 'winners' causes people to in-breed in the hope of having a 'winner' themselves, and as dogs of the same 'line' 'win', back-massing begins to occur. Thanks to the practice of picking 'winners' in both the show ring and the bite sport arena, show ring dogs are looking back at a hundred years of back-massing and sport dogs fifty.

Sport dogs, however, did not start 'even' so to speak. They already had fifty years of the show ring back-massing behind them (with, perhaps, slightly less intensity) when they started their own death spiral into 'popular sire' in-breeding. Because of that, they won't have another fifty years to in-breed before the back-massing catches up with them. Few people, even the 'experts', truly know or understand the breeding behind their dogs. They know the winners in their own milieu, they know the females with a record for producing winners and they know maybe four generations behind them. That knowledge doesn't even begin to present them with the full scope of the problem of back-massing in this breed. (Or any breed, most likely.)

That's the first effect of judging dogs to come up with 'winners'. It's the obvious one. The second effect is much more insidious, but like the breeders of popular sires who graduate from in-breeding to back-massing before they know it, people who make judgments about which dog ought to be number one, start the dogs on a path that inevitably leads to extremes. It really doesn't matter what is being judged, it is the action of choosing a first place dog (or anything, really) that creates the movment into extremity.

Think about the act of judging. A person walks into a circle of, say, a dozen dogs. That person is charged with choosing one dog out of all of that dozen dogs to call the 'best'. How do they choose? They all look pretty. They've all been spiffed up for the occasion, bathed and fluffed to look their best. If they are all the same breed, most of them will look at least a little like all the others. So how does a judge choose one?

The judge does it the only way it can be done. The judge looks for the dog that gives a little bit more, that has a little bit more. On the sport field maybe that more is more drive. Maybe it's more aggression. In the show ring, maybe it's a tad bit longer thigh, or a touch lower stifle, or a little more angulation behind. More is better, right? At least it's something by which to separate one dog from the others.

But none of this happens in a vacuum. The other exhibitors look at the 'more' that's winning and immediately start striving to produce it. In the beginning, that more isn't really all that big a deal. Anything too markedly different from all the rest would be discarded as out of the norm. And because it's not that much 'more', the competitors don't have that much trouble turning out dogs who all possess that 'more' nor any real qualms about doing it, because after all, it's just 'a little' more. All it takes is one generation, maybe two at the most especially with the tool of in- breeding at their elbow with which to do it. This puts the judges right back where they started, trying to find a way to separate the dogs in front of them out again so they can again choose a first place dog, a 'winner'.

They're not going to go back to where they started. People don't do that. It's not the way they think. So the judge picks another dog with a little bit 'more' again. And again, all the other exhibitors scramble to catch up, so that the 'norm' is always changing to something less 'normal'. It becomes a sort of Unnatural evolution, driven by the act of judging the dogs itself. Add the ego of the competitors who congratulate themselves for 'improving the breed' and the ego of the judges who get paid to pander to them, and mix in the money generated by successful studs in stud fees and puppy sales, and you have a juggernaut virtually impossible to change and completely impossible to stop.

The result has been a show dog with hind legs so weak and wobbly that the dog can hardly stand up, staggers when he walks and squats most of the rest of the time. He either has a back that runs downhill like a ski slope due to his weak hocks, or is humped up like a camel's, due to his roach back. And his gait, so desired in the show ring, is unnatural and even bizarre, an artificial construct of no earthly use to any true working dog. He's lost most of his genetic obedience, he's afraid of his own shadow and God help you in a thunder storm.

For the bite sport dogs, the 'courage' test has evolved from the action of the dog to get between his handler and a 'bad guy' simulating an attack on that very same handler, to a dog that runs down a football field to make an UNprovoked attack of his own on a stranger wandering around minding his own business. Good high bite thresholds have been ditched for low bite thresholds, prey drive suited to a herding dog has been exchanged for the kind of extreme prey drive which will support an unprovoked attack on someone no where near the dog's handler, and genetic obedience, which supports cooperation with a human towards a common goal has been thrown out the window because it doesn't support an unprovoked attack on a human.

As far as the popular sire syndrome, as it has come to be known, the effect on show dogs has been little less than catastrophic and the effect on sport dogs has been nearly as serious. The only real difference between the two groups is that the damage to the genetic diversity of the show dogs has had an additional fifty years to snowball but give the sport dogs time—they're already headed down that in-breeding road full speed ahead. Knowledgeable sport dog breeders already note that it is difficult to find a 'working-line' dog that doesn't carry one or more of a small coterie of bite sport competition 'titled' dogs, known familiarly by their first names, such as Held, Mink, Fero, Crok, Yoschy and Troll. What most sport folks don't understand is that these dogs are not only related themselves, but are, in their turn in-bred on Lex v Preussenblut and Maja v OsnabruckerLand. Nor do they understand the in-breeding behind Lex and Maja, and it is that very lack of understanding which will bring their dogs down.

In-breeding on popular sires in both groups has distilled out a devil's brew of genetic disorders which can kill the dog unfortunate enough to be affected by them, or just make his life a misery to him and a nightmare for his owner (as well as a pit down which said owner pours his or her money in a hopeless attempt to ameliorate that misery in at least some small way). All the genetic tests in the world won't help if we don't stop the proliferation of these conditions that in- breeding causes. As one pernicious genetic disorder is eliminated, another will merely take its place—and the odds are good that what takes the place of the eliminated disorder will be even worse. Remember the guide dog program that all but eliminated the relatively mild problem of hip dysplasia by adding a good foster program of prevention to their genetic culling, only to find themselves dealing with a far more serious problem in Mega E. More puppies were lost to their program through death and through their short, difficult and expensive lives than had ever failed due to hip dysplasia!

It is no accident that a tremendous upsurge of genetic disorder followed the short-sighted and ignorant decision to declare the traditional colors of grey and tan and red and tan 'faulty'. Today's drive to ratchet the acceptable size of the breed to a narrow and genetically UNdiverse 'ideal' of 25 inches may be even worse. If it catches on, and people actually attempt to limit the breed's genetic diversity again, the results may be catastrophic. One might suggest that the pundits of the breed suggesting this course of action get their heads out of their butts, but it would be impolite.

The best thing the breed could do for itself now would be for the breeders to get completely away from the competition models, be it bite sport competition or the even worse beauty contest venue, and instead encourage the use of the broadest spectrum of dogs for breeding. Dogs of all sizes, colors and working types (as opposed to 'working-line' types) such as herding, guide/assistance/alert dogs, Search and Rescue dogs, Police dogs, lots of 'old-fashioned' dogs, a soupcon of the best temperamented and structured and most moderate and solid in nerve of the sport dogs, the most moderate and best temperamented of the show crowd in sharply limited numbers, and all of them mixed judiciously, with dogs of similar structure and temperament put together to minimize the discontinuity, so that all the 'lines' are thoroughly mixed. The disparity of the results, litters containing dogs of different colors, light and dark, big dogs, small dogs, tall dogs, short dogs should all be celebrated, and if short dogs are desired, they can be bred to other short dogs to produce more short dogs, as long as they're not related and their overall structure and mentality are stable and similar in type.

The same can be done for tall dogs, for those who want them, big dogs, small dogs, and so on, but extreme care needs to be taken to keep the breeders from falling back into the in-breeding trap. Perhaps no dogs more closely related than second cousins should be allowed to be bred and only one generation of such in-breeding should be allowed out of three generations— or more practically, no pups of parents more closely related than 4-4 (second cousins) should be allowed to be registered.

Will anyone follow this prototype? Of course not. Few if any individual breeders could afford to follow such a program by themselves. To produce enough numbers of these unrelated dogs to make any kind of a difference for the breed, only breeding groups could be effective. And, to be successful, people would have to be actively discouraged from decrying the dogs of people who have chosen to perpetuate a type of dog different from the type or color or size of dog than the dog they have chosen to preserve.

The 'title' folks will continue to insist that no matter what, in order to make it in the breeding stakes, the dog has to be 'tested' and the bite sport folks are equally insistent that the breed test should be that of a dog biting a human without any provocation for the bite whatsoever. They assert that this tests the nerve of the dog as no other action or reaction of the dog can or will and that it is the only 'right' test of a German Shepherd. Whether you can accept this or not depends on how much you know about German Shepherds and whether you know what the actual breed standard says about temperament. If you believe in the commonly agreed upon (albeit unwritten and unofficial) bite sport breed standard, which considers hostile, 'naturally suspicious', dog aggressive, people aggressive, low bite threshold, 'reactive' dogs perfectly acceptable because they can pass a Schutzhund test then you may accept this premise and hold to it regardless of the increasing lack of mental and physical health in bite sport dogs.

If, on the other hand, you ascribe to the actual, written breed standard which has been in effect with only a few changes, since 1943, the one that says that hostility is a severe fault in a German Shepherd dog, you might have a bit of a problem with this premise. If you also know that the standard calls for an approachable dog, one who is calm and quiet and confident and who accepts the friendly advances of strangers with courtesy, the idea that modern Schutzhund and the rest of the bite sports as they are done today are any kind of arbiter of 'breed-worthiness' might start to seem a little specious. Then, when you add the over the top prey drive so necessary to the bite sports as they are done now, the low bite thresholds and extreme levels of drive and aggression, and you just might start to get a really bad feeling about the bite sports as breed tests, if you have any real sense at all.

Once you start to compare the kind of temperament needed for a dog in the world outside the bite sport arena, reality comes into focus. In the real world, dogs don't (or shouldn't) bite anyone they come into contact with at the drop of a hat. If you take them out into public, the general hostility towards other dogs and any person you might meet exhibited by bite sport bred dogs so commonly may give you a wake up call. You just may start to see how really problematical the bite sport standards are for dogs that have to live in the real world.

As long as dogs can remain in the bite sport world, as long as they can stay in the military, or be used by the police, dogs of bite sport standard are fine. The problems arise when they start filtering into the real world. While some pet people do exist who are both willing and able to create lives which revolve around confining, training and exercising their dogs and who can provide for a bite sport standard dog's needs and still protect the rest of the world from him, those people are not thick upon the ground. So where is the market for bite sport standard dogs? While bite sport homes do tend to have multiple dogs, and the people who do bite sports are fanatic about their sport, there just aren't that many of them.

That's where the hype that pups from bite sport titled dogs are best comes from. It's a sales ploy. And some of it is genuine, of course. The bite sport folks do genuinely believe that their dogs are the best. It's when they start cutting down on other types/lines of German Shepherds that the problems start. The bite sport folks, mostly, are sincere, but they want that pet money too, and people who breed dogs expressly for the solid nerve, high thresholds and genetic obedience that suits most families and actual work, like herding, guide work, Sar, and the rest become their targets, as the bite sport dog folks battle for every pet market dollar they can get. After all, bite sports are expensive. They need that money to fund their hobby.

But, you say, the bite sport people don't want their dogs in the pet families they so despise. They say they only want to let their dogs go to 'working' homes. So what is a 'working' home? One active in bite sports? Or in Agility or Flyball or Dockdiving or Sar or some other activity which has the family and dog out and about and in training every weekend year around? Well, no. When pinned down, 'working' family turns out to be any family which can represent themselves as 'active', which in the final analysis, after much more examination, turns out to be pretty much any family who wants a German Shepherd and can come up with the money to pay for one.

So much for the elitist view. The bite sport folks are fond of saying that they don't want their dogs in the hands of people who don't 'work' their dogs (which translates as trains their dogs constantly so they can keep them from biting people) but somehow they wind up out there anyway. Then when the family complains that the dog bites their kids, the neighbors' kids, or the family themselves, they're told to train more and exercise the dog more. When that doesn't work, they're told the dog is fine, they're the problem. Sometimes they are, but often in those instances, if the dog had less extreme prey drive, a higher bite threshold, or was a little more mentally stable, the family wouldn't be the problem.

The truth of the matter is that the bite sport crowd wants the pet dog dollar as much or more than anybody else, and they'll do just about anything short of actually breeding an appropriate dog for pet families to get it. Both show folks and bite sport fans are adamantly against the breeding of good, solid, stable dogs for families who want pet dogs. They are determined to force people who want German Shepherd dogs for their families to take their cast-offs, and pay a pretty penny for them, too. Whether you are willing to yield to their pressure and swallow their propaganda is, of course, up to you. And if you don't mind feeding enzymes every day for the term of your dog's life, or you don't mind having to keep your dog on steroids to keep them alive, or seeing your dog die from Bloat, or vWildebrand's or Mega E or DM, well, that's certainly your choice. One feels a little sad that your choices will make it that much more certain that dogs will suffer from these and other genetic disorders, but if you are willing for them to do so in order for you to be assured that your pup comes from dogs that have 'proven' their worth by 'earning' 'titles' well, there's not much that anyone can do about it. It is your choice.

Reflections from the Dog House: Breeding and People

By now, if you started at the beginning and have worked your way through to this point, you are aware that in German Shepherds, there are three main groups of people breeding German Shepherd dogs and that each of these groups of people have their own belief system about what the German Shepherd dog ought to be. One group, the old-fashioned folks, believe that their dogs ought to conform to the actual breed standard for temperament in place at this time and that their dogs should conform structurally and in variety of colors to the standards, sizes and versatility of purpose that belonged to the breed from its inception. They particularly like and are drawn to the foundation dogs of the Swabian/Wurttemberger strain and preserve and protect that strain as best they can in the modern world.

Another group, calling themselves 'working-line' but who would more accurately be labeled {'bite-sport' people, have crafted their own breed standard for temperament which has little in} common with the actual written standard, but which they believe in religiously (and I do mean religiously). Constant repetition of the tenets of this divergent breed standard for temperament, for instance, the insistence on 'natural suspicion' in place of the correct 'the German Shepherd dog should be alert' has so set the incorrect standards into their collective mentality that they are constitutionally unable to see or hear the correct breed standard when it is presented to them. This group pays little or no attention to matters of structure in their dogs but religiously require their dogs to be of small stature and dark in color. These folks derive their dogs from the yard dogs of Thuringia, with a soupcon of aggression from the Saxony and Brunswick dogs, sharing the attitudes of the rich landowners who developed yard dogs for the express purpose of attacking people less wealthy or privileged than they are, themselves. They do not care that the temperament and the structure they find so satisfying creates dogs who will suffer from Bloat and the Torsion Bloat leads to, and who will die early because of it. What they 'like' is more important to them than the good health and longevity of their dogs.

Unfortunately for this group, people no longer give the privileged the right to allow their dogs to attack and bite other people and other people's dogs with impunity. Some of the people of this group don't quite 'get' that, insisting on taking their 'aggressive' dogs out into public and allowing the dogs to threaten and menace other dogs and people at will and without apology. It is their right, they contend, to take their 'reactive' dogs out into public regardless of how uncomfortable the dogs raging makes other people with their well-behaved dogs. Those who will admit to attempting to correct the behavior uniformly use ineffective means to do so. Others insist that there is nothing wrong with the behavior, as the dogs can achieve their 'titles' anyway, despite their 'reactivity' and if other people don't like their dogs ill-nature, they can just stuff it. (And if anyone is unfortunate enough to actually get bitten by one of these rage-aholics, well, tough toenails, it was their fault anyway, for just existing in the dog's cosmos, if for nothing else.)

This group could quite accurately be described as a cult, and like a cult, they have followers, who, like followers everywhere, often don't understand the real tenets of the cult particularly well, but attach themselves to it anyway. Many of these followers are attracted by the certainty of the core members of the group, or cowed by their bullying ways. And like followers everywhere, they are often even more judgmental and bullying and rude than the more knowledgeable members of the group. Members of this group who are knowledgeable, reasonable, somewhat friendly and even courteous are rare, but do exist. If you manage to find one, cherish them. You can learn a lot from them.

The third group, a group becoming more marginal all the time, are the show-dog people. Their dogs, a largely Thuringian-Swabian/Wurttemberger blend, have long become homogenized into a breed in themselves by a literal century of in-breeding. Either black and tan or black and red in color with structure that doesn't even begin to approximate the existing breed standard (look at the picture in the breed standard and then look at any champion or best in show winner and even someone who knows nothing at all about conformation can tell the difference!) the dogs are bred with no regard for the breed standard in temperament whatsoever. Dogs are judged upon what they look like and how they move in the ring.

The breed standard says that any dog which bites the judge should be disqualified, but in the ring, handlers are asked to 'show' the judge the dog's bite (to check for missing teeth) because it has become common-place for show dogs to bite judges. Like the 'working' (bite)-line folks, the show-dog folks have invented their own breed standard to replace the actual written one, and again like the 'working' (bite)-line folks, the show folks believe in their own standard to the point where they are actually unable to recognize or comprehend the real standard. Only their own divergent standard exists for them.

Just as the 'old-fashioned' dogs tend to have a kinder, gentler nature and more diversity of size and color, the people who choose 'old-fashioned' dogs tend to be more open, mannerly 'just folks'. They are generally friendly, welcoming, and tend to accept a wide variety of opinions and experiences in the people with whom they are willing to associate, as long as those people can present those variances in temperament and opinion with courtesy and friendliness. They can generally understand divergent points of view, even if they don't embrace them. This, along with the larger sizes in some of their dogs, tends to make them a more accessible target for the other two groups, particularly the 'working' (bite)-line' people.

'Working' (bite)-line people have their own group mentality, leaning (like their dogs) towards a bullying disposition. They do NOT accept anyone who does not espouse the party line. Rudeness towards people who don't have their code words and phrases on the tip of their tongues is almost de rigueur. They tend to be hostile and aggressive towards people they perceive as outsiders and are often manipulative and controlling, even towards people they perceive as belonging to their own in-group. At best, you can expect members of this group to be arrogant, dismissive of other people's opinions and experiences or at best, brusque. Do not ask or expect them to be friendly or to welcome you, as a newcomer, to their midst. If you want to join them, you will have to be persistent, you will have to accept all their opinions and attitudes unquestioningly, and be prepared to swallow them whole and even to espouse them fervently if you are to be able to join their ranks. Like any other cult, the 'working' (bite)-line' people tend to be very fluent in their own dogma and this vocabulary, like the quotations spouted off by the members of other religious cults, gives them a verbal advantage over more courteous people of a less overbearing and aggressive temperament.

Show folks into German Shepherds are a beleaguered group these days. The results of a hundred years of competition breeding and the in-breeding it engenders have created a dog that no longer even resembles a dog in many instances. Show 'champions' with hind legs stuck out a country mile behind them or hocks so weak the hind leg collapses when the dog moves (or both) look awkward, ungainly and even unstable even to the most ignorant observer, and sensible people know exactly what to think of the show folks' self-serving fantasies. They know BS when they hear it. There is a very good reason fewer and fewer people are interested in joining the ranks of the German Shepherd show fanciers' crowd, no matter now glib the supply of smoke the show folks can blow. People are beginning to realize that all that in-breeding has created a monster of genetic disorder which will not be so easily overcome, and those people not foolish or outright idiotic know it won't be done by continuing to do the same old in-breeding on the same old lines and judging the dogs the same old ways.

Being beleaguered, however, exacts its own price. Show folks have always been elitist and arrogant, but now they are defensive as well. They pretty much have to be. People are telling them they've done wrong, and like people everywhere, they don't want to hear it. They don't intend to change anything, they don't intend to learn anything, and they DO NOT want to be criticized for those intentions (or lack of them). When you add that they tend to have, at the higher echelons, a lot more money than the rest of us, and control (for practical purposes) of the German Shepherd Dog Club of America (the group setting the standards and controlling what goes on in the show ring—or does not go on!) you have a group that simply doesn't have to do anything they don't want to and who are in the driver's seat so that they can cram anything they want to down the rest of our throats any time they want to.

Show folks would LOVE to welcome you to their ranks, but ONLY if you're willing to partake of their own particular fantasy and to do it not only unquestioningly, but with adulation for their wonderful, know-it-all selves and their pre-eminent dogs. (They may be wonderful only in their own minds, their knowledge may fit into a thimble, and their dogs pre-eminent only in fearfulness and their lack of ability to be useful for any reasonable kind of service, but they will never recognize or accept it and if you do, they will never accept you!) Buy their dogs, sit at their feet, join them in their chosen fantasy, and they will welcome you with open arms. Expect a little bit of back-stabbing and jockeying for position as normal—it is, it goes arm and arm with any kind of competition based on subjective criteria—and enjoy the ride. It will be expensive, but as in any community under siege, you will have the opportunity to make lifelong friends—as long as you continue to adhere to the community standards. Diverge from the fantasy, from those community standards, and you may wind up with lifelong enemies.

Are their exceptions to these generalities? Of course there are. There are always exceptions. It has been said that if your head is in an oven and your feet on a block of ice, on average, you are room temperature. It's the old Bell curve all over again. There are always some people (or dogs) out at either end of the curve which form an exception to the norm. Just remember that the view from inside the group as to the group disposition may be very different from that of an outsider. The point of view at which you stand may make all the difference in your perception of the group temperament, and of your treatment by the group.

A dog person you know who belongs to a 'working' (bite)-line' group may insist that their group is friendly and welcoming and made up of great people and that you just 'must' join them. I would suggest that if you want to partake of any friendliness or welcome, that you make arrangements to attend that meeting with your friend, so that your friend can directly sponsor you to the group. If at all possible, travel to the meeting place in their car with them. It may make all the difference in the treatment you receive from the group. Arrive in your own car a few moments in advance of your friend, and you may see a very different view of the group than your friend does. 'Working-line' folks can do a 'cold shoulder' with the best of them.

The odds that your 'friend' will perceive any coldness, rudeness, or hostility directed at you by the group, are just about nil. You'd have a better chance of winning the lottery. Your friend has already made up their mind about the attitude of the group, has already accepted the group norms of behavior as acceptable and appropriate, and already considers these folks their friends. They are not going to 'see' any behavior that does not correspond to their preconceived notions about those friends.

This is true, to some extent, with all exclusive groups. It is always better if, when joining a new group, you are 'sponsored' in your entry to the group by a member in good standing with the group. When it comes to dog groups, Search and Rescue groups are often heavy with 'working' (bite)-line' members, and thus partake of the 'working' (bite)-line mentality as a group and, as already mentioned, show-dog groups are, to some extent, under siege, so tend to regard newcomers with some suspicion. People in groups working on general obedience/behavior in their dogs (as opposed to bite work or tracking or herding or something else task specific) tend to be the most accepting of dog groups. They have joined the group specifically to work on their dog's behavior, so they will accept some deviation from whatever they deem correct behavior as long as they perceive that you are working on improving that behavior. These groups tend towards friendly, helpful, welcoming behavior. They also tend to have a wide variety of dogs and to welcome dogs of various breeds and types.

The same person and dog attending a 'working' (bite)-line' group, a show group, a SAR group, and a general obedience training group are apt to have very different experiences with the disparate groups. Unless they are very dedicated, or sponsored by someone in good standing with each individual group, the odds that they will want to return to any group other than the obedience training group are very low.

A couple of years back (this is a true story) a group of people started a guide dog school in an area of the country which had not, to that point, had one. Money was tight, so the people in the group went to the various factions of the German Shepherd constituency, and asked about their dogs. The show folks turned their backs on them and ignored them. The 'working' (bite)-line folks told them to go take a flying leap (only not quite that politely--'we don't have any stinkin' guide dogs here'!). The 'old-fashioned' folks conferred, rummaged around among their dogs, and over an almost 3 year period managed to come up with 6 dogs, 4 of which are now in service, 1 of which washed out, and 1 which looks like it will work out, but we don't know yet for sure.

That may say a good bit about the dogs, but it says a LOT more about the people.

'Ruby Tuesday', a contributor to this book, through our many discussions about dogs, once said that one of her friends told her she didn't like German Shepherds. When Ruby inquired more into her friend's dislike, her friend ruminated over her reasoning, and then concluded that it was not really German Shepherd dogs she didn't like, it was German Shepherd dog PEOPLE!

Whenever I come across 'working' (bite)-line dog people on the forums bragging about how they scream at other people, curse other people obscenely, kick other people's dogs, blame children for being afraid of the dogs that bite them, especially when they have done absolutely nothing to provoke a bite in the dog, and froth at the mouth when anybody else gets even close to their dogs, I have to admit that now and again I agree with her. A veteran of decades of raising, training and working service dogs, I've had many occasions when my dogs have been petted, clutched, impeded and even stepped on in their work. They take it in stride. 'Old-fashioned' folks just nod and admit that it's unfortunate that working dogs need to be able to tolerate such familiarity but what do you expect from John Q Public and good dogs just will have the ability to tolerate such things.

Service dog folks want to train John Q Public to behave better. (A laudable objective!) Show folks just don't get it. But 'working' (bite)-line' folks always respond that it's amazing that the dog didn't bite them and it would serve them right if the dog did. Unfortunately for German Shepherd dogs and the old-fashioned folks who have them, it is the 'working-line' folks who are in the ascendancy these days.

No wonder breed bans and insurance rates are on the way up.

Reflections from the Dog House: Breeding Philosophy

This is not a how-to breed your dog, or even a whether you ought to breed your dog. If you're determined to do it there are plenty of other dog books that will tell you how, and if you're undecided, there are plenty of forums to tell you NOT to breed your dog and why not. For the most part, the forums are right; the rescues and shelters are full of dogs and puppies bred by people who thought they could make a buck and found out they couldn't, or who learned the hard way just how much effort it takes to raise puppies safely and keep them clean, never mind give them proper socialization. And if that is not enough to discourage you, breeding good German Shepherds is not just putting one registered dog to another and getting good puppies. Managing to get good dogs doing it that way without knowing what is in what Cliff calls the 'bottom of the iceberg' - it is a little like hitting the lottery.

No, this is more of a what kind of dog do we want the German Shepherd dog to be, and how do we think we can get dogs to be that kind? For instance, what about the hip dysplasia paradox? Everybody believes that we ought to have dogs free of hip dysplasia, and breeders are supposed to give us only perfectly healthy puppies absolutely free of hip dysplasia, but the number one cause of hip dysplasia is not genetics, but the spaying and neutering of puppies when they're too young and their growth plates aren't closed yet. So on the one hand we have the pundits yammering on about hip dysplasia and on the other hand we have the Animal Rights people and all the people inundated with unwanted puppies and dogs dunning everybody to spay and neuter their dogs as early as four months of age and no later than six months of age despite the fact that our larger breeds aren't even close to being mature enough for their growth plates to have closed at that age. And since the hormones that we cut off when we spay and neuter our dogs are responsible for slowing and eventually stopping the growth of the long bones, the younger we spay and neuter our large breed dogs, the more we guarantee that the long bones will over-grow the hip sockets and create dysplastic dogs. (And I say dogs advisedly, because dogs mature more slowly than bitches, so the effect is even greater for males than for females.)

Today we live in an age when puppies are supposed to be 'products' rather than living, breathing beings, and breeders are supposed to 'guarantee' pups as if they're inanimate objects and the idea of buyer responsibility seems passé. How is a breeder supposed to survive in such a milieu? Do they play the odds and hope for the best and just pass puppies back and forth like interchangeable parts in a car? Big breeders and puppy mills can do that, but small breeders won't be able to substitute a puppy for another on a moments' notice, never mind the question of whether they should be doing that. If the majority of things that go wrong with puppies are the buyers' fault—and they are—how can a truly responsible breeder, in light of the fact that puppies are living, breathing and sentient individuals, give somebody a new puppy to break like a plastic toy the same way they did the old one?

Anybody who has spent any time at all on the forums can tell a breeder what they want to hear about how their puppy will be taken care of when the buyer gets said puppy. Will that actually be done, however? Ah, that's another question.

369

The expenditure of but a few minutes reading any forum in the section dealing with new puppies coming home from the breeder will find a plethora of people complaining about diarrhea in the new pup. Inevitably, the buyer has brought their new pup home and tossed out everything the breeder said about feeding that pup, trashed the samples of food the breeder sent with them in favor of some new food that was 'better' or 'cheaper' or anything, really, as long as it is different from that fed by the breeder and now they are complaining that there is something 'wrong' with the pup. Never mind that to the stress of a new home, new people, new places, and new house- mates, combined with the loss of the old companions and the attack on the pup's immune system from strange bacteria, viruses and parasites would be enough to send the best pup's digestion into a tailspin, now they have to change everything in the pup's diet as well! But Noooo, it's all the breeder's fault, the pup's not good enough, it's not like they did anything they shouldn't. They, the buyers, are perfect, right?!

Meanwhile, the Animal Rights and Peta People are only too ready, willing and able to jump onto the bash the breeders, the evil, evil breeders bandwagon. They will latch onto any pretext, however flimsy or unreasonable, and use it to inveigh against the breeding of any dog by anybody. While it is certainly true that our shelters and rescues overflow, in many cases, with unwanted dogs and cats, it might be wise to think very seriously before jumping on that bandwagon along with them. If ALL breeders, or even most breeders, were to give up on breeding dogs thanks to the efforts of these malcontents, where would you get your next dog? Or cat? Hummm? Give a good think about that before you behave in a manner calculated to make breeders throw up their hands and decide that it just isn't worth the time, effort, money and heartbreak to breed dogs (or cats) any more.

Now think about what kind of dog you want your next dog to be. A German Shepherd? What kind of German Shepherd? This is important, because you, the buyer, have a great deal to do with what kind of Shepherd will be bred. Right now, we have people buying the fantasy of the show dog, the hype for the bite sport dog, and others who long for the dogs of the old days who had 'genetic obedience' and made good all-around family dogs, who have found what they want in the old-fashioned dogs.

Think about this seriously. What kind of breeding do you want to support with your puppy buying dollar? For you, the buyer, do support whichever type of dog you buy. If you buy a puppy from 'titled' champion show dog parents, you are paying the stud fees, the entry fees, and the handler fees, as well as the feed, for show dogs. You are perpetuating, with your purchase, a way of life and a type of breeding that distills genetic disorders out of the chaotic stew of dog heredity and then disseminates them throughout the breed along with extreme and unsound forms of physical structure through in-breeding for beauty contest competitions. The sad truth is that if you want to 'do' something with your dog, this may not be the best source for a dog who can 'do' things.

If you buy the hype, and purchase a pup from bite sport 'titled' parents, then your dollars pay entry fees, stud fees, buys equipment, pays travel costs and feed so that the breeder of your pup can continue to pursue their hobby competing in bite sports. In this case, your dollars help to perpetuate the creation of dogs of increasingly extreme temperament and support the narrowing of the gene pool that happens when a few popular sires dominate the gene pool because someone put enough time, energy, money and skill into getting them to the top of their particular type of competition. If you buy one of these pups, while the pup may have the physical make-up to be able to 'do' the things you want to do, you will have to strongly consider how you mean to confine this dog as well as accept that the dog may die comparatively young of bloat. Not only will the dog have the physical make-up to 'do' things, the likelihood is that the dog will also have the mental 'need' to 'do' something— and given the genetic pre-disposition bred into the dog to bite people, absolute confinement for a dog of this type is a must.

If you buy a pup from one of the big guys (aka puppy mills) who always have a puppy ready for you, any time of the day or night, you put your money down, you get your puppy, no questions asked, well, a puppy mill by any other name may not smell very sweet. You may find yourself paying for your puppy twice over, whether that puppy is a cut-rate bargain or very expensive indeed, through the inordinate training fees it takes to make the puppy a comfortable member of your family, through the vet care costs which may go beyond those which a healthy, happy puppy from a more discerning breeder would generate, and most of all, through the taxes you pay to keep the public pet shelters where so many of these puppies end up in going so they can take care of these pups.

Remember, the easier it is to get a puppy, the easier it is to dump a puppy, because you don't have to assess your own situation in order to get such a puppy. You don't have to consider whether you are really ready for a puppy, whether you have the time or the temperament for any kind of dog, never mind a puppy, or even what you want to do with your new puppy. Do you really want to be paying twice for your puppy?

Truly good breeders of whatever type German Shepherd you choose, big or small, won't let you have a puppy of theirs unless and until you jump through the hoops experience and their own philosophies dictate. Some go for formal questionnaires, others for more informal conversations where they look for the little 'tells' that help them to spot lies and get through all the malarkey to the reality of what you will really be like as the new owners of their puppy. Good breeders don't want their pups winding up in a shelter somewhere, or having to be taken in by a rescue. Most of them want their puppy back, and even when circumstances prevent them from taking that puppy back into their own homes they will often try to find another place for the pup—even long after it has become a dog, and even into old age.

Old-fashioned breeders tend to be the whipping boys of the other two types of German Shepherd—but it was 'old-fashioned' dogs from 'back-yard breeders' who went to war in World War II and the Korean conflict and just this last couple of years, it was 'old fashioned' breeders who kicked in and donated pups to start a new guide dog school—pups most of whom are making the grade as guide dogs now. The folks with their bite sport dogs with their 'titled' parents pretty much told the guide dog people to take a flying leap—they bragged that their dogs aren't guide dogs, which they call 'German Shepherd- colored Labs'! (Never mind the breed standard that says outright that a German Shepherd dog SHOULD be 'fit and ready to serve' as a guide dog.) So much for the 'working' (bite)-line' dogs' crowd's adherence to the breed standard!

And this brings up another question. What kind of a dog should the German Shepherd dog become in the face of Peta and Animal Rights pressures, as well as those of an ignorant public with bite liability concerns? Police and the Military want to continue to be able to get a dog capable and fit to engage the bad guy and win the confrontation. Families want to be able to get a dog capable of acting as a deterrent to bad guys in a world which seems to increasingly favor the 'rights' of criminals to brutalize the innocent. Do we want SAR dogs who attack the lost children they search for when they find them? A recent court case regarding a SAR dog with bite sport training who bit the kid he found when he found him concluded that bite sport dogs were probably not the best choice for SAR work, or at least, SAR work where the dogs were looking for live people rather than dead bodies. Surprise! A court decision where commonsense was actually used.

For bite sport people for whom it is an article of faith that their dogs don't bite unless commanded to do so, such commonsense is anathema. Because their belief is an article of faith, it matters little how many of their most highly regarded dogs bite inappropriately, without a command. Articles of faith are not subject to critical examination by those who hold them, and such people are not likely to tolerate such applications of logic or reason on the part of others to whom they are not articles of faith. Any and all examples of the failure of that article of faith are dismissed without a hearing.

There have, however, been occasions when unbiased and knowledgeable sources have examined the problem, at least in the case of Fortunate Fields, as reported in 1934 by Elliott Humphrey and Lucien Warner. They chose to forgo attack training for their search and detection dogs. According to their account, in their original training of police dogs for search purposes, the dogs were given the same attack training as the regular patrol dogs, but such training was found to be counter-productive. By their report, dogs trained for attack depended too much on their eyes to make a perfect search. The dogs kept watching the bushes in anticipation of an opportunity to make an attack instead of keeping their noses and attention entirely on the search.

The writers of the "Working Dog" also commented that a second consideration which led them to divorce the two services was that most searches were not for criminals but for lost people, children and sometimes confused or injured adults and it was essential that the dog not attack in such situations. They tacitly agreed that once dogs were taught to attack at the end of a run after a criminal, they could, and sometimes did, either confuse the situation and bite innocent victims in a search and rescue situation, or they deliberately took the opportunity to bite the innocent on their searches. Hummm.

For the writers of the "Working Dog", no articles of faith were involved in this discussion. It was merely a report made objectively as a result of the training and use of literally hundreds of dogs for police work for over more than a decade. The writers had 'no ax to grind' in their report; they merely made their conclusions available to anyone who cared to take advantage of their extensive experience.

So we come back around again to the central question of what we want our breed to be. Are we willing to make the trade-off in good health and sound temperament for titles and uniformity? Or are we going to support the breeding of healthy, genetically diverse animals by supporting the breeding of a wide range of colors and a wide range of sizes in those animals? For those people who complain so bitterly about their dogs' health, I would advise them to put their money where their mouth is. Quit buying those cookie cutter black and red German High-line dogs with their intense in-breeding, turn your noses up at the Am-line show dogs with their ski-slope backs and intense in-breeding and same-old, same-old colors and sizes.

Turn your back on the dark colored bite sport dogs lurching from Troll to Fero to Mink to Held v Ritterberg and all the other popular sires who once hit a podium, and set your sights on dogs with diverse colors and sizes, the colors once so common-place and acceptable to the breed, before short-sighted and wrong-headed people started ratcheting down the standard to fewer colors and sizes. Celebrate dogs who adhere to the breed standard in temperament for a change, instead of the show-ring's fearful spooks and the reactive, low threshold, high prey drive dogs of the bite sports. Learn to recognize the lies spouted by both the show world and the bite sport world, and to understand the jargon deliberately designed to mislead—the use of the word 'civil' for instance, to refer to a profoundly Uncivil dog.

Remember that when Stephanitz started surveying the sizes of the dogs presented to him to pick and choose among to find each year's Sieger, that many of the dogs varied from 26 inches in height to 28 inches, and that was at 2 years of age, before many of the dogs had reached their mature heights!

That, in fact, many of the icons of the breed, Hettel Uckermark, Horst v Boll, Luchs v Kalsmunt-Wetzlar, Tell and Jung Tell v d Kriminal Polizei, Nores v d Kriminal Polizei, Arno v d Eichenburg, even Erich v Grafenwerth himself, would have been considered over-sized by today's sharply restricted and historically inaccurate standards. And you can add to that group Dolf v Dusternbrook, Donor v Overstolzen, Harras v d Juch, Erich v Glockenbrink and Arras a d Stadt-Velbert, all Siegers as well, and all of them but Arras chosen by Stephanitz, himself.

Remember too, that Horand v Grafath, Hektor v Schwaben, Horst v Boll, and Klodo v Boxberg, were all grey and tans—the dreaded blue—as well, making today's strictures against the color nonsensical as well as genetically unsound from the standpoint of genetic diversity. Think of Grief, and all the healthy, sound herding dogs that followed him into the breed, as well as all the breeds of herding dogs whose base color is white—the Maremma (which looks like a white German Shepherd), the Kuvasz, the Tatra, the Pyrenees Shepherd, and the rest. The more of the original colors and sizes of the breed that are welcomed back, the less prevalent things like Degenerative Myeopathy, Cardiomyeopathy, von Wildebrand's and all the rest can be become.

As far as cancer is concerned, that's on you. The more vaccinations you give, and the more often you give them, the regularity with which you dose your dog up with those spot on products, the more you pour poison down your dog in those heart-worm preparations, the more you mess with your dog's hormones by spaying and neutering them w-a-ay too young, and the more you drench your house and yard with pesticides, and your garden with herbicides, the closer you bring your dog to death by cancer. If we're talking spaying your bitch, for the 1 point 5 percent chance of mammary cancer you save her by spaying her early (because your money hungry vet insisted on it with scare tactics about cancer) you just traded that small percentage for a far larger one that your girl will die years early because of other cancers, among them hermangiosarcoma.

And when it comes to those yearly vaccinations your vet insists upon? They're money in his pocket coming and going. He gets to charge you for a call charge, a charge to examine your dog and for the shot itself, and then, when the insults to your dog's immune system makes your dog sick with a laundry list of illnesses including allergies and skin disorders in addition to cancer, he gets to reach into your pocket once again to extract even more money. Reputable vets follow the new vaccination protocols which call for a measured program of vaccinations for your puppy and then for only the most limited of repeated vaccinations throughout the dog's lifetime, certainly NOT every year. In places where rabies vaccines are required, they should be given no more often than every THREE years, not every year.

Learn to look to genetics for the things that genetics can do for you and your dog—freedom from genetic disorders through a breeding program minimizing line-breeding and eliminating in- breeding while encouraging the return to a wide range of sizes and colors. Look for breeding where competition ('titles') is not a concern, which will minimize the over-use of small numbers of males of like types, to the detriment of the breed. Consider supporting the breeding of purpose-bred dogs rather than competition-bred dogs to minimize the birth of genetically fearful dogs and dogs of extreme aggression, extreme prey drive, and extremes of structure.

Purpose-bred dogs don't have to out-point any other dog in some subjective contest where only one dog wins. Purpose-bred dogs only need a reasonable physical structure and sound mental structures in order to complete their tasks. Breeders of such dogs will place a premium on general biddability, intelligence, and good, sound nerve and make them a priority in their breeding. And, with the exception of the bite dogs, which are, after all, sport dogs in competition with each other, breeders of purpose-bred dogs will want good longevity for their dogs as well as good health, so that once their dogs are trained, they can continue to serve their purposes for many happy, healthy years to come.

All dogs are a compendium of genetics and environment. It matters not how good any particular dog's genetics are, that dog must be raised in a healthy manner, socialized and trained and then competed or worked in order to achieve any degree of success. All dogs exist on a continuum on what we call the Bell curve. Some dogs are more influenced by their genetics than others, whether for good or ill, and some dogs are more influenced by their environment, whether for good or ill. Dogs out at the extreme ends of the continuum are comparatively rare but no matter how far out on the end of the spectrum of 'good' genetics a dog may seem, without good environment those 'good' genetics will simply go to waste.

Today we are being spoon-fed the idea that everything is genetics. It is NOT. Yesterday we had the notion that good environment could overcome any genetics, no matter how bad. That was wrong too.

Good socialization when a puppy is young can minimize fearfulness. Depending on how bad the fearfulness is genetically, however, will to some extent, dictate how far the dog can go, even with the best of training—for that dog. Training, however, MUST fit the dog. The training that might be perfect for one dog can be perfectly WRONG for another.

Good socialization expands the dog's brain and increases his cognitive abilities. Regardless of whatever discipline the subsequent training will be geared towards, good socialization will help the dog to do better in whatever that form of training is than the dog would be able to do without the socialization. Good socialization is environmental.

Good diet, like good socialization, enriches the dog's health, and, again like good socialization, allows the dog to make the most of his genetic endowment, whatever it might be. Good diet is environmental.

Pesticides are known carcinogens. Consistently expose your dog to pesticides on a regular basis and you might as well be giving him cancer outright. This is environmental. I am continually seeing complaints on the forums by people wanting breeders to breed dogs that don't get cancer. That is impossible, as long as people insist on dumping pesticides onto and into their dogs every month of their lives.

Cancer is, in most cases, an autoimmune disease. Mess around with your pup's immune system with constant vaccinations, and you might as well shoot cancer into your pup with that syringe, because that's exactly what you're doing when you go into the vet's for those yearly vaccinations.

Insist on early spaying and neutering? Your choice, but then don't complain when your spayed or neutered young puppy winds up dying two years before his or her time because of it. Because that's it, two years that studies show your pup won't live if you insist on following that vet's urging to spay or neuter your 6 month old or LESS puppy. Bear in mind, too, that early neutering hits your male puppy harder than early spaying will your girl, because she will mature more quickly and will be farther along the maturity road at six months of age than your boy will.

And that hip dysplasia you're told to obsess on? Spay or neuter your pup before his or her growth plates close and you are GIVING your pup hip dysplasia just as surely as you would if you took a hammer to your pup's joints. Stop blaming the breeder for what YOU did. Get some of those joint supplements and toss them into your pup's kibble and get over it. If you do, your pup most likely will too.

Consider too, while you are at it, how your choice of the kind of German Shepherd you are bringing into your family will affect you. If you insist upon getting that 'titled' dog from the bite sport (working-line) folks, you know, the ones who tell you that they don't need no stinkin' guide dogs, and that the breed standard for temperament is for a hostile, edgy, 'civil', naturally suspicious dog who can and will bite anybody at the drop of a hat regardless of whether that body presents any realistic threat to you or not, you need to remember that you will have to confine that dog very carefully if you are not to drive up everybody's insurance rates and fuel breed discrimination.

Learn at least this much of the actual breed standard for temperament: hostility is a disqualifying fault, and any suspicion, 'natural' or otherwise is faulty and improper. Dogs are supposed to be calm and confident, approachable, and to accept friendly overtures from strangers quietly and with courtesy. And in order to meet the breed standard, a dog must be fit and ready to serve either as a guide dog for the blind or as a livestock herding dog. Dogs are supposed to be 'Alert', but neither wary nor suspicious. Anybody who calls guide dogs

'German Shepherd colored Labs' obviously doesn't adhere to the breed standard and therefore cannot be expected to produce breed standard pups.

When you find people on the forums touting their out of standard temperamented bite dogs, bragging on their titles and their dogs' drives, 'natural suspicion' and their 'good, full grips' (which means a 'good, full' and hard Bite!) and insisting that these dogs are the only good dogs, try to do a little critical thinking about what they are saying and doing. In a day and age when insurance companies are refusing to insure people who have dogs known for biting, and municipalities are passing legislation to ban dogs that bite people readily, does it really make sense to deliberately choose a dog bred to aggressively bite people? How much training are you really willing to commit to? How much confinement are you willing to provide? How rigourous are you prepared to be in supervising your dog's every moment with another person, up to and including your own children and the rest of your immediate family?

A 'titled' dog in any one of the bite sports, the biggie, of course, Schutzhund, but also PSA, SDA, KNPV, Mondio, French Ring, Personal Protection, etc, is a dog bred for multiple generations to aggressively bite people on command with no provocation required whatsoever. The extreme prey drive the people who put the 'titles' on their dogs are so proud of, is a strong element of that dog's ability to run down a field and bite a complete stranger minding his own business as hard as he can. Any puppy from this kind of breeding will not be the kind of dog your children can play with without a great deal of care and supervision on your part and will probably never be safe with your neighbors or your neighbors' children. If you believe the breeders' hype that this type of dog can be a 'good' (good, here, depends a LOT upon your interpretation of 'good') family dog you may be letting yourself in for a nasty surprise and some real liability.

If you stop and THINK about this, it will make sense to you. Do you REALLY want a dog expressly bred to bite people quickly and easily and without any provocation whatsoever? Are you willing to train this dog for years so that you can reliably control him? Are you willing to build the kind of fencing it will take so that the dog can be confined in your yard safely, and then to use it without fail? Or to keep your dog on leash (a short, 6 ft leash) at all times when the dog is outside your home? Will you crate or confine your dog consistently every time a friend or neighbor enters your home so that the dog cannot come into any contact with them? And especially when (if) someone else's child enters your home?

If you can guarantee this kind of responsible stewardship, then go ahead and get that Schutzhund/bite sport bred puppy. But if you can't, please don't get this puppy, because your failure to safely confine and to train this kind of pup to the level they must achieve to live safely in this world (safely for the people who know you!) is a liability not just for you, but for all of us and for the breed itself. Bite sport (working-line) dogs in the hands of people who do not respect or understand their genetic makeup do nothing but create fuel for the fire of the breed ban folks and make it that much more expensive and difficult for those of us responsible folks to get home insurance.

On the other hand, maybe if you think that breeding that kind of dog in today's world is irresponsible, inappropriate, or just plain downright stupid, you might want to take some care to use your puppy purchasing dollar towards a puppy bred with a higher bite threshold, more moderate drives, and a closer approximation to the actual breed standard for temperament. Give it some serious thought. What kind of dog do you think the German Shepherd should be? Do you think he ought to be the calm, confident, approachable dog the breed standard actually calls for? A guide dog? A dog capable of helping out around the house, the farm, the ranch? An alert dog, capable of warning his person of impending seizures or a sudden drop in blood sugar? Or do you buy the hype about the 'titled' biting machines, the prey 'monsters' being the better dogs? Maybe you seriously believe that the title of 'champion' means something more or better than a half (or fully) crippled animal riddled with genetic disorder after more than a century of incessant in-breeding. If you do, then support the kind of dog you believe in with your puppy purchasing dollar.

What you do with your puppy purchasing dollar is important. Please think about it seriously before you spend it, because it is your breeding philosophy that will influence which direction the breed takes in the future. If enough people turn away from the in-bred and disordered show dog, fewer show dogs will be bred to stagger around pitifully. Show people desperately need the money from the pet market in order to be able to make the money they need to keep on breeding their genetically disordered mental and physical cripples. Same goes for the bite sport/ Schutzhund crowd.

Schutzhund and all the rest of the bite sports are expensive. They need the pet market money they get for their puppies in order to keep buying the equipment and driving the miles they need to drive to get to their training meets and their trials so they can get those 'titles' they insist are so important. When you buy one of their puppies you are supporting the breeding of their low bite threshold, high aggression, high drive prey monsters, and, inadvertantly or not, you are supporting the production of dogs that bite people readily and with little or no provocation. You are also, however unwittingly, supporting high insurance rates and breed discrimination when you support the breeding of 'titled' bite sport dogs.

When you purchase a puppy from a puppy mill—one of those places which always has a puppy available and all you have to do to get one of their puppies is to show them the color of your money—you are supporting breeders who often do not take very good care of their dogs. Puppies from puppy mills are often taken away from their mothers too soon to receive good Mom to puppy and puppy to puppy socializaton which can be crucial to your pup's later development, they often do not receive vaccinations before they come to you, so they are more prone to puppy illnesses, and they may have been passed from hand to hand or transported long distances without adequate immunity to disease (puppies found in pet stores). Your puppy purchasing dollar thus serves to perpetuate these breeding practices which are so detrimental to the health and mental stability of all the puppies produced in this manner.

If you think that puppy mills should be put out of business, then STOP buying puppy mill puppies. When puppy mills can no longer sell their puppies they will go out of business. Puppy mills are in it for the money and ONLY for the money. Stop the money and they'll stop breeding.

It has been estimated that the pet market spends 98% of the pet buying dollars spent in this country for dogs. The fate of the German Shepherd breed—of all dog breeds—is ultimately in the hands of pet buyers, not the miniscule show dog market, nor the even smaller bite sport market, the small military/police dog interests, nor the itsy-bitsy service dog group and the just as tiny real-life farm/ranch stock dog group. All of those 'special' interest groups put together make up only 2 % of the people who buy German Shepherds. Pet dog buyers have the ability— and the responsibility—of perpetuating the groups they feel are most important to the German Shepherd breed.

Which kind of German Shepherd do YOU want to support and perpetuate? Make up your mind. It's your choice.

Reflections from the Dog House in Pictures

When you consider that German shepherds have been bred for over 115 years, you may think that the genetics of the old dogs have long been gone. What we now know about genetics, some breeders have made it their mission to preserve the old genetics. Some of the original genetics still remain.

Functional conformation - notice the rear structure, shoulder angle, and top and bottom line of these two German Shepherds.

Frigga von Scharenstetten 1911

Snotahay Sierra Abiona 1991

Working dog conformation from yesterday and today

Tell von der Kriminalpolizel 1910

Fig. 130. Tell von der Kriminalpolizei, SZ 8770 PH, Champion 1910.

Snotahay Sierra Ransome Sensenstein 2012

Strong Swabian influence can still be seen in the German shepherd today.

Swabian Shepherd Dog 1890

Black Magic's Abby 2010

Herding dogs of yesterday and today.

Hettle Ukermark 1909

Snotahay Sierra Ross Sensenstein 2009

Bibliography

Stephanitz, Captain Max von, The German Shepherd Dog in Word and Pictures, Published inGermany in 1922, translated into English 1925 and reprinted in 1994

This is the 'Bible' for the history and origins of the German Shepherd

Willis, Malcolm B, PhD, The German Shepherd Dog: a Genetic History, Howell Book House, New York, c1991

Extremely important for the study of the breed. Used in conjunction with:

Padgett, George A, DVM's Control of Canine Genetic Diseases, Howell Book House, New York, c 1998

and,

Ackerman, Lowell, DVM, A guide to Health Problems in Purebred Dogs: The Genetic Connection American, Second Edition, Animal Hospital Press, Lakewood, Colorado, c2011

Garrett, Gordon, German Shepherd Dog History, published by Gordon Garrett online, c2012

This is an extremely valuable history of the German Shepherd dog, I highly recommend it. The study of the pedigrees working forward is very insightful and valuable to anyone wanting to learn about the breed.

Lanting, Fred L. The Total German Shepherd Dog, Alpine Publications, Inc. c1990.

Contains historical and genetic information on the breed, with a section on the breed standard from the frist standards to the present. A good place to start for people who don't want to go to the expense (or can't afford the expense) of the Stephanitz or the Willis books.

Denlinger, Milo G. The Complete German Shepherd, Third Edition, Denlinger's Press, Richmond, Virginia, c1952.

Denlinger, Milo G., Paramoure, and Umlauff, Gerda M. The Complete German Shepherd Dog,

New Edition edited by Jane G. Bennett, Howell Book House, New York, c1972.

Bennett, Jane G. The New Complete German Shepherd Dog, Fifth Edition, Howell Book House, Inc, New York, c1982.

The first edition of Denlinger's Complete German Shepherd was published in 1949, but these three editions of the book, 1952 through 1982 give the reader a very good view of the why and how show conformation in the breed evolved from good working structure to the modern fad driven show conformation.

Goldbecker, Captain William and Hart, Ernest H., This is the German Shepherd, New revised edition, TFH Publications, New Jersey, c1967

Notable for its first hand accounts of dogs and events not to be found in other sources.

Wootton, Brian H. The German Shepherd Dog, Howell Book House, New York, c1988.

Some new early historical photos and information with a careful discussion of bloodlines; a good complement to the Garrett book.

Humphrey, Elliot and Warner, Lucien, Working Dogs: an attempt to produce a strain of German Shepherds which combines working ability and beauty of conformation, Johns Hopkins Press, c1934, reprinted by Dogwise Publishing, Wenatchee, Washington c2005

Fascinating report of the findings at Fortunate Fields regarding the breeding of service dogs for guide dogs for the blind, police and military dogs in the 1920s and '30s.

Derry, Margaret E. Bred for Perfection: Shorthorn Cattle, Collies and Arabian Horses since 1800, Johns Hopkins University Press, Baltimore, Maryland c2003.

An absorbing study of the creation and development of purebred animals.

Pugnetti, Gino, Simon and Schuster's Guide to Dogs, edited by Elizabeth Meriwether Schuler. A Fireside Book, Simon and Schuster, New York, c1980.

A good introduction to dog archaeology with a brief over-view of the various recognized breeds.

Coppinger, Raymond and Lorna, Dogs, a New Understanding of Canine Origins, Behavior, and Evolution, University of Chicago Press, c 2002

Interesting new ways of thinking about dogs, wolves, dominance, pack structure and how behavior evolved.
Which leads us too. . .

Coren, Stanley, How Dogs Think: What the world looks like to them and why they act the way they do, Free Press, Simon and Schuster, New York, c2004.

Important discussion as to how dogs think and why. We have a lot to learn about this subject, but this takes us into a new realm of discovery in this area.

Donaldson, Jean, The Culture Clash, A revolutionary new way of understanding the relationship between humans and domestic dogs, James and Kenneth Publishers, Berkeley, California c1996.

A discussion of the use of behavior modification techniques in training. Useful.

Ryan, Terry and Mortensen, Kirsten, Outwitting Dogs: Revoluntionary techniques for dog training that work! The Lyons Press, Guilford, Connecticut, c2004

Another discussion of behavior modification, very accessible and done with a light and very practical touch.

McConnell, Patricia B., PhD and Moore, Aimee M., Family Friendly Dog Training: A six-week program for you and your dog, Dog's Best Friend, Ltd, Black Earth, Wisconsin, c2006

Building on Donaldson and Ryan. Also, Patricia McConnell's Other End of the Leash is recommended.

McDevitt, Leslie, MLA, DCBC, CPDT, Control Unleashed: Creating a Focused and Confident Dog, Clean Run Productions, LLC, South Hadley, Massachusetts, c2007.

A necessity for the owners of reactive, fearful dogs.

Wright, John C., PhD, with Lashnits, Judi Wright, The Dog Who Would Be King: Tales and surprising lessons from a pet psychologist, Rodale Press, Inc., Emmaus, Pennsylvania, c1999.

Dodman, Dr. Nicholas, The Dog Who Loved Too Much: Tales, Treatments and the Psychology of Dogs, Bantam Books, New York, c1996.

A pair of books about dealing with the more severe problems of behavior via both behavior modification and medical modification.

And for a little historical perspective. . .

Meek, Colonel S. P. , So you're going to get a puppy: A Dog Lover's Handbook, Alfred A Knopf, New York c1947.

Duncan, William Cary, Dog Training Made Easy for You and Your Dog, Bell Publishing Company, Inc., New York, c1940. Contrast with the later.

Woodhouse, Barbara, Dog Training My Way, Berkley Books, New York, c1970.

One wonders who has changed more, the people or the dogs. Commonsense seems to be becoming less common and a lot harder to find in the dog keeping audience. No wonder people have to resort to 'outwitting' dogs.

Then again, at the same time we're losing the old ways of working with dogs, we're learning new ways of using them to serve us, or perhaps just recognizing for the first time ways in which they have always helped us.

Sakson, Sharon Paws and Effect: The Healing Power of Dogs, Alyson Books, New York, c2007.

A discussion of the ways in which dogs help people to live better lives.

Goldstein, Bruce Puppy Chow is better than Prozac: The True Story of a Man and the Dog Who Saved His Life, Da Capo Press, c2008.

An account of the effect of working with a dog on one mentally ill person.

Pfaffenberger, Clarence The New Knowledge of Dog Behavior: The landmark work that established the science of puppy testing and socialization, Howell Book House, Inc., New York, c1963, reprint, Dogwise Publishing, Wenatchee, Washington, c2002.

A discussion of the establishment of the School for Guide Dogs for the blind at San Rafael, California and of the methods used to determine which pups will grow up to be successful guide dogs. Revolutionary in its time.

Bergin, Bonnie, with McNally, Robert Aquinas, Bonnie Bergin's Guide to Bringing Out The Best In Your Dog, First Edition, Little, Brown and Company, Boston, c1995.

Bonnie Bergin is the founder of both Canine Companions for Independence and of the Bonnie Bergin Institute in northern California which trains assistance dogs for the disabled. She is, in some ways, the heir to Pfaffenberger.

Nordensson, Stewart and Kelley, Lydia, Team Work: A Dog Training Manual for People with Disabilities, Book One: Basic Obedience, revised and expanded, Top Dog Publications,
  Tucson, Arizona, c2007.

Nordensson, Stewart and Kelley, Lydia, Teamwork II, A Dog Training Manual for People with Disabilities, Book Two: Service Exercises, Top Dog Publications, Tucson, Arizona, c1998.

Companion volumes for those people who would like to train their own service dogs. Contains lots of examples of what other people have trained their dogs to do for them.

Assistance Dogs International, a website for the organization setting the standards for the training and use of assistance dogs throughout the world.

Explains the recognized types of assistance dogs, lists member training programs and provides other information for people interested in assistance dogs.

The Standard of the German Shepherd Dog, adopted by the German Shepherd Dog Club of America, 1943, published by the Shepherd Dog Review, Lancaster, Pennsylvania, c1953.

Ollivant, Alfred Bob, son of Battle, Grossett and Dunlap, NY, c1898

Interviews

Frawley, Ed, A Conversation with Karl Fuller, published by Leerburg on the Leerburg website.

Kintzel, Ulf, Herding Dogs and the Golden Middle, published by Working Dog Cyberzine.

German Shepherd Herding Home: Nickelsberg's Farms website
An Interview with Schafermeister Manfred Heyne on the Genetic Origin of the Breed, translated by Anka Andrews and Astrid Bortolucci, and

A visit with Schafermeister Manfred Heyne by Jurgen Rixen and Ellen Nickelsberg translated by Kerstin Braeckelmann and Astrid Bortolucci, reprinted from Der Gebrauchshund Magazine, 1/2004, and

Manfred Heyne's Letter to Helmut Raiser On the occasion of Dr. Raiser's Election to SV National Breed Wardenin 2002, translated by Anka Andrews, Feb 17, 2003.

Documentaries

Nature: Dogs that changed the world: Part One, The Rise of the Dog and Part Two: Dogs by Design, narrated by F. Murray Abraham, Thirteen/WNET, New York, and Tigress Productions Limited. C2007.

Nature: Yellowstone, In the Valley of the Wolves, Thirteen/WNET, New York and National Geographic Television, c2008.

Nova: Dogs Decoded: Understanding the Human-Dog Relationship, Produced and Directed by Dan Child. Produced for Nova by Melanie Wallace. Executive Producer for BBC Horizon, Andrew Cohen. c2010 by the BBC.

Secrets of the Dead: Bugging Hitler's Soldiers, narrated by Jay O. Sanders, October Films Ltd. Production for Thirteen, c2013.

Studies and Articles: Bloat

Arndt, Linda, Bloat and Torsion: Is Nutrition a factor? GREATDANELADY.COM

Arndt, Linda, Bloat and Allergies: The Relationship to Yeast Overgrowth and/or Pathogenic

Bacteria. GREATDANELADY.COM

Milani, Myrna, BS, DVM Canine Bloat and Temperament originally printed in Dogwatch,
  Cornell University College of Veterinary Medicine

Johnson, Dudley E., MVSc, Gastric Torsion in dogs.   Dog Owners Educational League, Inc.

Lee, David and Tracker, Dr. Leon, ADDL Director, Acute Gastric Dilation-Volvulus in Dogs.
  Indiana Animal Disease Diagnostic Laboratory

Glickman, L. T., Glickman, N. W., Schellenberg, D. B., Raghavan, M., and Lee, T. L., Incidence
  of and breed related risk factors for gastric dilation-volvulus in dogs Journal of the American
  Veterinary Medical Association, 34:64-73

Raghavan, M., Glickman, N., McCabe,G., Lantz, G., Glickman, L. T., Diet related rish factors
  for gastric dilation-volvullus in dogs of high risk breeds. (2004) Journal of the American
  Animal Hospital Association 40: 92-203

Studies and Articles: Vaccinations

Dodds, W. Jean, DVM Vaccination Protocols for Dogs: Canine Vaccination Protocol – 2011.
  It's For the Dogs.com

O'Driscoll, Catherine, Vaccinosis. From the Truth About Vaccines website published by Magda
  Aquila.

Tsumiyama, Ken; Miyazaki, Yumi and Shiozawa, Shunichi, Plos One: Self-organized criticality theory of autoimmunity, published by PLOS/ONE, December 31, 2009.

Stevenson, Heidi, Vaccinations Inevitably cause Autoimmune Diseases: Plos Study, published by Gaia Health.

Annual pet vaccinations may be useless, even fatal: Minnesota Issue Watch, October 1, 2002.

Blanco, Dee, DVM, Vaccines: Are they safe for your dog? From the Truth About Vaccines.

Ford, R. B. and Schultz, R. D., Vaccines and vaccinations: Issues for the 21st Century In: J. D. Bonagura, ed., Kirk's Current Verterinary Therapy XIII, W. B. Saunders, Philadelphia, Pa, 1999, pp 250-253.

Rentko, V. T. and Ross, L. A. Canine Leptospirosis. In: J. D. Bonagura, ed., Kirkk's Current Veterinary Therapy XI, W. B. Saunders, Philadelphia, Pa 1992. pp260-63.

Studies and Articles: Spay and Neuter and Cancer

Warner, David J., DVM, PhD, A Healtheir Respect for the Ovaries, Published by Gerald P Murphy Cancer Foundation

Torres de la Riva, Gretel, Hart, Benjamin, Farver, Thomas B., Oberbauer, Anita M., McVessam, Locksley, Willits, Neil and Hart, Lynette A., Neutering Dos: Effects on Joint Disorders and Cancers in Golden Retrievers.

Davol, Pam, Early Spaying and Neutering and the dangers that can be involved.

Sanborn, Laura J. M. S. Long Term Health Risks and Benefits Associated with Spay/Neuter in Dogs. May 14, 2007

Spain, C. Victor, DVM, PhD, Scarlett, Janet M., DVM, PhD, Houpt, Katherine A. DVM, PhD, DACVB, Long Term Risks and benefits of early age gonadectomy in dogs. Dept of Population Medicine and Diagnostic Science, College of Veterinary Medicine, Coornell University, Ithaca, NY. Journal of the American Veterinary Medical Association, February 1, 2004 Vol. 224, no 3, pp380-87

Salmer, K. R., Bloomberg, M. S., Scruggs, S. L. and Shille, V., Gonadectomy in immature dogs: Effects on skeletal, physical and behavioral development. Journal of American Veterinary Medical Association 1991; 198: 1193-1203.

Grumbach, M. M., Estrogen, bone growth and sex: a sea change in conventional wisdom. Journal of Pediatric Endocrinol Metab. 2000: 13 Suppl 5:1439-1455.

Katz, Larry S., PhD, Associate Professor and Chair Animal Sciences, Rutgers University, A Comparison of Healthy and related Risks between Intact and Early Spayed and Neutered Canines. Rutgers University.

Thomason, Dr. Jeannie, Neutering Dogs: Effects on Joint disorders, Cancers and More. February 19, 2013.